The Same Solitude

The Same Solitude

Boris Pasternak and Marina Tsvetaeva

CATHERINE
CIEPIELA

CORNELL UNIVERSITY PRESS
Ithaca & London

Publication of this book was made possible, in part, by a grant
from Amherst College.

First published 2006 by Cornell University Press

Printed in the United States of America

Library of Congress Cataloging-in-Publication Data

Ciepiela, Catherine.
    The same solitude : Boris Pasternak and Marina Tsvetaeva /
    Catherine Ciepiela.
        p. cm.
    Includes bibliographical references and index.
    ISBN-13: 978-0-8014-3534-8 (cloth)
    ISBN-10: 0-8014-3534-X (cloth)
    1. Tsvetaeva, Marina, 1892–1941—Criticism and interpretation.
    2. Pasternak, Boris Leonidovich, 1890–1960—Criticism and
    interpretation.   I. Title.
    PG3476.T75Z62 2006
    891.71'4209—dc22

                                                            2006040269

Cornell University Press strives to use environmentally responsible suppliers
and materials to the fullest extent possible in the publishing of its books.
Such materials include vegetable-based, low-VOC inks and acid-free papers
that are recycled, totally chlorine-free, or partly composed of nonwood fibers.
For further information, visit our website at www.cornellpress.cornell.edu.

Cloth printing   10 9 8 7 6 5 4 3 2 1

for Robert and Carolyn Ciepiela

Contents

Acknowledgments

I have been generously supported through all stages of my work on this book. I began my research with support from the National Endowment for the Humanities and the Social Sciences Research Council. The early interest in the book expressed by Cornell University Press in the persons of Bernard Kendler and John Ackerman was a constant encouragement. My sabbatic leaves from Amherst College provided valuable work time. At a crucial juncture Irina Shevelenko and Elena Korkina shared with me the typescript for their edition of Tsvetaeva's and Pasternak's correspondence. Much of this material was inaccessible until Tsvetaeva's archive at the Russian State Archive of Literature and Art was fully opened in 2000. I am deeply grateful to them for this collegial act. Stephanie Sandler, a loyal friend and reader for years, read drafts of portions of the book, as did Burlin Barr and Kim Brandt. Michael Wachtel gave excellent comments on several versions of the manuscript, and I thank him for his careful labor. Susanne Fusso, Sibelan Forrester, Alexandra Smith, Honor Moore, and Karen Evans-Romaine all helped me improve the final manuscript. I also thank Karen, and Konstantin Polivanov, for patiently fielding questions about Pasternak, and I thank Irina Shevelenko for doing the same with my questions about Tsvetaeva. Evgeny Pasternak kindly gave permission to quote from his father's works and supplied images for the book cover and illustrations from the archive of his remarkable family. The Tsvetaeva House Museum in Moscow also provided images from its collection.

Others have helped in more general, equally important ways. Without the work of scholars dedicated to Russian poetry, I would not have been able to arrive at my readings of Tsvetaeva and Pasternak. My annual summer meetings with a group of such scholars—Stephanie Sandler, Katherine O'Connor, Gerry Smith, Michael Wachtel, Sarah Pratt, and Susanne Fusso—have kept alive for me the pleasures of close reading and of reading poetry together. My companions at the MacDowell colony taught me to write however I needed to write. Then there are the dear friends who have endured with me throughout—Kim Brandt, Meredith Hedges, Mark Shapiro, and Pam Thompson. Finally, there are my very dearest, Burlin and Gareth Barr. My genuine thanks to all.

Note on Editorial Method

All citations of Pasternak's and Tsvetaeva's writings appear in the text and refer to the following multivolume collections:

Boris Pasternak, *Sobranie sochinenii v piati tomakh,* ed. A. A. Voznesenskii, D. S. Likhachev, D. F. Mamleev, A. A. Mikhailov, E. B. Pasternak (Moscow: Khudozhestvennaia literatura, 1989–92).

Marina Tsvetaeva, *Sobranie sochinenii v semi tomakh,* ed. Anna Saakiants and Lev Mnukhin (Moscow: Ellis Lak, 1994–95).

The two other publications cited in the text are:

DL   Rainer Maria Rilke, *Dykhanie liriki: Perepiska s Marinoi Tsvetaevoi i Borisom Pasternakom,* ed. K. M. Azadovsky, E. V. Pasternak, E. B. Pasternak (Moscow: Art-Fleks, 2000).

DNV   Marina Tsvetaeva and Boris Pasternak. *Dushi nachinaiut videt': Pis'ma 1922–1936 goda,* ed. E. B. Korkina and I. D. Shevelenko (Moscow: Vagrius, 2004).

All translations are my own unless otherwise indicated in the endnotes. I have used the Library of Congress system for transliteration, modifying it for surnames to make them recognizable to readers unacquainted with Russian.

The Same Solitude

Introduction

This sickness is incurable and it is called soul.
—Marina Tsvetaeva to Olga Kolbasina-Chernova (January 8, 1925)

. . . One sublime malady / Is still called song.
—Boris Pasternak, "A Sublime Malady" (1928)

When Marina Tsvetaeva and Boris Pasternak discovered each other's poetry in 1922, they were just emerging as essential poets of their generation. Although they both began publishing in the early 1910s, around the same time as Anna Akhmatova, Osip Mandelstam, and Vladimir Mayakovsky, their achievements and their reputations were longer in the making. The appearance of Pasternak's *My Sister Life* (*Sestra moia—zhizn'*) in 1922 led many to declare him the best contemporary poet. At the same time, a flood of new books by Tsvetaeva—six appeared over 1922–23—established her as Akhmatova's equal. It is fair to say that much of the story of Russian modernist poetry in the 1920s belongs to Tsvetaeva and Pasternak. Mayakovsky remained a prominent figure, but his political commitments largely supplanted his poetry; Akhmatova and Mandelstam, after publishing lyric collections in the early twenties, turned to writing prose. But Tsvetaeva and Pasternak continued not only to write but also to publish poetry and were the most discussed poets of the period. It was during these years that they entered into an intense, often romantically inflected friendship that would last into the early 1930s and resonate for the rest of their lives.

The salient fact about the poets' relationship is that it was conducted "blind" (*zaochnoe*), or at a distance. As members of the same cultural milieu in Moscow, Tsvetaeva and Pasternak were casually acquainted, but neither had read the other's poetry with attention. They discovered each other only after Tsvetaeva emigrated from Russia in 1922. Pasternak read her lyric collection *Milestones* (*Versty,* 1921) just three weeks after she left to rejoin her husband, who had fought with the defeated White Army and was waiting for her in Berlin.

The poets soon missed another opportunity to meet when Pasternak traveled to Berlin at the end of the summer, only to find that Tsvetaeva had just moved to Prague. This "missed meeting" (razminovenie), as Tsvetaeva named it, set the pattern for the entire relationship. They made almost annual plans to meet in Europe, but for various reasons these plans were never realized. Pasternak did not travel abroad again until 1935, when Stalin forced him to represent the Soviet Union at the Anti–Fascist Congress in Paris. There he finally met Tsvetaeva and her family. By then the poets' relationship had altered and the meeting was a disappointment, another sort of missed meeting. But the intervening years yielded an extraordinary long-distance exchange, possibly the most significant conversation to take place across the growing cultural divide between Soviet Russia and the Russian emigration.

The poets' relationship, then, was conducted almost entirely through texts. As Tsvetaeva said to Pasternak, "We have nothing except words, we're fated to them" (*DNV* 514). The task of telling this story, therefore, is largely one of textual interpretation—above all of the letters and poems they explicitly addressed to each other, but also of their major writings during the 1920s. Tsvetaeva and Pasternak were each other's most important readers throughout the decade and into the 1930s. Tsvetaeva's daughter Ariadna Efron even speculated that Tsvetaeva's poetic language grew more hermetic once Pasternak became her addressee: "The deepening complexity of her poetic language during this period . . . is also partly explained by Marina's focus on Pasternak: a language understood by two, encoded for everyone else!"[1] In fact, the language they developed together simply placed another layer of opacity over their already challenging modernist writing. When they met as mature poets, both were known to write very difficult high-modernist poetry. These were poets for whom the greatest poetic achievement was Goethe's inscrutable *Faust,* part two, a text they actually considered translating together.

To say that Tsvetaeva and Pasternak shared a hermetic language is not to say that they always understood each other. In fact, their long-distance romance allowed them free rein for invention. Their exchange is most interesting for how they misread, under-read or over-read each other, in patterns I attempt to trace in this book. Above all, they read themselves in each other's texts; their imaginings of each other were at the same time imaginings of themselves. Tsvetaeva's first poem to Pasternak, for example, was inspired by the appearance of the rhyme word "marina" in one of the poems of *My Sister Life;* Pasternak's poem renders an erotic episode between the poet and his lover, and in her answering poem, Tsvetaeva wrote herself into the scene. Later on, Pasternak read himself into Tsvetaeva's "Poem of the End," about the end of an affair. These examples highlight the fact that the poets relied on the familiar script of the heterosexual romance in shaping their relationship. In general, Pasternak and Tsvetaeva were highly conscious of addressing each other as male and female poets. Their relationship is an exceptionally well documented instance of a modernist "couple" working through ideas about gender and writing in the context of an enduring mutual preoccupation.

In many ways, though perhaps least of all romantically, Tsvetaeva and Pasternak were meant for each other. Their backgrounds were uncannily similar. Born two years apart, Pasternak in 1890 and Tsvetaeva in 1892, they grew up in the Moscow intelligentsia, and in an especially privileged corner of it, thanks to their fathers' impressive rise from modest provincial origins. Ivan Tsvetaev was the son of a village priest who launched a distinguished academic career after earning a degree from St. Petersburg University. His work in classical philology led him to the study of antiquities, and in 1889 he was appointed professor of the theory and history of art at Moscow University. His life's achievement was the creation of the Pushkin Museum of Fine Arts in Moscow, which he labored over throughout Tsvetaeva's childhood. Leonid Pasternak, the son of a Jewish Odessan innkeeper, was a gifted artist who, after a peripatetic existence of study and exhibiting, gained the attention of the Moscow establishment and was offered a teaching post at the Moscow School of Painting. The school provided the on-campus apartments where Pasternak spent much of his childhood. Leonid Pasternak's appointment was unusual, since Jews were prohibited from holding academic positions, but the artistic intelligentsia were more accepting, and the Pasternaks themselves were thoroughly assimilated. In fact, their sphere of acquaintances was more brilliant than that of the Tsvetaevs, and included Lev Tolstoy, whose novels Leonid Pasternak illustrated. Leonid Pasternak may have met Tsvetaev, and their work intersected once, at least, when Leonid made a drawing of the opening ceremony of the Pushkin Museum in May 1912.[2]

Their mothers, too, had similar vocations. Rozalia Kaufman, who came from a middle-class Jewish Odessan family, was a child prodigy at the piano. She had a successful concert career from age eleven, touring Russia and Poland and inspiring comparisons to Rubinstein and Liszt. Nervous exhaustion and a heart condition interrupted her touring, which she definitively gave up once she married Pasternak and had a family. Tsvetaeva's mother, Maria Mein, was also gifted at the piano, studied with one of Rubinstein's best students, and aspired to become a concert pianist. Her wealthy father, however, a high government official in Moscow, objected to a stage career. After a youthful infatuation with a married man, Mein married the older, widowed Tsvetaev and became an able collaborator on her husband's museum project. At home she continued to play the piano and initiated her children into her musical and literary passions, which were thoroughly romantic.

Both Tsvetaeva's and Pasternak's families, then, were deeply engaged with the arts, and with perfect symmetry: the visual arts were the realm of the father, music the domain—a domestic domain—of the mother. The reigning spirit in both households, though, was not bohemian but ascetic and even Victorian, as Pasternak's sister Josephine described their family home.[3] Pasternak's brother Alexander called the atmosphere one of moral idealism, and linked it to their friendship with Tolstoy. As Christopher Barnes has pointed out, Tolstoy's ethics were in some tension with the family's musical culture; Tolstoy preached against the seductive, immoral power of music, most famously in *The Kreutzer Sonata.*[4] Nevertheless, the famously conflicted Tolstoy loved music and sometimes heard Rozalia play. Pasternak recalled an evening when Tolstoy attended a house concert of Tchaikovsky's "On the Death of a Great Artist," an event that for the four-year-old Pasternak was "a boundary between the unconsciousness of infancy and my later childhood." Relating this story, Pasternak emphasized both his complete subjection to the music ("I was aroused by a sweet and oppressive torment") and the aura of Tolstoy's presence (4:299).[5] He thus represented himself as shaped by the simultaneous claims of romanticism and asceticism.

A similar combination of strictness and high feeling defined the atmosphere of Tsvetaeva's childhood home, as she later described it to Pasternak: "Principal influences: my mother's (music, nature, poetry, Germany, passion for Judaism, one against all, Eroica). The less evident but no less strong influence of my father. (Dedication to work, absence of careerism, simplicity, self-denial). The combined influence of mother and father—Spartanism. Two leitmotifs in a single home: Music and Museum. Atmosphere of the home neither bourgeois nor intelligentsia; chivalrous. Life on a lofty plane" (4:621–22). Tsvetaeva's family ideology of discipline, like Pasternak's, was set to the mother's romantic music. When Pasternak read this portrait of her family, he "sang it, ballad by ballad, nocturne by nocturne, all that you were brought up in—you and I. Mama never played in public again after we were born. I remember her as being always sad and loving" (*DNV* 185). Tsvetaeva also remembered her mother as sad, though rather less loving, in her autobiographical essay "Mother and Music" ("Mat' i muzyka," 1934). She describes her mother "flooding" her with music, much as Pasternak was overwhelmed on the night of Tolstoy's visit. Under their mothers' influence, Tsvetaeva and Pasternak studied piano as young children. Tsvetaeva fought and finally abandoned her lessons, while Pasternak for a period during his youth studied to become a composer. For both poets, though, the mother's music was a language of strong emotion and an ideal for their own writing.

In light of their shared sentimental education, it is not surprising that Tsvetaeva and Pasternak were drawn to the same poetic school. When each began writing poetry around 1907–9, Russian symbolism was in its final years as an organized literary movement.[6] In this atmosphere of decline, Andrey Bely and Viacheslav Ivanov took the lead in codifying symbolism and creating venues for disseminating its tenets. In Petersburg, they established the Society for Admirers of the Poetic Word—or "the academy," as it was more casually known—where symbolist luminaries read lectures and led debates about the "crisis of symbolism." In Moscow, they created the publishing house Musagetes, which published their major theoretical works.[7] Another "academy," the Society of Free Aesthetics, took shape around Musagetes, and its seminars were frequented by Tsvetaeva and Pasternak. The two poets did not actually meet there, but their simultaneous presence marks a central fact about their creative biographies: both were deeply and similarly influenced by their symbolist apprenticeship.

The fin de siècle in Russia, as in the rest of Europe, was an era of "sexual anarchy," to borrow the title of Elaine Showalter's book.[8] Writers of the period, including figures such as Anton Chekhov and Lev Tolstoy, openly treated the subject of erotic love, which, however, was the special provenance of the so-called "decadents" and "symbolists." As a later commentator observed, "Love opened up for the symbolist or decadent writer direct and instant access to an inexhaustible mine of emotions. . . . The symbolists wanted to nourish themselves on the strongest distillations of emotion."[9] Roman Jakobson designated Pasternak an heir to Russian symbolism precisely for his creation of "a romantic language of the emotions," and the same certainly may be said of Tsvetaeva.[10] Svetlana Boym has identified a "structure of love" that organizes Tsvetaeva's writing, and Joseph Brodsky discussed Tsvetaeva's "emotional" poetic form.[11] Both Pasternak and Tsvetaeva not only wrote love poetry but conceptualized their lyric creativity in terms of erotic feeling, also in the symbolist mode. The symbolists, like the romantics before them, imagined the moment of lyric inspiration as the poet's erotic encounter with the muse. They thereby linked creative agency with sexual agency, as Tsvetaeva and Pasternak did in their own writing.

The following two poems are representative in this regard. The first is a short poem by Tsvetaeva from 1918:

> I am a page for your pen.
> I will take everything. I am a white page.
> I am a steward of your wealth:
> I will increase and return it a hundredfold.
>
> I am the country, I am black earth.
> You are a ray of sun and rain's moisture.
> You are Lord and Master, and I—
> I am black soil—and a white page!
>
> Я—страница твоему перу.
> Всё приму. Я белая страница.
> Я—хранитель твоему добру:
> Возращу и возвращу сторицей.
>
> Я—деревня, черная земля.
> Ты мне—луч и дождевая влага.
> Ты—Господь и Господин, а я—
> Чернозем—и белая бумага!

Pasternak's somewhat earlier "Spring" ("Vesna," 1914) uses similarly suggestive imagery in the last two stanzas:

Poetry! If you were an absorbent Greek sponge,[12]
Amid the verdure I would place you
Like mortar on the wet plank
Of a green garden bench.

Grow yourself magnificent frills and farthingales,
Suck in clouds and ravines,
And by night, poetry, I will wring you out
To the health of the greedy page.

Поэзия! Греческой губкой в присосках
Будь ты, и меж зелени клейкой
Тебя б положил я на мокрую доску
Зеленой садовой скамейки.

Расти себе пышные брыжи и фижмы,
Вбирай облака и овраги,
А ночью, поэзия, я тебя выжму
Во здравие жадной бумаги.

Both poems suggest a homology between the act of writing and the sexual act. Both imagine the page as a vessel that eagerly, even greedily, receives moisture dispensed, in Tsvetaeva's poem, by a "Lord and Master" and in Pasternak's poem by a poet who squeezes out an engorged sponge. This is already to remark how the poets differently position themselves even as they resort to the same scenario: Tsvetaeva assumes a passive feminine posture, while Pasternak is a poet-agent who satisfies the "greedy paper." Most commentators have refrained from discussing the sexual meanings these poets trade in. Acknowledging the pervasive eroticism of their poetry, however, helps situate Tsvetaeva and Pasternak as the heirs to symbolism and helps account for the special intensity with which they responded to each other's writing.

These poems, like the topos of the poet's encounter with the muse, rely on a conventional gender scheme that associates masculinity with agency and femininity with passivity. With the rise of the "woman question" in the late nineteenth century, however, this very scheme became a question. By the early twentieth century, modernist writers were openly concerned with working changes on traditional gender identities, a famous example being Virginia Woolf's novel *Orlando*.[13] Tsvetaeva and Pasternak also experimented with these categories, though in a less explicit and iconoclastic fashion. This fact has been better recognized with respect to Tsvetaeva than to Pasternak. There exists a considerable literature on Tsvetaeva's uses of gender, with a wide range of emphases and conclusions. An early and still influential view holds that Tsvetaeva was interested in gender only as a category to escape, and that she puts forward a gender-neutral, androgynous ideal.[14] More recent interpreters emphasize Tsvetaeva's sympathetic portrayal of a powerful femininity (Chester, Burgin, Dinega), while others criticize her as male-identified and, relatedly, a bad mother (Heldt, Kelly, Bethea).[15] Still others (Cixous, Boym, Forrester, Sandler) acknowledge the tensions attending Tsvetaeva's views of gender, sex, and the body; my own analysis pursues this line of thinking.[16] These tensions strongly emerge in Tsvetaeva's engagement with Pasternak, which provides a defined context in which to explore them.

Similarly, Pasternak's experiments with gender are uniquely highlighted in his relationship with Tsvetaeva, though I also argue that they inform his work generally. The question of how gender functions in Pasternak's writing has been flagged as an important one but has not been vigorously pursued by Pasternak scholars. The notable exception is Alexander Zholkovsky, who has written a number of articles cataloguing "invariant" gender-related themes in Pasternak's work.[17] Christopher Barnes and Viacheslav Ivanov also have made important contributions to the discussion.[18] No one, however, has yet given a thorough account of Pasternak's use of gender, an account I supply as part of interpreting his response to Tsvetaeva. My reading is attentive to the frequent scenes of cross-dressing in Pasternak's poetry, such as the one in the quoted stanzas, where the phallic "Greek sponge" that comes all over the paper is dressed in women's clothing ("Grow yourself magnificent frills and farthingales"). On the basis of both Pasternak's poetic practice and his theorizing about poetry, I argue that his self-declared obsession with femininity helped shape the themes and forms of his art.

My analysis of gender in both poets' writing centers on their relation to femininity as it was constructed in the Victorian culture of Tsvetaeva's and Pasternak's childhood. Barbara Johnson's analysis of gender in French symbolist poetry is central to my argument.[19] I also have found it useful to appeal to Freudian theory as reformulated by later feminist critics such Luce Irigaray, Juliet Mitchell, and Elisabeth Bronfen.[20] I especially rely on Claire Kahane's argument about the historical relation between modernism and the cultural phenomenon of hysteria in *Passions of the Voice: Hysteria, Narrative, and the Figure of the Speaking Woman, 1850–1915*.[21] Freud identified hysteria as a malady of representation, in which the sufferer represents her trauma through mobile and dramatic bodily symptoms and by disordered speech. In her book, Kahane argues that a discourse modeled on the hysteric's speech gained cultural currency in the late nineteenth century. Analyzing selected works from English literature of the period, she finds that they share a psychopoetics characterized by "excessive splittings and displacements of the subject of a story, frequent paralyses of plot, phonemic rather than semantic continuities, and seemingly gratuitous and often bizarre disruptions of narrative sequences." She goes on to demonstrate that by the early decades of the twentieth century, hysterical discourse had become a resource for modernist writers, both male and female, both as a trope for their writing and as a poetics "that could more adequately represent the dislocations of the modern subject."[22] Hysterical discourse is well suited to such representations in part because, in Freud's and later Lacan's interpretations, the trauma being symbolized was a bisexual conflict, a refusal to accept an exclusively masculine or feminine sexual identity. The conflict for both men and women, however, is at root an ambivalence about femininity. As Kahane puts it, "What is repudiated in both sexes is *femininity*, specifically defined as passive desire. . . . [B]oth female and male hysterics were—are—involved in conflictual feminine identities that they both desire and fear."[23] In sum, the modernists appealed to hysterical discourse as a way of situating themselves with respect to femininity and, relatedly, questioning gender roles in the heterosexual romance.

While Freud was a less important figure in Russia than in the rest of Europe, Alexander Etkind has argued that many of the issues and insights of psychoanalysis were broached by the symbolists in their metaphysical vocabulary.[24] It is also possible that Freud's influence on Russian artists and thinkers of the period has been underestimated, as recent research by Nina Gourianova suggests.[25] Also in recent years an argument has been made that the discourse of hysteria was used to represent women in Russian fin-de-siècle culture.[26] Indisputably, hysterical discourse was recognizable to Russian readers of the period; one of the most revered symbolist poets, Alexander Blok, was accused by one reviewer of "hysterical psychopathology" (istericheskaia psikhopatiia).[27] Tsvetaeva herself was frequently charged with writing hysterically. Rather than countering such criticisms, I believe that they usefully remark, however unsympathetically, a dynamic in Tsvetaeva's work that can be understood within the cultural history and theorizing of hysteria. Thus contextualizing her writing allows one to read more fully the gender dynamics in her work.

Kahane's argument also makes it possible to theorize the relation between modernist explorations of gender and modernist poetics in a way that is useful for reading both Tsvetaeva and Pasternak. In particular, it allows one to interpret critically the heightened affect they craft in such a masterly way in their poetry. Like Tsvetaeva, Pasternak wrote poetry that dramatized emotion, though he was generally praised rather than criticized for doing so. This feature of their poetic discourse may be understood to mimic the discourse of the hysteric as a subject of passive desire. As I show in the first two chapters, both Tsvetaeva and Pasternak celebrate passive desire in their writing and understand their lyric creativity in the same terms—as an eroticized act of submission. As male and female poets, however, they are differently situated with respect to femininity. As Kahane argues, "Clearly, hysteria means one thing to a woman inhabiting a contested female body while resisting its significations, another to a man for whom the female body represents an unutterable alterity that can unman him." In a chapter on the use of hysterical discourse by male modernist writers (Eliot, Conrad, Ford), she argues that they made "a strategic use of hysteria as a defense, a form of mimicry through a first-person narrator that became part of the formal poetics of anxiety that was modernism."[28] Pasternak similarly attempted to control and aestheticize his performance of femininity.

My main purpose in making this argument is to give a full critical reading of how Tsvetaeva and Pasternak responded to each other. G. S. Smith once acutely suggested, in an essay on Tsvetaeva's "Poem of the Hill" ("Poema gory," 1923), that "perhaps the most promising avenue for further study would be the possible connection between what has here been seen as Tsvetaeva's view of the sinfulness of volition and this idea in the work of Pasternak—to whom, of course, 'Poem of the Hill' was despatched by the author."[29] Kahane's framework allows one to understand the "sinfulness of volition" as related to gender, or as naming the normative condition of femininity. What Pasternak and Tsvetaeva mainly shared, that is, was an investment in femininity, the issue around which their relationship unfolded. As they play the muse for each other, Tsvetaeva and Pasternak raise fundamental questions about identity and lyric creativity. Is the poet masculine or feminine, active or passive? Who speaks when the poet speaks? My account of their exchange in the 1920s emphasizes their changing replies to such questions.

Along the way, I supply the cultural and historical detail needed to understand the full resonance of their situation as poets writing across the cultural schism of postrevolutionary Russia. The first two chapters describe a prehistory of Tsvetaeva and Pasternak's engagement that both introduces the poets and makes the argument about their hysterical poetics, the first chapter focusing on Tsvetaeva and the second on Pasternak. The remaining three chapters track the poets' evolving relationship in chronological fashion, moving back and forth between both sides of the conversation. Chapter 3 mainly concerns Tsvetaeva's fascination with Pasternak during 1923–25, which fueled an entire body of lyric writing and a fantasy about having his child. Chapter 4 shifts to Pasternak's writing crisis in the early twenties, which led to both obsession and conflict with Tsvetaeva in 1926. Chapter 5 describes how both poets, after the crises of 1926, developed increasingly different personal and creative aspirations, primarily as expressed in their respective attitudes toward Rainer Maria Rilke, who briefly became a third party in their exchange before his death in December 1926. This last chapter addresses a stage in their correspondence that until recently was very poorly documented.[30] By contrast, the poets' correspondence during 1926 has been available for many years in German, Russian, and English editions.[31] It was therefore assumed that the rift that occurred in late 1926 was decisive, and that the poets exchanged few letters thereafter. But a volume of previously unavailable letters from Tsvetaeva's archive, which Elena Korkina and Irina Shevelenko have edited and published in 2004, reveals that their correspondence remained very frequent from 1927 until 1929, then trailed off in the early thirties. My discussion follows their exchange until its end in 1936, and a brief conclusion traces its lasting impact in their later lives and works.

I

The Girl Muse

"A second Pushkin" or "the first woman poet"—that's
what I deserve and may achieve while I'm still alive.
—Marina Tsvetaeva (1914)

My mother was the lyric element itself.
—Marina Tsvetaeva (1940)

Pasternak, in a reminiscence about Tsvetaeva, described her early work as symbolist, indeed, as the acme of Russian symbolism: "With the exception of Annensky and Blok, and with a few caveats, Andrey Bely, the early Tsvetaeva was what all the symbolists taken together wanted to be but could not be" (6:339). Tsvetaeva's engagement with Russian symbolism, however, has not been sufficiently studied or appreciated, although her own stories about her early career concern her symbolist apprenticeship.[1] As a beginning poet, Tsvetaeva attended the Society of Free Aesthetics (Obshchestvo svobodnoi estetiki), which the Moscow symbolists founded, along with the publishing house Musagetes, to promote their aesthetic program. There she met the symbolist luminaries whom she memorialized in her essays—Valery Briusov ("A Hero of Labor" ["Geroi truda," 1925]), Maximilian Voloshin ("A Living Word about a Living Man" ["Zhivoe o zhivom," 1932]), and Andrey Bely ("A Captive Spirit" ["Plennyi dukh," 1934]). In these essays Tsvetaeva offered a gender-conscious critique of her symbolist teachers, even as she paid them tribute. When she shaped that critique in the late 1920s and 1930s, she did so from a mature perspective and with the authority of an established poet. Yet one may already find a similarly critical, or at least contrarian, stance in her earliest writings.

When the unknown Tsvetaeva published her first book of poems, *Evening Album* (*Vechernyi al'bom*, 1910), at age eighteen, she sent out two copies for review, one to Musagetes, the other to the influential symbolist poet and critic Valery Briusov. Maximilian Voloshin discovered the book at Musagetes and hailed it as an example of the new "women's lyrics" (zhenskaia lirika), and Briusov praised it in similiar terms.[2] As Irina Shevelenko has argued, the enthusiastic response to the book's virtues can be explained in terms of the cultural moment.[3] The year 1910 was the year of the "crisis of symbolism" and the search for new developments in poetry. "Women's lyrics" emerged as a popular trend in the early teens partly in the context of women's more marked presence in professional and economic life generally, and partly under the influence of ideas about femininity promulgated by Otto Weininger, whose *Sex and Character (Geschlecht und Charakter, 1903)* was a best-seller in Russia at the time. The most important context, however, was symbolism itself, which fostered a cult of the feminine, and the young Tsvetaeva wrote as a woman poet in response to the symbolist example. Before we consider the version of femininity Tsvetaeva presented to the symbolist masters, though, a brief survey of symbolist representations of femininity will be useful.

In contrast to their European contemporaries, the Russian symbolists tended to conceptualize love and sexuality in metaphysical terms rather than in terms of the developing science of psychoanalysis.[4] Many of them understood their literary and cultural endeavors within the context of the religious renaissance that took place in Russia at the turn of the century. Most particularly, their writing and thinking were informed by the thought of the religious philosopher and poet Vladimir Soloviev. Soloviev's philosophy of love, elaborated in his tract "The Meaning of Love" ("Smysl liubvi," 1892–94), is a Christian philosophy that asserts the transformative power of eros in achieving union with the divine.[5] This notion also belongs to the tradition of European romanticism, which is informed by the same Platonic and Christian sources as Soloviev's philosophy.[6] The romantic poets and thinkers found metaphysical significance in erotic love, giving it central place in their philosophy and aesthetics. For them, as for Soloviev, love was a unifying force in a fragmentary world, a means of universal redemption, and they, too, imagined the end of history as a "divine marriage," drawing on the same imagery from the Book of Revelation.[7] As the marriage metaphor suggests, this metaphysical schema relies on a heterosexual model of love,[8] a model that draws with it two related gender ideals: the Eternal Feminine and the androgyne. In Soloviev's mystical philosophy, the Eternal Feminine is named the goddess Sophia, the World Soul who has fallen into base materiality and must be respiritualized through masculine agency. The task of love is to fuse the masculine with the feminine in the figure of the androgyne: "A true human in the fulness of his ideal personality, obviously, cannot be merely male or merely female, but must be the higher unity of both."[9]

What was most distinctive about Soloviev's vision—and similar ones elaborated by Russian philosophers of the period—was his insistence on the task of love as a realistic plan of action. As Olga Matich has shown, this emphasis was the legacy of nineteenth-century Russian social thought, a combustible mix of materialism and utopianism.[10] Soloviev's theory of love was urged as a practice, a practice known as *zhiznetvorchestvo,* or "life creation."[11] "Life creation" was explicitly divorced from procreation, and from sexuality generally. Like his teacher Plato, Soloviev advocated against sexual love and reproduction as activities that direct man's erotic energies away from self-transformation and toward "the bad infinity of the physical reproduction of organs."[12] Attempts to build relationships around unconsummated eros were understandably plagued by tension and confusion. Andrey Bely, probably Soloviev's most energetic and anxious disciple, was simultaneously involved in two celebrated symbolist love triangles.[13] The first formed around Alexander Blok and his wife, Liubov Dmitrievna Mendeleeva, whom Bely and Blok for a time regarded as the human embodiment of the Sophia.[14] Bely was also engaged in a duel with Valery Briusov over Nina Petrovskaya, a writer in the symbolist milieu. Petrovskaya dismayed Bely with her unmistakably sexual passion, but Briusov was glad to succumb; the couple made a passionate pilgrimage to Lake Saima in Finland, the setting for Soloviev's most famous erotic poems.[15] Petrovskaya's story later became the basis for Vladislav Khodasevich's essay "The End of Renata" ("Konets Renaty," 1928), in which he censured symbolist life creation as destructive to its practitioners, particularly to the women involved.[16]

Contemporary critics have similarly questioned the gender politics of Soloviev's metaphysics. As Eric Naiman has argued, despite Soloviev's cult of the Sophia, his ideal androgyne appears to subsume the feminine in an essentially masculine ideal.[17] He also observes that Soloviev's rhetorical assumption of woman's reproductive capacity in the notion of "life creation" is an appropriation of the feminine.[18] (Similar critiques have been made of the Romantic poets' "colonizing of the feminine.")[19] In general, Soloviev's theory of love preserved the romantics' heterosexual and masculinist orientation, reinfusing it with philosophical authority. It mapped neatly onto—and was partly produced by—the traditional love lyric, with its heterosexual structure of address, in which the male poet addresses an idealized female beloved. Relatedly, Soloviev helped introduce into the Russian poetic tradition the vocabulary of chivalric love.

The poem Soloviev put forward as the best Russian rendering of the "feminine shade" (zhenstvennaia ten') was Iakov Polonsky's "Tsar-Maiden" ("Tsardevitsa," 1876).[20] The phrase comes from Konstantin Balmont's translation of Shelley's "Epipsychidion," to which Soloviev compared Polonsky's poem.[21] Polonsky follows the convention used by Shelley—and later by Soloviev himself in his poem "Three Encounters" ("Tri svidaniia," 1898)—of "regarding a youthful vision as the romantic origin of a transcendent one."[22] In Polonsky's poem the feminine ideal assumes the form of the "tsar-maiden," a popular heroine of Slavic folklore, a virgin queen who possesses both strength and beauty; his tsar-maiden has the same solar attributes ("the sun shone on her brow"), and she inhabits the same "inaccessible castle," locked by "golden keys."

The poet first observes her in his youth, in what he describes as "a marvelous adolescent delirium" (chudnyi, otrocheskii bred). Later in life he sometimes senses that she "followed him with a bright, damp eye" as he walks home at night after holiday revels (iarkii, vlazhnyi / Glaz ee sledil za mnoi). She finally tracks him to his bedroom, appearing at his window one spring morning:

And how did this happen—
While awake or in a dream?!
Once in spring, at daybreak,
She blushed at my window:—

The curtains stirred,
A thick rosebush flared,
And when I closed my eyes I felt
The kiss of fragrant lips.

But barely, barely did I glimpse
The brightness of her face,
As my guest slipped away and burned
Her mark into my brow.

Since that time I've been unable
To wash away her mark.
And I don't have the strength to betray
The ever youthful tsar-maiden.

I wait until the beauty—granting
My lips a second kiss—
Opens for me the gates
To her secret castle.

И уж как случилось это—
Наяву или во сне?!
Раз, она весной, в час утра,
Зарумянилась в окне:—

Всколыхнулась занавеска,
Вспыхнул роз махровый куст,
И, закрыв глаза, я встретил
Поцелуй душистых уст.

Но едва-едва успел я
Блеск лица ее поймать,
Ускользая, гостья ко лбу
Мне прижгла свою печать.

С той поры ее печати
Мне ничем уже не смыть,
Вечно-юной царь-девице
Я не в силах изменить . . .

Жду,—вторичным поцелуем
Заградив мои уста,—
Красота в свой тайный терем
Мне отворит ворота.[23]

In typical romantic fashion, the poet's muse is fused with nature, appearing first as the moon and then as the sun at dawn. But the sun's kiss is also a kiss in this erotic scene, where the muse's visitation takes place in the poet's bedroom.

In addition to eroticizing the poet's encounter with the muse, Polonsky's rendering features a reversal of conventional gender roles: the feminized poet is seduced by an Amazonian muse. While a Solovievan reading of the poem might see a match made in heaven between two androgynes, a critical reading discerns an allegory about sexual agency. Although we observe the muse in the role of pursuer, the poem closes with the poet's fantasy that she finally will succumb to him. The match between the poet and the muse becomes perfect only when his fantasy is realized and customary gender roles are restored. With this turnabout, Polonsky reproduces the logic of the Slavic folktale on which he drew: the hero, after undergoing many trials, gains entrance to the tsar-maiden's castle and subdues her, after which his powers wax while hers wane, since her strength derives from her chastity.[24] The logic is similar to the logic of numerous romantic texts in which "the woman must finally be enslaved or destroyed, must disappear or die."[25] The ultimate end of the logic, as Karen Swann has argued in a reading of John Keats's "La Belle Dame sans Merci" (1819), is to confirm the poet's membership in an all-male community of "kings and princes" seduced by the same beautiful lady.[26]

The first among princes, the most influential poet of the "feminine shade," was Alexander Blok. Blok created her most famous hypostasis in his first book of poems, *Verses on the Beautiful Lady* (*Stikhi o prekrasnoi dame*, 1904). When the book appeared, his contemporaries hailed Blok as Soloviev's heir.[27] He also drew on Polonsky's example, and on "The Tsar-Maiden" in particular, in representing his own Beautiful Lady; as he noted in his diary, Polonsky's poem "preoccupies all poets."[28] Like Polonsky's tsar-maiden, Blok's muse has solar attributes and lives in an inaccessible castle.[29] As he states in another poem, however, the muse threatens to change her appearance: "I'm fearful: you will change your aspect" (Mne strashno: izmenish' oblik ty). With this line, Blok was already shaping a narrative about his poetic career, which he later called a "trilogy of humanization" (trilogiia vochelovecheniia).[30] In this narrative, the Beautiful Lady of the "first book" becomes in the "second book" a seductive Stranger sitting in a tavern, while the disillusioned poet sinks into debauchery ("Neznakomka," 1906).

Blok's renderings of the muse were also clearly influenced by Baudelaire, or if not by the French poet himself, then by the preceding generation of "decadent" Russian poets who embraced Baudelaire's work, including Konstantin Balmont and Valery Briusov.[31] Briusov, in particular, was known for poems that cast women as demonic temptresses in scenes of cruel eroticism. Joan Delaney Grossman has argued that Briusov's influence is detectable even in Blok's earliest representation of the "Beautiful Lady," confirming Blok's own claim that Briusov was just as important a teacher for him as Soloviev.[32] The claim has puzzled scholars, since Briusov publicly and polemically rejected the "second-generation" symbolists' metaphysical orientation, espousing instead a Nietzschean aestheticism. As Grossman persuasively shows, however, Blok saw Briusov as similarly engaged in exploring "the full horror of the secret . . . of the feminine soul" (ves' uzhas tainy . . . zhenstvennoi dushi).[33] Blok's achievement was to fuse successfully the metaphysical and decadent strains of Russian symbolism to produce a canonic image of femininity as both idealized and dangerously sexual.

In Blok's work, the symbolist fantasy of the poet's encounter with the muse achieves its fullest expression; he enhances and makes explicit the erotic character of the fantasy and its ambivalent fascination with the feminine. Many of Blok's later poems feature scenes of cruel eroticism with gender reversals like the one staged in Polonsky's "Tsar-Maiden." There are frequent sadomasochistic scenarios in which the poet is the masochistic partner, leading one critic to characterize Blok's muse as a dominatrix.[34] A famous example is "Humiliation" ("Unizhenie," 1911), which describes the poet's visit to a brothel. The first four stanzas render the interior—the red silk divans, pornography, and filthy service bell, all bathed in the light of a lurid sunset. The poem ends with the poet addressing a whore who beckons him to her bed:

> You are bold! So be even more fearless!
> I'm not your husband, your lover, or friend!
> So pierce my heart, yesterday's angel,
> With your sharp French heel.

> Ты смела! Так еше будь бесстрашней!
> Я—не муж, не жених твой, не друг!
> Так вонзай же, мой ангел вчерашний,
> В сердце—острый французский каблук!

Like the speaker of Polonsky's "Tsar-Maiden," the poet appears in a sexually submissive posture, now tinged with masochism: his angel delivers a phallic thrust instead of a mere kiss. Even in poems where Blok's poet is a sexual agent, he thematizes his "feminine" passivity. In "Song of Hell" ("Pesn' ada," 1909), from the same cycle, he appears as a vampire who nightly drinks the blood of a captive woman. The poem ends with the poet-vampire grinding his signet ring into his victim's flesh, a phallic gesture like the one he invites the whore to perform at the conclusion of "Humiliation." Yet the lyric hero of "Song of Hell" also finds his dominant role degrading, describing himself as a "fallen, humiliated maiden" (padshaia unizhennaia deva).

This dynamic is already found in Baudelaire's writing, as Barbara Johnson has shown in an important essay, "Gender and Poetry: Charles Baudelaire and Marceline Desbordes-Valmore."[35] Baudelaire's own "Le Vampire" begins with the vampiric beloved delivering a phallic thrust to the poet's heart ("Toi qui, comme un coup de couteau, / Dans mon coeur plaintif es entrée"). Her miserable captive, the poet, contemplates freeing himself by murdering her ("J'ai prié le glaive rapide / De conquérir ma liberté"). But the knife and the poison he considers using declare his abjection: were he to murder her, he would immediately resurrect her body with his kisses. As Johnson observes, "There is no simple correlation here between femininity and passivity, masculinity and action."[36] She goes on to observe that male masochism is present throughout the Petrarchan tradition of love poetry, and it is very clearly present in the Russian symbolist extension of that tradition.

Johnson speculates that the male poet's masochism has not been recognized because it is read rhetorically: the male poet simply performs femininity, in an instance of what she calls the "male feminine." By contrast, the masochistic scenarios rendered by Baudelaire's contemporary Marceline Desbordes-Valmore are read literally, as an expression of her feminine nature: "When men have described love as an experience of fragmentation, wounding, or loss of psychic intactness and control, it has been read as an analysis of the Nature of Desire. When women have described something analogous, it has been read as an expression of What a Woman Wants."[37] Johnson thus describes how the woman poet is differently situated with respect to the canonic love lyric, that is, as a poet who normatively writes as a passive subject. She supplies a useful framework for reading the work of women poets writing at the fin de siècle, including Tsvetaeva, to whose work I now turn.

Russian women poets of the symbolist period found creative ways to write within the tradition, one of which was to use a male persona.[38] Voloshin noted in his review of Tsvetaeva's *Evening Album* (*Vechernyi al'bom*, 1910) that younger women poets like Tsvetaeva, by contrast, openly claimed a female persona. For precedents Tsvetaeva turned not so much to Russian poetry (probably, like most of her contemporaries, she did not know Karolina Pavlova's work at the time)[39] but to autobiography, which, as Barbara Heldt has shown, was the most established mode for Russian women writers.[40] Tsvetaeva was already working in this mode before she began writing poetry, keeping a journal from a young age and writing her autobiography as a teenager. The voice she found most compelling, not surprisingly, was that of an ambitious young woman artist, Maria Bashkirtseva, whose *Journal de Marie Bashkirtseff, un portrait* (1887) was published after her premature death from tuberculosis at age twenty-four, a circumstance that helped make it a literary sensation. In her preface, Bashkirtseva explained that she decided to publish her journal when she became fatally ill: "If I should not live long enough to become famous, this journal will be interesting to the psychologist. The record of a woman's life . . . is always interesting."[41]

This autobiographical principle governed the making of *Evening Album*, which Tsvetaeva dedicated to Bashkirtseva, as well as her second book, *Magic Lantern* (*Volshebnyi fonar'*, 1912).[42] (Tsvetaeva also contemplated writing a third book titled *Maria Bashkirtseva*.) She included in these poems authentic details from her life—her age (seventeen), her family life, school, friends, and infatuations. It was this quality of "intimacy" (*intimnost'*) that struck contemporary readers as a new note in Russian poetry. But also at issue was the kind of intimacy Tsvetaeva offered: the intimacy of the teenaged girl, or as Voloshin put it "girlish/virginal intimacy" (*devich'ia intimnost'*).[43] He described her persona as "wholly at the threshold between the last days of childhood and first youth."[44] Mikhail Tseitlin similarly remarked that "she has her own theme: an intimate, mainly half-child and half-adolescent world."[45] With *Evening Album*, Tsvetaeva demonstrated that the record of an adolescent girl's life is always interesting.

The two central and interwoven concerns of this unfolding life are mortality and sexuality. Bashkirtseva wrote in the awareness of her impending death, and Tsvetaeva's autobiographism has a similar compulsion. Just a few years earlier, in 1905, her mother, like Bashkirtseva, died prematurely from tuberculosis. (That Tsvetaeva linked the two deaths is apparent from her attempt to correspond with Bashkirtseva's mother.)[46] In the aesthetic manifesto she included in an edition of her selected early poems (*Iz dvukh knig*, 1913), Tsvetaeva essentially reiterates Bashkirtseva's rationale for writing her *Journal*: "All of us will die. . . . So write, write more! Fix every moment, every gesture" (5:230). She makes repeated attempts in her early poems to recuperate her lost mother through language.[47] In numerous poems titled "Mama" or "To Mama" she includes the kinds of details she urged the poet, in her manifesto, to preserve, such as "the precious stone on a favorite ring": "Your slowed breath over your notebook / And your ring of bright rubies" (Zamedlennyi vzdokh nad tetradkoi / I v iarkikh rubinakh kol'tso).

In "To Mama" ("K mame"), the second poem in *Evening Album*, she also assesses the impact of her mother's death on her daughters:

> We first heard your quiet call
> In an old Strauss waltz,
> Since then all the living are strange to us
> And the fleeting chime of the clock is comforting.
>
> We, like you, welcome the sunsets,
> Rejoicing in the end's approach.
> All we own in the best of evenings
> Was laid in our hearts by you.
>
> Tirelessly watching over children's dreams
> (Without you only the moon looked into them!)
> You led your little ones past
> A bitter life of hopes and actions.

A silhouette of Tsvetaeva made by her daughter Ariadna Efron
with the inscription "C'est formidable" (undated)

From our earliest years we have been drawn to sad people,
Laughter is boring and the domestic hearth is alien.
Our ship set out at a bad hour
And sails at the will of all winds!

The azure island—childhood—grows ever more pale,
We stand alone on the deck.
It's clear you left a legacy of sadness,
O mama, to your little girls!

В старом вальсе штраусовском впервые
Мы услышали твой тихий зов,
С той поры нам чужды все живые
И отраден беглый бой часов.

Мы, как ты, приветствуем закаты,
Упиваясь близостью конца.
Все, чем в лучший вечер мы богаты,
Нам тобою вложено в сердца.

К детским снам клонясь неутомимо,
(Без тебя лишь месяц в них глядел!)
Ты вела своих малюток мимо
Горькой жизни помыслов и дел.

С ранних лет нам близок, кто печален,
Скучен смех и чужд домашний кров . . .
Наш корабль не в добрый миг отчален
И плывет по воле всех ветров!

Все бледней лазурный остров—детство,
Мы одни на палубе стоим.
Видно грусть оставила в наследство
Ты, о мама, девочкам своим!

The poem is an expression of loyalty to the dead mother, whom her daughters love to the exclusion of all "the living." Their loyalty is such that they want to share her condition; they hasten their young lives and look forward to "the end." This poem supplies a crucial context for the poems in the collection about young suicides and about the speaker's own desire for death. While the figure of the girl suicide is common in the literature of the period, the logic of her appearance in this collection is the logic of mourning: the speaker does not wish for death so much as she wishes to rejoin her mother. As she famously exclaims in "A Prayer" ("Molitva"), addressing God, "You gave me a childhood better than a fairy tale / So give me death at age seventeen!" (Ty dal mne detstvo—lushche skazki / I dai mne smert'—v semnadtsat' let!). In fact, as "To Mama" states, the little girls are already moving beyond the "island of childhood" into the uncharted waters of adolescence, without maternal guidance.

In this way the theme of the mother's death intertwines with the book's other main concern, the girl's first experience of love. In Tsvetaeva's case, her first romance was literally a symbolist one. Even before she published *Evening Album*, Tsvetaeva was personally acquainted with the Moscow symbolists. In 1909 she was introduced by a family friend to Lev Kobylinsky, better known simply as "Ellis." A symbolist poet who was a translator and fanatical proponent of Baudelaire, he collaborated with Andrey Bely in founding the Argonaut group and later the publishing house Musagetes. When he met Tsvetaeva, he was preparing a book on Balmont, Briusov, and Bely, *Russian Symbolists* (*Russkie simvolisty*, 1910), and probably brought her attention to their poetry; he also pressed Baudelaire's work on her, as Tsvetaeva ironically recorded in a later poem ("We've had enough of Baudelaire!" ["Nam tak dovol'no o Bodlere!"]).[48] Ellis, who was thirty-four years old at the time, was on unusually familiar terms with Tsvetaeva and her younger sister Asya, who were left relatively unsupervised after their mother's death. He regarded his relationship with Tsvetaeva seriously enough to make a marriage proposal, which she refused. She was better disposed toward the young man who delivered Ellis's offer, his friend Vladimir Nilender, a young classical philologist and translator of Heraclitus. Nilender also fell in love with Tsvetaeva and proposed to her, but she refused him as well.

Like her symbolist elders, Tsvetaeva made her triangular romance the subject of verse. A number of the poems in *Evening Album* are linked to Ellis and

Nilender, and the book as a whole was conceived "in place of a letter" to Nilender.[49] The title itself refers to an album the Tsvetaeva sisters kept, recording their conversations with their suitors. Tsvetaeva even made her own contribution to the symbolist array of oddly configured relationships: the love quadrangle. In "Two in a Square" ("Dva v kvadrate"), and in several other poems, Tsvetaeva's sister Anastasia figures as a fourth player in the drama. What is most interesting about Tsvetaeva's writing of the symbolist romance is that she plays the role of the poet's beloved. In her later memoir of Bely, she made this fact explicit, juxtaposing her affair with Nilender to Bely's famous union with Asya Turgeneva. As a young woman poet, that is, she found it useful to write from the position of the symbolist muse.

In a rare analysis of the influence of symbolism on the early Tsvetaeva, Omry Ronen has traced the prosodic models for particular poems to Zinaida Gippius, Mirra Lokhvitskaia, Briusov, Blok, and Balmont. Juxtaposing these with Tsvetaeva's poems allows him to detect a tendency to "clean up" the older poets' language, in a manner appropriate to her young girl's persona. When she does a variation on Gippius, she sheds the poem's metaphysical argument; when rewriting Blok, she tones down his "language of tormenting passions" (iazyk muchitel'nykh strastei).[50] Naturally, she does the same with Briusov, whom Tsvetaeva adapted with especial frequency. Ronen's argument that Tsvetaeva responds with "elegance" and "modesty" to symbolist eroticism is an essential observation about her response to symbolism, but one that needs refinement. The very fact that Tsvetaeva turned to these overheated poems shows her interest in them, which is to say that her resistance was a form of attraction. This dynamic is most apparent in her performance of the symbolist muse as a girl on the cusp of sexual maturity.

Tsvetaeva, in fact, created this role for herself under the influence of Valery Briusov, the symbolist poet with whom she was most intensely engaged when writing the poems of *Evening Album*. Tsvetaeva was avidly reading Briusov at the time of her affair with Nilender, and his poetry seemed to her to capture her own experience. In her extant copy of Briusov's collection *Paths and Crossings* (*Puti i pereput'ia*, 1908), Tsvetaeva entered the dates of her crisis and breakup with Nilender next to two of the poems.[51] In the first poem, "The Meeting" ("Vstrecha," 1906–7), the poet's love reincarnates the love of the Egyptian god Osiris for his sister Isis, which lasted for a "fateful and brief time" (v rokovoi i kratkii chas). The second poem, "In the Train Car" ("V vagone"), describes the poet's erotic encounter with a green-eyed beauty on a train. Both poems, like many others in Briusov's oeuvre, represent a love that is sexual and ephemeral.

That Tsvetaeva was drawn by precisely these qualities is apparent from a short essay she wrote about *Paths and Crossings* sometime during 1910. The essay, which Tsvetaeva copied out and preserved in a separate notebook, is titled "Magic in the Poetry of Briusov" ("Volshebstvo v stikhakh Briusova"). Writing in the genre of the literary review, Tsvetaeva adopts a tone of critical authority, perhaps emulating Briusov himself, an influential critic.[52] She identifies Briusov as a poet who has many female muses rather than a single "princess and enchantress." Tsvetaeva focuses on the figure of the "girl-muse" (devushka-muza), although, as she remarks, the girl-muse appears only rarely in his poetry. The "magic" of Tsvetaeva's title is the magic of love which, in language she borrows from Briusov's poems, draws girls like "butterflies" but leaves them "to yearn for the green leaves they have lost forever" (5:227). The doomed girls of Briusov's poetry end by wallowing in sensuality, with only the memory of innocence as solace. This "fairy tale," she says, "has a sad ending, like all the best fairy tales" (5:226).

By way of illustration Tsvetaeva adduces the final stanzas of Briusov's poem "The Condemned Priestess" ("Osuzhdennaia zhritsa"). The poem is written in the voice of a prostitute reflecting on her sordid fate:

> And if God sends me a dream
> About the unattainable, and about happiness,—
> He will not speak to me of love,
> I will not dream of passion.
>
> But I will be a child again
> Under the snowy sheets of my little bed,
> And my mother will sit next to me,
> Illumined by the flame of the icon lamp.

> И если Бог пошлет мне сон
> О недоступном и о счастье,—
> Мне про любовь не скажет он,
> Мне не приснится сладострастье.
>
> Но буду вновь ребенком я
> Под белым пологом кроватки,
> И сядет рядом мать моя,
> Озарена огнем лампадки.

The fallen woman, or ruined girl, dreams of being a child again, of being rejoined with her mother. As in the poems of *Evening Album,* being with the mother means remaining secure against sexual love and its tragic consequences.

The force of Tsvetaeva's emotional connection with the poems she singles out in Briusov's book is such that in the next paragraph the line between poetry and life simply disappears: "The poems 'Solitude' and 'First Meetings' resound with the music of youth called forth by the power of remembrance. In these poems the magic killed by life revives. Before us is the image of two sisters who once heard the poet's first avowals; the shady garden before us is the garden of his youth: 'For we're children, we're all children, butterflies around the fires!'" (4:228). Tsvetaeva quotes the line "For we're children" from "First Meetings"

("Pervye vstrechi," 1904), which does indeed feature a garden in which the poet recalls an innocent love. But the "image of two sisters" is Tsvetaeva's importation of a scene from her own life—Ellis's visits to the Tsvetaeva girls. This poem, and several others Tsvetaeva selected, features the inflammatory sexual imagery for which Briusov was renowned. By placing herself and Asya in this garden, Tsvetaeva marks her proximity to the dangerous sexual world to which Ellis and Nilender belonged. Tsvetaeva's adolescent sexual yearnings and fears blossomed in the symbolist hothouse, and she found a language for them in Briusov's poetry. Hence her readiness to see herself in the prostitute of "The Condemned Priestess," who regards her sexuality with regret and ambivalence.

It is ironic, then, that when Briusov reviewed *Evening Album,* he stated that her poems "always take their departure from some real fact, from something actually experienced," unaware of how his own work entered into shaping that experience.[53] (He did, though, observe on his copy of *Evening Album* that she had had "good schooling" [khoroshaia shkola], presumably in symbolist poetics.) He might have recalled Tsvetaeva's attempts to draw him into a dialogue with her. Even before Tsvetaeva mailed him a copy of *Evening Album,* she wrote him a letter after encountering him in a bookstore and overhearing him declare his dislike of Rostand—an opinion Tsvetaeva contested in her letter (6:37–38). She also mentioned that her sister Asya "thinks about him a lot" after a similar anonymous encounter, which Tsvetaeva memorialized in a poem titled "The Quandary" ("Nedoumenie"). According to Asya's memoirs, she was reading Briusov's poems on a bus when she noticed him sitting opposite her. When she began to recite his poems in a half-voice, she says, Briusov fled in discomfort. In her poem, Tsvetaeva suggests he feared being seduced by the girl-muse:

> Were you afraid of her amber eyes,
> Those childish, too-red lips,
> Did you, fearing her sly enchantments,
> Not dare to drink the foaming cup?

> Испугался глаз ее янтарных,
> Этих детских, слишком алых губок,
> Убоявшись чар ее коварных,
> Не посмел испить шипящий кубок?

This poem reveals Tsvetaeva's own pleasure in playing the girl-muse, despite her powerful sense of the dangers involved. It emerges that the adolescent girl can play two games: she may declare her childlike innocence, and she may claim and act on sexual feeling. The persona of the girl-muse, that is, allowed Tsvetaeva some strategic flexibility, even while conforming to the conflicted symbolist representation of idealized and sexualized femininity.

Briusov was not entirely comfortable with the way Tsvetaeva performed his girl-muse. In his review of *Evening Album,* he spoke of a "terrible intimacy" (zhutkaia intimnost') that placed the reader in the position of the voyeur: "When you read her book you sometimes feel awkward, as though you had indiscreetly looked into someone's apartment through a half-open window and glimpsed a scene passersby should not see."[54] Tsvetaeva, in a poetic reply, interpreted his response as merely condescending: "Smile into my 'window', / Or consider me a fool" (Ulybnis' v moe 'okno' / Il' k shutam menia prichisli). But Briusov, like Tsvetaeva's other readers, was likely responding to the virginal/ sexual ambiguity of her lyric persona, which she powerfully exploits.

A clear example may be found in Tsvetaeva's continued exchange with Ellis, who made Tsvetaeva his symbolist muse in his lyric collection *Argo*, published by Musagetes in 1914. The book, which is dedicated "to the memory of Vladimir Soloviev," contains several poems to Tsvetaeva and Asya. They recapitulate the central themes of *Evening Album*: the mother's death and the loss of sexual innocence. In the first of two poems dedicated to Tsvetaeva, titled "To Paradise" ("V rai"), the dead mother hovers over the poet's tryst with her daughters (a reference to an actual painting of Tsvetaeva's mother in the grave, which hung in her father's study[55]):

> The children are settled on the couch,
> There's night and cold outside the window,
> And in her portait that hangs above them
> Their mama sleeps her final sleep.

> На диван уселись дети,
> ночь и стужа за окном,
> и над ними, на портрете
> мама спит последним сном.[56]

The poet offers the children a choice of fantastic destinations, all of which they reject in favor of "paradise." This paradise, described in the final two stanzas of the poem, is a place where angels and children pray for the mother's return to life (chtoby mama na portrete / ulybaias', ozhila!). Ellis's second poem to Tsvetaeva, "Guardian Angel" ("Angel khranitel'"), describes a mother drowsing on a bench while her child moves to grasp a snake on a nearby rock. The child is protected by an angel's wing, however, and the snake crawls away defeated. The poem's message is thrown into relief by the poem that precedes it in the collection, "The Poisoning" ("Otrava"), in which a young boy is bitten by a snake and loses his sexual innocence (Ia ne ditia!).

In both of Ellis's poems to Tsvetaeva, the poet is a guardian angel who attempts to replace the absent mother. But one may also detect in them a prurient strain. Ellis, after all, imagines the child in "Guardian Angel" reaching for the snake, actively seeking sexual knowledge. In fact, in responding to this symbolist creation of herself in an answering poem, Tsvetaeva reminds him that she rejected his advances.[57] "The Enchanter" ("Charodei," 1914), Tsvetaeva's first long poem, renders Ellis as she knew him, that is, as an adopted member of her family household. Pointedly, and perhaps in response to his poems to her, Tsvetaeva paints him not as a guardian angel but as a tempter, though an ineffectual one, who tries to take advantage of the mother's, and father's, absence. (Ivan Tsvetaev, as the head of the Pushkin Museum, often traveled to make acquisitions):

> "You, whose father's now in Cairo
> Whose mother's gone without a trace—
> Know that in this world you two
> Cannot be saved!
>
> Shall I tear away your blindfold?
> Shall I reveal to you a new path?"
> "No, you'd better tell some kind
> Of fairy tale."

> «Вы, чей отец сейчас в Каире,
> Чьей матери остыл и след—
> Узнайте, вам обеим в мире
> Спасенья нет!
>
> Хотите,—я сорву повязку?
> Я вам открою новый путь?»
> «Нет,—лучше расскажите сказку
> Про что-нибудь.»

The sixteen-year-old heroine, as her age is identified in the poem, handily dismisses her symbolist seducer, insisting that he confine himself to telling fairy tales. This abrupt undercutting of Ellis's attempts to show her a "new path" is in keeping with Tsvetaeva's fond but mocking tone throughout.

Tsvetaeva's entanglements with Briusov and Ellis show her both inviting and resisting the symbolist poet's advances, testing the waters as an adolescent girl. Her male readers, though, tend to describe her lyric persona as innocent and childlike, even as they note her threshold age. Of the reviewers of *Evening Album*, only Marietta Shaginian remarked that she also articulates "an extremely subtle and interesting view" about "the element of passion." On these grounds she contrasts Tsvetaeva to Mirra Lokhvitskaia, whose speaker is so consumed by passion that she cannot be reflective about sexuality. Tsvetaeva, though, "addresses the question of sex, and addresses it very significantly, i.e., not from a general human or philosophical point of view and not with Otto Weininger's macho self-assertion [s muzhchinstvuiushchim samoutverzhdeniem]; she says, standing her ground, that her position is one of an eternal, conscious femininity, her instinct is hostile recoil from the masculine. Submission, but submission after a battle, submission to something outside, alien, enemy. For every pure (meaning typically virginal) woman, man is the enemy, and the story of love for a man is always a tale of military engagements, siege, and capture. Inevitably—

capture."[58] Whether or not Tsvetaeva's speaker is "typically virginal," she describes a view of sexual relations that is far from innocent and certainly informed by symbolist poetry's sadomasochistic scenarios. By identifying men as "the enemy," as she does in her poem "Into the Enemy Camp" ("V chuzhoi lager'"), the girl attempts to control a game she seems bound to lose.

Tsvetaeva found her girl's wisdom about the sexual romance bolstered by a woman poet, the nineteenth-century French poet Marceline Desbordes-Valmore, the very poet Barbara Johnson contrasts to Baudelaire in her essay mentioned earlier. Although scholars have sought to identify the women poets who influenced Tsvetaeva,[59] they have passed over a poem in which she directly equates herself with Desbordes-Valmore, "In the Mirror of M. D.-V.'s Book" ("V zerkale knigi M. D.-V."):

> This heart is mine! These lines are mine!
> You live, you are in me, Marceline!
> Your frightened verse is no longer silent in oblivion,
> And the ice has melted in tears.
>
> We gave ourselves together, we suffered together,
> We, loving, fell in love to our torment!
> The same grief pierced us and with the same lance,
> And on my exhaustedly scorching brow
> I feel a cool hand.
>
> I, asking for kisses, received a lance!
> I, like you, did not find my master! . . .
> These lines are mine! This heart is mine!
> Who is Marceline—you, or I?
>
> Это сердце—мое! Эти строки—мои!
> Ты живешь, ты во мне, Марселина!
> Уж испуганный стих не молчит в забытьи,
> И слезами растаяла льдина.
>
> Мы вдвоем отдались, мы страдали вдвоем,
> Мы, любя, полюбили на муку!
> Та же скорбь нас пронзила и тем же копьем,
> И на лбу утомленно-горячем своем
> Я прохладную чувствую руку.
>
> Я, лобзанья прося, получила копье!
> Я, как ты, не нашла властелина! . . .
> Эти строки—мои! Это сердце—мое!
> Кто же, ты или я—Марселина?

What the two poets share is the pain inflicted by love's "lance," though in this masochistic logic she continues to seek a true "master" (vlastelin). They are not quite identical, however: Desbordes-Valmore is older and more experienced than Tsvetaeva's girl, and she comforts her after the love disaster. She appears, in fact, as a mother soothing her daughter's forehead after her first adult trauma, a conjuring of maternal guidance through the transition to maturity.

As a substitute for her deceased mother she conjured, first of all, a woman poet, and a poet of good reputation among her contemporaries, though Desbordes-Valmore has since disappeared from the canon. A strong psychological draw for Tsvetaeva would have been the mythology of Desbordes-Valmore's ruined love life, a mythology of the great love affair followed by the compromise marriage. This was precisely the story of Tsvetaeva's mother, as Tsvetaeva learned it from reading her mother's diaries. But the mythology also had cultural power, as Barbara Johnson has discussed in her essay on gender and poetry.[60] Johnson argues that this mythology supported Desbordes-Valmore's construction of herself as perfectly feminine and therefore appealing to the nineteenth-century literary establishment, as represented here by Baudelaire. In his admiring words, Desbordes-Valmore was "a woman, always a woman, and absolutely nothing but a woman . . . nothing but the eternal feminine." Paradoxically, she achieves this by situating herself "elsewhere than as the 'beloved object' of traditional love poetry," whether as the unloved, abandoned woman, or as the feeling wife and mother.[61] Baudelaire particularly appreciated her performance of the latter: "but only in the poems of the ardent Marceline can you find that warmth of the maternal nest." As Johnson argues, Baudelaire finds in Desbordes-Valmore a poetic mother, his response to her poems reenacting "the drama of separation/individuation from the Mother which can be seen as *the* topic of Baudelaire's poetry."[62]

Tsvetaeva also chose Desbordes-Valmore as a poetic mother, and her poem dramatizes the same difficulty around individuation: "Who is Marceline—you, or I?" (Kto zhe, ty ili ia—Marselina?). Tsvetaeva's identification with the poet-mother, though, resonates differently from Baudelaire's because the two poets are in a different relation to femininity. As Johnson describes, Baudelaire enacts the "male feminine," or "male privilege as the right to play femininity."[63] Tsvetaeva also plays femininity, but her performance is taken literally because of her gender; she simply "is" feminine. The performance earned her the love of the male critic in the fashion of Desbordes-Valmore. Voloshin praised Tsvetaeva in the very same terms in which Desbordes-Valmore was praised, as "naïve" and "sincere," and he may have had Desbordes-Valmore in mind when he began his essay by invoking the example of the French women poets. As I have emphasized, however, Tsvetaeva's girl is also a bad girl, displaying a sexual agency that is very different from Desbordes-Valmore's passive emotionalism. Tsvetaeva's agency was possibly less readable in her work, or read rhetorically, as posturing by an inexperienced young woman.

The strategy Tsvetaeva most openly pursued in her early work, in fact, was Desbordes-Valmore's enactment of naïve femininity. In a much-quoted poem titled "In Luxembourg Garden" ("V Liuksemburgskom sadu"), she chooses motherhood, understood as a kind of captivity, over the agency of the Amazon:

> I love women who have not quailed in battle,
> Who have mastered the sword and lance,—
> But I know that only in thrall to the cradle
> Is my typical—woman's—happiness!

> Я женщин люблю, что в бою не робели,
> Умевших и шпагу держать, и копье—
> Но знаю, что только в плену колыбели
> Обычное—женское—счастье мое!

This girl's fantasy about becoming a mother, though, carries an implicit tension, since she must abandon girlhood in order to have a child. Her early poems generally inscribe a contradictory double desire to have children and to remain a child, to be the mother and to have the mother.

Both desires compel a poem addressed to Sergey Efron, the young man she met in Voloshin's bohemian milieu and married in 1912 at age twenty. The poem, "Out of a Fairy Tale—into a Fairy Tale" ("Iz skazki—v skazku"), describes a fantasy about continuing childhood's idyll in her marriage:

> My dear, on this winter evening
> Be like a small boy with me.
> Don't disturb my marveling,
> Keep, like a little boy, a scary secret

Wedding photograph of Sergey Efron and Marina Tsvetaeva, 1911

And help me remain a little girl
Even as a wife.

Милый, в этот вечер зимний
Будь, как маленький, со мной.
Удивляться не мешай мне,
Будь, как мальчик, в страшной тайне
И остаться помоги мне
Девочкой, хотя женой.

This desire to remain a "little girl" is interestingly framed by the fact that Tsvetaeva was already pregnant when she got married. In the poem's title, a dash stands in the place where the marriage would be consummated and the transition to adulthood achieved. In a manner typical of her early writing, the poem obscures the sexual moment in the experience of marriage and even motherhood, creating an idealized portrait of both.

In the poetry Tsvetaeva began writing a few years later, however, the sexual moment became a poetic focus. After publishing her first books, marrying, and giving birth to her daughter Ariadna in 1912, Tsvetaeva experienced a fallow period during which she shifted away from her early style and toward a decade of vertiginous creative growth. This decade is known as her "Borisoglebsky period," after the street where Tsvetaeva lived with her young family from 1914 until she emigrated in 1922.[64] Her own autobiographism demanded that she move beyond her "young girl" persona, which she did by boldly exploring new identities. As Olga Revzina has stated about the poetry she wrote during this period, "perhaps at no other time did Tsvetaeva so frequently ask the question 'Who am I?,'" giving fantastically varied and even contradictory poetic self-representations.[65] As though entering a kind of creative late adolescence, she is now explicitly preoccupied with love and sexuality. It is as though the suppressed "bad girl" of her early verse fully emerged. Through a wide range of personae, she speaks as a sexual woman, and a woman who is a sexual agent. She claims instinctive knowledge of the *ars amandi* ("Kak zhguchaia, ottochennaia lest'," 1915) and revels in her skills at seduction: "And how can I / Not lie—when my voice is more tender,— / When I lie" (I kak mogu / Ne lgat',—raz golos moi nezhnee,— / Kogda ia lgu . . .) ("Bezumie—i blagorazum'e," 1915). This poem is typical in celebrating sexual passion as immoral, as related to the lie. She represents her sexual agency as overriding moral law, a Nietszchean claim to power earlier made by symbolist poets such as Briusov and Balmont. The symbolist example, that is, remained the framework within which Tsvetaeva conceptualized sexuality and power even as she claimed them for herself.

Sexual agency, however, was most powerfully modeled for her by another woman poet. Tsvetaeva's boldly sexual personae began to appear in her work around the time of her love affair with Sofia Parnok, also a member of

Voloshin's circle. The affair began in late 1914 and lasted more than a year, contributing to a serious marital crisis.[66] Parnok was openly lesbian and wrote about her love for women in her verse, an exceptional practice in Russia to the present day.[67] Tsvetaeva learned from her example, writing a cycle of poems to Parnok titled "The Girlfriend" ("Podruga," 1914–15), though she did not publish it. In representing her love for Parnok, Tsvetaeva was no less explicit than Parnok about its sexual nature. Her representation of Parnok, however, is colored by a symbolist vision of the doomed, corrupt woman, as Diana Burgin has persuasively shown.[68] In one of her poems to Parnok, Tsvetaeva addresses her as "the stranger" (neznakomka), Blok's name for the fatal muse of his late poetry. As in Blok's scenario, the matter of the poet's agency is obscured: "And I can't tell: did I conquer? / Or was I conquered?" (Tak i ne znaiu: pobedila l'/ Pobezhdena l'). In her poems to Parnok generally, Tsvetaeva represents herself as conquered, emphasizing her relative youth and inexperience; she is "Kay" to Parnok's "Snow Queen," referring to Andersen's fairy tale about a little boy abducted by an icy supernatural entity.[69] Because her seducer is a woman, Tsvetaeva may also create her as a mother, as she did in a loving poem written after the end of their affair, "In those days you were like a mother to me" ("V ony dni ty mne byla, kak mat'," 1916). If Tsvetaeva earlier found in Desbordes-Valmore an idealized mother, in Parnok she discovered a mother who initiated her into sexual love.

During this period Tsvetaeva claimed a powerful and sexualized maternal persona, as Sibelan Forrester has shown.[70] Forrester analyzes Tsvetaeva's appeal to Russian Orthodoxy's "feminine" church architecture as a prime example of her use of the womb as "a crucial metaphor for the poetic process."[71] She describes how, in her cycle "Annunciation" ("Blagoveshchenie," 1916), Tsvetaeva contrasts her own active poetic creativity to the Virgin Mary's passive procreativity, whereby Mary is the passive vessel of God's word. The Annunciation also, and just as centrally for Tsvetaeva, concerns the virgin birth and therefore the role of sexuality in creativity. In this cycle she claims both sexual and creative agency over and against the Marian model. Tsvetaeva represents herself as the sexual mother, one who carries both children and the word, who exists as both voice and body. As Forrester concludes, Tsvetaeva remains in a "medial space" that embraces "a complex relationship of body and soul or spirit."[72] This self-representation is perhaps the most transgressive aspect of her writing in the context of Russian symbolism. As described earlier, Soloviev's theory of love urged the sublimation of sexuality and procreation in aesthetic creation. In his own act of sublimation, Soloviev used the rhetoric of maternity to shape his notion of "life creation."[73] In her "Annunciation" and other poems, Tsvetaeva takes back maternity from the symbolist master, both claiming the male poet's creativity and naming her own literal procreativity. She casts maternity as a form of female agency that is possibly even more potent than her sexual agency.

Even when Tsvetaeva renders these varieties of female potency, however, they are often framed, as they are in these poems, by scenes of moral judgment. Whatever power she derives from transgression, she still registers what she is doing as transgression, that is, as damnable within a moral code she continues to honor. This tension is played out somewhat differently at various moments in her career. The adolescent girl of the early poetry is sexually aware but chaste; the sexual personae of her middle period flaunt their transgressions in the face of moral law. But the crucial and enduring shift occurred at the end of the Borisoglebsky period, in the late teens and early twenties. These years saw the revolutions, the loss of her personal wealth, the disappearance of Efron into the Civil War, the birth and death by starvation of her second daughter, Irina, and her decision to emigrate when Efron resurfaced in Czechoslovakia in 1921. In the midst of these events, Tsvetaeva, if anything, intensified her exploration of love and sexuality.[74] Over 1918–19, Tsvetaeva was caught up in her "theatrical romance," her involvement with the actors of the Vakhtangov Studio in a set of overlapping bisexual infatuations. She rendered the experience in a sequence of verse dramas written with these players in mind, and in related lyric poems, drawing on eighteenth- and early-nineteenth-century discourses of romantic love.[75] As Jane Taubman has phrased it, "Tsvetaeva's theatrical romance was a last fling with the romanticism of her youth," as her art "tilted away from 'the great baseness of love' toward a denial of the flesh and a Platonic 'love without bodies.'"[76] Generally speaking, Tsvetaeva seems to have resolved her ambivalence about the sexual romance by renouncing it.

Irina Shevelenko has put forward an important new interpretation of the shift that occurred at this moment in Tsvetaeva's career, linking Tsvetaeva's retreat from sexuality to a wholesale change in self-conception, arguing that her sexual, as well as her social, identity was replaced by her creative identity as a poet.[77] In other words, Tsvetaeva decided that she would be no longer a woman but a poet. As she phrased it in lines Shevelenko quotes, she is "not a woman but a bird" (ne zhenshchina, a ptitsa), "your swallow—Psyche" (lastochka tvoia—Psikheia).[78] Her renunciation of her woman's body meshes with what Shevelenko describes as her return to the symbolist mythologies she absorbed in her youth.[79] Specifically, Tsvetaeva found in the Solovievan scheme of sublimating sexuality in eros a suitable mythology for her new creative identity.

This is a sharp and unexpected reversal for a poet whose creative identity to this stage was so centered on female sexuality, and it requires explanation. Shevelenko interprets Tsvetaeva's retreat into an exclusive identity as "poet" as her response to the newly hostile social and cultural environment of postrevolutionary Russia.[80] This argument, however, does not satisfactorily account for why Tsvetaeva would find it necessary to eschew femininity. That response would seem to be more immediately produced by the challenge to her maternal identity presented by her second daughter, Irina. Irina was born in April 1917 in the absence of Efron, who was already in southern Russia with the White Army. Whether because of Irina's own difficulties—she seems to have suffered neurological complications—or the difficulties of single parenting in the midst

Tsvetaeva's daughters, Ariadna and Irina Efron, 1919

of a civil war, Tsvetaeva had a different relationship with Irina than with her first daughter. Ariadna—or Alya, as she was called—was a precocious child who absorbed her mother's sensibility and mythologies, and her childhood poems and diaries were written in Tsvetaeva's poetic language. Tsvetaeva's relationship with Alya possibly helped underwrite her simultaneous claim, in "Annunciation," to literal and figurative fertility.

Tsvetaeva implicitly remarked the difference between her daughters in a series of poems to Alya she wrote during Irina's infancy. One of these poems declared Alya a perfect mirror for herself, as she once imagined Desbordes-Valmore: "I don't know which is you and which is I. / We have the same songs and the same cares. / What friends we are! / What orphans we are!" (Ne znaiu, gde ty i gde ia. / Te zh pesni i te zhe zaboty. / Takie s toboiu druz'ia! / Takie s toboiu siroty!). Here Tsvetaeva's reflexive identification with the child casts her as a sister to her daughter, making them sisters without parents. In another poem, Alya appears as a "son," and as such presumably less vulnerable to Tsvetaeva's maternal failure, which she confesses in the final lines: "Instead of all my studies— / A mother's womb / Would be better for you" (Vmesto vsei moei ucheby— / Materinskaia utroba / Lushche—dlia tebia byla b) ("If you fall— I won't lift a finger" ["Upadesh'—perstom ne dvinu," October, 1919]).

These poems were written not long before Tsvetaeva decided to send both of her daughters to the Kuntsevo orphanage so they might be fed during the famine of 1919. When she visited them a month later, she found Alya seriously ill and brought her back home to nurse her, which took another month. By then Irina had died, either from abuse or from starvation.[81] Although some critics have complained that Tsvetaeva suppressed the subject in her poetry, I would argue that it is readable everywhere in her work of the 1920s, most clearly in her declared retreat from the life of the body. The sexual and maternal body Tsvetaeva celebrated in her poetry of the Borisoglebsky period was now strongly connoted as a mortal body, in a way that harked back to Tsvetaeva's earliest experience and writing. This context helps explain her return to symbolism, which supplied a powerful mythology for negating and transcending the body at a moment when her relation to femininity was especially conflicted. Even so, her adoption of these mythologies was not complete, as indicated by my readings of two important poems.

The main vehicle for Tsvetaeva's new orientation was the long poem, or *poema,* a genre she would explore and transform over the course of the next decade.[82] She began, perhaps on Pushkin's model, with a series of narrative poems based on Russian folktales, for which she developed a fragmentary, high-modernist "folk" poetics.[83] Although each is based on a different folktale, they feature the same basic plot: a human being sacrifices his or her earthly ties to be joined with a supernatural being.[84] At issue is not just the "grammar" Propp identified for all folktales but Tsvetaeva's eye for the same story—a story onto which she could map the symbolist theory of love, as Shevelenko persuasively argues.

This mythology is quite apparent in Tsvetaeva's first long poem, "The Tsar-Maiden" ("Tsar'-devitsa," 1920), the same figure Polonsky canonized as the symbolist muse. She certainly knew Polonsky's poetry, and her "Tsar-Maiden" contains possible allusions to Polonsky's.[85] Tsvetaeva repeats the scene his poem describes, in which the tsar-maiden visits the poet's bedroom, preserving the reversed gender roles of Polonsky's active muse and passive poet. (As all commentators have remarked, both characters in Tsvetaeva's poem are androgynous.)[86] In Tsvetaeva's lengthy narrative treatment of the fairy tale, the tsar-maiden falls in love with the young tsarevich—a poet figure—and makes three nocturnal visits. The lovers' meetings are foiled, however, by the tsarevich's lustful stepmother, who each time renders the tsarevich unconscious with a sleeping potion. The stepmother then seduces him, and the tsar-maiden disappears when she learns of this betrayal. The tsarevich dies attempting to bring her back, the stepmother is transformed into a snake, and the tsar's rule collapses in a concluding scene reminiscent of social revolution.

Shevelenko states that the poem's allegory describes the symbolist "refusal of sex in the name of Eros."[87] The allegory is perhaps more precisely stated as "sexuality ruins the ideal union of androgynes." Tsvetaeva narrates how ideal love collapses under the pressure of sexual desire. In fact, she dramatizes the power of sexual love, which is such that it cannot be refused or renounced. Moreover, it is not so clear that sexual love should be renounced. The stepmother, the sexual mother who causes the love tragedy, is not an unsympathetic figure. As G. S. Smith has pointed out, the narrator is as sexually engaged as the stepmother, at one point stepping out of the text to kiss her lover.[88] Similarly, another of Tsvetaeva's folktale poems, "Side Streets" ("Pereulochki," 1922), is written in the voice of a Russian sorceress who seduces young men and transforms them into beasts. She continues to create compelling images of female sexual agency, although in line with symbolist thought she represents it as destructive.

Tsvetaeva's next long poem, "On a Red Steed" ("Na krasnom kone," 1921), stages a more profound self-reversal, as she renounces not only sexuality but maternity as well, and indeed her entire life's experience as a woman. In this poem she invents a "fairy tale" about her muse, adapting for her own use the symbolist scenario of the poet's encounter with the muse. Here the woman poet is visited by her male "Genius" ("Genii"), as she addresses him in the poem. Ariadna Efron, in a memoir of her mother, identified Alexander Blok as the model for Tsvetaeva's Genius.[89] More precisely, she identified the later Blok, "creator of 'The Twelve,'" a poem whose imagery and poetics deeply influenced the idiom Tsvetaeva developed in her long poems.[90] But Blok's relevance for "On a Red Steed" lies just as much in his depiction of the poet and the muse, which Tsvetaeva already appealed to in the lyric cycle she devoted to him in 1916, "Poems to Blok" ("Stikhi k Bloku").[91]

In that earlier cycle, Tsvetaeva remade Blok in the image of the symbolist muse. Her half-worshipful, half-erotic address mimics Blok's own relation to the Beautiful Lady, and he shares the solar attributes of the Eternal Feminine: "Rays shone from him— / Burning strings along the snow! / Three wax candles— / In honor of the sun! The lightbearer!" (Shli ot nego luchi— / Zharkie struny po snegu! / Tri voskovykh svechi— / Solntsu-to! Svetonosnomu!) ("They thought he was human" ["Dumali—chelovek," 1916]). Tsvetaeva's Genius in "On a Red Steed" is another such radiant figure. She addresses him as "Light!" (Svet!), and he wears armor that is "like the sun" (Dospekhi na nem— kak solntse). At the end of the poem, she prophesies his return in standard symbolist topoi: he will approach like the sunrise (A Voskhod svetel) and whisk her into the azure (v lazur'). She also addresses the Genius as "Angel," just as she addressed Blok in the lyric cycle. These two imaginings of Blok as muse, however, are very differently connoted in terms of gender. In the lyric cycle, he appears as a passive, feminized Christ figure. Although he is also named a knight, he is a gentle one: "Gentle shade, / Knight without reproach" (Nezhnyi prizrak, / Rytsar' bez ukorizny). By contrast, Tsvetaeva's Genius is a powerful and cruel warrior. His extreme masculinity sets him apart not just from her earlier imagining of Blok but from male figures in her poetry generally. When Tsvetaeva created this muse for herself in "On a Red Steed," she was adopting the masochistic scenario of Blok's encounter with the muse.

In her opening invocation to the muse, Tsvetaeva's poet asks him to stamp on her breast, in a more abstract, elevated version of Blok's cry, "So pierce my heart, yesterday's angel, / With your sharp French heel!" (Tak vonzai zhe, moi angel vcherashnii, / V serdtse—ostryi frantsuzskii kabluk!)[92]:

> And my two arms are
> Wide, wide open.
> And I tumble back!—Trample, rider!
> So my spirit, breaking from my chest, may fly to You,
> Not Born of Mortal Woman.

> И настежь, и настежь
> Руки—две.
> И навзничь! Топчи, конный!
> Чтоб дух мой, из ребр взыграв—к Тебе,
> Не смертной женой—
> Рожденный!

Tsvetaeva infuses this masochistic scenario with the symbolist metaphysics of love: the muse's violence will liberate her spirit from her body, allowing her to join with an angel. The climax of the poem is such a moment of liberation, and is prepared for by a series of earlier encounters with the Genius.

The first half of the poem describes three encounters at different stages of the poet's life, much like Soloviev's "Three Encounters" ("Tri svidaniia, 1898"), a poem about his visions of the Sophia.[93] Tsvetaeva's encounters with the Genius are described as "dreams" that have the same structure. In the first dream, Tsvetaeva appears as a little girl rescued by the Genius from her burning house. When she discovers that her doll was left behind, he charges back into the blaze and recovers it. He then orders her to destroy what he has saved: "I saved her for you—now destroy her! / Liberate Love!" (Ia spas ee tebe,—razbei! / Osvobodi Liubov'!). In the next dream, the poet stands with her lover by a flooded stream. She tests him by asking if he would retrieve a flower or handkerchief should she toss it in, and to her horror he dives into the torrent. Again the Genius saves him, only to demand that she kill him to "liberate Love." The third dream finds the poet urging her son along as they climb a steep mountain. When eagles snatch him away, the Genius swoops down to save him, once again to demand that she kill him: "I saved him for you—now kill him! / Liberate Love" (Ia spas ego tebe,—ubei! / Osvobodi Liubov'!).

The Genius's repeated command to "liberate Love" evokes symbolist metaphysics, as Shevelenko points out.[94] In line with Solovievan principles, he orders her to renounce both her sexuality and her maternity in the name of a higher, non-corporeal love. She obeys, and in the next scene she appears mounted on a white horse, pursuing her elusive Genius across a Russian steppe swept by snowstorms. The Genius gallops just out of reach until they both thunder into a church along with the storm. The church collapses, and she is thrown to the ground with her arms in the shape of a cross, a blasphemously erotic posture. A "pure and sweet" Christ asks her to accept him, but the Genius's horse stamps on her breast, as she had invited him in her opening invocation. This scene is interrupted by the appearance of an old woman (babka), who explains its meaning to the poet: "Your dream means: Your Angel doesn't love you" (A son takov: / Tvoi Angel tebia ne liubit). This wise female figure unmasks the Genius's love as non-love, which the poet now recognizes. Enraged, she calls on the elemental forces of nature to go to war with her against her Genius. Her encounter with the muse then becomes the Amazon's engagement with her male enemy in an evocatively rendered battle scene. The struggle ends with the Amazon defeated, her left breast pierced by a ray of light emanating from the Genius. He now claims her as his bride in a symbolist-style marriage that transforms her into an "angel," wearing the same wings as her Genius.

There is a disturbing asymmetry in this pairing, however, since the marriage was forced upon her. The poem ends with the poet lying tied up in a trench on the battlefield, awaiting the final return of her Genius:

> It was no Muse, no Muse,—not the mortal ties
> Of Kinship—not your shackles,
> Oh Friendship!—Not a woman's hand—but a cruel one
> Tied this knot
> Around me.
>
> A horrifying union.—In a black trench
> I lie—but the Sunrise is bright.
> Oh who hung these two
> Weightless wings
> On my shoulders?
>
> A mute witness
> Of the storms of the living—
> I lie—and watch
> Shadows.
>
> Until my Genius
> Sweeps me
> Into the azure—
> On a red steed.
>
> Не Муза, не муза,—не бренные узы
> Родства,—не твои путы,
> О Дружба!—Не женской рукой,—лютой,
> Затянут на мне—
> Узел.

Сей страшен союз.—В черноте рва
Лежу—а Восход светел.
О кто невесомых моих два
Крыла за плечом—
Взвесил?

Немой соглядатай
Живых бурь—
Лежу—и слежу
Тени.

Доколе меня
Не умчит в лазурь
На красном коне—
Мой Гений!

This final image of the unhorsed and captive Amazon recalls that of the symbolist muse. The logic of the action is the logic of the tale of the tsar-maiden, the virgin queen who loses her powers when she succumbs to the hero. When Tsvetaeva invents a male muse for the woman poet, that is, she ends up in the position of the female muse, deprived of agency. This conclusion flows from her adoption of the symbolist creative fantasy, a male fantasy that yields pleasure by temporarily reversing gender roles, by putting the "woman on top." For the woman poet to put the "man on top" is to risk being caught within a conventional notion of femininity as passive and abject.

In his reading of "On a Red Steed" as a rape fantasy, David Bethea rehearses a certain kind of feminist argument about why a woman writer would take such a risk: Tsvetaeva wanted to disown responsibility for her desire to claim a "male symbolic order" represented by the Genius.[95] Bethea seems closer to the mark, though, when he contextualizes his reading with the story of Irina's death. Tsvetaeva herself did so in a fashion that has not been remarked. She first published "On a Red Steed" in a small volume of poems titled *Parting* (*Razluka*, 1922). The only other poems she included were a cycle addressed to Efron, "Parting" ("Razluka," 1921), which appears before "On a Red Steed" and which seems to serve as preface to that poem. The "parting" of the title names her separation from her husband, but it also names the loss of Irina, which she addresses in the fifth and sixth poems of the cycle. In these poems she owns the act of abandoning her child. In the first poem, she disentangles herself from "tiny hands" (ruchonki), mounts a winged horse, and flies toward the sunset; in the second, her child pulls at her cloak as she departs for "that gleaming city / Where a mother / Doesn't dare take / Her child" (Tot grad osiannyi, / Kuda— vziat' / Ne smeet ditia / Mat'). Their logic is similar to the logic that led Tsvetaeva to remove her children to Kuntsevo: she must abandon them in order to protect them. These poems read like a tortured apology to Efron for her failure to save their daughter, surely the most difficult issue they confronted when Tsvetaeva rejoined him in Berlin in the summer of 1922. She had apparently told a similar story to Alya back in 1919 to help prepare her to leave for Kuntsevo. In a letter Alya wrote to Tsvetaeva from that period, she said, "I really love one fairy tale: about the horse and the girl with blond curls who runs away from her beloved children: Irina Efron and Ariadna Efron"—a fairy tale that may have been the basis for "On a Red Steed."[96]

This tale of maternal abandonment was reworked in "On a Red Steed" as a tale of abduction: Tsvetaeva was forced to abandon her child by a cruel muse. More precisely, though, the poem is structured by a confusion over whether her child's death was willed or fated, whether she was a mother or a murderer. "On a Red Steed" narrates the speaker's loss of agency as a story with reversals and complications, that is, it represents agency in a conflicted manner. In each dream, the poet destroys something—childhood home, lover, son—before the Genius does. Her delight in the blaze that destroys her home suggests complicity; she orders her lover to make a suicidal leap into a torrent; and she urges her child to scale the mountain from which he falls. In every instance the Genius saves her victims only to command her to destroy them a second time. This puzzling repetition deliberately complicates the question whether the poet's path was chosen or forced. In fact, these dreams seem to work on the principle of wish fulfillment, as the Genius accomplishes acts she has already set in motion. She is repeatedly punished for imagining or exercising an aggressive agency and punished in the same way—by losing her femininity. First she is "a little girl without a doll" (devochka—bez—kukly), then "a girl without a lover" (Devushka—bez—druga), then "a woman without a womb" (Zhenshchina—bez—chreva), and finally a genderless "angel." The suggested logic is that because she killed, or wanted to kill, her child, she can no longer be a woman.

It is not surprising that Tsvetaeva made use of Soloviev to shape this logic. As described earlier, the most powerful example of Soloviev's appropriation of the feminine was his ban on procreation in the service of creativity. In that context, Tsvetaeva's earlier flaunting of female sexuality and maternity was the most transgressive aspect of her writing. In "On a Red Steed," however, she hands over her womb to the Genius in an eloquent concession of her female potency. The Genius, in fact, functions as a kind of mother to the speaker. At the beginning of the poem he sings over her cradle, and at the end of each dream the poet reaches after him like a child reaching for its mother: "It is two hands—reaching for—the rider" (To dve ruki—konnomu—vsled). The speaker herself appears in the poem as an abandoned child, although she narrates her own act of abandonment. There is a prior ground for thus substituting herself for the child: Tsvetaeva's own mother "abandoned" her by dying, and Tsvetaeva wrote her earliest poetry from the position of the abandoned child. She appears to revert to that position in the face of her own maternal failure. The confusion about agency inscribed in "On a Red Steed" is at some level a confusion over whether she is a cruel mother or a neglected child.[97]

The speaker's paralysis at the end of the poem, then, does not simply mark

her loss of agency. Rather, it resolves by forceful means the tension that structures the poem, the tension between claiming and disowning agency. Hers is a
hysterical paralysis that can be understood in the terms laid out by Freud and
later modified by Lacan and by a number of feminist theorists, above all Luce
Irigaray and Julia Kristeva. Although Freud understood hysteria to afflict both
men and women, in his classic analysis and in later theorizations it is the daughter's disease. This understanding crystallized around the insight that the mother
plays a prior and more crucial role than the father in the family romance. As
Claire Kahane has summarized this development in later Freudian thought,
"the first lost object, which is also the first object of identification and the first
object of rage, is the mother, the most ambivalently constructed other, who
bears at the same time the traces of self."[98] The mother is ambivalently constructed because although she is an overwhelming presence at the earliest (pre-
oedipal) stage of development, she later becomes a diminished figure. In strictly
psychoanalytical terms, she is seen to be "castrated," or more generally, in terms
of the schema of gender polarities that typified Victorian culture, she is seen to
have no agency. The daughter's identification with a devalued mother causes a
hysterical conflict: although she wishes to negate the mother, she cannot do so
without negating herself. As Kahane puts it, "The daughter who succumbed to
hysteria typically turned her rage against herself in a kind of masochistic biting
of her own tongue instead of using it aggressively against the other and silently
mimed in her body the script that had entrapped her."[99] That script is the normative heterosexual romance, in which the daughter, like her mother, is a passive object of desire.

This is the same script that shaped the symbolist scenario of the poet and the
muse, which Tsvetaeva rewrites in "On a Red Steed." In this poem, though, she
rewrites this script in a manner that enforces it, imagining herself at the end of
the poem as a passive feminine subject. She makes use of the male tradition of
lyric masochism to resolve masochistically an anxiety about female agency.
From her earliest writing, Tsvetaeva explored the matter of female agency
around the figure of the mother. Her youthful poems were inspired by the death
of her mother, with whom she sought the total fusion described in her poem to
Desbordes-Valmore. She represents the same model of mother-daughter fusion
in her poems to Alya, but Irina's childhood and death brought that model to
ruin, exposing its conflictual nature.[100] Tsvetaeva addressed that maternal crisis with the allegory of "On a Red Steed," in which she is punished for desiring to separate from her child. With this poem, she describes a paradoxical logic
that will govern much of her later poetry, a logic according to which the only
form of agency she can confidently embrace is renunciation.

In describing this logic, "On a Red Steed" describes a kind of "etiology" of
her mature poetics. This poetics was first displayed in her lyric collection *Craft*
(*Remeslo*, 1922), which Simon Karlinsky has described as follows: "*Remeslo*
[*Craft*] does not have a unifying theme or leitmotif. . . . Its essential unity is due
to the great energy and expressiveness of its verse. The combination of a pas-

sionate tone with the wide use of syntactic ellipsis in this collection has led some hostile critics to speak of obscurity and hysteria—the two charges that have been repeatedly made against Cvetaeva's poetry from *Remeslo* onward."[101] These charges are justified not as terms of judgment and dismissal but as diagnoses of a hysterical tension in her writing. Karlinsky mentions the "great energy" of her mature verse, which is produced by a severely condensed verse form. Tsvetaeva always exercised strong formal discipline, but she now brings it to bear with special intensity. Her favored trope, which Karlinsky also mentions, is ellipsis: she eliminates all but the most essential components of expression. Her strong rhythms are packed into shorter lines, which are sliced into dramatic enjambments and broken up further by excessive punctuation. The words themselves are shorter, and there are denser accumulations of consonants. Tsvetaeva also eliminates words altogether, especially verbs, for which she expressed hostility. She cast her dislike of verbs as a protest against the "power of time," but that dislike may also be understood as an eschewal of agency. In a similar fashion, Freud's hysterical patient Anna O. used infinitives in place of subject and verb constructions, divorcing the subject from its action and "asserting instead the hovering stasis of potentiality in a linguistic version of hysterical paralysis."[102] In general, Tsvetaeva's condensing and shredding of language is a way of resisting its materiality. It expresses at the level of poetics what she states outright in the poems: the hysteric's rejection of corporeality.[103] In her writing, and in her thinking about writing, Tsvetaeva begins to represent language as "voice," and she begins to represent herself as a bodiless Psyche. The paradoxical effect of her disciplining of language and self is to create an impressive force of utterance that, like the hysteric's performance, is a kind of power.

At the same time, Tsvetaeva began to represent poetic power as masculine, in line with the mythology she created in "On a Red Steed." In poems she was writing shortly after emigrating in the summer of 1922, she named her poetic ideal "the Eternal Masculine."[104] Tsvetaeva was perhaps inspired to use this rhetoric by Andrey Bely, who was living in Berlin and befriended her on her arrival from Russia. He published an ecstatic review of *Parting*,[105] which inspired him to write a new book of poems under the title *After Parting* (*Posle razluki*, 1922).[106] The title refers not just to Tsvetaeva's book but also to his final break with his wife, Asya Turgeneva, the famous symbolist muse Tsvetaeva knew from her time at Musagetes.[107] At this time Bely was also writing his memoir of Blok, in which he recounts the story of their love triangle with Mendeleeva, whom they regarded as the living embodiment of the Eternal Feminine. According to Tsvetaeva, Bely told her "about the young Blok, Blok's young wife, and his young self" (4:258).

Bely's failed symbolist romances likely prompted Tsvetaeva to make ironic reference to the Eternal Feminine in her poem "So in the wearisome toil of days" ("Tak, v skudnom truzhenichestve dnei," 1922), from a cycle linked to her brief affair with Abram Vishniak, her editor in Berlin. The poem represents her posture in the love relationship as independent and unsentimental, in contrast to the "eternal femininities" (vechnye zhenstvennosti) of her rivals.[108] In a poem she wrote about a week later, "You can see from the sunburns—axe and plow" ("Po zagaram—topor i plug," 1922), Tsvetaeva again rejected the feminine for a masculine ideal. Here she names the Eternal Masculine for the first time:

> You can see from the sunburns—axe and plow.
> It's enough—tribute to dark-skinned dust!
> The early morning work hour
> Is dear to craftsmen's hands.
>
> Hello!—amidst Old Testament gloom—
> Sweep of the eternal masculine.
>
> Smoking fruit of honey and fur—
> Get away, you latest beast!
> Abandoning the Sarah-commandment
> And Hagar-heart in fur heaps
>
> Of somnolences . . .
>   —rejoice in mornings,
> Sweep of the eternal masculine!

> По загарам—топор и плуг.
> Хватит—смуглому праху дань!
> Для ремесленнических рук
> Дорога трудовая рань.
>
> Здравствуй—в ветхозаветных тьмах—
> Вечной мужественности взмах!
>
> Мхом и медом дымящий плод—
> Прочь, последнего часа тварь!
> В меховых ворохах дремот
> Сарру-заповедь и Агарь-
>
> Сердце—бросив . . .
>   —ликуй в утрах,
> Вечной мужественности взмах!

Tsvetaeva's use of the Old Testament story of Sarah, Hagar, and Abraham was prompted by Vishniak's Jewishness, a theme in her poems to him. Abraham had a son by his servant Hagar at the request of his wife, Sarah, who was barren; Sarah later gave birth at age ninety by God's command (Genesis 16–21). In an earlier poem to Vishniak, Tsvetaeva addressed him in the guise of a passionate Hagar eager to bear his son: "Son, kick!" (Synok, udar'!) ("I sit, a bare-headed

Hagar" ["Prostovolosaia Agar' sizhu," 1921]). In "You can see from the sun-burns," she rejects not only Hagar's role but Sarah's as well. Tsvetaeva's mention of Sarah was likely directed toward her part-Jewish husband, Efron, with whom she was lately reunited: she will serve neither as Vishniak's mistress nor as Efron's wife. The way out of the claustrophobic female world of sex and pro-creation is upward toward the sun ("rejoice in mornings"). Like "On a Red Steed," these poems link the Eternal Masculine with a notion of writing as tran-scendence—transcendence, in particular, of her femininity.

On June 27, a few days after naming the Eternal Masculine in this poem, Tsvetaeva received Pasternak's first letter.[109] On July 1 she received a copy of his *My Sister Life* inscribed to her, and Tsvetaeva discovered a poet who em-bodied her own creative ideal.[110] Upon reading *My Sister Life,* she wrote a re-view essay titled "A Downpour of Light (Poetry of the Eternal Masculine)" ("Svetovoi liven' [Poeziia vechnoi muzhestvennosti]"). The phrase "Eternal Masculine" receives no comment and appears only once in the body of the es-say: "Light-writing: that's what I'd call it. A poet of *lightnesses* (as there are po-ets, for instance, of darknesses). Light. The Eternal Masculine.—Light in space, light in motion, gaps (drafts) of light, explosions of light—very feasts of light. He is flooded and overwhelmed. Not just with the sun, but with all that radi-ates—and for Pasternak everything gives off rays" (5:235).[111] "Light," "sun," "rays": these are the solar attributes of the Eternal Feminine transferred to Tsvetaeva's masculine ideal. They are the same rays her Genius emits and which penetrate her breast in "On a Red Steed." They seem to shoot off Pasternak's pen as he enacts his "light-writing."

Yet Pasternak also appears subject to light's action, "flooded and over-whelmed" by the downpour of light named in the title. He appears, that is, both passive and active, both poet and muse. Tsvetaeva not only acknowledged the contradiction but cultivated it in a related passage:

> Pasternak is the most penetrable poet, and hence the most penetrating. Every-thing beats into him. (Evidently, there's justice even in inequality: thanks to you, a unique poet, more than one human dome is delivered from celestial thunder!) A blow—a rebound. . . .
> Sometimes he is knocked down: life's pressure through the suddenly flung-open door is stronger than his stubborn brow. Then he falls—blissfully—on his back, and is more effective in his knocked-down state than all jockeys and couriers of Po-etry, panting this very moment in full gallop over the barriers. (5:234)

Tsvetaeva's reference to "the jockeys and couriers of Poetry . . . in full gallop over the barriers" makes apt use of the title of one of Pasternak's early lyric col-lections, *Above the Barriers* (*Poverkh bar'ierov,* 1916). As a young poet, Paster-nak wrote in a futurist poetic idiom and was publicly aligned with the futurist poets Vladimir Mayakovsky, Sergey Bobrov, and Nikolay Aseev. These are pre-sumably Tsvetaeva's "jockeys and couriers," with whom Pasternak rides. Unlike them, however, Pasternak gets knocked off his horse (oprokinut). He looks less like his fellow futurists than like Tsvetaeva's female poet in "On a Red Steed."

What Tsvetaeva describes in these passages is the dynamic of her own hysterical creativity by which trauma is converted into forceful utterance ("A blow—a rebound"). Sometimes the trauma exceeds the poet's capacity for conversion, however, and he is thrown to the ground. Tsvetaeva includes in her vision of the Eternal Masculine a moment of vulnerability and paralysis that sharply distinguishes it from that of the futurists, to take the example she invokes. The Russian futurists, in their polemic with the symbolists, also claimed a new masculine aesthetic: "What naïf will turn his ultimate Love to the perfumed lechery of Balmont? Does this really reflect the masculine soul of today?"[112] But Tsvetaeva's "masculine soul" is a hysterical miming of masculinity, understood by Irigaray as "the little girl's or the woman's effort to save her sexuality from total repression and destruction" by engaging in "phallic activity."[113] It is a strategy of compensation for Tsvetaeva's lost feminine agency. Her imagining of poetic creativity in "A Downpour of Light" emerged from her own crisis. Yet it was also a canny reading of Pasternak's *My Sister Life,* to which we now turn.

2

The Boy Poet

I am homesick beyond description
Tears cloud my vision
I feel distant and feminine . . .

Ich habe Heimweh unbeschreiblich
Von Tränen ist der Blick verhängt
Ich fühle ferne mich und weiblich . . .

—Johannes Becher, quoted by Pasternak
in a letter to Tsvetaeva
(July 11, 1926)

In the late 1920s, around the same time as Tsvetaeva, Pasternak turned to autobiographical prose in which he explored the origins of his creativity. In his essay *Safe Conduct* (*Okhrannaia gramota*, 1931), he traced his birth as an artist to a sympathetic interest in femininity:

> I shall not describe how in the spring of 1901 a troupe of Dahomeyan Amazons was put on display in the Zoological Garden, nor how my first awareness of woman was bound up with a sense of their naked ranks and serried suffering, a tropical parade to the sound of beating drums. Nor shall I describe how, earlier than I should, I became a captive of forms because I saw in them too early the form of captives. Nor will I describe how in summer of 1903 at Obolenskoye, where the Scriabins were our neighbors, the young ward of some friends who lived across the Protva was almost drowned while bathing, how a student perished when he plunged in to help her, and how she later went mad after several suicide attempts from the same precipice. I shall not describe how later on when I broke my leg and escaped two future wars in a single evening and lay motionless in plaster, the same friends' house across the river went up in flames, and the shrill village fire alarm went crazy and shook in a fever. (4:150)[1]

Pasternak withholds an essential detail about the events of that summer, one that he supplied in a later autobiography: he broke his leg in a riding accident. The detail illuminates Pasternak's concern for the "Dahomeyan Amazons." The Amazons were equestrian performers hired by a circus in Moscow, but Pasternak recalls seeing them paraded like war captives. Pasternak's fall similarly kept him from the field of battle: his leg did not heal properly, forcing him to wear an orthopedic shoe and later disqualifying him from military service. The figural substitution of the Amazons for Pasternak—of female victims for male—is repeated in the story of his neighbors, in which the young man drowns trying to save a drowning girl. As described here, Pasternak's art is founded on an identification with the suffering woman, and specifically the woman who suffers a loss of agency—who has been, like the young Pasternak, unhorsed.

Pasternak's scenario is uncannily similar to Tsvetaeva's in "On a Red Steed": both poets link lyric creativity with the fallen Amazon. The coincidence testifies to the poets' shared tastes, interests, and education as largely shaped by the culture of Russian symbolism. As I have argued, the symbolist creative scenario stages the poet's seduction by the Amazonian muse, and Pasternak and Tsvetaeva make use of that scenario to imagine the dynamics of their own creativity. They are drawn to the symbolist model for how it conceives of poetry in relation to love and sexuality, and particularly for how it imagines creative agency in relation to sexual agency. I have argued that the way Tsvetaeva works out this relation in "On a Red Steed" is realized in her mature work as a poetics of paralysis. In this chapter I examine how the same nexus of issues shaped Pasternak's singular poetics, a poetics that has been described as "expressive" or "ecstatic," but which I describe as hysterical, in Kahane's cultural-historical sense. This poetics is on display in the passage from *Safe Conduct,* as Pasternak piles on the romantic clichés—young wards, drownings, suicide, madness, conflagration—to heighten the story in ways that are both agitating and pleasurable. This style is fully achieved in *My Sister Life,* the book that made his reputation and that he always considered his best. It is also the book through which Tsvetaeva first came to know him.

Strictly speaking, when Pasternak described his birth as an artist in 1903, he meant his aspiration to write music.[2] This was a natural choice for the child of Rozalia Pasternak, who, though she stopped performing after her marriage, was well known and respected in the musical world and took part in private concerts. That summer when "the Scriabins were our neighbors," Pasternak was captivated by Scriabin's music and began studying to become a composer. He studied successfully under several teachers, and in 1909 had the opportunity to hear Scriabin's spectacular performances of "Poème de l'ecstase" and to show him his compositions. Although Scriabin, among others, saw genuine promise in Pasternak's efforts, the encounter crystallized Pasternak's doubts about his abilities, and he gave up his musical vocation. Nevertheless, this period of immersion in late romantic and modernist music, and its association with his brilliant mother, helped form his poetic sensibility.

In 1909 Pasternak enrolled in the history and philology department of Moscow University; he completed his degree in the spring of 1913 with an honors essay on Hermann Cohen. During that time he spent one summer, in 1912, studying philosophy at the Marburg School, a center of neo-Kantianism led by Cohen and Paul Natorp.[3] In *Safe Conduct,* Pasternak identifies Marburg as the scene of his dramatic break away from philosophy and toward poetry. Actually, Pasternak had started writing poetry several years earlier, at about the time he entered Moscow University, and was a regular member of a salon of poets, artists, and musicians called "Serdarda," where he was regarded as "more of a theoretician than a poet."[4] Pasternak's simultaneous explorations in philosophy and poetry brilliantly suited him to participate in the landmark debates of the early 1910s over Russian symbolism. One might say that he developed these twin interests in emulation of the symbolists. As one critic has suggested, Pasternak's visit to Marburg conformed to Bely's dictum that in order to understand the theory of symbolism, "it wouldn't hurt to make more frequent pilgrimages to Marburg."[5]

Pasternak also attended the Society of Free Aesthetics (Obshchestvo svobodnoi estetiki), the symbolist "school" at Musagetes. During 1910 the society offered three seminars: one led by Ellis on European symbolism, especially Baudelaire; another on Russian prosody led by Bely; and a third led by the philosopher Fedor Stepun, on Kant's aesthetics. While Tsvetaeva attended at least some meetings of Ellis's and Bely's seminars, Pasternak chose to study Kant.[6] He later claimed that he avoided Bely's lectures on principle, since they focused on rhythm and neglected his own concern with semantics (4:319).[7] (Tsvetaeva also later dismissed Bely's tuition but on different grounds: she disliked the nasal sound of "gnoseology" and "gnostics," and was distracted by the personalities [4:228].) Pasternak may not have attended Bely's seminar, but he certainly read his book *Symbolism* (*Simvolizm,* 1910), which laid out many of the metrical possibilities Pasternak explored in his poetry.[8] While in Marburg, Pasternak undertook, with scholarly rigor, to read the complete works of the major symbolists,[9] and his early verse bears the traces of this reading.[10]

Pasternak's first published poems appeared in the 1913 miscellany *Lyric Poetry* (*Lirika*) put out by the Serdarda group, who advertised their symbolist bent by taking a quotation from Ivanov as the volume's epigraph. One of the poems by Pasternak's friend Sergey Bobrov, titled "Legacy" ("Zavet"), openly proclaimed their debt to symbolism: "Blessed symbolism / Has revealed to us shores and forests" (Otkryl nam berega i pushchi / Blagoslovennyi simvolizm).[11] By 1913, however, Bobrov and Nikolay Aseev, like their acmeist and futurist peers, were already distancing themselves from their symbolist fathers.[12] Pasternak aligned himself with Aseev and Bobrov as they moved on to form the futurist group Centrifuge (Tsentrifuga), and when he first became known to the reading public, he was known as a futurist poet. Pasternak participated in the internecine quarrels among different futurist groups, publishing several short manifesto-style essays. It was at a futurist "duel" at the Café

Pasternak in Vsevolodo-Vil've, 1916 (collection of E. B. Pasternak)

Grec that Pasternak began a complicated but enduring friendship with Vladimir Mayakovsky.

Pasternak's first book of poems, *A Twin in Clouds* (*Bliznets v tuchakh*, 1913), included a pugnacious introduction by Aseev announcing that Pasternak had supplanted his symbolist forebears. Unlike Bobrov and Aseev, however, and certainly unlike Mayakovsky, Pasternak never disowned the symbolist legacy.[13] In fact, he consistently acknowledged it, emphasizing in sometimes idiosyncratic ways those aspects of the symbolists' work he found most sympathetic. Important among these was the notion of lyric creativity as involving a passive and "feminine" element. This was precisely the aspect of symbolism the futurists disparaged in their defiantly masculinist posturings, and Pasternak's view strongly distinguishes him among his peers.[14] Pasternak always conceived of poetry in relation to femininity in the neoromantic fashion of the symbolists.

This is apparent in Pasternak's early theorizing about the nature of the poet's subjectivity, the topic of his first public statement of his views on symbolism. In February 1913 he gave a lecture at the Circle for the Study of the Problems of Aesthetic Culture, a group that evolved out of Ellis's Musagetes seminar. The lecture, "Symbolism and Immortality" ("Simvolizm i bessmertie"), has survived as a handout Pasternak distributed to his audience. According to his notes for the lecture, Pasternak argued that objects—or more precisely their "attributes" (kachestva)—partake of a "primordial subjectivity" (iskonnaia sub"ektivnost'). The poet joins himself to this subjectivity in the process of creation, achieving an immortality that transcends his person.

> The poet devotes the visible richness of his life to timeless meaning. A living soul, alienated from the individual in the service of a free subjectivity—that is immortality. Thus immortality is the Poet; and the poet is never an entity—but a condition of possibility for the attribute.
> Poetry is madness without the madman. Madness is natural immortality; poetry is immortality that "culture accepts." (4:683)

This notion of a supraindividual creativity implies a limited poetic agency. In fact, Pasternak imagines the poet submitting to a higher subjectivity that suffuses the surrounding world: "The reality available to individuals is penetrated by the searchings of the free subjectivity that belongs to the attribute. Signs of these searchings, which emerge from reality and are not confined to it, are perceived by the poet as signs of reality itself. The poet submits to the movement of these searchings, takes them up and conducts himself like the objects around him. This is called observation and writing from nature" (4:683). Pasternak's philosophical idiom suggests the influence of contemporary theories of the subject, probably those formulated by Husserl[15] and Natorp.[16] But Pasternak was also expressing a general romantic view of creativity as the loss or transcendence of self, a view that was important in symbolist aesthetics.[17]

As several commentators have remarked, Pasternak's "free subjectivity" resembles the notion of the Dionysian, which plays a central role in Ivanov's theorizing and which Ivanov borrowed from Friedrich Nietzsche.[18] When Pasternak describes the poet "succumbing to the movement of these searchings [of universal subjectivity]," he could be viewed as faithfully reproducing some of Ivanov's own ideas about the nature of poetic creation in his classic statement, "Two Elements in Contemporary Symbolism" ("Dve stikhii v sovremennom simvolizme," 1909). Ivanov's discussion of symbolism actually turns on the matter of the poet's agency. Remarking the familiar objection that his poet-theurge resembles the Nietzschean superman, Ivanov asserts the opposite—that the poet must adopt a passive posture toward the object world: "We think that the theurgic principle in art is the principle of the least forcing and the greatest receptivity. Not to bring to bear one's will on the appearance of objects but to see them fully and to proclaim the secret will of essences—this is the artist's highest testament."[19] Ivanov speaks here of symbolist "realism," as distinct from "idealism," the two elements of the essay's title.[20] If the realist poet passively perceives the essence of things, the idealist poet exercises creative will and thus shapes a purely subjective vision. Ivanov goes on to describe the realist poet as "feminine," in line with a conventional view of femininity as passive: "Realism and idealism . . . are always distinguished as forms of the feminine, receptive type (realism) and the masculine, initiatory type (idealism)."[21]

Pasternak similarly linked the poet's passive receptivity to femininity in his early work. The boundary between theoretical and creative writing is fluid in Pasternak's oeuvre; his creative work tends to be metapoetic, and his thinking about poetry relies on figurative language. An early fictional work, extant only in fragments, concerns an artist named Reliquimini. (The name is based on the Latin *relinquere,* "to leave behind.") He is a passive, feminized figure who falls to the ground in a faint in two different episodes. As Angela Livingstone has remarked, in Pasternak's early writing "the idea of a fall, of falling, or merely of lying down (being already in a fallen position) is rather frequent" and is associated with artistic emotion.[22]

Another early prose fragment supplies an evocative image of the force that moves reality, or "fact" ("byl'"), and to which the poet joins himself:

I have always experienced such fact as the stressed syllable in the final foot of a line of verse which has to have a feminine ending. Reality gave only the heavy syllable; the first half of the foot; a kind of melodic meaningfulness demanded the second half—evening twilight—in which this fact, or its bandages, would weaken. (Bandages fastened onto ailing fact by the healing hand of culture: the hand of the creative work of science and morality [fastened on by this hand and undone by the hand that does not know cures and wants sicknesses: of eternal faith: undone by the hand of lyricism, of lyric asceticism].)

See: the thirst for something unstressed, eternally unstressed, which cannot begin, for all fact—even its twilight—is without exception stressed, is a single masculine blow, blunt, cut off: which is sometimes sung for us only because we feel: this isn't the final syllable, for the native element of dreams is *disyllabic,* and reality is truncated, meaningless, and irrational, it trembles in a half-word. (4:776)[23]

Pasternak introduces gender as it is conventionally used to identify the two basic kinds of rhyme: masculine rhyme ending on a stressed syllable and feminine rhyme adding an unstressed syllable. He models the dynamic of creativity as a line-final trochaic foot, a sequence that combines masculine "fact" and feminine lyricism ("melodic meaningfulness," "dreams"). As Pasternak unfolds the metaphor at the end of his discussion, this sequence of syllables is produced by fact's desire to become feminine: "Fact (strange word—of masculine gender)[24] is always imbued with a thirst for unstressed chaos, with the yearning will to be feminine, whenever it's at the threshold of inspiration" (4:777). This is indeed the logic of Pasternak's figure, since the sequence of a "masculine" and "feminine" syllable yields a feminine rhyme.

Like the symbolists and the romantics before them, Pasternak imagines the creative event as the union of the sexes. Moreover, he imagines the poet as a feminized male and femininity as a kind of force—the force of lyricism understood as movement. Lyric creativity very simply is the dynamic power of the feminine. At the same time, lyricism's mobility is ambiguously, even rather darkly, connoted. Reality has been rendered motionless by the healing work of science and morality, which have "fastened bandages" on it. Lyricism not only undoes this healing action but also "wants sicknesses"; it is a chaos that works against the ordering forces of culture; it is the madness to which the poet succumbs in "Symbolism and Immortality." Taken together, these statements define the character of "free subjectivity" as chaotic, natural, sick, and feminine.

The two contemporary poets who most strongly modeled a feminine lyricism for Pasternak were Rainer Maria Rilke and Alexander Blok. In *Safe Conduct*, Pasternak relates how at age seven, thanks to his father's friendship with Tolstoy, he glimpsed Rilke and Lou Andreas-Salomé during their trip to Russia in 1900. Several years later he read his father's copies of *In Celebration of Myself* (*Mir zur Feier*, 1899) and *The Book of Hours* (*Das Stundenbuch*, 1905). Michel Aucouturier has suggested that reading Rilke was what inspired Pasternak to write his own poetry.[25] In fact, extant drafts of Pasternak's earliest poems, written during 1911–13, are mixed in with his translations of several poems from *The Book of Images* (*Das Buch der Bilder*, 1902, 1906).[26] The poems he elected to translate, especially "Music" ("Musik") and "The Boy" ("Der Knabe"), have clear biographical resonances and served as a mirror for his youthful poet-self, in the same way Marceline Desbordes-Valmore's poetry was a mirror for Tsvetaeva.[27] The translations suggest that Pasternak learned from Rilke not so much a poetic technique as an imagining of the poet and the creative process.[28] As Donald Rayfield has rightly remarked, both Rilke and Pasternak "combine a primaeval sexuality with a reworked myth of inspiration, in which the poet is a passive receptacle for a dynamic force."[29] Rilke explicitly cast lyric creativity in terms of female experience, and his poetry enacts the male feminine with exceptional consistency and power.[30]

Alexander Blok exerted a similar influence on Pasternak. Although most of the critical literature on Blok and Pasternak focuses on Pasternak's late period, more recent scholarship has documented numerous Blok subtexts in his early poetry.[31] One could observe more generally, as Elena Pasternak has done, that the dominant imagery of Pasternak's early verse—of wind, winter storms, and the city—are unmistakably Blok's.[32] Pasternak's comments on Blok in his 1956 autobiography reprise this very imagery: "The page contained a piece of news. It seemed as though that news, of itself, without prompting, had spread itself over the printed surface and that no one had written or composed the poems. It seemed that the page was not covered with verse about wind and puddles, lampposts and stars, but that lampposts and puddles chased breezy ripples across the surface of the journal, leaving behind damp, powerfully affecting traces" (4:309). In describing the effect of Blok's poetry, Pasternak expresses his notion of the poet's non-agency: it is as though "no one had written or composed the poems." In the same context, he also remarks Blok's dynamism as the feature that influenced him the most.

When Pasternak praises the impersonality and dynamism of Blok's poetry, he assigns them to a particular period, "to the Blok of the second volume of the Alkonost edition" (4:310). As noted earlier, the second volume of Blok's "trilogy" marks the turn from his idealization of the Beautiful Lady to his masochistic obsession with the Stranger. It is the period of poems such as the cycle "Snow Mask" ("Snezhnaia maska," 1907), where Blok represents femininity as a dangerous, elemental force (stikhiia).[33] Although Pasternak never spoke about Blok as a love poet, he was a key influence in this regard. When he reread Blok's "first volume" in 1946, he privately remarked this influence. Next to Blok's poem "It's dark and stuffy in the rooms" ("Temno v komnatakh i dushno," 1901) Pasternak wrote, "This is where *A Twin in Clouds* starts from. 'Hearts and Companions'" (Otsiuda poshel 'Bliznets v tuchakh.' Serdtsa i sputniki).[34] "Hearts and Companions" was the title of a poem from Pasternak's first verse collection *A Twin in Clouds;* it was dedicated to Elena Vinograd, who later became the muse of *My Sister Life*. With this notation, Pasternak traced to Blok not only his early poems but also his greatest book of love poetry. One can say further that Pasternak's poetic imagination, like Blok's, was tethered to the figure of woman throughout his career.[35]

Pasternak was writing within a literary tradition of lyric masochism that linked passivity with femininity. But his interest in femininity also reflected contemporary psychological theories, including, I would argue, Freudian theory. Pasternak was explicitly concerned with female sexuality and its relation to consciousness, and particularly to artistic consciousness. In his important essay on "the theme of woman" in Pasternak, Viacheslav V. Ivanov has shown how Pasternak cast his own artistic development in terms of female sexual development, from little girl, to adolescent, to mature woman.[36] The clearest example is "The Childhood of Luvers" ("Detstvo Liuvers," 1918), another of Pasternak's metapoetic fictions from his early career. Events are narrated as perceived by the young girl Zhenya Luvers, in the naïve, associative fashion that Pasternak, like many modernists, ascribed to the poet. As Tsvetaeva later put it, Luvers is "Pasternak if he were a girl, Pasternak himself, all of Pasternak" (5:381). The story concentrates on a crucial period in Luvers's adolescence from which she emerges a mature moral being, someone who comprehends the biblical injunction to love one's neighbor as oneself. The events that precipitate her moral awakening all have to do with female sexuality and reproduction. Luvers has an upsetting first experience of menstruation, described in some detail; she falls ill on the day one of the servants gives birth; and the climax of the story is her mother's miscarriage, obscurely linked to a carriage accident in which her parents' horse, named Foster Child (Vykormysh), tramples and kills a lame man. These details have yet to be fully interpreted, but they establish Pasternak's tendency to conceptualize his own art in terms of women's bodily traumas and powers.[37]

Early in "The Childhood of Luvers," the narrator steps forward with a metatextual comment rejecting the relevance of psychology for interpreting Luvers's evolving consciousness. Speaking about how "life informs very few about what it is doing with them," he names the useless means man employs to discover that knowledge: "For this purpose all true religions were established, all abstract ideas and all human prejudices, and most shining and entertaining of these—*psychology*" (4:38). When Pasternak scholars have addressed the matter of his interest in women, however, they have reasonably turned to psychological theories. Ivanov invokes Jung's notion of female anima as part of the complete human personality; Ronen has also suggested the influence of Otto Weininger, whose linking of passive femininity and Judaism may have resonated with Pasternak.[38]

Pasternak himself referred to Sigmund Freud when later reflecting on his similarity to his heroine Luvers. He did so to none other than Tsvetaeva, in a letter of July 11, 1926:

> I have certain painful inclinations, paralyzed only by lack of will. They are completely familiar to Freud, which I say for the sake of brevity, to indicate their type . . .
> . . . I have an abyss of feminine features. I know too many sides of what is called passivity [stradatel'nost']. For me this is not just one word that names one fault: for me it is more than the entire world. The entire actual world, that is, the actuality I have reduced (in my tastes, my painful response, and in my experience) precisely to that passivity, and the fact that my novel has a heroine and not a hero is no accident. (*DNV* 257)[39]

Here Pasternak claims a feminine knowledge of "passivity," and by mentioning Freud he suggests that he is speaking about passive desire, or masochism. (The noun I have translated as "passivity" is derived from the verb "to suffer"; another translator has rendered it as "penchant for suffering.")[40] Pasternak described his femininity similarly in a later context, his 1956 autobiography, where he cast it as a childhood fantasy: "At the dawn of life when such foolishness is possible, I imagined, perhaps owing to my memories of the first little tunics [sarafanchiki] they dressed me in earlier, that at some earlier point I had been a girl, and I needed to bring back that more fascinating and charming crea-ture, tightening my belt until I fainted. Or I imagined that I was not my par-ents' son, but a foundling they had discovered and adopted" (4:306). In this passage, as elsewhere in his work, gender is marked by clothing. The way the child Pasternak gains access to his fantasized femininity—the way he gets back into his "little tunics"—is to masochistically cut off his breath until he loses consciousness. In these passages Pasternak declares how he enacts femininity: he mimics woman's passive condition through masochism.

The point is not to diagnose Pasternak, or even to accept his own self-diag-nosis, but to get at the particular character of his lyric masochism. When he represents himself dressed like a girl, tightening his belt until he faints, he is also representing his vision of the poet when he creates, the poet when he becomes feminine. One of his early poems, "The Northern Seamstress" ("Poliarnaia shveia," 1916), directly represents the poet as a cross-dresser: the poem opens with the poet in "a little girl's white boots" (Na mne byla belaia obuv' de-vochki). The action is motivated by the governing metaphor of winter as a "northern seamstress" who dresses the poet in snow, hence the white boots. Pasternak thus takes up and alters the romantic and symbolist topos of ad-dressing nature as feminine muse.[41] Specifically, he loads the scenario with psy-chosexual meaning. First of all, he makes explicit its gender dynamics, whereby the male poet borrows femininity from the muse: Pasternak's poet appears as a male mannequin whom the seamstress puts in a dress ("She didn't care that the stuffed figure— / Was a wooden block of masculine gender" [Ei ne bylo dela do togo, chto chuchelo— / Churban muzhskogo roda]).[42] He also represents the poet's cross-dressing as part of a sexual fantasy: his desire to dress like a woman is inseparable from his desire for her ("I loved because, wearing my sweetheart's dress / I saw my sweetheart with no dress" [Ia liubil ottogo, chto v plat'e miloi / Ia miluiu videl bez plat'ia]). Finally, Pasternak assigns the fan-tasy to adolescence, the period of transition to sexual knowledge ("Many other adolescent boys, I'm sure, dream / Of the pattern-maker" [Eshche mnogim po-drostkam, verno, snitsia / Zakroishchitsa]). As the second poem of the cycle suggests, it is an anxious period.[43] The poet's agitation is rendered by a Mayakovskian image of "a wall clock for measuring feelings" (stennoi pribor dlia izmeren'ia chuvstv), feelings Pasternak characterizes as neurotic: "The neurasthenic on the wall knows us on sight" (Stennoi nevrastenik nas znaet v litso).

"Northern Seamstress" identifies the kind of femininity Pasternak performs in many of his early poems, namely, a femininity defined by sexual anxiety or trauma and expressed through hysterical affect. This femininity resembles the "free subjectivity" of the lyric poet, which Pasternak described as sick, chaotic, and feminine. There is a strong accord, that is, between Pasternak's theorizing and his poetic practice, whose most distinctive aspects may be linked to the poet's "yearning will to be feminine." The most unusual feature of Pasternak's poetics is his treatment of the lyric speaker. In his 1935 essay on Pasternak, Ro-man Jakobson put forward the influential argument that Pasternak's writing is driven by metonymic association.[44] This principle, he argued, also governs Pasternak's "invisible" lyric speaker, who rarely speaks in the first person. Rather, he is metonymically present in every aspect of the described world: "The hero is as if concealed in a picture puzzle; he is broken down into a series of constituent and subsidiary parts; he is replaced by a chain of concretized situations and surrounding objects, both animate and inanimate." From this feature of Pasternak's poetics Jakobson deduces that Pasternak's basic thematic material is the passive experiencing of external impulses. The action of his lyric narratives tends to be reactive; entities are surprised, confused, delighted, or disappointed, but they never actually do anything. Jakobson concludes that "the lyric 'I' in Pasternak's work is a *patiens*."[45] It is not simply that Pasternak achieves impersonality by sidelining the lyric subject; he achieves it by adopting the passive voice. Jakobson's description of Pasternak's dispersed and reactive persona, I would suggest, is a profile of the hysteric. The very figure of metonymy, with its continual slippage from one object to the next, might be seen as mimicking hysterical mobility.[46]

A poem from 1916, "Anguish, crazed, crazed" ("Toska beshennaia, beshennaia"), well displays the confluence between Pasternak's performance of femininity and his distinctive poetics. The poem features Pasternak's impersonal persona; there is no lyric subject, just the entity "anguish." It stages a scene Pasternak repeatedly returns to in his work: the poet at his window.[47] We follow the actions performed by his "anguish," the first of which is to shatter the window and run outside:

> Anguish, crazed, crazed,
> Anguish in two or three leaps
> Reaches the window frame hung
> With the castoffs of a garden spider.
>
> Anguish breaks the window
>   And like a wet marten rushes
> To where across the moon-hilled plateau
> The night forests moan,
> Swinging, without unclenching their mouths,
>   Eaten away by the sulphuric moon.

> Тоска, бешенная, бешенная,
> Тоска в два-три прыжка
> Достигает оконницы, завешенной
> Обносками крестовика.
>
> Тоска стекло вышибает
>   И мокрою куницею выносится
> Туда, где плоскогорьем лунно-холмным
> Леса ночные стонут
> Враскачку, ртов не разжимая,
>   Изъединные серною луной.

The poem displays Pasternak's cherished lyric dynamism, which is catalyzed by a particular affect—the affect of "crazed anguish." The landscape has the same affect, also set into motion by trauma: the forests have been injured ("eaten away") and moan without speaking ("without unclenching their mouths"). Similar responses are forwarded along a metonymic chain to other parts of nature—to oaks whose mouths are shut by the moon (Luna dubam zazhala rty) and leaves that excitedly perceive "the sky's debauch" (neba debosh). We then return to the activity of "anguish," which in several more leaps reaches a thrusting branch and "hoists a wail" (vodruzhaet vopl') in a thinly veiled rendering of heterosexual copulation. ("Anguish" is grammatically feminine and "branch" masculine.) The act leaves "the mark of anguish" (kleimo toski) on the branch, and that mark, or anguish itself—the chain of substitutions makes the difference unclear—begs the branch "to pull the thorn out of her paw" (Vynut' iz lapki zanozu). Both partners, it seems, have been painfully marked by the sexual encounter. The poem thus rehearses a second scene repeatedly staged by Pasternak, a scene of contact that yields a painful ecstasy.[48]

The semantic connection to the final stanza is the act of "pulling out," which has both sexual and psychological nuances. The final stanza begins with the untranslatable sentence "I hope her [missing noun] is pulled out" (Nadeius', ee vynut). Logically it would read, "I hope it is pulled out," referring to the thorn, but Pasternak's strange syntax does not allow such a reading. In any case, what follows is an act of "putting in":

> I hope hers is pulled out. Then into the opening
> In the embrasure—glazier—insert it,
> The caustically corroded photograph
> Of my soul with a woman's name in the world.

> Надеюсь, ее вынут. Тогда, в дыру
> Амбразуры—стекольщик—вставь ее,
> Души моей, с именем женским в миру
> Едко въевшуюся фотографию.

The architectural "embrasure" recalls the window at the poem's beginning—the window that was broken by the poet's anguish. The final stanza imagines a kind of repair: the glass will be replaced by a photograph of the poet's "soul with a woman's name," which is to say, a photograph of his anguish. This image of the window as photograph establishes the speaker's full identity with his feminine soul: the window surface/photograph reflects the poet's own face as he looks out onto the landscape. Pasternak renders this identification with rare explicitness, as the poet steps forward to speak in the first person ("my soul"). These concluding lines establish the equivalence that sets Pasternak's metonymic chains into motion: the poet's soul is the anguished feminine soul.

This final episode of framing also suggests an aesthetic allegory: the hysterical movement of "anguish," in the end, is captured as an aesthetic artifact. It is an allegory that is reflected in the poem's form, which is highly unstable. Although Pasternak primarily uses his favorite four-line stanza, the second and third stanzas have six lines. His use of rhyme is irregular: some stanzas, like the first, have a recognizable *abab* rhyme scheme, some stanzas rhyme only two lines, while some contain no rhyme at all. When rhymes do appear, they are strenuously inexact, even in the context of futurist practice ("znaet"/"skvoznaia ikh").[49] As for the poem's rhythmical structure, there is a general impression of a three-stress *dol'nik*, but four-stress lines make random appearances. The poem also features the syntactic and semantic complexity that is a signature feature of Pasternak's difficult early poetics.[50] The line "I hope hers is pulled out" (Nadeius', ee vynut) is a fine example of how grammatical units may not line up logically in a Pasternak sentence. The challenge of interpreting Pasternak's figuration is also evidenced by the way actions and affects are continually displaced from one entity to the next. The "tenor" undergoes so many metonymic transformations that it is unrecognizable as any particular thing. As Lazar Fleishman has phrased it, "All the vehicles of language at the author's disposal seem, in fact, to be mobilized to blur the distinction between a trope and nontrope."[51] In sum, this poem might well be said to capture and frame the dramatic, mobile representations of the hysteric.

Whether because "Anguish, crazed, crazed" was too chaotic or because it was too readable, Pasternak never republished it. (It appeared in the second Tsentrifuge miscellany.) But the poem remains fairly typical of the poems Pasternak was writing in 1914–16. These poems made up his second book of poetry, *Above the Barriers* (*Poverkh bar'erov*, 1917), which represents the acme of Pasternak's experimental poetics. By the time the book appeared, he was already honing and moderating that poetics in the poems that became the basis for *My Sister Life* (*Sestra moia—zhizn'*, 1922) and the companion volume *Themes and Variations* (*Temy i variatsii*, 1923). Although these books were not published until the early 1920s, they are close in conception and technique to his futurist poems.[52] In particular, as I will show, *My Sister Life* realizes to perfection an allegory whereby dramatic emotionality—an emotionality marked as feminine—is shaped into aesthetic artifact.

By way of beginning, I offer a reading of one of the book's key poems, "The Mirror" ("Zerkalo"), which shows strong though not immediately obvious continuities with "Anguish, crazed, crazed." These become more apparent if we read "The Mirror" in conjunction with its companion poem, "The Girl" ("Devochka").[53] "The Mirror" and "The Girl" appear sequentially in the first section of *My Sister Life* and form a diptych. (In the 1919 manuscript, "The Mirror" is followed by the instruction "without a pause," with an arrow leading over to "The Girl.") Together the two poems name the romantic conception of the beloved as a mirror of the poet's self. This concern—defining the poet's self—was more directly announced by the first poem's original title, the Mayakovskian "I Myself" ("Ia sam"). Characteristically, however, the lyric subject is difficult to locate in these poems. The mirror of "The Mirror" reflects not the poet's image but a garden, which is visible outside the window. Just as in "Anguish, crazed, crazed," the window marks a boundary between the poet and nature, a boundary that is broken:

> In the mirror a mug of hot chocolate is steaming,
>   A swirl of tulle—and right
> Into the garden, its crush and its chaos,
>   The mirror runs to the swing.
>
> There pine trees, swinging, sting the air
>   With tar; and there the fence
> Feels around in the grass for its glasses,
>   There Shadow reads a book.
>
> And toward the background, the gloom, the gate,
>   The steppe and the smell of sleeping potions,
> Along the road covered in branches and snails
>   Runs hot and sparkling quartz.
>
> In the hall the enormous garden pesters
>   The mirror—but doesn't break the glass!
> It seemed like collodium covered it all,
>   From dresser to rustling trees.
>
>   It seemed that the mirror gushed over it all
>   With ice that doesn't sweat,
> So the branch wasn't bitter, the lilac unscented—
>   But it couldn't cover the hypnosis.
>
> The multitudinous world minces in mesmerism
>   And only the wind can bind
> What breaks into life, and breaks up in prisms
>   And is pleased to play in tears.
>
> The soul can't be blown up like a deposit of ore,
>   Or dug up with a spade like treasure.
> In the hall the enormous garden pesters
>   The mirror—but doesn't break the glass.
>
> And out in that hypnotic fatherland
>   Nothing can extinguish my eyes.
> As when after it rains slugs crawl over
>   The eyes of the statues.
>
> Water gurgles over their ears, and a siskin,
>   Giving a chirp, hops on tiptoe.
> You can smear their lips with bilberry
>   And still not stop their mischief.

In the hall the enormous garden
    Raises its fist to the mirror,
Runs to the swing, chases, tags,
    And shakes—but doesn't break the glass!

В трюмо испаряется чашка какао,
    Качается тюль,—и прямой
Дорожкою в сад, в бурелом и хаос
    К качелям бежит трюмо.

Там сосны враскачку воздух саднят
    Смолой; там по маете
Очки по траве растерял палисадник,
    Там книгу читает Тень.

И к заднему плану, во мрак, за калитку,
    В степь, в запах сонных лекарств
Струится дорожкой, в сучках и в улитках,
    Мерцающий жаркий кварц.

Огромный сад тормошится в зале
    В трюмо—и не бьет стекла!
Казалось бы, все коллодий залил
    С комода до шума в стволах.

Зеркальная все б, казалось, на́хлынь
    Непотным льдом облила,
Чтоб сук не горчил и сирень не пахла,—
    Гипноза залить не могла.

Несметный мир семенит в месмеризме,
    И только ветру связать,
Что ломится в жизнь, и ломается в призме,
    И радо играть в слезах.

Души не взорвать, как селитрой залежь,
    Не вырыть, как заступом клад.
Огромный сад тормошится в зале
    В трюмо—и не бьет стекла.

И вот, в гипнотической этой отчизне
    Ничем мне очей не задуть.
Так после дождя проползают слизни
    Глазами статуй в саду.

Шуршит вода по ушам, и, чирикнув,
    На цыпочках скачет чиж.

Ты можешь им выпачкать губы черникой,
   Их шалостью не опоишь.

Огромный сад тормошится в зале,
   Подносит к трюмо кулак,
Бежит на качели, ловит, салит,
   Трясет—и не бьет стекла!

Roughly summarized, the poem's message is that art can, and presumably should, render the world in motion, echoing Pasternak's theoretical statements about dynamic realism. The poem opens with the mirror racing out into the garden, which the next two stanzas describe in long perspective. In the fourth stanza, the garden races into the house and up to the mirror, at which the poet exclaims, in the line that becomes the poem's leitmotif, "but doesn't break the glass!" The reflecting medium of art retains its integrity even as it frames nature's unceasing and sometimes violent dynamism.

As Anna Ljunggren has shown, the poet's presence in the poem is marked by several references to eyes and to vision: "The eye is written into the poem's focus, the depths of the mirror."[54] The poet's eyes, like the reflected image of the garden, are covered by a transparent film—his tears, in which the world "plays." But he retains his power of vision: "And out in that hypnotic fatherland / Nothing can extinguish my eyes." Ljunggren identifies this "burning gaze" as the chief attribute of the symbolist poet-prophet but does not follow out its implications for the poem's aesthetic allegory. The poet of "The Mirror" is the poet possessed—a madman, as the poem's most peculiar image vividly conveys: "As when after it rains slugs crawl over / The eyes of the statues." The statues, the only human shapes in the poem, are stand-ins for the hypnotized poet, whose rigid body sets into relief his crazily mobile eyes. This is poetic seeing, as distinct from the 20/20 vision made possible by the lost pair of glasses remarked in stanza two. The poem thus recalls Pasternak's statements in "Symbolism and Immortality" about poetic inspiration as the loss of self, echoing Ivanov's concept of the Dionysian. In fact, the poem reproduces exactly the Nietzschean formula Ivanov adopted, in which Apollonian form contains the destructive force of the Dionysian: Pasternak's poet, though in a state of inspired madness, is nonetheless preserved by the liquid film that coats his eyes; his "soul" cannot be "unearthed." Nature's hypnotizing power (gipnoza) is similarly preserved by a coating of collodium, a substance used to develop photographs—and a word that phonically evokes "Apollonian."

The word "collodium" also points to the theme of sickness, since it names a substance used to seal wounds. Boris Gasparov unburied this thematic in his clarifying reading of the poem, in which he reconstructs the action preceding the depicted scene. He has demonstrated that "there begin to emerge the contours of an illness that has passed: the painful sensation of the scratches, the sharp 'medicinal' smells, the 'mesmerising' effect of impressions and recollections that flared up in consciousness during a fever."[55] On the basis of these and other details, he speculates that the illness is suffered by a child who has spent too much time in the summer heat playing a game of stickball (*igra v chizha* or *chilika*). This allows him to place the speaker with respect to the mirror and the garden: he is in bed, with a view of the mirror in which the garden is reflected—a garden whose movement reminds him of the mischief that caused him to fall ill and from which he is now recovering.

Like most commentators, Gasparov does not go on to consider the relevance of the next poem, "The Girl," though it offers strong support for his argument. Gasparov notes parenthetically that the sick child in "The Mirror" may be the young Pasternak, who was confined to bed for six weeks after the riding accident that broke his leg. The action of "breaking a limb" is rendered in "The Girl" and takes place within the same space configured in "The Mirror":

The Girl

> A little golden cloud spent the night
> On the breast of the giant cliff.

From the garden, the swing, and the higgledy-piggledy
  The branch runs right into the mirror!
She's huge and up close, and an emerald drop hangs
  From the tip of her ramrod brush.

The garden's obscured, lost behind her disorder,
  The commotion that beats in your face.
She's akin, huge, as big as the garden, but by nature
  A sister! A second mirror!

But that branch is now taken and put in a glass
  And set near the frame of the mirror.
Who is it, she wonders, that moistens my eyes
  With this human, confining torpor?

Девочка

> Ночевала тучка золотая
> На груди утеса великана.

Из сада, с качелей, с бухты-барахты
  Вбегает ветка в трюмо!
Огромная, близкая, с каплей смарагда
  На кончике кисти прямой.

Сад застлан, пропал за ее беспорядком,
  За бьющей в лицо кутерьмой.
Родная, громадная, с сад, а характером—
  Сестра! Второе трюмо!

Но вот эту ветку вносят в рюмке
И ставят к раме трюмо.
Кто это,—гадает,—глаза мне рюмит
Тюремной людской дремой?

The branch is the garden's synecdoche, in a most literal fashion: the branch is a part that is "as big as" the whole garden. At the same time, the poem announces the branch's difference. She is a "sister," a female, in contrast to the masculine garden. Her different nature, or more literally "character," is "disorder," as emphasized by Pasternak's pairing of a dactylic with a feminine rhyme: "besporiadkom"/"kharakterom." Her frenzied motion obscures the poet's view, so that he cannot see the garden for the branch. Her hyperactivity apparently becomes intolerable; between the second and third stanzas, the branch is broken off by an unknown hand and placed in a glass by the mirror. The aesthetic allegory ends in the same way it ended in "Anguish, crazed, crazed"—with the containment of a chaotic feminine element.

What does "The Girl" add to "The Mirror"? The masculine garden and the feminine branch act similarly: both the garden and the branch rush at the window, attempting to break or penetrate it, and their violence is successfully deflected. The feminine branch even has the same phallic shape as the "fist" raised by the garden; she is a phallic girl, an Amazon. Unlike the garden, however, she is not simply contained but also injured and immobilized, in the way Pasternak was injured and immobilized by his riding accident. The image of the broken branch represents that laming as a kind of castration: it is not broken but broken off. Pasternak himself later represented his riding accident as a kind of castration. In his 1956 autobiography, Pasternak attributes his fall to his father's aesthetic agency, describing himself as riding into one of Leonid Pasternak's paintings: "That autumn I had an accident which kept us in the country later than usual. Father was painting a picture, *To the Night Pastures*. It was a sunset scene of girls from a nearby village, Bocharovo, riding at full tilt and driving horses to the water meadows at the bottom of our hill. One evening I joined them, but my horse ran away with me and, as it jumped a wide stream, I fell off and broke my leg."[56] The painting features Pasternak's beloved Amazons, sisters of "the girl." With Pasternak's accident, their motion comes to a halt, and in a sense his father's as well. As Fleishman has clarified, the painting Pasternak associated with his fall was a new kind of work for Leonid Pasternak: "It was to have been one of his largest and most important canvases (with the horses and riders life-size)," presenting new artistic challenges.[57] But as Leonid Pasternak related in his memoirs, his son's fall prevented him from finishing the painting. The broken branch, then, is also his father's paintbrush, as indeed it appears in "The Girl." ("an emerald drop hangs / From the tip of her ramrod brush" [s kaplei smaragda / Na konchike kisti primoi]). Pasternak's story about his accident represents the male artist attempting to keep pace with the Amazons and to capture their power and movement for his own art, and in this instance the father's attempt is foiled by his son.

Leonid Pasternak's sketch for his unfinished painting "Into the Night Pastures," 1903 (collection of E. B. Pasternak)

In "The Mirror" and "The Girl," Pasternak makes the experience of castration the ground of his creativity. He does so by imagining his injury as the girl's "castration," which Freud believed was key to female sexual development ("The discovery that she is castrated is a turning point in the girl's growth").[58] As Irigaray has argued, Freud's—and Victorian culture's—conception of sexuality as phallic places the girl in a difficult relation to sexuality. Her best option in this predicament is hysteria, as a kind of phallic activity that substitutes for her own devalued sexuality. This is the affect to which Pasternak lays claim when he imagines himself sharing the girl's injured condition. As early as 1913, Pasternak linked his accident to his first creative impulses, expressed in the medium of music. He recalls himself as a thirteen-year-old boy lying "in his fresh, still hardening cast, and through his delirium rush the three-beat, syncopated rhythms of the gallop and the fall" (4:684). He describes here the same allegory I have traced in his poems, an allegory about movement arrested and then reproduced in the aesthetic artifact. This is a matter of both allegory and form, both metapoetics and poetics. As Gasparov has shown, the syncopated rhythm Pasternak mentions is a leitmotif not only in Pasternak's musical compositions but also in his verse.[59] It reproduces a kind of tripping forward move-

ment that suggests a gallop, as well as Pasternak's limping gait after the accident. This rhythm, along with the other aspects of Pasternak's art I have described as "hysterical," arises from an experience of paralysis and confinement
that mirrors the condition of Victorian woman.

When configuring the poet's relation to the girl in "The Mirror" and "The
Girl," Pasternak made deliberate use of grammatical gender. Katherine
O'Connor has drawn attention to this issue by reading Pasternak's use of the
epigraph, two lines from Lermontov's poem "The Cliff" ("Utes"): "A little
golden cloud spent the night / On the breast of the giant cliff." O'Connor points
out that the grammatically masculine garden and the feminine branch repeat
the masculine cliff and feminine cloud of Lermontov's poem.[60] Pasternak also
introduces the neuter gender into this scheme. The Russian "mirror" (zerkalo)
is grammatically neuter, and the analogous "pier glass" (triumo) is also neuter.
The mirror's neutrality allows it to reflect a natural world that has two genders
(the garden and the branch), allowing the poet a fluid gender identity. He exploits the possibilities throughout the "garden cycle," as O'Connor has named
the five-poem sequence that includes "The Mirror" and "The Girl." In all these
poems a window looks out into a garden, which attempts to penetrate the window, usually with a branch. The erotic suggestiveness of this action is never
noted, perhaps because of its unusual gendering: the poet's window is being
probed by a phallic object that is nevertheless identified as feminine. But this is
precisely the kind of freedom allowed by Pasternak's metonymic poetics,
whereby the poet can not only be everywhere but also be anything, even any
gender. It is an aspect of what Michel Aucouturier has described as the "hidden eroticism" created by Pasternak's metonymies.[61]

In the first poem, "The Weeping Garden" ("Plachushchii sad"), the garden
appears, as it will throughout the cycle, dripping from a recent rain shower:

> He's awful!—He'll drip and he listens,
> Is he alone in the world as he
> Presses a branch in the lacelike window,
> Or is there a witness?

> Ужасный!—Капнет и вслушается,
> Все он ли один на свете
> Мнет ветку в окне, как кружевце,
> Или есть свидетель.

The "he" is the masculine garden, whose concern about being observed suggests that he is engaged in a private act. In the second stanza, a spongy feminine earth chokes from the volume of water she has absorbed; in the third, the
garden "gets up to his old tricks" (berets'ia za staroe) after making sure no one
is watching. There is, nevertheless, a witness, the lyric speaker, who steps forward in the fourth stanza:

> I will raise [it] to my lips and I listen:
> Am I alone in the world,—
> Ready to sob in a second,—
> Or is there a witness.

> К губам поднесу и прислушаюсь,
> Все я ли один на свете,—
> Готовый навзрыд при случае,—
> Или есть свидетель.

Like the garden, the poet is wary of being caught in the act, here the act of raising something to his lips—impossible to say what, since Pasternak does not supply the direct object required for the transitive verb "raise." It is clear enough, though, that he remains "ready to sob," just as the garden is ready "to drip," in a state of anxious arousal as he waits for the beloved: "Not a trace of a sign, except for the awful / Gulps and splashing in slippers / And sighs and tears in the interim" (Ni priznaka zgi, krome zhutkikh / Glotkov i pleskaniia v shlepantsakh / I vzdokhov i slez v promezhutke).

There follow "The Mirror" and "The Girl," then an untitled poem that begins "You are in the wind, which tests with a branch" (Ty v vetre, vetkoi probuiushchem). The addressee is a another girl-branch, who is dressed like a man: the branch is soaked with raindrops that have "the heaviness of cuff links" (tiazhest' zaponok). The garden is similarly covered with raindrops as a result of his nocturnal exploits:

> All night he thrust at the window
> And the shutter shook.
> Suddenly a breath of damp rankness
> Ran down his dress.

> Всю ночь в окошко торкался,
> И ставень дребезжал.
> Вдруг дух сырой прогорклости
> По платью пробежал.

The garden achieves orgasm without penetration, in what looks like a scene of onanistic pleasure. The event also seems to involve cross-dressing: the garden wears a dress, as well as cuff links.

The last poem of the cycle, "Rain" ("Dozhd'"), announces the beloved's long-anticipated arrival: "She is with me" (Ona so mnoi). The speaker urges the rain to "beat against the window" like a silkworm, thus making midday as dark as night (Snui shelkopriadom tutovym /I beis'a ob okno). This small phallic shape grows in size when the rain becomes a downpour and beats against the beloved "like entire trees / Coming at eyes, temples, jasmine!" (I—tselymi derev'iami / V glaza, v viski, v zhasmin!). As in the preceding poem, nature's movement reaches a climax, again signaled by an abruptly released scent: "And suddenly it smelled of discharging / From a thousand hospitals" (I vdrug pakhnulo vypiskoi / Iz tysiachi bol′nits). Finally, the sexual event is connoted beyond traditional heterosexual coupling. In the last stanza the pair runs out into the "garden St. Gotthard / Washed in linden mist" (Omytyi mgloiu lipovoi / Sadovyi Sen-Gotard). As O'Connor has pointed out, Pasternak refers to the St. Gotthard tunnel in Switzerland, through which he once traveled.[62] The image supplies a final instance of ambiguous gendering in the cycle: the male garden possesses a vaginal, or anal, opening. It also heightens the erotic meaning of the poet's train trips to visit the beloved, most famously evoked in the title poem, "Life is my sister and today in a downpour" (Sestra moia—zhizn′ i segodnia v razlive"). In sum, the garden of *My Sister Life* is a garden of the Fall, a sexual garden in which the poet explores various erotic configurations. In these poems, he is "polymorphously perverse," to use Freud's famous phrase about the child's constitutional bisexuality.[63]

The poet's erotic experiments are conducted in the context of the heterosexual romance that is the subject of *My Sister Life*. Although many of the poems are not easily recognized as love poems, as "The Mirror" and "The Girl" are not, Pasternak carefully composed *My Sister Life* as the story of a summer love affair. More accurately, he structured the book to create the "illusion of a narrative," as O'Connor has demonstrated.[64] Pasternak presents the book as telling a story, for example, by supplying "chapters" with titles such as "The Beloved's Diversions"("Razvlechen′ia liubimoi") and "The Return" ("Vozvrashchenie"). At the same time, he creates lyric "cycles" that in counterpoint with the "chapters" create a unique temporality that embraces both moment and eternity;[65] events occur "instantaneously forever," to borrow a phrase from one of the poems ("Groza, momental′naia navek"). Despite the book's complex structure, the general outline of events remains clear: the lovers meet in the spring in Moscow, where the poet resides; during the summer he travels to visit her in the countryside; and the relationship ends in the fall.

The story is anchored in a specific autobiographical and historical context, as announced by the book's subtitle, *Summer 1917* (*Leto 1917 goda*). The "revolutionary summer" of 1917 was framed by the February and October revolutions, to which Pasternak makes significant allusion (as I will show in a later chapter). During that summer Pasternak had an affair with Elena Vinograd, details of which appear in the book, including the fact that she spent the summer doing social work in southern Russia. Pasternak's inclusion of prosaic details and diction in his love lyrics was distinctive and became a hallmark of his poetics.[66] In *My Sister Life*, these details were so markedly personal that one contemporary critic referred to the book as a "diary."[67] But Pasternak does not, like the young Tsvetaeva, set out to capture individual experience, nor does he speak through literary and mythological personae, as she does in her later poetry. Rather he creates an interplay between the particular and the archetypal in his telling of the love story.

In the poem "With Oars Crossed" ("Slozha vesla"), which renders the classic scene of two lovers boating on a river, the poet does not simply acknowledge his affair's conventionality but celebrates it: "And this could happen to anyone!" (Eto ved' mozhet so vsiakim sluchitsia). As Nils Åke Nilsson has stated in his landmark essay on this poem, Pasternak here "rejects the false claim of poets and lovers to the exclusiveness of their feelings."[68] Nilsson goes on to conclude that Pasternak's controlled, ironic performance demonstrates his freedom from romantic cliché and prejudice. This is a claim the speaker himself seems to make when, in another of *My Sister Life*'s "rowboat poems," he takes pains to distinguish his own role-playing from the beloved's:

> You played the role so wonderfully!
> I quite forgot that I'm the prompter!
> And that you'll sing a second one,
> Whoever the first one attracted.

> Ты так играла эту роль!
> Я забывал, что сам—суфлер!
> Что будешь петь и во второй,
> Кто б первой ни совлек.

He identifies himself as the "prompter" (sufler), the one who knows they are working from a script. Yet a prompter is also an actor of sorts, who, though he remains offstage, is very much part of the play. And though he possesses the script, he also appears liable to be possessed by it, to "forget" that they are playing roles.

The roles the poet and his beloved play are the conventional roles of the heterosexual romance. Nilsson, along with other commentators, perceives Pasternak as transcending or transforming the role of the romantic lover.[69] I would argue that Pasternak's performance of the role is more in the spirit of exploring and giving himself over to the romantic script of love. For example, in "From Superstition" ("Iz suever'ia"), the poet tries to prevent the beloved from leaving his room:

> I would not let the door latch go,
>   You tore yourself away,
> My forelock touched your lovely bangs
>   And my lips, your violets.

> Из рук не выпускал защелки,
>   Ты вырывалась,
> И чуб касался чудной челки
>   И губы—фиалок.

According to Elena Vinograd, this episode occurred when she visited Pasternak's Moscow apartment: "I went up to the door . . . , preparing to leave, but he held the door closed and smiled, that's why the forelock and bangs drew close. But 'you tore yourself away' is an exaggeration, because Boris Leonidich by his very nature was incapable of exerting the slightest force even just to embrace a girl if she didn't desire it. All I did was reproachfully say 'Boria' and the door immediately opened."[70] Vinograd undercuts the drama of the scene by insisting that Pasternak was incapable of acting the male aggressor. Pasternak's poem, by contrast, heightens the action, making it something to relish. Juxtaposing Vinograd's memoir with the poem highlights how Pasternak makes a pleasurable performance of the love drama. Here he plays the male lead, but as we shall see, he also plays the woman. Pasternak does indeed transform the male role, not so much through ironic distance as by enacting both active and passive desire in a fluid gender performance.

In shaping the love story of *My Sister Life,* Pasternak draws on classic literary texts that dramatize the roles of male predator and female victim. The opening poem, "In Memory of the Demon" ("Pamiati demona"), is based on the narrative poem "The Demon" ("Demon," 1829–39) by the Russian romantic poet Mikhail Lermontov, to whom Pasternak dedicated the book. Lermontov's poem tells the story of a demon who falls in love with the mortal Tamara, then seduces and unwittingly destroys her. Pasternak's poem supplies a coda to Lermontov's by depicting the demon's nightly vigil at Tamara's grave. The two other narratives prominently featured in *My Sister Life*—Goethe's *Faust* and Shakespeare's *Hamlet*—also feature the story of an innocent young woman's demise, for which her male lover is to some degree culpable. These stories are invoked together in a poem called "To Helen" ("Elene"), referring to both Pasternak's lover Elena Vinograd and Helen of Troy ("Sleep, queen of Sparta" [Spi, tsaritsa Sparty]). Pasternak refers not to classical mythology as such but to part two of *Faust,* where Faust marries Helen of Troy, the embodiment of the Eternal Feminine ("das Ewig-weibliche"). Ophelia also is named in the poem: "A pearl from the necklace / On Ophelia's shoulder" (Zhemchug ozherel'ia / Na pleche Ofeliinom).

Ophelia appears earlier in the book, in a poem titled "English Lessons" ("Uroki angliiskogo"). The poem belongs to the chapter "The Beloved's Diversions" ("Razvlecheniia liubimoi"), and here her diversion is reading Shakespeare's *Hamlet* and *Othello*. The first two stanzas are devoted to Desdemona's swan song, the second two stanzas to Ophelia's. Pasternak, that is, juxtaposes Desdemona and Ophelia as victims who sing before they die. Pasternak was not the first Russian poet thus to bring together Shakespeare's heroines. The nineteenth-century poet Afanasy Fet, who strongly influenced Pasternak,[71] wrote a cycle of poems "To Ophelia" ("K Ofelii," 1847) in which the poet exorts her to "sing of the willow, the green willow / The willow of Desdemona your sister" (Pro ivu, pro ivu zelenuiu spoi, / Pro ivu sestry Dezdemony). But it was Aleksander Blok who most deeply influenced Pasternak's representation of

Elena Vinograd, 1916

Ophelia, as Igor Smirnov has shown.[72] Blok himself was influenced by Fet, whom he ranked with Polonsky as a singer of the Eternal Feminine. He praised him both as the translator of Goethe's *Faust*—that is, as the poet who rendered the Eternal Feminine into Russian—and as the author of the lyric cycle "To Ophelia": "In the four poems of 'To Ophelia,' Fet, bringing Shakespeare into modernity (not simply a poetic but a philosophical and cultural achievement), incarnates his feminine ideal in a foreign image and thus masters the image and his own genius."[73] Ophelia is the second foreign image, after Goethe's Helen, of the symbolist feminine ideal; they are the "beautiful ladies" of Blok's early verse. When Pasternak brought together Helen and Ophelia in "To Helen," he united what were for Blok the two great incarnations of the Eternal Feminine.

While Pasternak could not have known this passage from Blok's diary, he certainly understood Ophelia's significance for Blok. As Smirnov has shown, Pasternak's early poem "The Dream" ("Son," 1913) reworks two of the "Ophelia" poems in Blok's *Ante Lucem*.[74] The first, "I dreamed about the death of a beloved being" (Mne snilas' smert' liubimogo sozdan'ia), imagines the poet at her coffin, a coffin covered with flowers. The second, "I once again dreamed of you wearing flowers on a famous stage" (Mne snilas' snova ty, v tsvetakh, na shumnoi stsene), renders a performance of *Hamlet* in which the beloved plays Ophelia and the speaker plays Hamlet. The poem refers to the well-known fact that Blok, an enthusiastic theater amateur, played Hamlet opposite Liubov Dmitrievna Mendeleeva during the summer of their courtship in 1898.[75] Blok later declared himself the Russian Hamlet in a poem of 1914, a claim his contemporaries honored ("I am Hamlet. The blood chills" [Ia—Gamlet. Kholodeet krov']).[76] Blok's relationship with Mendeleeva was, of course, a highly scripted one: she was the woman who, for both Blok and Bely, was the human embodiment of the Eternal Feminine. Pasternak took another such Ophelia for the muse of *My Sister Life*. As remarked earlier, Pasternak traced to Blok's *Ante Lucem* an early poem he dedicated to Elena Vinograd.[77]

Pasternak's "English Lessons," like the Blok poems just mentioned, focuses on the heroines' fatal end. The poem's leitmotif—it is time for them to sing—suggests the rightness of their fate, which the women themselves appear to sense. In fact, Pasternak suggests that they choose death and welcome it as a release from painful emotion:

> Slipping passions from their arms like rags,
> With sinking hearts they slowly waded into
> The pool of the universe that loves
> To drown and mute its body within worlds.

> Дав страсти с плеч отлечь, как рубищу,
> Входили, с сердца замираньем,
> В бассейн вселенной, стан свой любящий
> Обдать и оглушить мирами.

Although Othello's murderous act is evoked in the second stanza, Desdemona's and Ophelia's lovers are curiously irrelevant at the moment of death; they appear only metonymically, as the "passions" of which these heroines divest themselves.

The same discarding of emotion like clothes occurs in Pasternak's representation of Helen. Katherine O'Connor has argued that Helen's image underpins the epigraph to *My Sister Life*, four lines from a poem by Nicolas Lenau: "The forest rages, across the sky / Fly stormy thunderclouds, / Then into the weather I draw, / O maiden, your features" (Es braust der Wald, am Himmel ziehn / Des Sturmes Donnerflüge, / Da mal' ich in die Wetter hin, / O Mädchen, deine Züge).[78] O'Connor notes that in part two of *Faust*, when Helen leaves Faust after the death of their son, she rises into the sky leaving behind her garments, which are transformed into a huge cloud. The Lenau epigraph renders Helen as a "stormy thundercloud" that is metonymically associated with the forest's "raging." In Pasternak's "To Helen," by contrast, she is a remote, statue-like figure who sleeps peacefully while the poet rages, tormented by fruitless, obsessive thoughts about the end of their troubled affair:

> Her dear departed apron
> And her temple pulsing.
> Sleep, you queen of Sparta,
> It's early yet, and damp still.
>
> Sorrow now in earnest
> Got worked up and tipsy.
> Awful to be alone with.
> If it goes mad—can it be managed?
>
> Weep, it whispered. Choking?
> It burns? Then give her one on the cheek!
> Let fate be the judge:
> A mother or a stepmother?
>
> Милый, мертвый фартук
> И висок пульсирующий.
> Спи, царица Спарты,
> Рано еще, сыро еще.
>
> Горе не на шутку
> Разыгралось, навеселе.
> Одному с ним жутко.
> Сбесится,—управиться ли?
>
> Плачь, шепнуло. Гложет?
> Жжет? Такую ж на щеку ей!
> Пусть судьба положит—
> Матерью ли, мачехой ли.

In these stanzas the poet displays the strong affect Helen wore in the Lenau epigraph. Pasternak's rendering of the heterosexual romance in *My Sister Life*, that is, enacts the same aesthetic allegory as Pasternak's earlier verse, where the poet "dresses" as the traumatized woman.

Pasternak himself identified his muse as a hysteric in a remarkable poem called "Earth's Illnesses" ("Bolezni zemli").[79] The poem gathers together some of the book's main semantic fields, namely, "illness," "darkness," and "despair."[80] It represents a thunderstorm as the "crazed spittle" of a raving monster, and offers several diagnoses of its condition. The diseases named in the poem—tetanus and rabies—both affect the nervous system, causing symptoms of madness. Another version of the poem points to hysteria with a mention of "Charcot's black soul," referring to the French psychiatrist Jean-Martin Charcot, who specialized in hysteria. (Freud studied with him at the start of his career.) Charcot also introduced the use of photography to study his patients' condition, a fact that provides a suggestive context for the photographic imagery in *My Sister Life*. "The Substitute" ("Zamestitel'nitsa"), for example, features a photograph of the beloved performing a frenzied dance, like a scene from the Salpêtrière asylum.[81] Charcot's patients also, at his direction, sometimes played Ophelia for the camera[82]—Ophelia being the exemplary hysteric in nineteenth-century European culture.[83]

Pasternak's lyric speaker turns in a similar performance in *My Sister Life*, making it the most sustained example of his hysterical poetics. Throughout the volume, the lyric speaker sobs, faints, and suffers fits of paranoia. He also frequently struggles for breath, the kind of speech disturbance Kahane identifies as hysterical. Moments of choking or drowning are underscored at the acoustic level; as Donald Plank has shown, "A Stuffy Night" ("Dushnaia noch'") renders a nocturnal attack of asthma. (The word-final velar stop *k* "signifies the stoppage of breath" and the onset of faintness.[84]) Pasternak's speaker also openly performs the role of the tragic heroine. In "To love, to walk" ("Liubit', idti"), he sings and dies like Shakespeare's heroines:

> And so I sang, I sang and died
> And died and then returned,
> A boomerang, into her arms
> And said farewell, as I recall.

> Так пел я, пел и умирал.
> И умирал, и возвращался
> К ее рукам, как бумеранг,
> И—сколько помнится—прощался.

Pasternak has more trouble divesting himself of passion than the Desdemona and Ophelia of "English Lessons"; he obsessively returns to the beloved, unable to make a final break. In this poem filled with references to opera, among them Gounod's *Faust,* the poet wears the costume of the diva, prolonging his agony in an endless aria. His performance is also reflected in the way the volume is structured. As O'Connor has pointed out, *My Sister Life* has two concluding chapters, the last of which has two concluding poems.[85] The affair—and the book—ends only when he is too exhausted to continue his performance: "But the bitterness, numbness, lumps / In the throat, but the anguish of so many words / One grows tired of befriending!" (No s oskominoi, s otsepenen'em, s kom'iami / V gorle, no s toskoi stol'kikh slov / Ustaesh' druzhit'!). It ends, that is, only when the lyric speaker succeeds in his attempt to "separate out his soul," as he puts it in one of the chapter titles ("Popytka dushu razluchit'"), and recovers his subjectivity from its merging with hysterical femininity.

Boris Pasternak during his sickness in 1918, as sketched by Leonid Pasternak
(collection of E. B. Pasternak)

The process of "separating out his soul" is treated at greater length in *Themes and Variations,* which includes a number of poems that, like the poems of *My Sister Life,* concern Pasternak's affair with Vinograd. One of his proposed titles for *Themes and Variations* was "The Other Side of the Coin," referring to the fact that he wrote these poems on the back of the typescript of *My Sister Life.*[86] They do indeed represent the "underside" of the love story, with their emphasis on pain and anger. Vladimir Alfonsov also has identified in these poems a new and different treatment of the love theme, namely, the realistic psychological mode of Akhmatova's love lyrics.[87] Although the basic elements of Pasternak's poetics remain in force, the lyric speaker and his beloved are now recognizable human agents, in keeping with the dominant theme of separation.

The process of separation is represented as a process of recovering from "The Sickness" ("Bolezn'"), the title of an eight-poem cycle about the poet's suffering after the end of the affair. The densely employed vocabulary of madness, raving, fainting, floating, and trembling renders a heightened and prolonged episode of hysterical emotion, whose destructive power is repeatedly compared to that of the snowstorms outside. (It is now winter, "the end of 1918," as one of the poem titles specifies.) The ecstatic emotion of *My Sister Life* has devolved into madness; the poet has suicidal thoughts and is confined like an invalid. In the sixth poem, "January 1919" ("Ianvar' 1919 goda"), he does have premonitions of recovery: "There is no anguish in the world, / That snow couldn't cure" (Na svete net toski takoi, / Kotoryi sneg by ne vylechival). But the final poem shows him still tormented at night, in a famous rendering of insomnia:

"Like a horse's eye, from the pillow, hot, aslant / I stare, fearing an immense insomnia" (Kak konskii glaz, s podushek, zharkii, iskosa / Gliazhu, strashas' bessonitsy ogromnoi).

The cycle that follows, titled "The Breakup" ("Razryv"), returns to the moment that caused that year of suffering.[88] The first poem opens with an attack on the beloved: "Oh lying angel, instantly, instantly, / I would poison you with pure sadness!" ("O angel zalgavshiisia, srazu by, srazu by, / I ia b opoil tebia chistoi pechal'iu!). This act of poisoning is just revenge, since she poisoned him first with "eczema" of the heart, and a "skintight sickness of the soul" (dushi bolezn' natel'naia). (The adjective I translate as "skintight" describes an article of clothing worn close to the skin, and the root of the word is "body" [na-tel'noi].) Pasternak thus supplies a precise description of hysteria as that illness of the soul whose symptoms are somatic. The poem establishes that the poet's case of hysteria was communicated to him by the beloved, so that strictly speaking it is not his disease but hers.

"The Breakup" goes on to describe his efforts to distance himself from her as an agent of infection. The second and third poems thematize his helplessness: he is unable to "attack his shame," and thinks obsessively about the beloved. His condition worsens in the fourth poem, where he dares her to try to stop his accelerating hysteria. The fifth poem moves us out of the immediate situation, as the speaker imagines himself and his beloved as the mythological characters Actaeon and Atalanta. As Alexander Zholkovsky has shown, Pasternak does some rearranging of mythological sources, but the character types—the masculine hero and the Amazon—are consistent.[89] As he has further shown, Pasternak reverses the roles scripted by those mythologies: although the Amazon remains unconquered in those precedents, Pasternak has her taken by the hero. The poem describes a scene that recalls the natural, primeval eroticism of *My Sister Life,* a scene in which Actaeon hunts down Atalanta and they make love. The lyric speaker, that is, begins to achieve his distance from the beloved by reclaiming active male desire.

A similar staging of the Amazon's sexual subduing appears earlier in *Themes and Variations* in a poem titled "Margarethe" ("Margarita," 1919).[90] The title character is Margarethe (also called Gretchen) of part one of *Faust,* who succumbs to Faust's seduction and pays for it with her sanity and finally with her life. She is an Ophelia-like figure; as one commentator has remarked, "the Gretchen tragedy is, in a sense, *Hamlet* rewritten from Ophelia's point of view."[91] Pasternak, however, imagines her as an Amazon, while Faust appears as a poet-nightingale:

Margarethe

Tearing the bushes away as though caught in a snare,
More violet than Margarethe's clenched mouth,
Burning hotter than Margarethe's rolled eyes,
The nightingale beat, trilled, ruled, and shone.

It dispersed like the fragrance of grass. Like the mercury
Of crazed rains it hung among the cherries.
It stupefied the bark. Gasping for breath it went up to
Her mouth. It stayed and hung on her braid.

And when passing an astonished hand over
Her eyes Margarethe drew close to the silver,
It seemed as though, under a helmet of branches and rain,
An Amazon fell in a faint in the woods.

And her nape was on familiar terms with it,
And her hand was flung backward, where lay,
Where caught, where hung her spectral helm,
Tearing the bushes away as though caught in a snare.

Маргарита

Разрывая кусты на себе, как силок,
Маргаритиных стиснутых губ лиловей,
Горячей, чем глазной Маргаритин белок,
Бился, щелкал, царил и сиял соловей.

Он как запах от трав исходил. Он как ртуть
Очумелых дождей меж черемух висел.
Он кору одурял. Задыхаясь, ко рту
Подступал. Оставался висеть на косе.

И, когда изумленной рукой проводя
По глазам, Маргарита влеклась к серебру,
То казалось, под каской ветвей и дождя,
Повалилась без сил амазонка в бору.

И затылок с рукою в руке у него,
А другую назад заломила, где лег,
Где застрял, где повис ее шлем теневой,
Разрывая кусты на себе, как силок.

The nightingale, performing a kind of wild mating dance, approaches Margarethe, who succumbs, leaving her helmet hanging in the bushes above. As so often, the poet and the beloved are hard to distinguish. They are in a comparable state of agitation; both "fall" (the nightingale is compared to rain); and by the end of the poem Margarethe's helmet literally has assumed the nightingale's place, "trapped" by the bushes. The final line enacts their total merging by repeating the first line. This repetition, however, also marks their reversed positions. Moreover, the nightingale and the helmet do not have the same figurative status. The helmet is a synecdoche for Margarethe—a part of her—and calls attention to the fact that in the final stanza her body appears dismembered.

The final stanza of "Margarethe," that is, suggests a rape scene in which the poet's agency is subtly downplayed: Margarethe, in defiance of spatial logic, "draws close" to the nightingale, though it already "hangs on her braid."[92]

The scene in poem five of "The Breakup" is similarly ambiguous. Although the lovemaking between Actaeon and Atalanta is mutual (rendered in the third-person plural), it takes place in the atmosphere of violence that follows the hunt. In the context of the cycle, the sexual attack, while only imagined, is pivotal; it marks a shift in the poet's posture from helplessness to aggression. In the poem that follows, he derides the beloved's dramatic scenes and suicide threats and regrets the lack of a whip. These moments of ridicule and imagined violence seem to allow him to draw back into a more detached perspective. In the final three poems, he addresses her as "my friend," urges her to calm down and sleep, and finally blesses her departure, though she continues to demand a dramatic finale. In contrast to her agitation, his affect is flat and his attitude resigned, as he rejects suicide in the famous line "Werther has already been written" (Uzhe napisan Verter). By the end of the cycle he is ready to reject the hysterical violence the beloved continues to display. "The Breakup" suggests that the poet is able to cure his hysteria with a fantasy about sexual violence—to cure it by reverting to the conventional male posture.[93]

The love story Pasternak shapes in *My Sister Life* and *Themes and Variations* dramatizes the gender dynamics of the romantic lyric without fundamentally transforming them. In fact, his writing so perfectly enacts those dynamics that it might be considered "the culmination of romanticism," to borrow Pasternak's own phrase about his fellow poet Aseev (4:363). The literary models he draws upon in the German and English romantic traditions are the same ones on which his symbolist forebears drew to create the contradictory image of a muse who is both Ophelia and the Amazon, both innocent victim and powerful aggressor. (How else to understand Pasternak's extraordinary rendering of Goethe's gentle, pious Gretchen as "an Amazon in the woods"?) His poetry dramatizes a tension in the lyric tradition's rendering of the sexual romance, in which the poet both covets and violates the feminine.[94] Pasternak's rehearsal of this dynamic is distinctive for its explicitness and for its psychosexual emphasis. He develops a poetics that renders the poet's merging with the feminine, and he narrates a necessary separation that is achieved through sexual violence, in effect "giving back" hysterical affect to the beloved.

My Sister Life had only recently been published when Pasternak discovered Tsvetaeva's *Milestones* in the summer of 1922. I have argued that Tsvetaeva's notion of the Eternal Masculine was taking shape at the moment when she received his first letter, and that after reading *My Sister Life* she was able to cast Pasternak in this role. Pasternak experienced a similar moment of recognition, since in the poems of *Milestones* Tsvetaeva resembles his Amazonian muse. In his letter he cites the second line of her poem "Dear travelers who share our camp bed!" (Milye sputniki, delivshie s nami nochleg!):

Dear travelers who share our camp bed!
Miles, and miles, and miles, and stale bread . . .
Thunder of gypsy carts.
Thunder of rivers running
Backward . . .

Милые спутники, делившие с нами ночлег!
Версты, и версты, версты, и черствый хлеб . . .

Рокот цыганских телег,
Вспять убегающих рек—
Рокот . . .

Tsvetaeva's persona in this poem, and throughout the first half of *Milestones*, is a gypsy woman who rides freely over the steppe and shares her bed with whomever she pleases. These poems celebrate her sexual agency, along with a powerful maternity ("Who's the father?—A tsar, perhaps. / Perhaps a tsar, perhaps a thief" [Kto otets?—Mozhet tsar'. / Mozhet tsar', mozhet vor]).

Pasternak remarks her Amazonian force indirectly when he calls the book "your milestone Swinburniada" (Vasha verstovaia Suinburniada). His idol Swinburne, he says, must have influenced Tsvetaeva indirectly, even if she had never read him. As Omry Ronen has decoded, Pasternak was referring to the lines from Swinburne's "By the North Sea": "Miles, and miles, and miles of desolation! / Leagues on leagues on leagues without a change!"[95] Swinburne's poem hymns the poet's union with the force of the elemental, which Pasternak likely perceived in Tsvetaeva's unbound gypsy heroine. (In one of the poems he loves she is "daughter of the sky" [neba doch'].) The poem's final stanza supplied Pasternak with an epigraph to *Above the Barriers*, lines that capture his aspiration toward a natural, impersonal writing: "To the soul in my soul that rejoices / For the song that is over my song."

Just as important for Pasternak, Swinburne's work in general represents the most unbridled example of lyric masochism in the English romantic tradition. In the winter of 1916–17, Pasternak translated Swinburne's *Chastelard*, the first play of a trilogy about the life of Mary Stuart.[96] His translation is not extant, but in "Several Propositions" ("Neskol'ko polozhenii," 1918), written a year later, he portrays Mary Stuart as a captive innocent whose "quiet plaint" becomes, in Swinburne's play, "the terrifying roar of five tragic acts" (4:368). Swinburne's Mary is indeed terrifying, "the Fatal Woman par excellence" as Mario Praz has described her in *The Romantic Agony*.[97] Her lover Chastelard might be termed the masochist par excellence, whose "heart feels drunken when he thinks . . . that her sweet lips and life will smell of his spilt blood." The same plot about the hero's fatal obsession with a powerful woman appears in Swinburne's "Atalanta in Calydon," the likely source for Pasternak's use of the myth in the fifth poem of "The Breakup." When Pasternak spoke of Tsvetaeva's "Swinburniada," he was linking Tsvetaeva with these Amazons.

The impact of Pasternak's discovery of Tsvetaeva was the impact of an encounter not simply with an Amazon but with an Amazon who was a poet, a poet who possessed the kind of feminine force he wished to bring to his own writing. In his letter, he very simply declares her the greatest contemporary Russian poet and takes care to elevate her above Akhmatova, to whom Tsvetaeva dedicated *Milestones*. For Pasternak this means elevating her above femininity, as he ostentatiously does in his manner of addressing her. At the end of his letter he threatens to go on writing to Tsvetaeva about her gift with this warning: "You don't need to read them [his letters]. It's a woman reading them. But it's a first-rate and rare poet who writes, forges, and cools—a poet whom even Marceline Desbordes-Valmore would envy for this rising above femininity" (*DNV* 13). Remarkably, Pasternak compares her to the very poet whom Tsvetaeva first mirrored and then moved beyond in her poetic development. The Tsvetaeva of *Milestones*, however, was not "rising above" femininity but modeling Amazonian power, as Pasternak himself registered in linking Tsvetaeva to Swinburne. Pasternak's impulse to divide the woman from the poet suggests an anxiety around being presented with such a powerful "native" version of his own feminized writing.

Pasternak's distinction between Tsvetaeva the woman and Tsvetaeva the poet also makes it possible for him to borrow her affect, in the same way he uses hysterical affect in his poetry. His letter opens with such a performance:

> Dear Marina Ivanovna!
> Just now in a shaking voice I started to read to my brother your "I know I will die at sunset, but which one . . ." and was overwhelmed, as though by someone else's rising and finally released sobbing, and when I directed my efforts from that poem to "I shall tell you of the great deception" I was thrown back by you in the very same way, and when I tried "Miles and miles and miles and stale bread," the same thing happened.
> You are no child, my dear, golden, incomparable poet. (*DNV* 11)

When Pasternak reads her poems, he channels a traumatic emotion that "overwhelms" and "throws him back." In her answering letter to Pasternak, Tsvetaeva jokingly observed that when she first read his letter, the words "thrown back" were the first ones she grasped, leading her to take it for an angry attack. She thus highlighted the difficulty of interpreting hysterical affect: Is it pained expression or threatened violence? This ambiguity remains in her response to the poems of *My Sister Life*, which she received soon after his first letter.

Tsvetaeva wrote "A Downpour of Light" in a few days immediately after reading *My Sister Life*. Her essay remains probably the best single commentary on the book, though she declines to discuss its formal qualities: "That is the business of poetry specialists. But my specialty is Life." She thus declares herself Pasternak's sister, and it is her rhetorical task throughout the essay to display their kinship. She does so through the character of her performance, which mimics Pasternak's both in *My Sister Life* and his letter to her. Pasternak even supplied Tsvetaeva with the metaphor of the "downpour" when he said of her book, "If you want to take a soulful briny thunderous shower—then read *Milestones*" (DNV 12). Tsvetaeva stages the experience of reading *My Sister Life* in exactly the same way, as an experience of submitting to an overpowering flood: "My Sister, Life"!—My first gesture, after taking it all, from the first blow to the last—was arms open: so that all my joints cracked. I fell under it like it was a downpour" (5:233). Both poets fall under the force of the other, and both are in danger of drowning. They are flooded by each other's affect—Pasternak when he is "thrown back" by her sobbing, and Tsvetaeva when she claims she is writing "not a review, but an attempt to get out, so I don't choke" (5:245). In a real sense, her essay is taken over by Pasternak's voice, since she packs it with quotations from *My Sister Life*. She thus sustains the circulation of hysterical emotion Pasternak set into movement when he read her *Milestones*.

When Tsvetaeva's essay was reviewed by émigré critics, it drew criticism for not being a proper review.[98] Even the sympathetic Alexander Bakhrakh, who found her essay "curious," took pains to point out that it was not "critical."[99] Georgy Ivanov openly ridiculed Tsvetaeva's "tone of ecstatic hysteria."[100] None of these commentators acknowledged how deliberately Tsvetaeva rendered her hysterical speech, nor did they remark its similarity to Pasternak's own. In fact, the motif of "difficult breathing" in *My Sister Life* generally was interpreted as "healthy" by reviewers. Osip Mandelstam famously described the poems as "breathing exercises," as a cure for disease rather than a symptom:

> To read Pasternak's verse is to clear your throat, strengthen your breathing, renew your lungs: such poems must help cure tuberculosis. There is no healthier poetry today. It's like *kumis* after American milk.
> Pasternak's book *My Sister Life* seems to me a collection of wonderful breathing exercises: every time the voice is in a new register, every time a powerful breathing apparatus is differently regulated.[101]

In "A Downpour of Light," Tsvetaeva also describes Pasternak as receiving and bestowing the energies of "Life." She concludes her essay with a claim about Pasternak's fundamental healthiness, quoting a line from his garden cycle: "And suddenly it smelled of discharging / From a thousand hospitals!" (I vdrug pakhnulo vypiskoi / Iz tysiachi bol'nits). But the heightened emotion that most readers found vital and uplifting also, in her view, had tragic possibilities: "What he takes in tragically exceeds what he expends" (5:244). Similarly, when she celebrates his poetic dynamism, she also sees it as a kind of death drive, "for the primordial temptation of such souls—undoubtedly—for all their brightness: is Death" (5:239). He appeared to her as a suffering figure, although this other side of the coin is not as visible in *My Sister Life* as it is in *Themes and Variations*, which Tsvetaeva read only later.

In sum, Tsvetaeva perceived Pasternak as a poet like herself, one who creates a powerful utterance out of painful experience. She read in his verse the same posture of submission to violent force she rendered in "On a Red Steed." She even, in the passage quoted earlier, imagines him "knocked off his horse" by the blow. Remarkably, she did so without being familiar with the poems in *Themes and Variations* that feature the fallen Amazon. Rather, she derived her insight from the eroticized imagery of *My Sister Life*. When she describes Pasternak's method of nature description, she invokes the phallic branch of the garden cycle: "And one wonders: who is writing whom? The answer: his penetrability. He so willingly allows the leaf, the ray, to penetrate him—that he's no longer himself but: a leaf, a ray.—A metamorphosis.—A miracle" (5:241). Like Tsvetaeva's poet, who becomes "like" the Genius after being run through by his lance, Pasternak is pierced and transformed, displaying the same eroticized passivity. Tsvetaeva, that is, recognized Pasternak's performance of femininity and understood it in her own terms. Her "Eternal Masculine" names a hysterical miming of masculine agency: the woman poet creates a forceful lyricism from a position of paralysis. Tsvetaeva perceived the same kind of power in Pasternak's writing, supplying in one of her letters to him the very definition of hysterical creativity: "Because you have no acts—all that crazed activity in your poems: nothing stands still" (6:234).

Pasternak, however, also performs the masculine agency of Tsvetaeva's Genius, as she also remarked. Several of the poems she calls attention to in *My Sister Life* feature the poet in the role of sexual aggressor. For example, she cites two lines from "Our Thunderstorm" ("Nasha groza") to illustrate her point that the poet bears an excess he seeks to dispense. The lines appear at the end of the poem:

> Where shall I put my joy?
> In poems, on ruled paper?
> Their lips are cracked already
> From the poisons of the page.
>
> In battle with the alphabet,
> They burn on your skin like a blush.

> Куда мне радость деть мою?
> В стихи, в графленую осьмину?
> У них растрескались уста
> От ядов писчего листа.
>
> Они, с алфавитом в борьбе,
> Горят румянцем на тебе.

This notion of writing on the beloved's body reprises an earlier moment in the poem when the poet invites a mosquito to "thrust the needle of mischief / Where the blood is like wet leaves?!" (Vsadit' strekalo ozorstva, / Gde krov'

kak mokraia listva?!). Pasternak equates the act of writing with an act of penetration that draws blood and leaves a mark on the beloved's body, thus modeling his creativity as masculine.

Pasternak's mosquito was the detail that made it into Tsvetaeva's poetic response to *My Sister Life,* which she wrote a day after finishing "A Downpour
of Light." She inscribed the poem, "Words to a Dream" ("Slova na son"), on
the last page of the copy of *Parting* she sent to Pasternak with the notation
"Berlin, July 8, 1922—after My Sister Life—Marina Tsvetaeva."

> Life lies inimitably:
> Beyond expectation, beyond the lie . . .
> But by the trembling of every vein
> You know: it's life!
>
> As though you lay in the rye: sound, azure . . .
> (So what if you're in a lie!)—heat, hill . . .
> Murmur—through the honeysuckle—of a hundred veins . . .
> Rejoice!—He called you!
>
> And don't reproach me, friend, so
> Easily are souls lured from us
> Bodies—that here already: I'm headfirst into a dream.
> For—why else did he sing?
>
> Into the white book of your quietnesses,
> Into the untouched clay of your "yesses"—
> I quietly lean my fragment of brow:
> For your palm is life.
>
> Неподражаемо лжет жизнь:
> Сверх ожидания, сверх лжи . . .
> Но по дрожанию всех жил
> Можешь узнать: жизнь!
>
> Словно во ржи лежишь: звон, синь . . .
> (Что ж, что во лжи лежишь!)—жар, вал . . .
> Бормот—сквозь жимолость—ста жил . . .
> Радуйся же!—Звал!
>
> И не кори меня, друг, столь
> Заворожимы у нас, тел,
> Души—что вот уже: лбом в сон.
> Ибо—зачем пел?
>
> В белую книгу твоих тишизн,
> В дикую глину твоих «да»—

Тихо склоняю облом лба:
Ибо ладонь—жизнь.

The word "life" (zhizn') is an obvious reference to Pasternak's book, but it also refers to a specific poem. The poem thickly repeats the "z" and "zh" sounds of the word "zhizn'," creating a buzzing effect when read aloud. This insect sound, produced also by the word for "rye" (rzhi), evokes Pasternak's poem "The Steppe" ("Step'"). As O'Connor has shown, the steppe is the primary setting of the love affair in *My Sister Life,* and in this poem the lovers lie in a field on a summer night.[102] Pasternak's poem opens with the small sounds that surround them:

How good were those exoduses into the quiet!
The shoreless steppe is like a marina,
The feathergrass sighs, the ants rustle
And the mosquito's wail floats.

Как были те выходы в тишь хороши!
Безбрежная степь, как марина,
Вздыхает ковыль, шуршат мураши,
И плавает плач комариный.

To the general reader, Pasternak's comparison of the steppe to a "marina" is simply a beautiful example of his habit of rhyming Russian with foreign words, or words of palpably foreign origin. When Tsvetaeva read these lines, she heard Pasternak saying her name—hence her line "He called you!"

The mosquitos in this poem, like the mosquito of "Our Thunderstorm," are implicated in an erotic scenario. The "mosquito wail" that rhymes with "marina" (komarinyi/marina) has a specific subtext, as Alexander Zholkovsky has discovered.[103] The phrase reappears near the end of the poem in lines that play with biblical rhetoric:

—In the Beginning
Did there Float the Mosquito Wail, did there Crawl the Ants,
Did there Stick Thistles to your Socks?

Close your eyes, love! It will powder us!
The entire steppe is like Paradise before the Fall:
Entirely ringed by the world, entirely like a parachute,
Entirely a rising vision.

. . .—В Начале
Плыл Плач Комариный, Ползли Мураши,
Волчцы по Чулкам Торчали?

Закрой их, любимая! Запорошит!
Вся степь как до грехопадения:
Вся—миром объята, вся—как парашют,
Вся—дыбящееся видение!

Zholkovsky traces Pasternak's playful eroticism to Goethe's *Dichtung und Wahrheit,* a favorite book of Pasternak's. Goethe relates how he went on innocent outings with one Frederika, which were sometimes ruined by mosquito swarms. When he complained about them, a pastor informed him that mosquitos and other biting insects probably were created after the Fall—or that if they existed in paradise, they didn't bite but pleasantly hummed. Although Pasternak compares the steppe to paradise in his poem, this paradise includes the "thistles" God sent to punish Adam and Eve in Genesis 3:8. In any case, Pasternak's vision of a swelling, bursting paradise is typically immodest.

Tsvetaeva possibly recognized the reference to *Dichtung und Wahrheit,* also a favorite of hers. She certainly responded to the poem's eroticism and wrote herself into Pasternak's love scene.[104] In typical fashion, she rejects love as a "lie" and succumbs to it anyway. She does so in the renunciatory spirit of the mature Tsvetaeva. The poem represents their erotic contact as mediated in two ways—through a dream in which the soul is separated from the body, and through a text, Pasternak's book, which she imagines as a hand cradling her brow. The peculiar image of the "fragment of brow" suggests the damaged heads of the classical busts and statues her father collected for the Pushkin Museum. It also renders Pasternak a kind of Pygmalion who will finish creating her out of pure and natural clay.[105] This expectation would continue to shape her response to Pasternak. Pasternak, in turn, when he thanked her for the poem, imagined his own disfigured, fragile head, redeemed by Tsvetaeva's example: "I like the poem terribly, and during those moments when Caligula thinks he has a glass head, and he sees in 'Words' that lovely, marvelous, sleepless, wonderful, wonderful head, beautifying everything it looks upon, he stops groping around his own and either completely calms down or, in the worst case, derives some measure of calm in thinking about the usefulness of glass. Need I explain to you that 'Words' is support in moments of self-doubt—of which I am an unrivaled master—need I explain, after the sometimes mysterious understanding you displayed in certain aspects of your article?" (*DNV* 19)

3

The Romance of Distance (1922–1925)

We have nothing except words, we're fated to them.
—Tsvetaeva, letter to Pasternak
(December 31, 1929)

Oh poet who depicts the body's movement as the movement of the soul!
—Pasternak, letter to Tsvetaeva
(January–February 1923)

When Pasternak wrote his first letter to Tsvetaeva, he was expecting to travel to Berlin in a few weeks and expressed the hope of seeing her there. In reply, she invited him to let her know how things stood with his trip, closing with the words, "I await your book and you" (*DNV* 16). The book in question was *My Sister Life*, which Pasternak mailed separately. About a week later, when she sent him copies of her *Poems to Blok* (*Stikhi k Bloku*, 1922) and *Parting* (*Razluka*, 1922), she inscribed the latter "To Boris Pasternak—toward you!" (Borisu Pasternaku—navstrechu!).They did not see each other in Berlin, however, and the "missed meeting," for which Tsvetaeva later coined the word "razminovenie," would become the leitmotif of their relationship.

Pasternak had several reasons to travel to Berlin. Chief among these was his desire to introduce to his family his wife, Evgenia Lurie, a young artist whom he had married a few months earlier, in February 1922. Pasternak had not met Lurie until after his parents and his sisters moved from Moscow to Berlin to get medical care for his mother's heart condition. The family did not anticipate staying abroad for long, nor did Pasternak when he decided to visit them; at this juncture it was still possible to travel across the border with relative ease. Pasternak and his wife arrived in August on a three-month Soviet visa, which they later extended by several months. They finally returned to Moscow on March 21, 1923, apparently at the urging of Evgenia, who was three months pregnant.[1] They left with the understanding that they would visit the Pasternaks in Berlin again the following year. Leonid Pasternak even began a new portrait of his son, expecting to complete it when Pasternak returned.[2] Pasternak's seven-month stay in Berlin, however, would be the last time he ever saw his parents, and the last time he would go abroad until 1935.[3]

Pasternak arrived in Berlin on August 15 to find that he had missed Tsvetaeva once again. Just two weeks earlier, on July 31, Tsvetaeva had left for Czechoslovakia to join her husband, Efron, who was studying at Charles University on a stipend provided by the Czech government. (The Czechs generously supported resident Russian émigrés with funding for education and grants to scholars and writers, one of which Tsvetaeva received and was for many years the mainstay of the family budget.) Tsvetaeva had spoken to Pasternak of wanting to move to Prague but indicated that it would not happen soon, so he was surprised to find her gone. Once in Berlin, Pasternak could easily have discovered her new address, but he did not write to her until November 12 to thank her finally for sending her books, "A Downpour of Light," and her poem "Words to a Dream." In a postscript he expressed his disenchantment with the émigré literary scene, which he had observed now for three months: "I was very distressed and discouraged not to find you in Berlin. When I parted from Mayakovsky, Aseev, Kuzmin, and several others, I was counting on seeing you and Bely along the same lines and in the same spirit" (*DNV* 21). Mayakovsky and Aseev belonged to Pasternak's old futurist circle, which immediately after the October revolution reinvented itself as the Left Front of Art, the literary avant-garde of socialism. Pasternak was ambivalent from the start about the futurists' polemical posturing, and he was no more comfortable with their newly politicized literary agenda. For example, when Mayakovsky himself visited Berlin that fall, Pasternak spoke disparagingly of his collaborations with the Soviet-funded journal *On the Eve* (*Nakanune*).[4] Nevertheless, Pasternak's exposure to literary Berlin cast the achievements of his confreres into flattering perspective: "I warmly, stubbornly love Bobrov, Aseev, and Mayak [Mayakovsky]. I, who belong to their squadron, didn't need to come here to appreciate their qualities. But here we seem like gods."[5]

Pasternak had reason to assume that Tsvetaeva shared his literary sympathies. In her first letter to Pasternak, Tsvetaeva recollected seeing him at Mayakovsky's famous reading of his poem "Man" ("Chelovek," 1917) in 1918, and reminded him that he once conveyed to her Mayakovsky's high opinion of *Milestones* (*Versty*, 1921) (*DNV* 15).[6] She also noted their mutual association with Ilya Ehrenburg, who separately befriended both poets in Moscow during 1919–20.[7] (He brought them together only later when he personally delivered Pasternak's first letter to Tsvetaeva.)[8] Ehrenburg, who had lived abroad before the revolution as a political exile, was critical of the Bolsheviks, but he enjoyed official favor and had extraordinary freedom to travel.[9] It was Ehrenburg, in fact, who reunited Tsvetaeva with her husband. While in Paris and Berlin in March 1921, Ehrenburg discovered that Efron had been evacuated with the White Army after the end of the Civil War and was living in Prague. Ehrenburg then facilitated the couple's correspondence, aided their plans for Tsvetaeva's emigration, and hosted Tsvetaeva and her daughter Alya when they first arrived in Berlin.[10]

Ehrenburg also escorted Tsvetaeva around the publishing houses and cafés of literary Berlin as one of the Moscow discoveries he was presenting to the émigré audience. Ehrenburg was pursuing a campaign for the "new poetry" in Russia, mainly in the pages of the journal *The New Russian Book* (*Novaia russkaia kniga*), whose stated purpose was to preserve the unity of Russian culture, Soviet and émigré, "au-dessus de la mêlée." In an article by that title, Ehrenburg attacked émigré critics for their political refusal to acknowledge that "living Russian literature is in Russia."[11] By "living" literature Ehrenburg meant the modernist canon he was helping to shape through his critical and editorial work, a canon that included artists as diverse as Akhmatova, Balmont, Esenin, Mandelstam, and Sologub.[12] He singled out Pasternak and Tsvetaeva for special praise, both in his journalistic articles on culture and in reviews of their recent work.

Ehrenburg was the first to review *My Sister Life,* a circumstance that informed Tsvetaeva's "Downpour of Light," which she dedicated to Ehrenburg. In the opening paragraphs she struggles with Ehrenburg's primacy: "Well, yes, Ehrenburg's praising him to the skies. Yes, but don't you know Ehrenburg? His front and back Fronde!" (5:231). With this reference to the eighteenth-century aristocratic rebellion, Tsvetaeva remarks Ehrenburg's simultaneous conflicts with both Soviet and émigré ideologues. Ehrenburg had similarly represented Tsvetaeva in the portrait he wrote for one of his anthologies: "I am convinced that to her it essentially makes no difference who she's rebelling against, like Vesuvius, ready to swallow up a lord's estate and a model commune with equal pleasure."[13] With her review of Pasternak, Tsvetaeva claimed the same political agnosticism as Ehrenburg, not so much above as against the fray.

When she replied to Pasternak's letter on November 19, Tsvetaeva did indeed engage him "along the same lines and in the same spirit" as his futurist comrades. She spoke of coming to Berlin to see both him and Mayakovsky, who also was visiting Berlin, as Tsvetaeva would have learned from the émigré press:

> I hate meetings in real life: banging heads. Two walls. You can't get through that way. A meeting should be an arch: then the meeting is—*above*. Heads thrown back.—
>
> But these days people part for too long, and so I want to know—clearly and soberly: how long you've come for, when you're going. I won't hide that I would be glad to sit with you in some godforsaken (god-remembered) pitiful cafe in the rain.—Elbow and brow.—I would be glad to see Mayakovsky, too. He's obviously behaving terribly—and it would put me in a very difficult position in Berlin.— Maybe I will. (*DNV* 25)

She sets their meeting in a cheap café that pointedly bears no resemblance to the Café Pragerdiele, the stomping grounds of literary Russian Berlin. Tsvetaeva shared Pasternak's conviction that contemporary Russian literature was being better served in Soviet Russia than in the emigration, and he offered a vital link to the culture she had left behind.

The Pragerdiele had an additional meaning for Tsvetaeva. In the same letter, she wished Pasternak a pleasant time with Ehrenburg, explaining that she herself was no longer friendly with him. Tsvetaeva's conflict with Ehrenburg emerged from a complicated set of love affairs involving them both. While in Berlin, Tsvetaeva had a short-lived affair with Abram Vishniak, the addressee of her poems about the Eternal Masculine. At the same time, Ehrenburg was involved with Vishniak's wife, Vera. As Tsvetaeva tells it, Ehrenburg did not appreciate Tsvetaeva's indignation when she discovered he was trying to get Vishniak to publish a book of Ehrenburg's erotic poems to Vera Vishniak.[14] Thereafter Tsvetaeva termed "Pragerdiele" any compromising behavior driven by sexual passion.

Though Tsvetaeva did not tell this story to Pasternak, she did direct him to a cycle of her own erotically charged poems about Vishniak, "The Youth" ("Otrok," 1922). Moreover, she advised him to get a copy from Vishniak himself, thus introducing him to her former lover.[15] She also copied out for Pasternak a poem she had written that September, "These are the ashes of treasures: / Of losses, of hurts" ("Eto peply sokrovishch: / Utrat, obid," September 27, 1922). The poem employs a favorite conceit that her prematurely graying hair attests to her bitter experience in love; she wears "Solomon's ashes," the burnt-out remains of sexual passion. A related image—her soul rises out of her gray hair "like a straight flame" (kak otvesnoe plamia)—evokes the descent of the Holy Spirit, suggesting that inspiration and writing have taken the place of love. By bringing these poems to Pasternak's attention, Tsvetaeva sought to affirm both her sexual experience and her capacity to rise above its debasements. She emphasized the latter by describing her life in the Czech countryside as confined to "poems," "family," and "nature." For now, at least, she addressed Pasternak on these grounds, inviting him to send more of his verse, being acquainted thus far only with *My Sister Life*.

Perhaps because of this very request, Pasternak took two months to respond to Tsvetaeva's November letter. Since the fertile period of 1917–18, when he wrote the poems of *My Sister Life* and *Themes and Variations* as well as a number of unfinished prose works, Pasternak had produced little. Like many of his literary peers, he spent the Civil War years clerking and doing translations in order to survive. Much of his earlier work, however, had circulated in manuscript and began to appear in print once the war ceased and he was being hailed as a major talent. Pasternak thus felt an uncomfortable gap opening up between his reputation and his productivity, which the trip to Germany was partly an attempt to bridge; as he succinctly put it in a letter to Briusov, written on his way to Berlin, "I'm going there to work" (5:133). If that was indeed the reason for Pasternak's silence, Tsvetaeva only made things more difficult by sending him more of her poetry. When *The Tsar-Maiden* was published in December,

Tsvetaeva inscribed a copy to Pasternak ("To Boris Pasternak—one of my muses") and mailed it to Roman Gul, asking him to deliver it for her (6:517). Presumably Tsvetaeva did not send it directly to Pasternak because she had not received a reply to her November letter. The gift of her book was a kind of invitation or inquiry, one she soon voiced to Gul in a postcard of January 4: "What is happening with Pasternak? I always ask people arriving [from Berlin], but no one's seen him" (6:518). Tsvetaeva did not hear from Pasternak until the beginning of February.

In the meantime, Tsvetaeva was at work on a narrative poem that was profoundly oriented toward Pasternak. She actually had begun work on "The Swain" ("Molodets," 1922) back in Moscow, but later said to Pasternak, "I lived by it from you (the fall) until you (February). Reading it will clarify a lot for you" (*DNV* 53).[16] What reading this poem would clarify for Pasternak, presumably, is Tsvetaeva's conflicted view of sexual love, which "The Swain," like her earlier narrative poems, elaborates. The poem is based on the Russian version of the vampire tale found in Afanasiev's *Popular Russian Tales* (*Narodnye russkie skazki*, 1855–64). The peasant girl Marusya falls in love with a strange young man, whom she observes one night eating a corpse in the church. When she will not admit what she saw, he kills her family and finally Marusya herself, who, with the help of her grandmother, is reborn in the form of a flower. A passing nobleman picks the flower and takes it home; when he observes its nocturnal transformation into Marusya, he falls in love with and marries her. They have a child and live happily until the nobleman insists she be baptized, at which moment the vampire reappears to claim her. This time, however, Marusya exposes the vampire and thereby destroys him.

To a degree unusual for her, Tsvetaeva followed the plot of Afanasiev's tale in her poem. She entirely rewrote the ending, however. Tsvetaeva's Marusya does not kill the swain but joins him in a flight away from earth into the heavens, the "blue fire" (ogon' sin'). As N. K. Teletova has argued, Goethe's *Faust*, part two, is the source for Tsvetaeva's new conclusion to the folktale.[17] "The Swain" repeats both the plot and structure of Goethe's tragedy. Like *Faust*, Tsvetaeva's poem is divided into two parts, each with five scenes. In part one of *Faust*, Gretchen succumbs to Faust's seduction, and as a result becomes complicit in her brother's death, drowns her own child by Faust, then goes mad and kills herself. As interpreted within the symbolist culture that Tsvetaeva and Pasternak absorbed, the first part of *Faust* was "a paradigm of failed love."[18] Part two, however, develops the love story in a new direction: Faust the demonic seducer is redeemed through the agency of his victim. A forgiven and resurrected Gretchen intercedes for him with the Mother of God, and the tragedy concludes with Faust's ascension into heaven to the accompaniment of a chorus. Referring to the final lines "The Eternal Feminine draws us upward" (Das Ewig-Weibliche / Zieht uns hinan), Teletova argues that Tsvetaeva's Marusya is the Eternal Feminine, the heroine of a "philosophical fantasy" about the power of passionate love.

With this celebratory finale, "The Swain" departs from previous literary treatments of the vampire tale, as Michael Makin has emphasized.[19] Drawing on feminist discussions of the vampire myth, he points out that canonic renderings purvey "a myth of sexual repression and male fantasy" in which women are the innocent victims of predatory male desire. He argues that "The Swain" subverts these sexual stereotypes by transforming the female victim into a "willing lover." To say simply that Tsvetaeva introduced female agency into the story, however, is to reduce the psychological complexity of her rewriting. Tsvetaeva revealed that complexity in her own later account of how she came to interpret the tale, in her essay "The Poet on the Critic" ("Poet o kritike," 1926). There she describes her poem as a form of dream interpretation: "The people, in a fairy tale, interpreted the dream of the elements, the poet, in a poem, interpreted the people's dream" (5:296). Her rendering of the unfolding drama of interpretation recalls Freud's in his *Interpretation of Dreams* (1900):

> I read Afanasiev's fairytale "The Vampire" and got to thinking about why Marusya, fearing the vampire, so stubbornly denied what she saw while knowing that to expose him was to save herself. Why instead of yes—no? Was it fear? But when people are afraid they don't just hide in bed—they also throw themselves out the window. No, it wasn't fear. Even if it was fear it was something else, too. Fear and what? When I'm told: do this and you are free, and I don't do that thing, it means I don't want freedom, it means my non-freedom is more precious to me. And what is that precious non-freedom between people? Love. Marusya loved the vampire, and therefore didn't reveal him and lost, one after another, her mother—her brother—her life. Passion and crime, passion and sacrifice. (5:295–6)

Tsvetaeva detects Marusya's unconscious desire for the vampire, the moment to which Makin calls our attention. But in Tsvetaeva's formulation, female desire is masochistic ("my non-freedom is more precious to me") and ineluctably linked to "crime"—specifically, the murder of her family and her own self-destruction. In the poem's finale, which is set in a Russian church, the ascending lovers are accompanied not by a Chorus Mysticus but a chorus of demons, who sing a discordant version of the "Kheruvimskaia," a canticle from the Slavic Orthodox liturgy. These lovers defy the morality enjoined by the institutions of the church, and of marriage and family, as Marusya leaves behind her husband and child. The rebellion the poem celebrates is traumatic; Marusya may claim her desire only through murder and abandonment. This tension is surely what motivates the "problematic employment of textual violence" that Makin remarks, citing the disorienting polyphony of voices, the words distorted by nonstandard stress, unintelligible language, and the disrupted metrical and stanzaic forms.[20] Again, when Tsvetaeva adopts the male poet's masochism—Baudelaire's and Blok's love for the vampire—it becomes more traumatic than pleasurable.

The same tension around desire drives the poem's narrative logic, according to which the lovers can be united only by leaving this world. "The Swain," that is, renders not a conviction but a fantasy: sexual love is glorified, but only as an impossibility. It is worth remarking that Tsvetaeva wrote "The Swain" during the first months of a troubled reunion with Efron, and the fantasy it purveys about escaping marriage could well be a response to her domestic situation. What is certain is that the fantasy was bound up with Pasternak. When Tsvetaeva entered the poem's final lines in her notebook, she interpreted them thus: "'Ho—ome: / Into the blue fire' sounds like an unsaid: amen: may it be so (with whom—I'm afraid to say, but I'm thinking of Boris)."[21] Later she was less equivocal on that point, regularly invoking "The Swain" to elucidate her relationship with Pasternak. With this poem, Tsvetaeva plotted her relationship with Pasternak as the heterosexual romance in which the male lover is a demonic seducer, a plot Pasternak also drew on in *My Sister Life.*

Not long after finishing "The Swain," Tsvetaeva finally heard from Pasternak. On January 29, 1923, he sent her a copy of the just published *Themes and Variations.* He inscribed the book "To the incomparable poet Marina Tsvetaeva, who is 'from the Don, fiery, and hellish,' from an admirer of her gift, who had the gall to publish these shavings and filings," referring to the fact that *Themes and Variations* was made up of poems left out of *My Sister Life.*[22] The line "from the Don, fiery, and hellish" comes from his poem "We are few. We are perhaps three" ("Nas malo. Nas mozhet byt' troe," 1921). The three are Pasternak himself, Mayakovsky, and Aseev, and with his dedication Pasternak welcomed Tsvetaeva into their company. She accepted the invitation, naming the cycle in which the poem appears one of her favorites ("I Could Forget Them" ["Ia ikh mog pozabyt'"]).

Tsvetaeva named, in addition, several individual poems she loved "to the point of passion": "Margarethe" ("Margarita"), "Clouds. Stars. And sideways" ("Oblaka. Zvezdy. I sboku"), and "Here is the trace of enigma's mysterious fingernail" ("Zdes' proshelsia zagadki tainstvennyi nogot'") (*DNV* 41). "Margarethe," as I have said, belongs to a cycle of Faust poems that appears at the beginning of *Themes and Variations;* the poem depicts Gretchen's violent seduction by the poet/nightingale, Faust. The poem "Here is the mark," which closes the volume, is another openly erotic poem that features a nightingale/seducer. Tsvetaeva makes this nightingale one of the book's emblems: "And suddenly—you: 'Wild, slippery, growing' . . . (a deer? a reed?), with your questions to Pushkin, with your devil's nightingale" (*DNV* 42). Tsvetaeva, having just drawn on Goethe's *Faust* to shape the love plot of "The Swain," discovered the same source and plot in the poems of *Themes and Variations.* A similar plot about love and destruction governs "Clouds. Stars. And sideways," which is based on Pushkin's poem "The Gypsies" ("Tsygany," 1824), and the phrase "wild, slippery, growing" refers to the poem in "The Breakup" in which Actaeon sexually subdues Atalanta.

When she read *My Sister Life,* Tsvetaeva was already drawn to Pasternak's most erotic poems and even, in "Words to a Dream," imaginatively placed herself in the erotic scene Pasternak renders. Tsvetaeva more openly expresses passionate feeling in her response to *Themes and Variations;* if the first book was a "downpour," this one was "fire," she says in her answering letter of February 10. She tells Pasternak that she is tempted to write a second review essay, but it is no surprise that she did not. Tsvetaeva now sought an exclusive and private exchange: "You'll get two more letters from me: one about your and my writings, and the other—with poems to you. Then I'll stop. Without an answer—I never write. Writing is like going in without knocking. But my home is always halfway toward you. Whenever you write, know that your thought is always in answer. Because how can there be knocking if the door has been flung open forever!" (DNV 38). Tsvetaeva wrote the letter "about your and my writings" in two installments, on February 11 and 14. She identified the "poems to you" in her notebooks as ten poems she wrote between February 7 and 17, which I refer to as the "February poems."[23] In the meantime, Pasternak sent an "inventory of his literary estate," perhaps an attempt to justify himself before his relentlessly prolific peer.[24] But as Pasternak would discover, his *Themes and Variations* had just touched off another burst of creativity on Tsvetaeva's part.

Tsvetaeva opened her first February letter by declaring Pasternak the only real poet among their contemporaries: "You are the first poet—in my whole life—I see." As she clarifies in the next sentence, he is the only real poet besides herself: "You are the first poet in whose tomorrow I believe like I believe in my own" (*DNV* 33). Tsvetaeva's tribute is from the first bound up with self-assertion; to elevate Pasternak is to elevate herself, and vice versa. In linking her poetic stature with his, the matter of gender immediately comes to the fore, as she recalls her earlier relationships with male poets.[25] She writes:

> You are the first poet whose verse is less than himself, though greater than anyone else's. Pasternak, I have known many poets: old and young, and none of them remember me. They were people who wrote verse: who wrote verse beautifully, or (more rarely) wrote beautiful verse.—And that's all.—I didn't see the convict's brand of the *poet* on any of them: that burns far off! . . . They were worse than nonpoets because *knowing* what writing cost them (months and months of possession, miserliness, non-being!), they demanded from those around them a huge price: incense, bowing and scraping, monuments during their lifetime. And I was never tempted to refuse them: I gallantly flattered—and left. And I loved the poet most when he was hungry or his tooth hurt: that brought us together on a human plane. I was a *nanny* around poets, a gratifier of their base demands—and not at all a poet! and not a Muse!—young (sometimes tragic, but still:)—a nanny! When I was with a poet I always forgot I was a poet. And if he reminded me—I disowned it.
>
> And—it's laughable—seeing *how* they were writing (poems), I began to consider them geniuses and myself, if not a nonentity, then a novelty of the pen, almost a prankster. "Am I really a poet? I just live, feel happy, love my cat, cry, get dressed up—and write poems." (DNV 33–34)

Tsvetaeva portrays her younger self as a mystified *naïf* who accepted the view that a woman cannot be a poet, so much so that she would disown the title when presented with it. The problem, she says, was that she complied with the male poet's demand that she be a "nanny." If being cast as a nanny excluded her from being a poet, however, it also excluded her from being an object of the male poet's desire. Both roles in the traditional romantic scheme have been denied her: "I was . . . not at all a poet! and not a Muse!" Tsvetaeva describes her own strategy of self-representation in her early verse, where she appeared as a girl who, however precocious, was sexually unavailable. Now, however, she wanted to be acknowledged as both poet and muse, and Pasternak promised to acknowledge her thus.

How was Pasternak different from his male peers? In Tsvetaeva's formulation, he was "greater than his verse," a poet who was an extraordinary individual. She invokes this romantic notion to criticize the narcissism of the male poet, who becomes available for human connection only when physically vulnerable, when "his tooth hurts." He becomes available, that is, only when he is feminized by injury. Pasternak, by contrast, was always available, as witnessed by the fact that he sought out Tsvetaeva to pay her tribute rather than demanding it from her. His essential availability was also legible in his writing; as Tsvetaeva phrased it in "A Downpour of Light," he was both "penetrated and penetrating." Pasternak was both masculine and feminine, both powerful and vulnerable, and in this fashion was "greater than" his gender. His double-gendering made him an ideal addressee, someone with whom Tsvetaeva might identify as both an agent and object of desire, both a poet and a muse.

In her letter Tsvetaeva describes Pasternak's special kind of subjectivity in the romantic vocabulary of the divine and the human: he is no mere mortal but a demigod (*polubog*), as she calls him at the end of her letter, pointedly contrasting him to her estranged lover Vishniak. More precisely, he exists between his mortal and immortal selves: "You are Pasternak's correspondence with his Genius" (*DNV* 36). The poet is a kind of third party, an effect of a dialogue between two selves, a dialogue that, in Tsvetaeva's rendering, takes the form of an exchange of letters. Her own letters to Pasternak unfold further ambiguities of this model: if Pasternak exists between selves, then she may address whomever she pleases. In this instance she claims to speak "not to you but to the Spirit [Dukh] in you," a Spirit that is masculine like the Genius ("By the way, this letter is a conversation with your Genius about you, you don't have to listen" [*DNV* 37]).

Tsvetaeva actually borrowed this scheme from Pasternak himself. He had represented her as "greater than" her gender when, in his first letter to her, he distinguished between the "first-rate and rare poet who writes" and "the woman who reads" his letters (*DNV* 13). Tsvetaeva mimics this gesture in her letter when she distinguishes between Pasternak the man and Pasternak the poet. She also took from Pasternak the notion of a dialogue with the poet's "spirit," which she found in a poem from *Themes and Variations*. (Tsvetaeva marked the poem in her copy of the book.)[26] Pasternak's "Voice of the Soul" ("Golos dushi," 1918) appears in the cycle "The Sickness" ("Bolezn'"), discussed earlier as treating the poet's distress at the end of the love affair:

Lay out everything in the wardrobe,
And gather up
All his warm clothes—his sobs
Are tearing them up.

Get away, don't waste your effort,
If you don't let go—I'll grab it,
If you tear it—who cares,
There'll be thread enough to mend it.

Man! You're afraid?
Can't do anything about it.
I am the soul. You're headed
For dust!

Why would I need
Ribbons and a dress.
Man, you dared?
Then you'll pay for it.

I'll light his eyes
With a wild thought—
"I said that!"
"No, those are my words."

I am taller than
Your like by a head,
I, who haven't been here,
And who haven't been.

Все в шкафу раскинь,
И все теплое
Собери,—в куски
Рвут вопли его.

Прочь, не трать труда,
Держишь—вытащу,
Разорвешь—беда ль:
Станет ниток сшить.

Человек! Не страх?
Делать нечего.
Я—душа. Во прах
Опрометчивый!

Мне ли прок в тесьме,
Мне ли в платьице.
Человек, ты смел?
Так поплатишься!

Поражу глаза
Дикой мыслью я—
—Это я сказал!
—Нет, мои слова.

Головой твоей
Ваших выше я,
Не бывавшая
И не бывшая.

The poem features a lopsided dialogue between the "voice of the soul," which is feminine, and the voice of a man, who speaks once ("I said that!"). The subject of their exchange—"he," the poet—does not speak but only sobs, undone by the love tragedy. The poet is literally in between his divine and human selves, in a complicated rendering of Pasternak's cherished "free subjectivity." This scenario, though, is charmingly deflated; he domesticates the romantic conflict between the poet's mortal and immortal selves, rendering it an undignified squabble, a tug-of-war over the poet's clothes.

We have seen Pasternak use clothing to signify gender in earlier poems, and in this poem it signifies familiar gender crossings. In his human incarnation, the poet's gender is masculine (chelovek), but one of the "warm things" he wears, as the next poem in the cycle reveals, is a comical "fufaika," a sort of knitted robe, and he weeps hysterically. His feminine "soul," by contrast, refuses to wear "ribbons and a dress," and behaves in an aggressive, domineering fashion. She is physically more impressive, a full head taller than the man (his "kind"), whom she browbeats for having "dared." With her height and power, exhibited next to the abject poet, she resembles the Amazonian muse. This depiction of the poet dominated by the muse conforms to Pasternak's lyric masochism, with its classic reversals: his masculine human self is feminized, while his feminine soul has masculine power and agency. The poem, that is, represents the poet's gender as "between."

Where did Tsvetaeva see herself in this configuration? One might expect her to embrace the role of Pasternak's feminine soul, given her self-proclaimed identity as "Psyche."[27] But in her copy of *Themes and Variations*, next to the final stanza of "Voice of the Soul," Tsvetaeva wrote "I am / is B.P." (Ia—B.P.).[28] This remark is ambiguous, since Russian has no present-tense form for the verb "to be," which the writing system simply marks with a dash. Tsvetaeva could be equating Pasternak with the poem's speaker, with the feminine "voice of the soul" ("I is B.P."). Just as likely she was equating herself with him ("I am B. P.")—a bold act, but one Pasternak's poem invites by putting into question who, or what, speaks when the poet speaks. Tsvetaeva, after all, is commenting on a poem in which Man and Soul fight for possession of the poet's language: "'I said that!' / 'No, those are my words.'"

Pasternak's condition—his existence "between" his humanity and his soul—means that his language, and his very self, are up for grabs, and Tsvetaeva grabs them. In her letter Tsvetaeva asked Pasternak to "mentally" dedicate to her his poem "Thus gypsies begin": "Give it to me. So I'll know it's mine. So no one will dare think it's his" (*DNV* 36). The poem appears in the cycle "I Could Forget Them," whose fourth poem Pasternak had already "given" her when he used it in his inscription ("We are few . . ."). In the notebook version of this letter, she also laid claim to a line from yet a third poem in the cycle: "And there's a cry that's wailingly mine:—'It is I and not you who's the proletarian' (which, however, I always recite this way: 'No, not you—it is I who am the proletarian')."[29] Pasternak's line so completely belongs to her that she takes the license of changing his word order.

More generally, Tsvetaeva claimed Pasternak's language by adopting features of his poetics in her February poems. In these poems she borrows his lexicon, his convoluted syntax, and his predilection for finite verbs.[30] Tsvetaeva earlier had reproduced aspects of other poets' voices in tribute poems to Alexander Blok and Anna Akhmatova. But her poems to Pasternak are a different matter. Her ventriloquizing of Pasternak occurs in the context of already present similarities. Tsvetaeva's poetics resembled Pasternak's in major respects, particularly in their strong reliance on intonation and syntactic parallelism. The most striking example is the very poem "Voice of the Soul," which sounds uncannily like a Tsvetaeva poem. With its short lines and central use of dialogue, it sounds so Tsvetaevan that one scholar introduced his commentary with a "guess the author" puzzle.[31] The question the poem raises about who possesses the poet's language—"'I said that!' / 'No, those are my words'"—has added meaning in the context of Pasternak's and Tsvetaeva's affinities, affinities that lend merit to Tsvetaeva's claim to his poetry.

For Tsvetaeva, it was not so much a matter of possessing language as of sharing it. (Pasternak was possibly less eager to share; he chose to cut "Voice of the Soul" from later editions of *Themes and Variations,* the only change he made to that book.) She attributed the authorship of her February poems to Pasternak, in a sense giving them back. She describes how reading Pasternak caused new poems to come upon her like a "burst dam": "You are *exhausting* me, my head is tired, how many times a day do I lie down, sprawled on the bed, *thrown back* by that skull and ribcage polyglossia dissonance: of lines, feelings, revelations . . . and simply noise" (*DNV* 42). She imagines the process as a sexual encounter in which she lies "sprawled on the bed, thrown back," which is to say she still plays Margarethe to the male poet's Faust. Her claim to poetic equality, that is, remains circumscribed by the heterosexual love plot in which the woman is not an agent but a victim. In her February poems, as she struggles to work out the best way to engage him, she addresses him doubly, as both poet and woman. When she sent him the poems a month later, she adduced them as evidence of her confusion: "Now, to the point. *What is this,* exactly? What's going on? I honestly and clearly—I swear!—do not know the *word* for it. I'll try them all out. (The degree to which I don't know you'll see from my February poems)" (*DNV* 50).

The first poem, "You must not summon her" ("Ne nado ee oklikat'," February 7, 1923), like her letter, depicts Tsvetaeva's penetration by Pasternak's voice.[32] Drawing on the musical imagery of *Themes and Variations*, she represents their voices in a kind of duet. The performance, though, is not harmonious. This duet is also a duel, in keeping with Pasternak's definition of poetry as "a duel of two nightingales" (poedinok dvukh solov'ev) ("Opredelenie poezii"):

> You must not summon her:
> To her a summons is a lash. To her
> Your call is a wound to the hilt.
> Down to her deepest organ notes
>
> She's shaken—the creator's fear
> Of penetration—so beware, from the heights
> —All fortresses stand on cliffs!—
> She may sing out like an organ.
>
> Can you take it? The mountain is steel and basalt,
> But, like an avalanche into the blue,
> She'll sing out at your seraphic alto
> With the full voicing of storms.
>
> And it will come to pass!—Beware!—One always
> Falls the hundredth time . . . Hark!
> I'll avenge the singer's gutteral call
> With an organ storm!
>
> Не надо ее окликать:
> Ей оклик—что охлест. Ей зов
> Твой—раною по рукоять.
> До самых органных низов
>
> Встревожена—творческий страх
> Вторжения—бойся, с высот
> —Все крепости на пропастях!—
> Пожалуй—органом вспоет.
>
> А справишься? Сталь и базальт—
> Гора, но лавиной в лазурь
> На твой серафический альт
> Вспоет—полногласием бурь.
>
> И сбудется!—Бойся!—Из ста
> На сотый срываются . . . Чу!
> На оклик гортанный певца
> Органною бурею мчу!

In the poets' duet, Pasternak sings in an alto voice, "al't," a word that also designates the viola.[33] Tsvetaeva sings like an organ. Because most Russian musical terminology is Latinate, "organ" implies the same double entendre it does in English, and Tsvetaeva brings the somatic meaning to the fore when she describes her wounding. Her self-representation as a heavy, bodily entity contrasts with her representation of Pasternak, whose voice is "seraphic." Tsvetaeva's voice, grounded in her body, is fuller than his: she sings out "with the full voicing of storms."[34] Her bass voice will easily drown out Pasternak's alto (or viola), reversing the typical gendering of voice.

Despite her power, though, the poem, like "On a Red Steed," depicts an attack on her, and is suffused with what she now openly names "the creator's fear of penetration." In this staging, her agency is defensive: she parries the Genius's thrust by overwhelming him like an avalanche. The image recalls the opening poem of *My Sister Life*, in which Lermontov's Demon, mourning at Tamara's grave, vows to "return like an avalanche" (lavinoi vernus'ia). Tsvetaeva thus replies to Pasternak with masculine force, though the unnatural upward movement of her avalanche still positions her, as in "On a Red Steed," below her partner—positions her, like Tamara, in a ditch/grave. She hears Pasternak's call as a dangerous, possibly fatal seduction, one that places her in the role of the male poet's muse, a role she both desires and fears.

The second February poem, "No, don't dispute the truth" ("Net, pravdy ne osparivai," February 8, 1923), continues and reimagines the action of "Do not summon her." Pasternak's voice now sings over a dead woman, identified as "the Muse," the "kindred deceased," who may be the fatally wounded speaker of the first poem.[35] The action occurs in the same setting, now identified as the "cathedral Alps." Both terms of the metaphor remain in force: the action seems to unfold simultaneously in the mountains and inside a church. The setting evokes Italy, as does the reference at the end of the poem to a cantata by the Italian composer Pietro Metastasio (1698–1782). The singer of this Italian composition is Pasternak, who again appears as an ethereal alto voice, this time the voice of a choirboy. The poem is devoted entirely to his vocal performance, which is to say it describes a solo rather than a duet:

> No, don't dispute the truth.
> Among the cathedral Alps
> Sometimes a fledgling alto
> Beats against a rosarium.
>
> A girl's voice and a little boy's:
> At the very boundary.
> One voice in a thousand—
> And already cracked.
>
> Constricted at its very source:
> A hundred and one pearls

Dissolved, in vain,
In the voice's ray.

Sing, sing—worlds will pay tribute!
But the choir director says: "That voice
Sings over the kindred deceased,
Sings over the Muse!"

I am expert in the voices
.Of boys . . .—that have scattered into blood and dust
Like a sheaf of rays
Against a burial shroud.

No, tell no fairy tales:
This is no rainbow scatter,—
It is a breast torn open
By Metastasio's cantata.

I swear by all the sacraments:
By my own living soul!—
I love your cracked voice
More than all heights.

Нет, правды не оспаривай.
Меж кафедральных Альп
То бьется о розариум
Неоперенный альт.

Девичий и мальчишеский:
На самом рубеже.
Единственный из тысячи—
И сорванный уже.

В самом истоке суженный:
Растворены вотще
Сто и одна жемчужина
В голосовом луче.³⁶

Пой, пой—миры поклонятся!
Но регент:—Голос тот
Над кровною покойницей,
Над Музою поет!

Я в голосах мальчишеских
Знаток . . .—и в прах и в кровь
Снопом лучей рассыпавшись
О гробовой покров.

Нет, сказок не насказывай:
Не радужная хрупь,—
Кантатой Метастазовой
Растерзанная грудь.

Клянусь дарами Божьими:
Своей душой живой!—
Что всех высот дороже мне
Твой срыв голосовой!

As the speaker in the first poem predicted, the male singer is destroyed: he throws himself against the muse's bier and is "scattered into blood and dust." This last phrase, and the image of his "breast torn open," render his voice corporeal, both sexual and mortal. His song is bound up with a tragic romance in which both poet and muse are destroyed.

The Italian setting Tsvetaeva chose for these poems amplifies the notion of a passionate but unrealizable love. The cathedral and its presumably Latin choir evoke the Catholic spirituality Tsvetaeva ascribed to Pasternak in her February 10 letter: "I know about you that you love Beethoven more than any other composer (even *more* than Bach!), that you more passionately succumb to Music than to verse, that you don't like 'art,' that you have often thought about Paganini[37] and wanted to write (and will write!) about him, that you are a Catholic (in your spiritual makeup, your breed) rather than Orthodox. Pasternak, I study you, but I, like you, don't know your final page.—However, a monastery glimmers on the horizon" (*DNV* 36). Pasternak's Jewishness is irrelevant here, as Tsvetaeva contrasts Orthodox and Catholic spiritual types. She associates the latter with masochistic passion, which she perhaps detected in one of the poems of Pasternak's "I Could Forget Them": "I am proud of this torture. Scar me!" (Ia gorzhus' etoi mukoi.—Rubtsui!). She herself had drawn on this lexicon in such poems as "Nailed to the Shameful Pillory" ("Prigvozhdena k pozornomu stolbu," 1920), casting herself as an Eloise to her lover's Abelard.[38] This story of passionate lovers who can reach each other only through letters also hovers behind this vision of Pasternak as monk.

Tsvetaeva invoked yet another Italian cultural legacy, the opera, to gloss the poets' impossible love. Pietro Metastasio was an eighteenth-century poet known for his librettos for the early Italian opera, or *melodramma*. As Michael Naydan has suggested, Tsvetaeva may have had a particular opera in mind, Metastasio's *Didone Abbandonata* (1724), which tells the story of Aeneas' seduction and abandonment of Dido.[39] It tells, that is, the paradigmatic story of the operatic tradition, the story of a tragic love. Tsvetaeva's own "Don't dispute the truth" describes such a tragedy, and with operatic staging: the male lead casts himself on his beloved's bier to the accompaniment of a chorus. In drawing on this model, Tsvetaeva was once again taking her cue from Pasternak. Pasternak, after all, represents himself "singing and dying" in the love tragedy of *My Sister Life*. He even placed an Italian opera reference at the heart of that volume's "Definition of Poetry" ("Opredelenie poezii"), which describes the same falling movement: "It's Figaro descending like hail / From music stands and flutes onto a garden bed" (Eto—s pult'ov i s fleit—Figaro / Nizvergaets'ia gradom na griadku).[40] For both Pasternak and Tsvetaeva, opera stands for poetry as a vehicle that blends words and music in passionate expression. Tsvetaeva invokes Metastasio as a librettist, a poet who makes words fit the requirements of music. As she wrote to Pasternak: "Your passion for words only evidences how much they are a *means* for you. That passion is the *despair of speaking.* You love sound more than you love the word. . . . You want the *impossible,* going beyond the realm of words" (*DNV* 39).

In the opera of "No, don't dispute the truth," the male lead is a choirboy who sings in a "fledgling alto" (neoperennyi al't). His voice is "at the boundary" of a girl's voice and a boy's, and his alto is beginning to crack. He is, in other words, an adolescent. The action of "falling," then, has another connotation in the context—the fall from sexual innocence, which is also a fall into gender roles, into the tragic romance of the male poet and the female muse. (She, "expert in the voices of boys," speaks with the voice of experience.) The trauma of sexual love is signaled by his "constricted" throat, which even the beauty ("pearls") of his gift cannot soothe. Tsvetaeva had recently used the same cluster of images in a poem about her own voice. In "The underwater light of Lethe" ("Lety podvodnyi svet," August 11, 1922), a pearl sticks in the singer's throat and cannot be removed by the bloody surgery imaged in the poem:

> For the pearl cannot be dissolved
> In the voice's
>
> Ray . . .
>   Hoarse from the iron
> Of a thousand saws and drills—
> The stuck thorn
> In the bitterness of singing throats.

> Ибо нерастворим
> В голосовом луче
>
> Жемчуг . . .
>   Железом в хрип,
> Тысячей пил и сверл—
> Неизвлеченный шип
> В горечи певчих горл.

Tsvetaeva's definition of poetry as constricted utterance resembles the definition Pasternak offered in a poem titled "Poetry" ("Poeziia") from *Themes and Variations*: "Poetry, I will swear / By you, and will end having wheezed out: / You are not the bearing of a sweet-voiced singer, / You are summer with a third-class train ticket" (Poeziia, ia budy klasts'ia / Toboi, i konchu, prokhripev: / Ty ne osanka sladoglastsa, / Ty—leto s mestom v tret'em klasse). As this last line suggests, poetry is the poetry of *My Sister Life*: a love story told in a prosaic rather than an elevated mode.[41] His lyric speaker is indeed far from sweet-voiced; rather, we hear him choke on emotion in what I have described as a hysterical performance. The love story of *My Sister Life* was to Tsvetaeva a familiar love tragedy, one that she linked to the "fall" into sexuality—hence her representation of Pasternak as an adolescent in "Don't dispute the truth."

My Sister Life's enthusiastic eroticism is probably well described as adolescent. But that is precisely why it is difficult to regard its story as genuinely tragic, especially given Pasternak's narrative, in the relevant cycles of *Themes and Variations,* about his recovery. Tsvetaeva's misreading highlights important differences in the two poets' views about sexual love. Pasternak would later state to Tsvetaeva that adolescence is the deciding moment in the poet's biography: the "electricity" of inspiration, he says, is "loaded from birth and almost always neutralized in adolescence, and only in rare cases of a great gift (talent) still preserved in adulthood" (*DNV* 94). His formulation suggests that sexuality poses some challenge to the poet's gift that he must meet to emerge as a mature artist. One might argue that Pasternak met that challenge with the erotically suggestive poems of *My Sister Life.* Tsvetaeva's own writing was just as profoundly sexualized, as Pasternak remarked when he addressed her, in his January letter, "Oh poet who depicts the body's movement as the movement of the soul!" (*DNV* 28). Tsvetaeva, however, viewed the fall into the sexual romance as a mortal danger, both for herself and for Pasternak.

The rest of Tsvetaeva's February poems render the two poets, in turn, as aggressive and vulnerable. Her three-poem cycle "Scythian Poems" ("Skifskie," February 11–14, 1923), for example, casts the two poets as members of the fierce equestrian tribe of the Black Sea region. She was taking her cue from Pasternak's "We are few, we are perhaps three / From the Don, fiery and hellish," which in turn refers to the futurists' self-identification as "Scythians." She joins their male company, however, as an Amazon. Her poet-warriors write not with pens but with arrows, which are also Cupid's arrows. In the second poem, a lullaby ("Kolybel'naia"), she warns Pasternak to stop his ears against her "fatal arrow" (strela smertnaia), which also takes the shape of a "flattering reed" (l'stivyi trost') on which she plays. In the third poem, she calls upon the goddess Ishtar to preserve her camp of "brothers and sisters" from the pursuing khan. In the cycle as a whole, the two poets appear as combatants and as equals; the khan is as likely to be wounded as the Amazon.

A poem she wrote the same day, "The Lute" ("Liutnia," February 14, 1923), also imagines the poets' love as a lethal contest. The poem is based on the Old Testament story of Saul and David. David entered Saul's court as a lute player whose music had the power to soothe Saul's fits of madness. Tsvetaeva remakes the episode as a story about a poet who placed his gift in the service of another poet's demons. "The Lute," that is, concerns her poetic subjection to Pasternak/Saul, whom she represents in her letters as perpetually on the verge of madness ("The froth of inspiration will change into the froth of madness. You need an *outlet*: daily, almost hourly" [*DNV* 40]). Rather as Pasternak did in his cycle "The Breakup," Tsvetaeva regards the beloved as a hysteric whose "disease" is communicable. In this poem, succumbing to Pasternak's madness means losing her own voice:

> This is like pouring tin down
> A nightingale's throat . . . and still worse:
>
> This is laying your immortal soul in the groin
> Of the first man who comes along . . .
> This is—but it's worse than smashing into blood and dust:
> It's—breaking with your voice!
>
> Это же оловом соловью
> Глотку залить . . . да хуже еще:
>
> Это бессмертную душу в пах
> Первому добру молодцу . . .
> Это—но хуже чем в кровь и в прах:
> Это—сорваться с голоса!

As so often in these poems, the notion of poetic voice is sexualized: singing for another poet is tantamount to succumbing to a random sexual advance. Here and elsewhere Tsvetaeva cannily interprets the relationship between Saul and David as a sexually charged relationship.[42] The fact that they are male does not alter the erotic dynamics of Tsvetaeva's imagined encounter with Pasternak.

Tsvetaeva's David, actually, is both masculine and feminine, in keeping with her view of the poet as existing "between." Here the poet's two genders are delineated by the poem's structure of address: her speaker addresses both David's lute, which is grammatically feminine, and David himself.[43] She first berates the feminine lute for succumbing to domination and then exhorts David to leave Saul and regain his "health": "Go, be well, / Poor David . . . There are neighboring towns!" (Idi, bud' zdrav, / Bednyi David . . Est' prigorody!). The male David has the power not only to escape the dangers of love but, if Tsvetaeva's plot follows that of the biblical story, to gather his forces and return to triumph over Saul. This notion about the relative safety of genders—that the woman succumbs to love and is destroyed ("smashing into blood and dust")—belongs to the canonic heterosexual romance, which Tsvetaeva resists without transforming.

Tsvetaeva used two words for "demon" in this poem, the Russian "bes" and the Greek "aggel" transcribed into Cyrillic. She used the same Greek term in her February letters when she spoke of being possessed by Pasternak's voices:

"With angels (with demons!) it's harder to play" (*DNV* 42). Juxtaposing "angel" with "aggel" allowed her to suggest that the difference between good and evil spirits hangs on a single phoneme.[44] This problem of identifying the true nature of spirits also emerged in the Book of Samuel, where the biblical author cannot say whether Saul's possession is evil or divine ("Is Saul one of the prophets, too?" [1 Samuel 19:24]). Tsvetaeva raised a similar question about Pasternak in her next February poem, "Azrael" ("Azrail," February 17): is he Eros or is he Azrael, the angel of death?[45]

In a now familiar configuration, the speaker of "Azrael" is "cast down" (nizlozhena) on her bed, while her addressee hovers over her. In this poem, however, the scene is recontextualized through the myth of Psyche, which, as Alyssa Dinega has shown, is Tsvetaeva's dominant myth during this period.[46] In Apuleius' canonic version, a jealous Aphrodite orders her son Eros to cause Psyche to fall in love with a monster. But Eros invents a scheme to have her for himself: he installs Psyche in a palace where he visits her nightly, warning her never to try to discover his identity. Psyche disobeys and lights her lantern while he sleeps, accidentally waking him with a drop of oil. Eros flees, and Psyche pursues him, performing impossible labors set by Aphrodite until she dies, and Zeus unites the couple by raising Psyche to divinity. The myth, like the symbolist mythology discussed earlier, serves Tsvetaeva's self-representation as "soul" rather than body. Her treatment of the myth, however, like her treatment of symbolist mythology, often reintroduces the repressed body. As she said in her cycle "Phaedra" ("Fedra," March 7–11, 1923), which she wrote a few weeks later, "It is impossible, pressing lips / Not to press Psyche, the fluttering guest of lips. . . . / Slake my soul: and thereby slake my lips" (Nel'zia, pripadia k ustam, / Ne pripast' i k Psikhee, porkhaiushchei gost'e ust. . . . / Utoli moiu dushu: itak, utoli usta).

"Azrael" well displays both the centrality and repression of the sexual moment. Tsvetaeva's speaker plays Psyche's part in the scene where she unmasks her mysterious husband in her bedroom. However, she plays it only hypothetically, since Tsvetaeva represents the action as never taking place:

> You didn't delight at the touch of my hand,
> You didn't cry on my breast . . .
> More inalterably and assuredly
> Than a spilled torch:
>
> Hovering over my soul at the head of my bed,
> Hovering over my sufferings at the foot of my bed,
> (You didn't shudder at the touch of my hand,—
> It was not your hand that cast me down)
>
> Azrael! In nights without a moon
> Or stars, all roads are steep.

In that heavily weighted hour
I won't become your burden . . .

Azrael? In nights without exit
Or stars: masks are torn away!
In that heavily breathing hour
I won't become your channel . . .

And then with your torchlike finger
Write in the greys of dawn
Of the wife who called you
Azrael instead of Eros.

От руки моей не взыгривал,
На груди моей не всплакивал . . .
Непреложней и незыблемей
Опрокинутого факела:

Над душой моей в изглавии,
Над страдой моей в изножии
(От руки моей не вздрагивал,—
Не твоей рукой низложена)

Азраил! В ночах без месяца
И без звезд дороги скошены.
В этот час тяжело-весящий
Я тебе не буду ношею . . .

Азраил? В ночах без выхода
И без звезд: личины сорваны!
В этот час тяжело-дышащий
Я тебе не буду прорвою . . .

А потом перстом как факелом
Напиши в рассветных серостях
О жене, что назвала тебя
Азраилом вместо—Эроса.

The poem's structuring negation lends the action a curious status: it is both narrated and suspended in a way that suggests repressed desire. Yet something does happen during the ellipsis between the fourth and final stanzas. The next words, "And then," set the narrative into motion—after the union of Tsvetaeva/Psyche and Pasternak/Eros. The final stanza moves the Psyche narrative forward to where Eros flees and the lovers are long and painfully separated. The speaker now knows her lover's name is Azrael; Pasternak is Death because he is Eros, who abandons his beloved. Even as she lies destroyed, however, she invites him to write their story ("And then with your torchlike finger / Write"). When she raised the torch, she precipitated the tragedy, but Pasternak wields it to create. The poem expresses the notion that the love tragedy will enable Pasternak's writing, as it had in *My Sister Life,* while leaving her in pain.

Back in November, Tsvetaeva had been content to have her own "soul meetings" with the absent Pasternak (*DNV* 35). Now, in February, despite her anxieties about meeting him, she insisted on coming to see him in Berlin:

> And now, Pasternak, a request: don't go to Russia without seeing me. To me Russia is *un grand peut-être,* almost the beyond. If you left for Guadalupe, snakes, lepers, I wouldn't summon you. But: you're going to Russia—and I summon you.— And so, Pasternak, prepare, I'm coming. Supposedly on account of business, but really to see you: on account of your soul: to say good-bye. You already disappeared once—at the Novodevichy cemetery: you *removed* yourself, you simply were no longer there. Remembering that, I get scared—and I'm fighting for: what? Just a handshake. In general, I doubt your existence, I can't conceive of it, it appears to me too much like a dream because of the disinterestedness (renew the word's original meaning!), the sureness, the *blindness* I feel toward you.
>
> I could write a book about our meetings, just resurrecting them, *without* invention. Being so convinced of your Being, I doubt your existence: you simply aren't there. I won't ask this again, but I await an answer. I won't ask this again, but if you don't do it (for whatever reason)—it's a *wound for life.*
>
> I don't fear your leaving but your disappearing. (*DNV* 37)

Tsvetaeva had already outlined "a book about our meetings" in her first letter to Pasternak, where she enumerated the several times their paths had crossed back in Moscow. The episode at Novodevichy took place in April 1922 at the burial of Scriabin's wife, Tatiana Scriabina, where the poets had a brief exchange before Pasternak, as Tsvetaeva tells it, "disappeared." These circumstances illuminate the distinction Tsvetaeva makes between "leaving" and "disappearing": "disappearing" signifies the irrevocable loss that is death. The stakes seem absurdly inflated until we recall her mother's death, echoed in the death of her older woman friend Scriabina, and the death of Irina, who truly disappeared: she died at the orphanage and Tsvetaeva did not have the courage to attend her funeral.

Tsvetaeva reiterated at the close of her letter that meetings are a matter of life and death. The death in question is that of Alexander Blok, which she also mentioned in her first February letter: as a footnote to her statement that Pasternak was the only poet she had ever "seen," she added, "Except for Blok, but he had already died!" As remarked earlier, Blok was the model for the Genius in "On a Red Steed," and he was the only poet other than Pasternak whom she regarded as a demigod. She now told Pasternak about a "missed meeting" with Blok that took place at a reading he gave at the Moscow Polytechnical Museum in May 1920, not long before his death:

> Pasternak, in my life—as willed by a line of verse—I passed up a crucial encounter with Blok (if we had met, he wouldn't have died!), I myself at age twenty

thoughtlessly cast the spell: "And I won't extend my hands."—And there was a second, Pasternak, when I stood *next* to him in the crowd, shoulder to shoulder (seven years later!), looked at his sunken temples, at his reddish, so *un*attractive (shorn, sickly) thin hair, at the dusty collar of his worn-out jacket.—The poems were in my pocket—my hand didn't make a move toward them. (I sent them through Alya, without an address, just before he left town.) Ach, I should tell you the whole story, you should learn from my life experience: experience of the most dangerous—almost fatal—games. (*DNV* 42)

Tsvetaeva describes a careworn, fragile, all too human Blok. She focuses, that is, on his mortal body, which provides both physical intimacy (she crowds up against him, "shoulder to shoulder") and a reminder of death. Her misplaced, grandiose claim that she could have saved him recalls, again, her guilty ambivalence about Irina's death. The logic is the same as the logic of "On a Red Steed": she lost Blok because she was commanded by her Genius, by "a line of verse." ("And I won't extend my hands" [I rukami ne protianus'] is a line from one of her 1916 poems to Blok.)[47] She did not wish to repeat her failure, and suggested to Pasternak that she would come to Berlin in early May, "if you don't leave before then" (*DNV* 38).[48]

By the time Pasternak received these letters, he was already preparing to leave for Moscow. He had long wavered about when to return, largely out of concern for his productivity. He did not work well in Berlin, and by December he wrote to a friend in Moscow that he wanted to return, but that his wife, Evgenia, whose painting was going well, was opposed.[49] In January he wrote to another correspondent that he was finally writing, but again complained of being trapped in Berlin by his wife's work: "But remember I warned that I wasn't going to do 'literature' in Berlin. Isn't that why I chose beforehand the countryside—Marburg? But I didn't make it to Marburg: my wife got sick, and then her work started going well (she's an artist)" (5:139).

The couple finally made the trip to Marburg in early February. By that time they had discovered that Evgenia was pregnant and decided to leave for Moscow in mid-March so she could see her pregnancy through at home. Being in Marburg, however, reminded Pasternak of his unrealized work plans, and he now became frustrated at having to leave, as he wrote in a postcard to a friend: "And why go home?—circumstances!"[50] He was just as irritable after returning to Berlin: "Go ahead and think this decision is pointless and rushed,—I have to go—the reasons will announce themselves and become known to you."[51] When he wrote to his brother, he tried to establish that he would have a separate room to work in, apparently not yet grasping the realities of life in a communal apartment.[52]

Pasternak received Tsvetaeva's February letters on returning to Berlin from Marburg in mid-February. These letters, in which Tsvetaeva praised his work and urged him on to still greater achievements, touched a raw nerve. She advised him to retreat to the countryside to write, expanding on the theme in her second letter: "Do you know, Pasternak, you need to write a big work. It will

Drawing of Evgenia Pasternak by Leonid Pasternak, 1923 (collection of E. B. Pasternak)

be your second life, your first life, your only life. You won't need anyone or any-thing. You won't notice anyone. You will be terrifyingly free" (*DNV* 38, 40). Tsvetaeva, of course, knew nothing about Pasternak's desire to stay in Mar-burg. But she surely knew that her counsel—to embrace complete solitude and write—was provocative in the context of Pasternak's young marriage. In fact, her letters did provoke a domestic crisis for Pasternak. As he later confessed to Tsvetaeva, he shared them with Evgenia, who was understandably dismayed by their passionate rhetoric. Evgenia refers in later letters to "that old hurt in Berlin that coincided with Evgeny's conception,"[53] one source of the distress Leonid Pasternak captured in a sketch he made of her on the day of their departure. Evgenia's jealousy and the couple's disagreement over the need to return to Moscow, as well as their busy preparations to leave, explain why Pasternak de-layed answering Tsvetaeva's invitation to meet in Berlin.

The effect of Pasternak's delay was to make it very difficult for Tsvetaeva to travel to Berlin to see him before he left. He first responded on February 22 with a short note apologizing for not being able to write; he did not mention his up-coming departure and closed with a cryptic "until our imminent meeting" (do skorogo svidaniia). Tsvetaeva wrote on March 8 after learning from Liubov Ehrenburg that he was preparing to leave; she was cool and brief, thanking him for his kindness and wishing him a good trip to Moscow (*DNV* 46).[54] The next day, however, she received a letter from him announcing his departure date and inviting her to Berlin. She responded with delight at his attention and anguish at his departure, since, as she begins by saying, she "will not come," it being too late to get a German visa ("I kept waiting for your letter, I didn't dare act without your permission, I didn't know if you needed this or not" [*DNV* 49]). Probably aware that this would be the case, Pasternak had offered an alterna-tive: if she couldn't make the trip, they should plan to meet in Weimar in two years' time. Tsvetaeva embraced this plan, saying she would "*live* on this through the next two years" (*DNV* 50).

When Pasternak made the suggestion to meet in Weimar in May 1925, he was responding to a remark Tsvetaeva had made in her February letters: "I would like to visit two places with you: Weimar, Goethe's, and the Caucasus (the one place in Russia where I *think* Goethe!)" (*DNV* 35).[55] Her desire to meet Pasternak on Goethe's ground possibly was a way of marking their shared interest in *Faust*. Along the same lines, she arranged for a friend in Berlin to de-liver personally to Pasternak a copy of Eckermann's *Conversations with Goethe* (*Gespräche mit Goethe*, 1836–48) before he left (6:524–26). Johannes Ecker-mann was Goethe's secretary, hired late in Goethe's life to help him bring his unfinished manuscripts to completion; when Goethe died, Eckermann became his literary executor. He made two noteworthy contributions to German liter-ature: he persuaded Goethe to write part two of *Faust*, and he wrote his own *Conversations with Goethe*, a reverential account of all he heard and witnessed as a member of Goethe's household.

As Avital Ronell has described, Eckermann's service to Goethe was far more than secretarial.[56] His task was to complete not just Goethe's oeuvre but Goethe's very persona, by creating him as "the great poet" in the *Conversations*. Ronell argues that this was a collaborative venture, in the deepest psychological sense: Eckermann was answering Goethe's desire, following Goethe's "dictations." The bulk of Eckermann's book, in fact, consists of Goethe's quoted utterances, in versions apparently sanctioned by the poet himself, thoroughly vexing the question of authorship: "Eckermann's style is, in the end, indistinguishable from Goethe's. Scholars have been unable to determine whether he copied from Goethe's diary or whether Goethe reconstituted his diary from Eckermann's notes."[57] The book's attraction for Tsvetaeva was precisely its "radical copulation of style," its modeling of an intimate relationship with a poetic master, a relationship in which the "apprentice" is an indispensible co-author. Also, like Eckermann, Tsvetaeva wanted to establish herself as the mediator between Pasternak's text and his audience ("About you, the poet, I will tell others" [*DNV* 51]). She was just as possessive of the poet's *Wahrheit*, insistently curious about Pasternak's daily life ("Describe your everyday life [byt], where you live and write, Moscow, the air, you in space" [*DNV* 53]). Finally, she took it upon herself to urge him on to greater achievements, particularly a "big work" ("And you know, Pasternak, you need to write a big work" [*DNV* 40]). She would help him, that is, write his own *Faust*, part two, and become the great poet. We cannot know what Pasternak made of Tsvetaeva's gift, but he endorsed the Eckermann-Goethe model in one regard, at least, when years later he proposed that they translate part two of *Faust* during their visit to Weimar (*DNV* 505–6).

What does Eckermann/Tsvetaeva get from this transaction? Ronell argues that Eckermann had his own psychological investment in fusing his language with Goethe's: "The loss of a close relative [his brother], most particularly, and his inability to complete what psychoanalysts call the 'work of mourning' (Trauerarbeit) appear to render Eckermann an eternally haunted figure. The presence of the familial phantom could well explain Eckermann's compulsive need to substitute for his own self (Ich, moi) that of another."[58] Ronell refers to Freud's famous discussion of melancholia as a failed process of mourning, in which the melancholic cannot let go of the lost object because the ego has become completely identified with it.[59] (Freud also notes a similarity to hysterical identification.) Tsvetaeva represents herself to Pasternak in strikingly similar terms: "I myself have tried to get away (to tear away!) from myself all my life, and I am calm only when there isn't the slightest trace of me—in me" (*DNV* 39). In a later context, she said of this need to leave herself, "This sickness is incurable and it is called: soul."[60] She seeks from Pasternak/Goethe if not a cure then a means of stabilizing her condition: "Manage, finally, to be the one who *needs* to hear this, be that bottomless vessel that doesn't contain anything (*read* CAREFULLY!!!!), so it can go through you—as through God—as through a channel" (*DNV* 43). The word for "channel" (prorva) is based on the verb "to tear through" (prorvat'), and refers to a new stream torn open during a flood.[61]

This vessel that provides a form but does not contain resembles a birth canal through which the child "tears." When she asked Pasternak to channel her, she was asking him to author her very self in a process that will never be completed. He would serve precisely because, unlike her mother, he was only leaving and not "disappearing."

In his March 6 letter, Pasternak gently resisted Tsvetaeva's demand that he "manage to be" her channel. In her reply, she nevertheless repeated her demand, with the following elaboration:

> Don't be afraid. This is the only such letter. After all, I've not gotten more stupid—or more needy because I've been transported by you. Not only is my praise difficult for you, but also the way I relate to you, you don't yet understand that you are the one who is giving. I will be restrained. Not in my poems. But in my poems you'll forgive it.
>
> My Pasternak, I may someday really become a great poet—thanks to you! Because I have to tell you an infinite amount: to turn my breast inside out! In conversation that's done by means of silence. But I have—only the pen! (*DNV* 51)

It emerges that the new self Pasternak will help author for Tsvetaeva is a great poet, a Goethe. This possibility arises thanks to the poets' "missed meeting," whose meaning Tsvetaeva is working out throughout this letter. She imagines that if they met, Pasternak would naturally complete her: "A meeting with you would have been a release from you, a legitimate one. Do you understand? An exhalation. I would (to be cured of you!) breathe myself into you" (*DNV* 50). This would take place, as she paradoxically states in the quoted passage, "in conversation . . . by means of silence." In this romantic fantasy, perfect embodiment is accomplished without recourse to language. Now that a meeting has been decisively postponed, however, she has "only the pen." Deprived of the love experience, she is forced into language as a lesser form.

Tsvetaeva's elevation of love and presence over language and absence is a familiar romantic hierarchy. But what precisely is the failure of language, according to Tsvetaeva? As she states at the end of her letter: "My despair concerning you (*already* despair) is that for me words are emotions THROUGH AND THROUGH: the deepest ones. If we met, you wouldn't know me, you'd immediately feel relieved" (*DNV* 52). Language, that is, does not supply the kind of form she seeks; it does not "give her limits" but leaves her emotions frighteningly untrammeled. This view of language entails a view of her own subjectivity as unbounded and chaotic. Tsvetaeva represents herself as wholly possessed by her feelings, "excessive feelings: *feelings* that by their nature exclude the idea of measure!" (*DNV* 50). She represents herself, that is, as a hysteric whose "infinite amount" pours uncontrollably from her person. As such, she cannot achieve form through her own agency but must have it bestowed upon her by the lover, by Eros. In Eros' absence she has no choice but to become a poet. As long as she is separated from Pasternak, she will generate an endless flow of emotion-words, an ever-proliferating body of poetic work. With this vision of a hysterical creativity, Tsvetaeva contrives to achieve poetic greatness not by renouncing femininity but by embracing it. The pain of abandonment will underwrite her creativity; she will become a great poet because she is an injured woman. Tsvetaeva thus shapes a feminine creative myth that allows her to be both a poet and a woman in relation to Pasternak.

She shaped this myth, above all, in her lyric cycle "Telegraph Wires" ("Provoda," 1923), which she began on the eve of Pasternak's departure.[62] The punning title is etymologically related to *provody*, meaning "a sendoff." The cycle dramatizes the speaker's efforts to retrieve her lost lover, like a Psyche pursuing a fleeing Eros.[63] In the first poems of the cycle, Tsvetaeva amplifies the Psyche myth by invoking other canonic tales of woman's thwarted desire—the myths of Ariadne and Theseus, and of Eurydice and Orpheus, and the plays of Shakespeare and Racine, presumably *Hamlet* and *Phèdre,* which she had recently used as sources for lyrics to Pasternak.[64] Together these narratives describe, for Tsvetaeva, the canonic female role in European culture, which is to lose the beloved either through rejection (Phaedra, Ophelia), abandonment (Ariadne), or error (Psyche, Eurydice). In "Telegraph Wires," the speaker plays this role to the hilt, giving full vent to the excessive feelings Pasternak might "forgive" in her poems, if not in her letters.

The first two poems have the speaker "clinging to the telegraph pole," sending her lover messages over the wires. They thus establish a distinction between "voice" and the vehicle of voice that becomes important in the cycle's argument.[65] In the first poem, her messages are set off as quoted speech and break up the poem's surface. The quoted words are themselves broken up graphically by means of dashes, recalling those earlier poems in which the poet's voice also was "torn" by painful emotion (liu—u—bliu). Here, though, the dashes also function to draw out her speech as though it were being sung; Tsvetaeva later spoke of being influenced by the way song lyrics appear on musical scores, the words elongated to fit the musical phrasing.[66] This lyric speaker sings in a tragic opera, a kind of performance strongly evoked in the third poem, where she "throws open her sleeves like banners."

In keeping with the opera metaphor, she is backed by a chorus, which includes not only Ariadne and Eurydice but all "the voices of Hades," who are also quoted in the poem. This confusion of voices makes the individual voice difficult to discern, as the speaker remarks when she asks, "Can you hear my voice in the chorus?" It is, of course, a deliberate confusion that allows her to inhabit all these narratives of loss. The poem's final words belong to Eurydice:

> Over hills—and—ditches
> Eurydice's: "a—a—las,
>
> Don't l—"
>
> Через насыпи—и—рвы
> Евридикино: у—у—вы,
>
> Не у—

The poem breaks off in mid-word, mimicking the action that concludes the story of Orpheus and Eurydice. Orpheus, when he was allowed to retrieve Eurydice from Hades, was enjoined not to look at or speak with her until they returned to earth; when he weakened and turned around, he lost her forever. Eurydice's command is cut off at its prefix "u-,"and the rhyme scheme suggests that the missing verb is *ukhodi,* yielding "Don't leave."[67] Ariadne's earlier command "Turn back" suggests, though, that the woman precipitates her loss by speaking her desire: by calling Orpheus back, Eurydice wrecks his resolve and causes him to look at her. The opening poem of the cycle thus asserts the tragic structure of language: in speaking your desire, you necessarily frustrate it.

As Bruce T. Holl has argued, Tsvetaeva's linking of desire and language resembles Lacan's theory of child development, viewed as "a metaphor for the normative human condition of desires and disappointments."[68] The important point, however, is that Tsvetaeva refuses that normative condition, or rather uses it to create a powerful utterance. The tragic structure established in the first poem makes possible the speaker's spectacular performance. She does not, like Eurydice, fall silent, but insists on speaking beyond the limitations of language, as the second poem both enacts and announces:

> So I can express to you . . . but no, words are cramped
> By these rhymes and rows . . . The heart—has space!
> I fear that our misfortune can't be told
> With all of Shakespeare and all of Racine!

> Чтоб высказать тебе . . . да нет, в ряды
> И в рифмы сдавленные . . . Сердце шире!
> Боюсь, что мало для такой беды
> Всего Расина и всего Шекспира!

Language's failure is rendered through a spatial metaphor—the narratives she invokes to tell the tragedy are "too small" for her feeling, as are the very poems she is writing. By the fourth poem, her feeling threatens to destroy its vehicle: "It's my heart, like a magnetic / Spark—that tears the meter" (Eto serdtse moe, iskroiu / Magneticheskoi—rvet metr). These poems address the failure of language through sheer force by bringing to bear a voice of overwhelming power. More precisely, this voice is created by that very failure of language, by the trauma it now performs with operatic volume.

In the poems that follow, the speaker battles language by distilling her "message" to pure, emotive sound—"moaning," "sighs," a "shout," a "hiss," a "wail." These are identified as a kind of bodily speech, as "the palpable news of lips" (Ust osiazaemaia vest'). The speaker, that is, adopts the representational strategy of the hysteric, who speaks through the body: "A cry—from my womb into the wind!" (Krik—iz chreva i na vetr!).[69] Her voice has an elemental power, as suggested in the preceding poem, where she sounds like "the wildest cacophony / Of schools and thaws" (Dichaishei iz raznogolosits / Shkol, otte-pelei), referring to the spring storms of Pasternak's *My Sister Life*. She thus imagines him receiving and understanding her message:

> Shh . . . And if suddenly (aren't poles
> And wires everywhere?) you've racked
> Your brain, it dawns: these tortured
> Words are just the wail
>
> Of a lost nightingale:
> "Without my love the world is empty!"—
> Since lo—ving the lyre of your hands,
> The Leila of your lips.

> Тсс . . . А ежели вдруг (всюду же
> Провода и столбы?) лоб
> Заломивши поймешь: трудные
> Словеса сии—лишь вопль
>
> Соловьиный, с пути сбившийся:
> —Без любимого мир пуст!—
> В Лиру рук твоих влю—бившийся,
> И в Леилу твоих уст!

Presumably, this poem stages the triumph of embodied voice over language: Pasternak will understand that these poems, these "difficult words," are just a cry of pain. Yet even this speaker must translate emotion back into language, must translate her "wail" as "without my love the world is empty." She thus reiterates the logic of her letter, according to which she must use language to reach the beloved, causing her to become a poet, a "nightingale." This is the nightingale of Tsvetaeva's favorite verses by Pasternak, the Faust nightingale, the poet/seducer, whose masculine gender is grammatically preserved in this poem (vliubivshiisia). Tsvetaeva mimics here the male poet's active relation to desire. Correspondingly, Pasternak becomes a feminized love object, even as he bears the poet's attributes ("the Lyre of your hands," "the Leila of your lips"). She achieves this reversal, though, only through the pain and loss she hysteri-cally performs; in order to become a nightingale, she must wail.

These first four poems of the cycle are dated March 17, 18, 19, and 20, each marking a day in Pasternak's journey. There is a temporal gap, however, be-fore the writing of the fifth poem, which is dated March 25. During this time, Tsvetaeva received a letter from Pasternak that affected her work on the cycle. He wrote to her on May 20, the eve of his actual departure, with a heartfelt confession about her importance to him and the complexity of his domestic sit-uation.[70] With surprising directness, perhaps inspired by Tsvetaeva's own soul-baring, he explained that they could no longer correspond because of his "dear, tortured wife," who could not understand that his friendship with Tsvetaeva in no way threatened his marriage, that it belonged to the realm of lyric "power." Yet he also gave their friendship a romantic cast: "You are a sister to me—and just think how painfully I bite my lips with every new line so as not to let through that word of our greatest masculine expressiveness, for fear that its burning truth would come to grief because of my pettiness or your youth, or for some other reason, which almost always happens with man's best, his very best possessions" (*DNV* 63). He calls Tsvetaeva his "sister," a term that would seem neutral and distancing in other contexts but here is loaded with the erotic meaning it accrued in *My Sister Life*. The word Pasternak refrained from uttering was presumably the word "love," as Tsvetaeva herself guessed ("Ah, you even are considering writing that word?" [*DNV* 67]). Had he met Tsvetaeva in 1917, he says, she would have been the muse of *My Sister Life*. He further clarified that Evgenia was emphatically not such a muse, that he married her "so there would be no poems and catastrophes, so as not to be ridiculous, so as to be a human being" (*DNV* 63).

Pasternak thus assigned Tsvetaeva the role she sought as his muse, but in a convoluted fashion she understandably misread. While he distinguished between his marital love for Evgenia and his unuttered romantic love for Tsvetaeva, he held both kinds of love "sacred." He also remarked a material difference between these kinds of love: marital love, though a mere "shadow of feeling" gives life "not to shadows but to living children" (*prizraki chuvstv, daiushchie zhizn'* na zemle ne prizrakam, *no zhivym detiam* [*DNV* 63]). He then revealed that Evgenia was expecting a child in the fall and that this was the reason they were leaving. He spoke of the fact with the same neutrality, even annoyance, he expressed earlier to his friends. But his decision, at least, was clear: he asked Tsvetaeva not to send any more letters until he wrote to her from Moscow.[71]

Pasternak's letter caused Tsvetaeva to stop working on "Telegraph Wires" while she registered his rejection in a poem she wrote on March 23. "Eurydice to Orpheus" ("Evridika—Orfeiu," 1923) is a monologue spoken by Eurydice, returning to the story that structured the first poem of "Telegraph Wires." While in the earlier poem Eurydice calls Orpheus back, here she begs him to abandon his quest and let her remain in the underworld. The poem's final lines invoke Pasternak's rhetoric of kinship: "Orpheus should not descend for Eurydice / Nor should brothers disturb their sisters" (Ne nado Orfeiu skhodit' k Evridike / I brat'iam trevozhit' sester). Eurydice resembles Desdemona and Ophelia from Pasternak's "English Lessons," as she removes her "woman's passion" (zhenskaia strast'):[72]

> For those who have slipped off the last chains
> Of the earthly . . . those who, on the bed of beds
> Have composed the great lie of seeing with your own eyes,
> Those who see inward—a meeting is a knife.

Для тех, отрешивших последние звенья
Земного . . . На ложе из лож
Сложившим великую ложь лицезренья,
Внутрь зрящим—свидание нож.

She also invokes Psyche, whose "seeing with your own eyes" was the subject of "Azrael." With the eloquent gesture of turning her gaze inward and away from her lover, this speaker renounces her desire, abandons her pursuit of Eros.

Tsvetaeva did not include "Eurydice to Orpheus" in "Telegraph Wires," presumably because it disrupts the cycle's logic.[73] While in this poem she renounces her lover, in the next poem of the cycle she claims him, now pursuing him with godlike potency: "I am, and I will be, and I will gain / Your lips, like God will gain your soul" (Esm' ia i budu ia, i dobudu / Guby—kak dushu dobudet Bog). Rather than turning her gaze inward, she celebrates the power of her gaze to find out her lover: "I am no sorceress! I honed my gaze / With the white book of the Don's expanse!" (Ne chernoknizhnitsa! V beloi knige / Dalei donskikh navostrila vzgliad!). Tsvetaeva refers to her years of separation from Efron, when he fought with the White Army on the Don River in southern Ukraine. That experience will be the model for her separation from Pasternak: she will endure, with no news of him, until he reappears. Like the poems she wrote about Efron during the Civil War, this poem employs epic motifs (The Swans' Encampment [Lebedinyi stan]). In this case, however, the enemy preventing her hero's return is "another woman" (drugaia), Pasternak's wife, Evgenia:

Like the Witch of Endor—I'll conjure
Samuel—and return alone:

For there's another woman with you, but on Judgment
Day there's no contesting . . .
    I writhe and endure.
I am and I will be and I will gain
Your soul—like the soother

Will gain your lips . . .

Как прозорливица—Самиула
Выморочу—и вернусь одна:

Ибо другая с тобой, и в судный
День не тягаются . . .
    Вьюсь и длюсь.
Есмь я и буду я и добуду
Душу—как губы добудет уст—

Упокоительница . . .

Tsvetaeva, in response to Pasternak's letter, concedes Evgenia's momentary triumph. She does so as the Witch of Endor, the Old Testament prophetess who, at Saul's request, conjured up the spirit of the prophet Samuel. Saul was seeking advice before a crucial battle with the Philistines, but Samuel predicted Saul's defeat and death. Tsvetaeva proves herself more cunning than Saul, who ignored the prophecy: when she learns of her impending defeat, she leaves the field to wait for a more propitious moment. That moment will arrive on Judgment Day, which is to say that her union with Pasternak is deferred beyond death, in keeping with the tragic structure of love.[74]

In fact, in terms of the love tragedy, little would seem to have changed. While in the first part of the cycle love was impossible owing to the nature of desire as invested in language, now the obstacle to love is "another woman." Yet as commentators have observed, at this point in the cycle there is a marked change in the speaker's performance.[75] In line with her declared intention to relinquish Pasternak for the time being, she no longer "calls him back," no longer employs the passionate address of the earlier poems. Instead, she "writhes and lasts" (v'us' i dlius'), displaying her capacity to endure through a disciplining of self and utterance. She remains a traumatized self, whose emotions exceed all vehicles of expression ("There were tears bigger than eyes" [Byli slezy—bol'she glaz]),[76] and her body and speech remain fragmented ("My speech lost its sounds, / My palm lost its fingers" [Zvuki rasteriala rech' / Pal'tsy rasteriala piast']). But in these poems, her emotion is stabilized by strong anaphora:

> Patiently as one breaks rock,
> Patiently as one faces death,
> Patiently as rumors grow,
> Patiently as one nurses revenge— . . .

> Терпеливо, как щебень бьют,
> Терпеливо, как смерти ждут,
> Терпеливо, как вести зреют,
> Терпеливо, как месть лелеют— . . .

The form of these poems, that is, no longer mimics the fragmentation of hysterical speech but enforces a strict pattern. This movement toward restraint is apparent in the speaker's own behavior. While in the sixth poem she appeared as a frenzied Witch of Endor ("My breast heaves, / My eyelids are blind, froth covers my mouth" [Persi vzmyli, / Veki ne vidiat, vkrug ust—sliuda]), in the eighth poem she waits for her lover "with gaze down, / Bitten lip. Stupor. Cobblestone" (v zemliu—vzgliad, / Zuby v guby. Stolbniak. Bulyzhnik), a posture that resembles paralysis.

As the quoted stanza conveys, self-mastery is a kind of punishment, yet it is also the mode of entities in gestation ("rumors grow"). Later stanzas render "waiting" as part of the creative process ("Patiently, as one waits for a rhyme" [Terpelivo, kak rifmy zhdut]), and a means of sexual gratification ("Patiently, as one slows pleasure" [Terpelivo, kak negu dliat]). The notion that her trauma will have a yield becomes explicit in the tenth and final poem of the cycle, when she returns to the matter of the other woman. Here Tsvetaeva casts her rivalry with Evgenia as a competition to procreate, responding to the news contained in Pasternak's letter[77]:

> Others draw you into rosy heaps
> Of breasts . . . into the hypothetical rhythm
> Of weeks . . .
>   But I'll remain
> A treasury of similes,
>
> Got by chance—overturned
> On beaches, roads—overheard
> In winds, on railroad tracks—in all the worst
> Parts of town, where my youth strayed.
>
> Recognize her, shawl? Wrapped up
> Like she's got a cold, opened
> More hot than hell . . .
>   It's the womb's
> Wonder under my skirt, a living child:
>
> A song! With this firstborn, greater
> Than all firstborns, and all Rachels . . .
> With such inventions I shall overcome
> The womb's most real mass.

> С другими—в розовые груды
> Грудей . . . В гадательные дроби
> Недель . . .
>   А я тебе пребуду
> Сокровищницею подобий
>
> По случаю—в песках, на щебнях
> Подобранных,—в ветрах, на шпалах
> Подслушанных . . . Вдоль всех бесхлебных
> Застав, где молодость шаталась.
>
> Шаль, узнаешь ее? Простудой
> Запахнутую, жарче ада
> Распахнутую . . .
>   Знай, что чудо
> Недр—под полой, живое чадо:
>
> Песнь! С этим первенцем, что пуще
> Всех первенцев и всех Рахилей . . .

—Недр достовернейшую гущу
Я мнимостями пересилю!

The theme of competitive pregnancies is amplified by reference to Genesis 30, which recounts how Jacob, who loved Rachel, was permitted to marry her only after marrying her older sister Leah. Out of pity for the unloved Leah, God blessed her with many children, while Rachel was barren. Later God "opened her womb" and Rachel bore two sons, Joseph and Benjamin, who became leaders of the Israelites. Nevertheless, Leah was the mother of the firstborn (pervenets) and gave birth to many more children, and these are the powers Tsvetaeva's speaker claims against all "Rachels."

Crucially, she makes this claim to being the first and more fertile wife on the grounds that she is a poet; she is a "treasury of similes," whose riches allow her to give birth to a "song." Her possession of language sets her apart from other women, who are purely creatures of the flesh. The "heaps of breasts" suggest a threatening proliferation, while the bizarre metonymy has the effect of severing the body part that would nourish children. In turn, the women enact their own kind of violence, dissecting time's infinitude into "the hypothetical rhythm of weeks." Their strongest threat is carried by their wombs, which Tsvetaeva names indirectly (nedr dostoverneishaia gushcha), avoiding the word "chrevo". The word "gushcha" is difficult to translate, but its various meanings—sediment, thicket, center—gather around the notion of thickness. It suggests something recalcitrant and blocking, like the amassed corporeality of "heaps of breasts," and strongly expresses a hysterical disgust for the female body.

In this poem, the other woman of the sixth poem is revealed to be a mother. With this image of the other woman's womb, Tsvetaeva identifies a final and perhaps definitive obstacle to her desire. This traumatic confrontation with the mute substance of the maternal body drives the speaker to claim it for herself. She uses the same word (nedra) to describe her own womb, and renders her pregnancy in graphic physical detail: she is "opened more hot than hell" and her "living child" is growing "under her skirt." Tsvetaeva's "living child" (zhivoe chado) echoes Pasternak's odd reference in his letter to the "living children" (zhivye deti) produced by marital love, but she inverts its meaning.[78] With it she assigns life and human form to her poems, in contrast to the shapeless, inert "mass" produced by other women, thus creating herself as a superior mother.

Most important, the poet-mother confers immortality upon her poem-child. The Old Church Slavonic form "chado" (child) picks up an earlier reference, in the sixth poem, to the birth of Jesus ("The hour when kings and tribute / Travel to each other in the heavens" [Chas, kogda vverkhu tsari / I dary drug k drugu edut]). This fantasy of giving birth to an immortal child, a "living child," registers as a response to the death of her own child. Her disassociation from other mothers is an attempt to disassociate herself from the deathlike and death-dealing mother she fears herself to be. She claims an impossible maternity, one that makes both mother and child secure against the body's mortality. She does so by means of language, a bodily language that violently strains against bodily limitation. In short, she speaks hysterically, as she declared earlier in the cycle when she described herself speaking from the womb, there correctly named "chrevo": "A cry from the womb into the wind" (Krik—iz chreva na vetr). "Telegraph Wires" dramatizes with exceptional force and clarity the hysteric's simultaneous denial of the body and her resort to the body as a means of expression. Her performance even yields a hysterical pregnancy, as the final lines concede by distinguishing between her "inventions" and a flesh-and-blood child.

If she does not persuasively vanquish the other woman, Tsvetaeva does newly position herself in relation to Pasternak with the writing of "Telegraph Wires." Specifically, she will become the mother of his poems, the enabler of his creativity ("I'll remain for you a treasury of similes"). Now it is Tsvetaeva who will help Pasternak become a great poet. She achieves this reversal through the evolution of her address: she speaks no longer from the vulnerable position of the beloved but with the power of the mother. Her maternal address, however, remains passionate, just as her "sisterly" address is always erotically charged.[79]

As Pasternak had warned, Tsvetaeva received no letters from him in the months following his departure, and as he had requested, she refrained from writing to him. Their silence lasted for an entire year.[80] In the meantime, however, Tsvetaeva wrote numerous poems addressed to him, all of which were later published in her lyric collection *After Russia* (*Posle Rossii*, 1928). In a real sense, the entire volume was addressed to Pasternak.[81] As Tsvetaeva herself said when she finally sent him the poems in 1924, "I've sent only the poems that are directly to you, point-blank. Otherwise I would have to copy out the entire book!" (*DNV* 90). Two poems she wrote that June, "The Chasm" ("Rasshchelina," June 17, 1923) and "A tuner of strings—I'll master" ("Stroitel'nitsa strun—pristruniu," June 30, 1923), address the fact of his silence, drawing on a familiar "treasury of similes" of penetration, channeling, and pregnancy. In "The Chasm"[82] she writes:

> How the episode ended
> Neither love nor friendship may know.
> With every passing day your answer grows more muffled,
> With every day you disappear more deeply.
>
> And so, no longer disturbed by anything
> —Only the tree gently moves its branches—
> As though you'd fallen into a crevasse—
> You've fallen into the breast that *so* smashed itself against you.
>
> From the treasury of similes,
> Here—at random—is a riddle for you:

You sleep inside me like you're in
A crystal coffin—inside me like you're in

A deep wound—the ice chasm is narrow!

Чем окончился этот случай,
Не узнать ни любви, ни дружбе.
С каждым днем отвечаешь глуше,
С каждым днем пропадаешь глубже.

Так, ничем уже не волнуем,
—Только дерево ветви зыблет—
Как в расщелину ледяную—
В грудь, что *так* о тебя расшиблась!

Из сокровищницы подобий
Вот тебе—наугад—гаданье:
Ты во мне как в хрустальном гробе
Спишь,—во мне как в глубокой ране

Спишь,—тесна ледяная прорезь!

Pasternak's silence means that his movement through her is frozen; he is now trapped inside her, presumably to awaken someday in the fashion of Sleeping Beauty in her "crystal coffin."[83] In the poem's final stanza, the speaker's "wound" becomes a volcano, an Etna who has "married Empedocles" (Sochetavshis's toboi kak Etna / S Empedoklom"). According to legend, the poet-philosopher Empodocles threw himself into Mount Etna to prove he was a deity. The image suggests Tsvetaeva's agency in helping to create Pasternak as a Goethe, which here involves his being dead to his family ("And tell those at home it's useless: / The breast will not give up its dead" [A domashnim skazhi, chto tshchetno: / Grud' svoikh mertvetsov ne vydast]).

"A tuner of strings—I'll master," written about two weeks later, pursues the idea of channeling Pasternak, this time by imagining him, as in "A Downpour of Light," as bearing a flood of emotion requiring an outlet. Tsvetaeva offers herself as a "master" (in the feminine form, *stroitel'nitsa*), who like David in "The Lute" will supply a form for the other poet's excess:

A tuner of strings—I'll master
This string, too. Hold off
Despairing! (This June
You are weeping, you are the rains!)

And if there's thunder—on the roofs,
Rain—in the house, a downpour—complete—
Then it's you writing me a letter
You don't send.

You furrow my brain like a poem
With the drum of your water voices.
(The most capacious mailbox
Won't hold them!)

You, scanning the horizon,
Abruptly set upon the field—like a silver
Flail . . . (Shouldn't I stop you?
My child! You'll ruin the crop!)

Строительница струн—приструню
И эту. Обожди
Расстраиваться! (В сем июне
Ты плачешь, ты—дожди!)

И если гром у нас—на крышах,
Дождь—в доме, ливень—сплошь—
Так это ты письмо мне пишешь,
Которого не шлешь.

Ты дробью голосов ручьевых
Мозг бороздишь, как стих.
(Вместительнейший из почтовых
Ящиков—не вместит!)

Ты, лбом обозревая дали,
Вдруг по хлебам—как цеп
Серебряный . . . (Прервать нельзя ли?
Дитя! Загубишь хлеб!)

The poem depicts Pasternak weeping and writing, much as he does in his celebrated early poem "February" ("Fevral'," 1912/1928) ("It's February! Grab
some ink and weep" [Fevral'! Dostat' chernil i plakat']). Tsvetaeva imagines
him, like the speaker of "Telegraph Wires," finding the printed text inadequate
and communicating by other means—in Pasternak's case, through the natural
elements his poetry celebrates. Her body will absorb their force, her brain serv-
ing as a page on which he expends himself through writing. And he has much
to expend: in the final stanza he literally "flails," reaping with dangerously un-
controlled energy. She promises to discipline his instrument ("master this
string") so that he will realize the poetic harvest ("You'll ruin the crop!"). In
further stanzas cut from the published poem, she repeats her invitation to channel him as Etna to Empedocles and commands outright, "My friend, send the
letter!" (Drug, opusti pis'mo!).

While waiting to hear from Pasternak, Tsvetaeva formed several attachments
to other men. In June, while she was writing the poems about Pasternak's silence, she entered an intimate "soul" correspondence with the émigré critic
Alexander Bakhrakh, who was living in Berlin. They exchanged about twenty

letters in the course of the summer, but the friendship suffered a fatal blow in August when Bakhrakh apparently failed to reply to one of her letters.[84] On the heels of this crisis, Tsvetaeva announced to him that she loved "someone else," meaning Konstantin Rodzevich, another Russian émigré and a close family friend who was living in Prague. Tsvetaeva's affair with Rodzevich was by many accounts, including those of her daughter and husband, one of her most serious, and the one that nearly broke up her marriage. But Tsvetaeva and Rodzevich separated in December 1923, and he soon married a mutual acquaintance. Tsvetaeva immortalized the tragedy in her long poem, "Poem of the End" ("Poema kontsa," 1924), which she wrote from February to June 1924.

"Poem of the End" would play a pivotal role in Tsvetaeva's relationship with Pasternak when he discovered it two years later. At the time she was writing the poem, however, she still had not heard from him. After his departure in March 1923 she periodically made efforts to learn news of him, and in October she asked Bakhrakh to find a courier to deliver a letter and poems. In January 1924, Tsvetaeva wrote again without asking for a reply, since she had "let him go for two years," that is, until the promised meeting in Weimar in 1925 (*DNV* 69). In this letter she made a veiled reference to her recent affair with Rodzevich, whom she claims she could not love because of Pasternak: "I tried so hard to love someone else, with all love's will, but to no avail, I tore myself away from him while looking back at you, looking greedily for you (as one looks for a train that should appear out of the mist)" (*DNV* 69). In the meantime, there are his verses, which allow her to remain "in" him: "I shudder from the coincidences. Because—not a single line I've written since then has gone beyond you, I write and breathe—into you (like a goal, a place, you write *into*)" (*DNV* 68).

Tsvetaeva finally heard from Pasternak in March after a year's silence. It is worth remarking that the gaps in their correspondence during this period were partly due to the unreliable and censored Soviet postal system, which both poets tried to avoid by sending their letters through acquaintances who traveled across the border. (Pasternak's March letter was delivered to her by Liubov Ehrenburg.)[85] Pasternak apparently wrote not in response to any letter he received but to mark the anniversary of his departure for Russia: "Today marks exactly a year since I have been holding back, hiding, and not existing for you. That intentional impoverishment is the wage of injustice" (*DNV* 72). The injustice, as he rehearsed at length in his letter, was his wife's continued hostility toward his friendship with Tsvetaeva. Pasternak essentially repeated his letter of the previous year, stating his desire to sustain both relationships; he even imagines them enriching each other, describing a vision of his family uplifted by the "celebration" (prazdnik) that is Tsvetaeva. For Pasternak himself, Tsvetaeva remained, as he riskily phrased it, "in the ranks of those great things that one may ignore without danger of offending them and losing them." He sincerely intended to flatter by elevating Tsvetaeva above the domestic troubles he described. The letter as a whole expresses a passionate idealization of Tsve-

Pasternak with his wife, Evgenia, and son Evgeny, 1924 (collection of E. B. Pasternak)

taeva; Pasternak calls her "his heart's air, which I breathe day and night" (*DNV* 70). He closed by announcing his desire to write letters to her, to hear about her life, and to read all the poems she is writing, since "only you are still a poet under our sky" (*DNV* 72). This aside is the first time Pasternak sounded the theme that would dominate his relationship with Tsvetaeva—the theme of the end of lyricism in Soviet Russia.

Tsvetaeva replied with ample evidence that lyricism was still alive, sending him copies of her cycle "Telegraph Wires" (including "Eurydice to Orpheus") and about a dozen other poems she wrote to him during their silence.[86] She took elaborate precautions when asking Roman Gul, on April 6, to forward her letter through friends: "Please ask them to deliver it personally, into his hands, with no witnesses (female ones)—in a word, without his wife there. Otherwise Pasternak's life will be spoiled for a month—and why should it be?" (6:534).[87] Pasternak received the poems in mid-May, as he reported to Evgenia.[88] He replied on June 14 and opened by addressing her as "Marina, my golden friend, my amazing, supernaturally akin fate, my early morning smoldering soul, Marina, my martyr, my pity, Marina" (*DNV* 93). He was writing under the impression of reading the poems she had sent, at the same pitch of excitement as when he wrote his first letter to her: "What amazing poems you write. How painful that now you are greater than me! But in general—you are an amazingly great poet" (*DNV* 95). The letter shows Pasternak engaged in defining the "world" he shares with Tsvetaeva as the world of lyric inspiration, rendered through an elaborate scientific metaphor as electric "polarization." He also quotes a "miserable poem" from his 1915 cycle titled "Paganini's Violin" ("Skripka Paganini"), possibly recalling Tsvetaeva's comment back in 1923 that he must be interested in Paganini:

> I love you black with soot
> From burned-up passages, in the ashes
> Of flamed-out andantes and adagios,
> With a ballad's white dust on your forehead,
>
> Wearing a rind coarsened by music
> On your *workday* soul, far away
> From the unskilled crowd, like a miner
> Who spends her day underground.
>
> Я люблю тебя черной от сажи
> Сожиганья пассажей, в золе
> Отпылавших андант и адажий,
> С белым пеплом баллад на челе,
>
> С заскорузлой от музыки коркой
> На *поденной* душе, вдалеке
> Неумелой толпы, как шахтерку,
> Проводящую день в руднике.

As he then clarified, he adduced the poem to explain the nature of his love for her: "No one will allow me to love you the way I need to—you, of course, most of all. Oh, how I love you, Marina! So freely, so instinctively, so enrichingly clearly. How easy it is for my soul, there's nothing simpler!" (*DNV* 95). The way he needed to love her, evidently, was as a poet, hard at work in the mines of inspiration. As he went on to declare: "How I want a life with you! And, above all, that part of life that is called work, growth, inspiration, knowledge" (*DNV* 96). One way he sought to nurture that life was to bring Tsvetaeva's poetry to his Soviet audience. He told of including her poems in a recent public reading he gave, and he arranged to have two of the poems she sent—"The Curtain" ("Zanaves," June 23, 1923) and "Sahara" ("Sakhara," July 3, 1923)—printed in the Soviet journal *Russian Contemporary*.[89] He also fostered connections with Tsvetaeva's sister Anastasia and her old friends Pavel Antokolsky and Evgeny Lann.[90] Finally, he spoke with anticipation of their meeting in Weimar the following summer: "It will be like a return to that distant homeland where they still married their sisters, when man was still rare, exemplary, and legendary" (*DNV* 96).

Tsvetaeva replied to Pasternak's desire for "a life with you" at the end of June with a two-poem cycle titled "The Pair" ("Dvoe," June 30–July 3, 1924).[91] The cycle marks an important shift in Tsvetaeva's orientation toward Pasternak. It conveyed Tsvetaeva's crystallized sense that the two poets would never be united as lovers, and thus constituted a kind of refusal. The first poem develops the conceit that Homer crucially failed to bring together Helen and Achilles, Sparta's most beautiful woman and its greatest hero. The euphony, in Russian, of their names (Eléna / Akhillés) is proof that they were meant for each other: "There are rhymes that are chosen / In *that* world. If you part them // *This* world collapses" (Est' rifmy—v mire *tom* / Podobrannye. Rukhnet // *Sei* —razvedesh'"). In her writings, Tsvetaeva habitually represented Helen, the desired woman, as a scorned rival. In this poem, however, she plays Helen to Pasternak's Achilles—the only time she ever claimed this role. She did so because Pasternak himself had called her the sister, the Helen, of *My Sister Life*. She also did so because, in accordance with the iron law of separation, she would never actually be called on to play the role.

This view of the love tragedy is subtly different from the view Tsvetaeva rendered in "Telegraph Wires."[92] Where earlier she had fought separation first by force and then by stubborn endurance, here she serenely contemplates it as law. In the first poem of "The Pair," Helen and Achilles might be said to be equal in stature, but only within their respective gender roles as warrior and beauty. The second poem introduces a pair that is more typically "Tsvetaevan" in that they meet each other as equals on the same ground, the field of battle. Achilles is paired with Penthesilea, queen of the Amazons. As Omry Ronen has shown, Tsvetaeva could only be referring to Heinrich von Kleist's play *Penthesilea*, since nowhere in classical mythology does Achilles meet Penthesilea.[93] (Also, Kleist sets their encounter during the siege of Troy, that is, in the neighborhood of Helen.) She invokes the moment in the play where Penthesilea is defeated by Achilles and lies wounded on the ground:

> Thus they passed each other by: Thetis' son
> And Ares' daughter: Achilles
>
> And Penthesilea.
>   O remember—her upward
> Look! The look of a fallen
> Rider! No longer directed from Olympus—her glance
> Is from the mud—but still haughty!
>
> Так разминулисяь: сын Фетиды
> С дщерью Аресовой: Ахиллес
>
> С Пенфезилеей.
>   О вспомни—снизу
> Взгляд ее! сбитого седока
> Взгляд! не с Олимпа уже,—из жижи
> Взгляд ее—все ж еще свысока!

In line with Kleist's plot, Tsvetaeva's Achilles falls in love with the wounded Penthesilea and wants her for his wife—in vain, because of the law she then repeats: "It is not fated for equals to be joined" (Ne suzhdeno, chtoby ravnyi—s ravnym). This is the model for her relationship with Pasternak, whom she addresses in the final line with the verb she coined to describe their "missed meeting": "Thus we pass each other by" (Tak razminovyvaemsia—my). The third and last poem of the cycle reprises the theme of equality, stating simply and directly that Pasternak, and Pasternak alone, can match her: "In a world where we / Desire so much, / I know—there is one / Who has my power" (V mire, gde stol' / Mnogogo khoshchem, / Znaiu—odin / Mne ravnomoshchen).

"The Pair" introduces a new aspect to the love tragedy: it is precisely love between equals that is impossible. Kleist attributes the disaster to Penthesilea, who, in love with Achilles but unable to bear the thought of her defeat, loses her mind and murders him. No such complexities are unfolded in Tsvetaeva's poem, but she chooses to dramatize the moment of the Amazon's defeat. It would seem that love between equals is not possible because equality is not possible within the heterosexual romance, which always stages the woman's humiliation. In her February poems Tsvetaeva had attempted various strategies to position herself as an equal within that structure. Now, however, she describes a double impossibility: the impossibility of female agency within the heterosexual romance, and the impossibility, for her at least, of abandoning or reinventing that structure. She now finds that the best way out of a bad gender scenario is simply "out." There will be no love with Pasternak.

What accounts for Tsvetaeva's serenity in the face of this conclusion? By the time Tsvetaeva wrote "The Pair" in June–July 1924, she knew that she was pregnant, as she announced to Pasternak. Her letter is not extant,[94] but a notebook entry dated July 8 is addressed to him: "I was hurt by the birth of your son (now I can say that because you'll be hurt by the birth of mine!). Now we are equal. I'm afraid to get your reply, how will you react?" (*DNV* 99). When she received no reply, she repeated the news in October:

> Boris, since the birth of my second daughter (she was born in 1917, died in 1920) seven years have passed, this is the first child who's knocked after these seven years. Boris, if you fall out of love with me because of this, I won't regret it. I acted properly, I didn't interfere with *life's workbench* (a completely Goethean observation and definition and even form, only Goethe would have said nature in place of *life*. About "Luvers's Childhood"—later), I didn't thrust a stick into the wheel of fate. That's the only thing I respect. [The right to existence—always—in everything: from the right to existence of a given line of verse, despite the most fateful consequences—to that of my son inside me.][95] Yes, Boris, even if I conceived him with the first man I ran into, he still would have been, because he wanted to be—*through me*. Yes, Boris . . .
> I will name him Boris and thus draw you into the circle. (*DNV* 100)

Tsvetaeva dismisses the question of the child's actual paternity, allowing her to choose the father, and she chooses Pasternak.[96] Back in 1923, when she was confronted by the news of Evgenia's pregnancy, Tsvetaeva cast herself as a mother to Pasternak's poems. Now, with her real pregnancy, she imagined herself as mother to Pasternak's child as well.

More generally, Tsvetaeva's pregnancy allowed her confidently to reclaim a maternal identity in all its manifestations. In a cycle about her pregnancy, "Under the Shawl" ("Pod shal'iu," August 5–November 11, 1924), her variegated fertility is conveyed by the image of her mouth as a second womb.[97] While in the earlier "Telegraph Wires" her shawl covered only poems, here it covers both poems and a child. A similar sense of magnified creative power may also be read in her memorial essay for her old teacher Valery Briusov. Tsvetaeva was five months pregnant when she began "A Hero of Labor" ("Geroi truda," 1925) after Briusov's death in October 1924. The essay mounts a scathing critique of Briusov as a poet and exposes him as a misogynist. It includes a lengthy account of an "Evening of Poetesses" Briusov organized in 1921, in which Tsvetaeva participated. Another of the "poetesses" was Adalis, who was Briusov's wife and pregnant by him.[98] Tsvetaeva introduced the subject of Adalis's pregnancy with this recollection of a backstage emergency:

> We lit up. Comrade Adalis's teeth were chattering. And suddenly, throwing off her furs: "You know, Tsvetaeva, I think I'm going into labor." "It's your imagination." "I'm telling you, I'm going into labor." "And I'm saying it only seems like it." "How do you know?" "It's too stagy: an evening of poetesses, and then . . . it's Pope Joan again. It happens in history, but not in real life." We laugh. And in a minute Adalis's singsong: "Tsvetaeva, I don't know whether I'm going into labor,

but could you do me a big favor?" I, sensing something, "Yes!" "Will you go tell Valery Yakovlevich [Briusov] that I need him—immediately." "And interrupt the reading?" "Well, that's up to you." "Adalis, he'll be furious." "He won't dare, he's scared of you, especially after today." "You seriously want me to?" "Sérieux comme la mort."

I go out during a break in the applause for the sable-fur woman, call Briusov aside, and, clearly and quietly, looking him straight in the eye: "Comrade Briusov, Comrade Adalis asks me to tell you that she's going into labor." Briusov makes a question mark with his eyebrows. "I don't know what it's about, I'm telling you what she said, she asks you to come: immediately." (4:46)

Tsvetaeva gleefully allows Adalis's pregnancy to disrupt Briusov's staged spectacle of femininity. The apocryphal story of Pope Joan, who posed as a man until a pregnancy exposed her true gender, establishes the swollen belly as the visible mark of the female, just as the phallus marks the male. It is also the visible mark of female power, and not, as Briusov had represented pregnancy in his poetry, the mark of her enslavement to the body. Later in the essay Tsvetaeva quotes from his poem "The Woman" ("Zhenshchina"), in which he describes a woman in labor becoming "a beast" in her pain.[99] She had praised this very poem in her youthful essay on Briusov but now rejects it as blasphemy: "This is about maternity, which *washes away* everything!" (4:53–54).

Tsvetaeva's formulation—maternity "washes away everything"—reveals the grounds on which she reclaimed her own maternity: she regarded her life-giving maternal body making up for the "sins" of the sexual and mortal body. Tsvetaeva described such a fantasy about compensatory maternity not long after Irina's death. In a poem called "The Son" ("Syn," 1920), she imagines having a son, also called a "poem" (poema), who is preternaturally vital, and who is linked to Christ by the poem's dating of "Easter." A similar fantasy helped shape her mythology about Alexander Blok after he died in 1921. In her lyric cycle "The Woman Friend" ("Podruga," 1921), she represented the recently deceased Blok as the father of a son, modeled as a baby Jesus.[100] These poems expressed Tsvetaeva's conviction that her friend Nadezhda Nolle-Kogan's child was fathered by Blok. Tsvetaeva later abandoned this idea, for which there is no evidence, but for years she baffled her acquaintances by insisting on its truth.[101] Tsvetaeva's interest in Blok's child may be understood, though, in the context of her own desire to have a child by him, achieved here through a surrogate.[102] The point was precisely to have an "immortal" child, a child fathered by a "god," as Tsvetaeva perceived Blok to be.

Pasternak was a second such god, and Tsvetaeva fully played out the mythology when she named him the father of her own child.[103] The notion that Pasternak in some sense fathered her child followed logically from the erotic scenarios Tsvetaeva had staged so many times during 1922–23. She had even staged an "Annunciation" involving Pasternak in her poetic cycle "The Sybil" ("Sivilla," 1923).[104] The first two poems, which she wrote on August 5–6 just after she left Berlin, represent her body as inhabited by Pasternak's voice. The

Drawing of Tsvetaeva's son Georgy
by Ariadna Efron (undated)

immortal, aged sibyl takes the form of a burned-out tree that is "entered by a god," an action compared to the Annunciation: "Thus did the Annunciation take place in that / Hour that never ages" (Tak Blagoveshchen'e svershilos' v tot / Chas ne stareiushchii). Tsvetaeva later included a third poem in the cycle, "The Sybil to Her Child" ("Sivilla— Mladentsu," 1923), which she wrote on May 17, a few weeks after Pasternak's departure from Berlin and his revelation of his wife's pregnancy. In this poem, the Sybil addresses the infant presumably fathered by the god Pasternak, describing the child's birth as a fall into death.[105] She thus represents the mother as a death-bearer, as she did in the tenth poem of "Telegraph Wires." With Tsve-

taeva's new pregnancy in 1924–25, however, her life-giving capacities were confirmed and the model of the Annunciation restored: impregnated with Pasternak's voice, she would give birth not just to immortal poems but to an "immortal" child. As she later said to Pasternak about her son, "I feel that with him I've won back what I lost [otygraius']" (*DNV* 109).

When Tsvetaeva gave birth to a son on February 14, 1925, she wrote again to Pasternak to announce the event. In the same letter she explained that although "he was Boris for nine months in my womb and ten days on this earth," in the end she acceded to Efron's desire and named him Georgy: "You know what feeling decided me? Embarrassment, some kind of awkwardness: about introducing you, Love, into the family, about reining in a wild animal—love, about domesticating a leopard. . . . Clear and simple: if I called him Boris, I would be parting forever with the Future: with you, Boris, and with a son by you. And so, having called him Georgy, I've retained my rights to Boris. (Boris remains inside me)" (*DNV* 103–4). Even though she relinquished the name "Boris" she did not give up the fantasy of having Pasternak's child.[106] As she stated still more strongly to her friend Olga Kolbasina: "I couldn't live with B.P, but I want a son from him so that *he might live in him through me*. If this doesn't happen, then my life, its meaning, will not be realized" (6:725). With this statement, she unfolded a final implication of her maternity—that she would give immortality to Pasternak himself.

Tsvetaeva's fantasy was also fueled by her reading of Pasternak's recent prose. As she remarked to him later, during the winter of her pregnancy she "lived on" his "Childhood of Luvers," reading it "like a diary" (*DNV* 101, 102). That story showed Pasternak writing about woman's sexual and reproductive life with a sympathetic fascination unthinkable for someone like Briusov. Reading it may have helped confirm Tsvetaeva in her maternal vocation generally, and it certainly helped her imagine herself as a mother to Pasternak. Commenting on the difficulty of his prose, which she compared to part two of *Faust*, Tsvetaeva described the process of reading him as the process of giving birth to him:

> BP comes into being only in the present reader, i.e., BP is pure blueprint, BP + the ideal reader = blueprint + action, i.e., a complete act: realization. BP is realized not in the printed number of pages, like Bunin, for example, who wants only one thing: admire me!—BP is realized only in the reader. He is not a given thing, he is thing *being given*. He is not a created thing, but a thing *being created:* a thing that is *being born*. His entire self is the very act of *rendering*.
>
> It is precisely due to this need for co-creation, this complete dependence on another, that he is so singular, isolated, and solitary. (4:596)

This model of co-creation recalls the rhetoric of her letters to Pasternak, in which they are "in" each other, "channeling" each other. In this passage she finally names this action "being born."[107] Remarkably, she asks Pasternak to "bear" her in the same way, supplying a vessel (prorva), a womb that does not trap her but allows her limitlessly to unfold. It was Pasternak's readable femininity—his receptivity, his penetrability—that allowed Tsvetaeva to shape this fantasy, as she did with no other male poet with the later exception of Rilke.

Pasternak received none of Tsvetaeva's letters about her pregnancy, nor did he write to her.[108] She wrote to him again on May 26, 1925, repeating the news of Georgy's birth and forwarding a copy of the recently published *The Swain* (*Molodets*, 1922). This letter he did receive, after a year-long break in their correspondence. He sent her a copy of his *Stories* (*Rasskazy*, 1925), inscribed, "To Marina, my amazing, wondrous friend, gifted by God. B.P."[109] And he wrote on July 2 what Tsvetaeva described as his "first human letter (the rest were Geisterbriefe)" (*DNV* 119). The letter was "human" in that Pasternak spoke openly about his frustrations and difficulties, especially his inability to earn enough to support his family. He found it especially difficult to pay the taxes and rent for their uncommonly large space in their communal apartment; one of their two rooms, a "real Manege," was his father's former studio, which still contained many of his paintings and other family property (*DNV* 114). Tsvetaeva responded in solidarity against the humiliations of "daily existence" (byt), comparing her own life to that of Katerina Ivanovna in Dostoevsky's *Crime and Punishment,* a woman driven mad by the strain of caring for her children and a dependent husband in the deepest poverty. She very simply equates the burdens of daily life with having a family: "NB! The everyday is your obligations to other people." Like Pasternak, however, she honored that commitment, declaring, "I have a Protestant sense of duty before which my Catholic—no!—

my sectarian love (for you) is trifling" (*DNV* 119). She also immediately tried to help Pasternak earn money by arranging for a Czech translation of his story "Aerial Ways" ("Vozdushye puti").[110] With these "human" letters, in which Tsvetaeva and Pasternak shared their mundane difficulties, their relationship entered a new phase of intimacy.

Pasternak's letter established another theme that would dominate their further exchange: "For a long time (about six years) I have been completely unable to write" (*DNV* 115). He dates the end of his creativity to 1919, the last year of his work on the poems of *My Sister Life* and *Themes and Variations*. Pasternak was speaking about lyric poetry, for as he goes on to describe, he did continue to write in other genres, such as the stories in the volume he sent Tsvetaeva. He names with distaste a long poem he recently published, "A Sublime Malady" ("Vysokaia bolezn'," 1924), which he also sent to her, and mentions several children's stories he wrote in order to earn money. He speaks more hopefully about "a novel in verse" he began in the spring, his novel *Spektorsky*. But just last fall, he says, he had decided to "give up literature," to which Tsvetaeva replied, "And then what? Jump off a bridge into the Moscow River? With poetry, my friend, it's like love: until *love* leaves you . . . You are the Lyre's serf" (*DNV* 120). Tsvetaeva would continue to supply encouragement and support, becoming not just Pasternak's muse but his main literary adviser. Pasternak now turned to Tsvetaeva as someone who would help him return to poetry, and by early 1926 they were exchanging letters almost every other week.

The date of their proposed Weimar meeting had come and gone, as Tsvetaeva remarked in her notebooks: "May 1, 1925—PASTERNAK—WEIMAR. Mur [Georgy] is exactly three months old."[111] She had also marked the second anniversary of Pasternak's departure for Russia with a famous poem that begins,

> Dis—tance: versts, miles . . .
> We're sep—arated, dis—persed,
> So we'll behave ourselves
> At our two ends of the earth.

> Рас—стояние: версты, мили . . .
> Нас рас—ставили, рас—садили,
> Чтобы тихо себя вели
> По двум разным концам земли.

The poem ends with a reference to the years they had waited for their planned meeting: "How many, say, how many Marches?! / They've cut us like a deck of cards!" (Kotoryi uzh, nu kotoryi—mart?! / Razbili nas—kak kolodu kart!). Tsvetaeva later marveled that what was for her a personal poem became an anthem for Russians living in emigration.[112] In a similar fashion political and historical circumstances began to encroach on her unfolding relationship with Pasternak. At the end of 1925, Tsvetaeva moved from Prague to Paris, the center of the Russian emigration, where she quickly became a controversial figure.

When she wrote to Pasternak about her plan, she proposed meeting him the following year in Paris rather than Weimar. They did not in fact meet in 1926, but it was to be a watershed year. The poet Rainer Maria Rilke would figure centrally in their relations, as bizarrely heralded when Tsvetaeva, in August 1925, erroneously reported to Pasternak that Rilke had died.

4

Lyricism and History (1926)

Corresponding with you is no easier than corresponding with myself.
—Pasternak, letter to Tsvetaeva
(January–February 1923)

Marina, we will be neo-Hegelians.
—Pasternak, letter to Tsvetaeva
(March 4, 1926)

After Pasternak returned to Moscow in 1923, his work turned in a "revolutionary direction," as Christopher Barnes has phrased it. For the next several years, Pasternak was preoccupied with the subject of the Russian revolution, as writers in Soviet Russia were generally during the 1920s. He rejected the idea of political art, however, and shaped his own evolving, conflicted, and idiosyncratic vision of revolutionary history. While this work answered Pasternak's strongly felt need to respond to the historical situation, it also deepened the writing crisis that set in after the completion of *My Sister Life* and *Themes and Variations*—hence Pasternak's confession to Tsvetaeva in 1924 that he had "given up literature." What Pasternak meant by "literature" was lyricism, for him the highest mode of creativity. He worked through this crisis primarily in relation to Tsvetaeva, whom he regarded as an exemplary lyric poet.

Pasternak had already addressed the subject of the revolution in an oblique fashion in *My Sister Life*.[1] The book's full title was *My Sister Life: Summer of 1917*, suggesting that it in some way concerned the revolutionary events of that year. There was a factual basis for introducing the subject, since Pasternak's muse Elena Vinograd, inspired by the reigning political idealism, spent the summer doing social work in the provinces, where Pasternak visited her from Moscow. But Pasternak was also responding in a substantive way to contemporary history, as his readers recognized.[2] Tsvetaeva, too, remarked this aspect of the book in her review, "A Downpour of Light." In a section devoted to the topic

"Pasternak and the Present Day," she culled a half-dozen political references from the volume, with the following commentary:

> About the riddles quoted above, one thing is clear: Pasternak did not hide from the Revolution in one or another intelligentsia underground. (There's not an underground in the Revolution—just a public square in a field!) He did meet it.—He saw it for the first time—somewhere over there—in the haze—as a scattered haystack; he heard it—in the groaning flight of roads. It succumbed to him (came to him) like everything else in his life—through nature.
>
> Pasternak's word about the Revolution, like the Revolution's word about itself—still lies ahead. In the summer of 1917 he walked in step with it: he was absorbed in listening. (5:240).

Tsvetaeva correctly discerned that despite the only muted presence of political themes in *My Sister Life*, Pasternak was and would remain deeply engaged by the subject of the revolution.

She also correctly intuited where his sympathies lay. The summer of 1917 was an interim period between the February and October revolutions. The February revolution that overthrew the Romanovs and ended tsarism was an unplanned popular uprising. A State Duma then was formed that gathered representatives of many parties, including the previously banned socialist parties, whose leaders, most notably Lenin, soon returned from exile. Alexander Kerensky was chosen as the head of a Provisional Government that lasted only until October, when it was overthrown by Lenin's Bolsheviks. One of the political references Tsvetaeva notes in *My Sister Life* was to Kerensky, whose May speech welcoming the socialists Pasternak celebrated in "Spring Shower" ("Vesennii dozhd'"). Tsvetaeva also wrote a poem to Kerensky that May, containing the lines, "The spirit of Bonaparte / Has wafted through my country" (Poveialo Bonapartom / V moei strane ["I kto-to, upav na kartu," 1917]). (When she later met Kerensky in emigration, she shared with him both her poem and Pasternak's "Spring Shower.")[3] In noting Pasternak's Kerensky poem, Tsvetaeva was highlighting his enthusiasm for the February revolution, which was widely shared among the Russian intelligentsia. When she said that Pasternak had yet to utter his "word about the Revolution," she was speaking about the October revolution.

Tsvetaeva also uncovered in the lyrics of *My Sister Life* the grounds of Pasternak's regard for the February revolution. Quoting from his poem "Summer" ("Leto"), she followed a trail of associations to the French revolution:

> A rain shower stamped at the doors,
> And it smelled like a wine cork.
> That's how the dust smelled. That's how the weeds smelled.
> And if you think it through,
> That's the way the nobility's maxims
> About equality and brotherhood smelled . . .

(Like young wine: like a storm! Is there not in this the entire "Serment du jeu de paume"?)

> Топтался дождик у дверей,
> И пахло винной пробкой.
> Так пахла пыль. Так пах бурьян.
> И, если разобраться,
> Так пахли прописи дворян
> О равенстве и братстве . . .

(Молодым вином: грозой! Не весь ли в этом "Serment du jeu de paume").
(5:237–38)

Tsvetaeva refers to David's painting of the National Assembly of 1789, the first assembly of the Third Estate convened after the French revolution, a gathering she presumably was comparing to meetings of the Provisional Government. Many of Tsvetaeva's contemporaries drew such analogies between the February and French revolutions, including Pasternak in his "Dramatic Fragments," which he worked on during the summer of 1917.[4] Pasternak later said that her comments on the politics of *My Sister Life* were so accurate that he suspected "the secret mischief of radio links not noticed in time"(*DNV* 19).

In fact, Pasternak described the book's political import similarly to none other than Leon Trotsky, who invited him to visit on the eve of his departure for Berlin. At the time, Trotsky was preparing his landmark article "Non-October Literature" ("Vne-oktiabr′skaia literatura") for *Truth* (*Pravda*). To judge from the questions Trotsky put to him, Pasternak was invited as a "non-October" writer, an intellectual sympathetic to the revolution but not a supporter of the Bolsheviks. Pasternak described their encounter a few days later in a letter to Briusov:

> He asked (referring to *Sister* and something else he was acquainted with)—why I "refrain" from responding to social themes. . . . I confined myself to general propositions and cautions about my future works, conceived even more individualistically. But instead of that, perhaps, I should have told him that "Sister" is revolutionary in the best sense of the word. That the stage of revolution closest to the heart and to poetry—that the *morning* of revolution and its eruption, when it returns man to the *nature* of man and looks on government through the eyes of *natural rights* (of the American and French declarations of rights)—are expressed by that book in its very spirit, the nature of its content, the tempo and sequence of its parts, and so on and so on. Obviously, I'm somehow going to have to write about this. (5:134)

Pasternak's conviction, which he restated in his letter to Tsvetaeva, was that his own *My Sister Life* captured the spirit of the revolution—a spirit that was ahistorical, that had also presided over the French and American revolutions. It was, moreover, a spirit akin to romantic feeling and creative inspiration, which is to say, to individual self-realization. In Pasternak's romantic philosophy, the "morning of revolution" is a moment when the lyrical and the historical ecstatically merge. What the fate of lyricism might become during later stages of the revolution remained for him a matter of concern; hence his promise to write works "conceived even more individualistically."[5]

In early Soviet culture generally, such concern for lyricism was perceived as anachronistic, as it was by Trotsky, who declared, "Our epoch is not lyrical."[6] This was also the view of Pasternak's old futurist comrades Mayakovsky and Aseev, who had regrouped after the revolution as the "Left Front of Art" (Lef). They claimed to be the standard-bearers of the new Soviet poetry, exhibited on the pages of their journal *Lef*, to which Pasternak contributed.[7] As Halina Stephan has described in her history of the group, during the postrevolutionary period "the lyrical perspective seemed incompatible with the desired social character of poetry."[8] Accordingly, the Lef poets favored long verse forms that could accommodate large political and historical themes, though there was little agreement about what those forms should look like.[9] Mayakovsky's first major postrevolutionary work was his long poem "150,000,000," a self-described "blood-soaked Iliad of the revolution" (revoliutsii krovavaia Iliada). Nikolay Tikhonov and Aseev wrote ballads about the exploits of the revolutionary period. Despite their formal variety, these works were broadly designated epic poetry (*epos*).

It was in this context that Pasternak wrote his own long poem about the revolution, "A Sublime Malady" ("Vysokaia bolezn'," 1923), which appeared in *Lef* in early 1924.[10] The title names the lyric mode Pasternak was defending before his comrades. Pasternak himself writes in this mode in "A Sublime Malady," avoiding plot and proceeding by the logic of metaphor.[11] The poem opens with a mini "epic," a sixteen-line rendering of the siege of Troy as an allegory of the revolution. As Ilya Serman has argued,[12] by invoking Troy, Pasternak was polemicizing with Mayakovsky, challenging his easy assumption of the role of epic bard in his "150,000,000":

> The Achaeans show their mettle.[13]
> The siege goes on, the days go by,
> Months and summers pass.
> One fine day the pickets arrive.
> Collapsing from exhaustion,
> They bring the news: the fortress is surrendering.
> They don't believe it, then believe it, they light fires,
> Blow up vaults, look for ways in.
> They go in and out,—the days go by.
> Months and years pass.
> One fine day
> They bring the news: an epic has been born.
> They don't believe it, then believe it, they light fires,
> Impatiently they wait to be dispersed,

They weaken, they go blind—the days go by,
And the years destroy the fortress.

Ахейцы проявляют цепкость.
Идет осада, идут дни,
Проходят месяцы и лета.
В один прекрасный день пикеты.
Не чуя ног от беготни,
Приносят весть: сдается крепость.
Не верят, верят, жгут огни,
Взрывают своды, ищут входа,
Выходят, входят,—идут дни.
Проходят месяцы и годы.
В один прекрасный день они
Приносят весть: родился эпос.
Не верят, верят, жгут огни,
Нетерпеливо ждут развода,
Слабеют, слепнут,—идут дни,
И крепость разрушают годы.

Pasternak's choice to narrate the revolutionary epic in the present tense carries his polemical point: the revolution is not an event but a process that is strangely, diffidently prolonged. Remarkably, this epic features no battle, or indeed any action at all. The Achaeans busy themselves, to be sure, but only reactively, and in a haze of uncertainty. This almost comical portrayal of "heroic waiting" suggests that time itself is the only agent. Moreover, as goes history, so goes the writing of an epic poem: a rhyming pair links the surrender of the tsarist "fortress" (kr*epost'*) and the creation of the revolutionary saga (*epos*). With this short prelude, Pasternak asserts that neither history nor poetry may be forced by human agency.

The more appropriate mode for rendering the revolution, according to Pasternak, is the passive, receptive mode of lyricism. After challenging the notion of epic writing, he counters with the notion of the "sublime malady":

I am ashamed and daily more ashamed
That in the era of such shades
A certain sublime malady
Is still called song.

Is it proper to call "song" sheer Sodom,
Which earth has labored
To assimilate, rushing from its books
To lances and bayonets?

The road to hell is paved with good intentions.
The view has taken hold

That if you pave it with verses—
All sins will be forgiven.

Мне стыдно и день ото дня стыдней,
Что в век таких теней
Высокая одна болезнь
Еще зовется песнь.

Уместно ли песнью звать сущий содом,
Усвоенный с трудом
Землей, бросавшейся от книг
На пики и на штык?

Благими намереньями вымощен ад.
Установился взгляд,
Что, если вымостить ими стихи,—
Простятся все грехи.

Pasternak's reference to poetry as "malady" has been traced to Mandelstam, who described second-rate revolutionary poets as suffering from "poetry sickness" (bolezn' stikhov) ("Armiia poetov," 1923).[14] Pasternak, however, reclaims the notion to name a genuine revolutionary lyricism. In his formulation, poetry is akin to revolution, a natural force that cannot be captured by the slight category of "song." This is the lyricism of *My Sister Life,* which similarly embraced the natural and the historical, and which Pasternak already cast as a malady. The earth that "rush[es] from its books / To lances and bayonets" is the same earth of "Earth's Illnesses" in *My Sister Life.*

Interpreters of "A Sublime Malady" have struggled to account for how Pasternak could align poetry with the revolution as "pure Sodom."[15] This association, however, is consistent with the political allegory he developed through *My Sister Life* and the relevant cycles of *Themes and Variations.* Just as those cycles address the aftermath of the affair, they address the political aftermath of 1917. When Pasternak rejects a hysterical recourse to suicide at the end of "The Breakup," he directly invokes the contemporary political context: "Werther has already been written, / And in our day the very air smells of death: / Opening a window is like opening your veins" (Uzhe napisan Verter, / A v nashi dni i vozdukh pakhnet smert'iu: / Otkryt' okno chto zhily otvorit'). Pasternak wrote these lines in 1918, which is to say, after the Bolshevik revolution of October 1917. In the allegory Pasternak developed in these lyrics, the revolution turns ugly as his relationship sours. If *My Sister Life* renders "the morning of revolution," then *Themes and Variations* renders the morning after the revolution. Yet he also looks for the recovery of health on all fronts. His cycle "The Sickness" ("Bolezn'") includes a poem titled "The Kremlin in a Snowstorm at the end of 1918" ("Kreml' v buran kontsa 1918 goda"). The poem ends with the lines, "I foresee that I, the broken one, / Will be educated anew / By this undawned year" (Predvizhu, kak menia, razbitogo, / Nenas-tupivshii etot god / Voz'metsia syznova vospityvat'). In the poem that follows, "January 1919" ("Ianvar' 1919 goda"), Pasternak uses the imagery of the winter storm to suggest that the revolution, like the poet, could recover from its illness: "There is no anguish in the world, / That snow couldn't cure" (Na svete net toski takoi, / Kotoroi sneg by ne vylechival).

The image of the revolution as a winter storm almost certainly derives from Blok's revolutionary poem "The Twelve" ("Dvenadtsat'," 1918). Blok's long poem was the masterpiece of his late career, combining epic, lyrical, and dramatic elements to shape an influential vision of the revolution.[16] The poem appeared in the summer of 1918 in *The Banner of Labor* (*Znamia truda*), where Pasternak published his "Dramatic Fragments" in May and June. The journal was associated with the Scythians, and Christopher Barnes has suggested that, at least during 1917–18, Pasternak shared their view of the revolution as an elemental phenomenon.[17] Blok, the most famous member of the group, had already begun to shape this "elemental" mythology after the revolutions of 1905. Influenced both by Nietzsche and by Christian mysticism, Blok understood the Bolshevik revolution as the cathartic unleashing of a force residing in the Russian people ("narodnaia stikhiinost'"), an event that would restore "the spirit of Music" to Western civilization. In line with this understanding of the revolution, "The Twelve" represents it as a blizzard ("metel'") through which a band of revolutionaries blindly struggle. The poem, however, ends with a kind of moral stabilization when "the twelve" encounter the figure of Christ, who leads them forward under a red banner.[18] Despite the poem's mystical conclusion, it supplied for early Soviet literature a canonic image of the revolutionary storm.

When Pasternak conflated lyricism and history as natural forces in *My Sister Life* and *Themes and Variations*, he was working within Blok's neoromantic paradigm. He was also reworking it, however, in line with his liberal convictions.[19] His image of a "healing" snowstorm in "The Sickness" envisions a revolution purged of elemental violence. This stands in stark contrast to Blok's celebration of "the destruction of humanism," as he named one of his essays ("Krushenie gumanizma," 1919). Here and elsewhere Blok called on the intelligentsia to put aside the enlightenment values that defined them as a class and embrace even the cruelest manifestations of the revolution. In effect, he called on them to accept their own demise, echoing the Bolshevik claim that the intelligentsia was a historical anachronism. Despite their historical role in opposing serfdom and tsarist rule, the educated elite was nonetheless regarded within early Soviet culture as an "enemy" class. Blok himself exemplified the paradoxical situation of the *intelligent* who helped bring about revolutionary change and was destroyed by it. Although Blok publicly supported the Bolsheviks and was an officer of the Soviet writers' organization in Petersburg, when he died in 1921 his final words, "I can't breathe," were taken to express a fatal alienation from the new order. One could say that Blok's lyric masochism devolved into a political masochism, that he succumbed to Bolshevism the way he fantasized about succumbing to the Stranger.[20]

Pasternak's "sublime malady," then, names the lyricism he shared with Blok, a lyricism that in the revolutionary period has become "pure Sodom." Although "A Sublime Malady" opens with a polemic with Lef, that is, the poem is more deeply engaged with Blok's legacy.[21] Pasternak renders the revolutionary period as one of "listening" rather than of heroic action; its lyrical plot traces the emergence of sound out of the postwar silence that reigns at the beginning of the poem. Pasternak borrowed this rhetoric from Blok's famous exhortation, "With all your body, all your heart, all your consciousness: listen to the Revolution" ("The Intelligentsia and the Revolution," 1918).[22] In "A Sublime Malady," the music of the revolution has yet to sound, even though the intelligentsia has already sung its swan song, its "motif / Of crumbling self-defeat" (motiv / Sypuchego samosverganiia). Their music has now fallen silent, as Pasternak conveys through the extended image of an organ clogged with dust, also a realistic detail of postwar ruin. The "garbage" lying around it, however, still senses the "inspiration" the organ silently preserves. Similarly, the polecats who "have bitten through the throat of the chorale" (Khoralu gorlo peregryzshi) nourish themselves on "the warmth and pain of the sublime malady" (Teplo i bol' bolezni vysshei). Despite the intelligentsia's demise, that is, its music remains an example for the postrevolutionary period. Pasternak rehearses this logic more directly in the famous stanzas that follow:

> We were music trapped in ice.
> I'm speaking of the whole milieu
> With whom I planned to
> Leave the stage and do.
>
> There is no place for shame here.
>
> I was not born to always
> Try to please somebody else.
> Even more meaningless than song
> Is the moronic word "enemy."
> I remain a guest.—The sublime malady
> Is a guest in every world.
>
> All my life I wanted to be like everybody else,
> But the epoch in its beauty
> Is more powerful than my whining,
> And wants to be like me.
>
> Мы были музыкой во льду.
> Я говорю про всю среду,
> С которой я имел в виду
> Сойти со сцены, и сойду.

Здесь место нет стыду.

Я не рожден, чтобы три раза
Смотреть по-разному в глаза.
Еще бессмысленней, чем песнь,
Тупое слово «враг.»—
Гощу.—Гостит во всех мирах
Высокая болезнь.

Всю жизнь я быть хотел как все,
Но век в своей красе
Сильнее моего нытья
И хочет быть как я.

Pasternak embraces his own irrelevance to postrevolutionary culture in a direct and honest fashion. His irrelevance frees him from any and all social roles, including that of class enemy, though he has always coveted conformity ("I wanted to be like everyone else"). Rather, his role will be to embody "the sublime malady," which in a remarkable turnabout is what the revolution wishes to emulate. Though the era of the intelligentsia has passed, it set the standard of creative genius that the revolution has yet to achieve. Pasternak offers in this poem a defense of the intelligentsia in Blok's own terms, as bearers of the "music of revolution."

This notion of the intelligentsia as an object of the revolution's desire is one Pasternak develops in explicitly psychosexual terms in the lengthy, sixty-three-line section that follows, which begins, "We were the music of embraces / Accompanied by injury" (My byli muzykoi ob"iatii / S soprovozhdeniem obid). In this section, Pasternak again borrows Blok's famous rendering of the revolution as a blizzard (metel') in "The Twelve." In Pasternak's poem, the revolutionary "blizzard" directs its violence against the *intelligent*: it breaks down his door and pursues him. The poet, however, characterizes the attack as an act of love when he warns the *intelligent* not to try to reason with "this hag who's fallen for you" (v vas vtiurivshaia'ia karga). Pasternak thus suggests that the revolution still needs, and even loves, what it harms.[23] The gender politics of this scenario are those of his lyric poetry, as the effeminate *intelligent* is dominated by the powerful "hag" (karga) of the revolution. The main difference is that the muse has "changed her aspect," as Blok said about the Beautiful Lady. Pasternak's horror of elemental violence, which he also expressed in other writings of this period, unsettles his revolutionary romanticism and distinguishes him from Blok.[24] That profound ambivalence was expressed in the idea of a "malady" that is nevertheless "sublime."

In tune with poem's rendering of a historical limbo, we are still listening for the music of revolution at the end of the poem. What emerges from the intelligentsia's silence is not music but pseudo-sounds that cancel sound itself: "Everything became sound: sound disappeared" (Vse stalo zvukom: zvuk ischez). A similar statement—"And all began to seem like sound" (Vse stalo pred-stavliat'sia zvukom)—introduces the poem's final segment, where the poet attends the Ninth Party Congress, which took place in December 1921. Thanks to his connection with Mayakovsky, Pasternak actually was in the audience, as he remarks in the poem. (He goes to the theater "with an orchestra ticket" [k teatru, s propuskom v orkestr].) The "sound" at the end of the poem, then, is the sound of the congress's debates and proclamations, which Pasternak openly ridicules. He pointedly chose, however, not to represent the main sound of the event, an important speech by Lenin. It was at the Ninth Party Congress that Lenin announced the New Economic Policy, a pragmatic measure to restart the ruined economy by granting some rights to private property and a degree of entrepreneurial freedom. Lenin's speech marked the end of so-called War Communism, when repressive measures were justified in the name of winning the Civil War. In an earlier poem, titled "The Russian Revolution" ("Russkaia revoliutsiia," 1917), Pasternak had depicted Lenin giving a crude speech urging his followers to violence; his advocacy of violence stands in grotesque contrast to the humane spirit of the February revolution.[25] In "A Sublime Malady," however, Pasternak draws back from judging Lenin's performance.[26] He even obliquely suggests that the congress captured something of the spirit of February, which he invokes by reminding the reader of the flight and capture of the tsar's family. Pasternak either predicted or hoped that the Bolsheviks, at the end of War Communism, would prosecute the "true" February revolution. He imagines the revolution, in a sense, starting over with the end of War Communism. The poem's vision was strangely confirmed by Lenin's unexpected death on January 21, 1924, around the time "A Sublime Malady" appeared.

After writing "A Sublime Malady," Pasternak continued to listen and abide, writing almost no poetry for about two years, though he published the aforementioned collection of stories (*Rasskazy*, 1924). This was the period when he "gave up literature," as he said to Tsvetaeva, and took a job compiling a bibliography of foreign Leniniana at the People's Commissariat for Foreign Affairs. He became more estranged from Lef and gravitated toward literary venues such as Maxim Gorky's journal *The Russian Contemporary* (*Russkii sovremennik*), which published a diverse array of writers and poets, including Mandelstam, Akhmatova, and, at Pasternak's instigation, Tsvetaeva.[27] When the Central Committee of the Communist Party made its first foray into literary affairs in 1925 with a resolution "On Party Policy in the Field of Literature," Pasternak responded with an agitated public statement. The Central Committee demanded "a style in accord with the epoch," one created by the working class as part of the cultural revolution. Pasternak, while condoning the search for new forms, argued that these must emerge organically in the course of history; to demand that they appear now is to fail to "love history." He cites "Blok's barricade-street style and Mayakovsky's superman-collective style" as examples of styles that emerged at the historical moment of the revolution, thus implying that they were no longer relevant (4:617–18). But they remained examples of art as "an extremity of the age," in contrast to the reigning Soviet "style of the epoch," which he described as a mix of mediocre forms, both revolutionary and non-revolutionary. Pasternak concluded his remarks by mentioning two new projects of his own in which, presumably, he would love history better: his long poem "1905" and a novel in verse, *Spektorsky,* both of which address the prehistory of the revolution. With this short statement, Pasternak publicly set forth the task he assigned himself and which he pursued throughout the 1920s—to write about the revolution, and to do so in historical perspective.

Already in "A Sublime Malady," Pasternak had suggested that one might solve the problem of writing epic poetry by turning to history. At the end of the poem, he speaks of "cherishing the memory" of the intelligentsia's role in creating the revolution as the prerevolutionary period receded further into the past, and of the importance of fine historical detail ("And time has obscured the details / But trifles were what prevailed" [I vremia sgladilo detali, / A melochi preobladali]). If one cannot write about the unfolding revolution, it is not only possible but urgent to write about the revolution's past. Pasternak's decision in 1925 to write a long poem about the 1905 revolution was guided to some degree by pragmatic considerations: works on the subject were being commissioned in honor of its twentieth anniversary. (The most famous of these was Eisenstein's film *Potemkin,* which Pasternak later said to Tsvetaeva "coincides exactly with my interpretation" [*DNV* 164].) But his work on the poem was entirely in keeping with the artistic task he conceived for himself.

Also in line with the argument of "A Sublime Malady," in these new works Pasternak appeals to narrative; although the unfolding event of the Bolshevik revolution cannot yet be grasped as a sequence, a past event can. Thus, "1905" features a recognizable timeline, as it moves in chronological order through the signal events of that year, though they are still rendered in Pasternak's lyrical idiom. The main event was the sailors' mutiny that took place on the naval ship *Potemkin* in the southern port of Odessa. Pasternak also decided to treat a similar rebellion at greater length in a second poem, "Lieutenant Schmidt" ("Leitenant Shmidt," 1926). The two poems were conceived as a diptych, and were published together in 1927 under the title *1905,* after appearing piecemeal in various journals. In these works, Pasternak "loves history" by scrupulously relying on documentary sources; he described "1905" as "not a long poem but simply a chronicle in verse form" (4:621). Preparing to write the poems, he acquainted himself with the major historical works about the 1905 revolution, including Trotsky's *1905* and the memoir of Afanasy Matiushenko, a leader of the *Potemkin* rebellion. As several analyses of the poems have demonstrated, Pasternak hewed closely to these historical accounts.[28]

Pasternak's carefully researched treatment of the 1905 revolution served to establish the intelligentsia's role in revolutionary history. As in "A Sublime Malady," in "1905" the speaker represents himself as a member of the intelligentsia, now with specific reference to Pasternak's own life. The second chapter, "Childhood" ("Detstvo"), evokes his privileged youth in the company of figures such as Scriabin. The autobiographical references drop away as the poem proceeds, but their inclusion at the beginning recalls Alexander Blok's long poem "Retribution" ("Vozmezdie," 1919), in which he charted his family's history as emblematic for the intelligentsia.[29] Similarly, Pasternak, in his "1905," used autobiographical references to make a point about the historical role of the intelligentsia. In a letter to his parents, he described his approach as "intimizing history": "I express not everything but a great deal about myself when I say that my singular feature consists in my drawing expanses and quantities and abstractions into my personal, isolated sphere: in my 'intimizing,' earlier, of the world, and now, of history; in my assimilating the mass of sifting infinitude." He then added, "I love this same feature in Marina."[30]

With this formulation, Pasternak imagines a way of bringing together lyricism and history. He identifies a common impulse behind the lyrics of *My Sister Life* and his new historical poems—the impulse to merge with his environment. He thus presents the historical poems as a natural development in his poetic career. In other contexts, however, Pasternak spoke as though this new work were forced upon him, and to his regret. In January 1926, when the newspaper *Leningrad Truth* (*Leningradskaia pravda*) sought his opinion about the current state of poetry, he replied: "You say that people haven't stopped writing poems, though they aren't being published, and those that are, aren't being read. A valuable observation, but that's not what convinces me that poetry is in decline—we are writing large works, being drawn to the epic, and that is definitely a secondhand genre [vtoroi ruki]. Poems no longer contaminate the air, whatever their merits. The acoustic environment for their sound was the individual. The old individual has been destroyed, the new hasn't yet been formed. Without such resonance, lyric poetry is unthinkable" (4:619–20). Pasternak, as always, identifies poetry with lyricism, and lyricism with individualism. Now, however, he definitively states that lyricism cannot exist at this moment in Soviet Russian history: "Poems no longer contaminate the air." Therefore, despite the superiority of the lyric mode, he has turned to the genre of the epic. This portrait of the lyric poet forced from his true vocation by history might appear simply an elaborate justification for Pasternak's prolonged writing crisis, which in some sense it is. Yet it also accurately reflects Pasternak's felt dilemma. In the cultural environment of the 1920s, two of his deepest values came into conflict: his regard for lyricism as the highest form of creativity, and his desire to assimilate himself to the unfolding history of Russia. The conflict manifested itself in Pasternak's labored progress in his work on the 1905 poems, and in his wildly changing evaluations of that work in letters to friends and family.

Pasternak's conflict was most strongly expressed in his relationship with Tsvetaeva. Around the time he began writing "1905" in the summer of 1925, he addressed her as the best living Russian poet, the only poet with whom he "would be glad to share a poetic rank" (*DNV* 115). Nevertheless, he did not place himself at her level, for as he went on to explain, "You are purer and stronger than me because you haven't changed. . . . You write with open gates, your lyricism is as young as ever, it retains its sacred posture" (*DNV* 116). Pasternak cast Tsvetaeva as the quintessential lyric poet, the standard by which he measured himself as he "changed." As a consequence, Pasternak began to involve Tsvetaeva in his ongoing work. He introduced the subject of his new historical poems in his lengthy reply to Tsvetaeva's next letter, in which she mistakenly reported that Rainer Maria Rilke had died.

When Tsvetaeva wrote to him about Rilke, she had no reason to believe that the news would touch him any more closely than it did herself, as the loss of a great poet whom, she said to Pasternak, she first began to read in Berlin (*DNV* 127).[31] In his reply, Pasternak extravagantly declared his grief, linking Rilke to his "childhood" and his "roots" but without explaining his family's connection to him. He told Tsvetaeva about having wanted to visit Rilke back in 1922 from Berlin, and about a dream he later had of visiting Rilke with Tsvetaeva: "You often asked what we would do together. One thing I knew for sure: we would go see Rilke. I even once dreamed about such a visit. In the scene there was much that was materially elementary, natural, what he gave expression to in his books, no small part of which was passed along to me and partly to you" (*DNV* 123). Pasternak names himself and Tsvetaeva as heirs of Rilke, poets who shared the world of his "natural" lyricism. But he also attempts to link that world to his new understanding of the poet's task: "We risk becoming cut off from what is profound if we do not in some fashion become historiographers. . . . Soon the air, the air of life, yours and mine and the dead poet's, the air of strong and gusting poetry, the air of the conceivable and desired novel will become for me completely identical with history" (*DNV* 124–25). Pasternak wished to breathe the air of Tsvetaeva and Rilke in a cultural environment where, as he said in his public statement, "poems no longer contaminate the air." Pasternak wished, that is, to bring the inspired lyricism of Tsvetaeva and Rilke to his new historical writing.

After making inquiries with his family abroad, Pasternak discovered not only that Rilke was still alive but that he was still writing as well. His sister Josephine sent him a copy of Rilke's *Sonnets to Orpheus* (*Die Sonette an Orpheus*, 1923), which along with *Duino Elegies* (*Duineser Elegien*, 1923) were the first books Rilke had published in more than a decade. Pasternak's desire to legitimate his new project in relation to Rilke shaped an odd evaluation of *Sonnets to Orpheus*. He wrote to Tsvetaeva in January 1926 that the poems were "poetically unbelievably pale for Rilke," and as such touched him "very personally, as the simple, mundanely understandable sickness of a great and precious soul" (*DNV* 133). Rilke, he says, had always belonged to the class of poets who write outside of history, harking back to the "absolute source" of the aesthetic. With Rilke's new book, though, he was writing like a contemporary poet, addressing, however unsuccessfully, modern themes such as "the car, the war, the airplane, etc." Pasternak was clearly tracing in Rilke's career the desired arc of his own, although in Pasternak's case, being a "contemporary poet" meant writing about revolutionary history.

In his letters to Tsvetaeva over the next months, Pasternak continued to unfold the meaning of his statement that they "must in some fashion become historiographers." For the first time, he declared to her his commitment to the socialist ideal: "Several propositions have become guiding ones for me. Our time is not an explosion of the elements, not a Scythian fairytale, not a point to apply Red mythology. It is a chapter in the history of Russian society, and a beautiful chapter, directly following the chapters about the Decembrists, the People's Will, and 1905. When it becomes condensed and clarified in a style, when it leaves its own style to posterity, it will turn out to be more elevated and serious than today's stylized clichés. Moreover, this chapter in world history will be called *socialism,* without any quotation marks" (*DNV* 139–40). Pasternak was well aware that Tsvetaeva would not be a sympathetic audience for this declaration, but he continued to insist that Russian history was searching for a "form" that would in some way meet up with Tsvetaeva's lyricism.[32] He also needed her to confirm that in his historical poems he was preserving "what makes poets good" and sent her a chapter of "1905" (*DNV* 141). The chapter depicts the *Potemkin* mutiny, which, as in Eisenstein's film, is sparked by the sailors' anger over being forced to eat tainted meat. Pasternak's naturalistic description of the meat crawling with worms horrified his wife and brother, who thought it had no place in a poem, and he sought Tsvetaeva's opinion on the matter.[33] Her reply is not extant, but her view may be learned from an essay she was working on at the time, a hostile review of Mandelstam's *Noise of Time* (*Shum vremeni,* 1925). Tsvetaeva objected to what she saw as Mandelstam's "aesthetic" depiction of the Civil War period in the Crimea, and invoked Pasternak's "worms" as proof of his more courageous confrontation of ugly realities (5:310). Whatever she said to Pasternak himself, it confirmed him in his chosen course: "I would distort my soul if I played down the joy caused by your words about 1905. So I'm not mistaken, and maybe not in other respects, either" (*DNV* 144–45).

In fact, no Tsvetaeva letters or drafts of letters from the period survive, so we do not know her full response to Pasternak's new historical project. Despite her encouragement about "1905," however, she could not have had any interest in his "socialism."[34] Her own very different documentary impulse was manifested by her plan to write a poem about the suicide of the Soviet poet Sergey Esenin, who hanged himself in the Hotel Angleterre in Leningrad on December 28, 1925.[35] Tsvetaeva wrote to Pasternak in January asking him to collect materials about the event for her to use in her poem. Pasternak studiously obliged but was disturbed by her interest in the matter, which she characterized in an extant fragment of her letter: "The internal aspect [of Esenin's suicide]—I entirely understand, every gesture—down to the last one. And all the prayers, spoken or silent. I know everything except the particulars."[36] It was Tsvetaeva's developing conviction, shaped largely against Pasternak's historicism, that the poet was necessarily and even fatally in conflict with his times; hence her interest in the myth and reality of "the poet's death."

Also during these months in early 1926 Tsvetaeva and Pasternak seem to have experienced the first crisis in their relationship. (Tsvetaeva's letters in January and February are not extant.) Pasternak wrote: "Ah, ·Marina, Marina! Whatever I might say to you now won't be any better than my past answers that finally provoked this explosion, which I've been expecting and fearing for a long time" (*DNV* 137). For some reason, Tsvetaeva had begun to doubt the sincerity of his attachment, to the extent that she wrote to him: "I laugh at myself for all these past years with you. I really laugh!" (*DNV* 144). She had apparently insisted that they address each other with the intimate second-person "ty" form, while Pasternak always used the formal "Vy." (Tsvetaeva had used "ty" for some time in the notebook versions of her letters, though not in her letters to him.) The conflict was rather artificially resolved when Tsvetaeva assured him that her "ty" meant something other than the ordinary, at which point Pasternak acceded and began to use the form himself (*DNV* 146).[37] Clearly, the conflicts that unfolded in the summer of 1926 were already under way before the famous date when Rilke was drawn into their exchange.[38]

On the same day in late March, Pasternak made two galvanizing discoveries: he read Tsvetaeva's "Poem of the End," and he received word from his father, Leonid, that Rilke had read and admired his poems.[39] Rilke offered this praise in a letter to Leonid Pasternak. Though the two men had not communicated for twenty years, Leonid wrote to Rilke in December congratulating him on his fiftieth birthday, which was being publicly celebrated. Rilke had recently spent time among Russian émigrés in Paris, where he came across Pasternak's poems in an anthology edited by Ehrenburg.[40] Pasternak was stunned by Rilke's unsolicited acknowledgment. His family abroad were equally excited and shared Rilke's letter among themselves before forwarding it to Moscow, as Leonid serenely informed his son: "Next time I will send you excerpts from his letter, copied out by Lydia—I'm afraid to send the original for fear it will get lost. I am forwarding it to Josephine—she will be delighted" (*DL* 34). Pasternak's sister Lydia and his parents were living in Berlin, while his sister Josephine lived in Munich with her husband, so the copy did not reach Pasternak until April 3, almost two weeks after he learned of it. He complained bitterly about the delay in a letter to Josephine ("What thieves you all are, and cannibals!" [*DL* 45]).

Pasternak's irritation at his family's delay was understandable, but they were right to hold back the original. In his letter, Rilke spoke feelingly about the suffering of the Russian people under the Bolsheviks, whose rule he implicitly compared to the Tatar yoke of the medieval age, and about Russia's capacity for eventual rebirth. Moreover, he ascribed to the Pasternaks, and to the Russian émigrés he met in Paris, a crucial role in sustaining this "real Russia" (eigentliche Rußland) (*DL* 31). These remarks might have led the Soviet censors to confiscate the letter, so Lydia cut them from the version she copied out and mailed to Pasternak. The version he received, then, contained Rilke's warm ad-

Sketch of R. M. Rilke by Leonid Pasternak (Deutsches Literaturarchiv Marbach)

dress to Leonid, his praise for Pasternak, and a brief account of his doings, including mention of a recent illness that had put him in a sanatorium in Switzerland. (Rilke was suffering from leukemia.) Reading the letter emboldened Pasternak to write to Rilke himself, on April 12. Amidst the effusive expressions of gratitude and admiration that open the letter, one claim stands out: "I am indebted to you for the basic features of my character, the entire composition [sklad] of my spiritual life. They were created by you" (*DL* 54). Pasternak also gave an accounting of his poetic work, a potentially painful exercise since, as he said, he had been unable to write poetry for the past eight years. Of course, Pasternak had not been silent, having completed or worked on "A Sublime Malady," "1905," and *Spektorsky,* but he clearly felt unable to justify these works as poetry before this particular addressee and therefore did not mention them. He did indirectly defend them, however, when he said that "even in my deepest depression I never forgot about the exalted tragedy of the revolution," a defense he might not have made had he known about Rilke's excised comments about the revolution's barbarism (*DL* 55–56).

Despite the historical context Pasternak invoked, he also wanted to reassure Rilke that "as far as poetry is concerned, everything remains as before." Inspiration, he said, was still a free, autonomous force that, having abandoned him for years, had now returned to him in the persons of Rilke and the poet Marina Tsvetaeva. Pasternak then introduced Tsvetaeva to Rilke: "On the very day that I received news of you, I also received, through the local circuit, a poem that was written genuinely and rightly, as none of us in the USSR can write anymore" (*DL* 56). Her genius, he says, is akin to Rilke's; just as he had described himself, he describes Tsvetaeva as a creature of Rilke's own making, as "a part of your biography, in her force and range." Pasternak then made an extraordinary gesture, whose consequences would be played out for years to come: he asked Rilke to send Tsvetaeva an inscribed copy of one of his books, saying he would consider the gift a reply to his own letter. Having received the greatest blessing of his life, Pasternak immediately made Tsvetaeva its recipient. He explained this substitution by claiming that all poets are one poet who "at different times has a different name," doubtless referring to a line from Rilke's *Sonnets to Orpheus:* "We must not concern ourselves / about other names. Once and for all / it is Orpheus when there is singing" (Wir sollen uns nicht mühn // um andre Namen. Ein für alle Male / ists Orpheus, wenn es singt).

Pasternak, of course, did not want entirely to dissolve his identity in the general identity of "the poet" but coveted an individual reply from Rilke. At the close of his letter, he suggested that if Rilke wanted to send him "a few lines," he should mail them to Tsvetaeva, who would forward them to Moscow.[41] And Pasternak desired still more than a reply from Rilke: he began making plans to realize his dream of visiting Rilke in Switzerland with Tsvetaeva, apparently at Rilke's invitation. He enigmatically remarked to Tsvetaeva, who still knew nothing about Rilke's letter to him, "About Rilke, a piece of our life, about the man who is inviting us to the Alps next summer—I'll write later, in another letter" (*DNV* 152). Earlier, Pasternak's and Tsvetaeva's projected meeting had been set for Weimar, conceived as a pilgrimage to Goethe. Now they entertained the prospect of visiting a living idol in the summer of 1927.

As Pasternak related to Rilke, he received "Poem of the End" in a copy circulating among friends rather than directly from Tsvetaeva. The last thing he had read of hers was "The Swain," which he compared to "Poem of the End" in a letter to his sister Josephine: "It's beautiful romanticism, but nothing like the best parts of 'Poem of the End.' There's something of me there. But Lord what amazing hands that something has fallen into!" (*DL* 46).[42] Reading "Poem of the End" reminded him of his own poetry—not the poetry he was writing in 1926 but the lyricism of *My Sister Life*. Tsvetaeva's poem made him see "how awful '1905' is!" He wrote: "All my 'historicism,' my pull toward contemporaneity, and in general my whole disposition has blown to pieces from Rilke's letter and Marina's Poem. It's like my heart has ripped open my shirt. I've gone crazy, splinters are flying, and something akin to me exists in the world, and what kin!" (*DL* 46). The immediate impact of "Poem of the End," along with Rilke's letter, was to make him question the value of his historical project. As he wrote to Tsvetaeva, he now saw that with his writings of the past year, he had "suffocated the child and the poet" in him (*DNV* 156).

As the process of contacting Rilke dragged on from March until May, Pasternak wrote letter after long letter to Tsvetaeva. In the first of these letters, written on March 25, Pasternak describes his feeling as "nothing new," as something he had expressed earlier "somewhere in my letters to you during the summer of 1924, or maybe during the spring, and maybe already in 1922–23" (*DNV* 152). But the letters he wrote after reading "Poem of the End" reached a new level of intensity. His rhetoric, in fact, resembles that of Tsvetaeva's passionate letters of 1923–25, so much so that one might say he borrowed it from her in another act of co-authoring. He addresses her as a divinity ("I worship you" [*DNV* 153]), and speaks of their encounter in sublime, elemental terms.[43] And he expresses the same neurotic fear that she will die before they get to meet, though Pasternak's particular fear, spurred by what he regarded as her excessive interest in Esenin's suicide, was that Tsvetaeva might kill herself.[44] At the same time, he was plagued by fears of his own death, as he confided to his sister Josephine (*DL* 51). In sum, he "somehow went off his head," as he put it (kak-to svikhnulsia) (*DNV* 154).

The first letter he wrote to Tsvetaeva about "Poem of the End" celebrates it in a fashion that recalls his very first letter to her about *Milestones:* he performs, rather than simply declares, his enthusiasm. He describes himself in an exalted state, reading the poem to everyone he meets, introducing them to its "abyss of wounding lyricism, its Michaelangelan sprawl and Tolstoyan deafness" (*DNV* 148). Pasternak rightly attributes the pleasure of reading the poem aloud to its intrinsic dramatism, calling it a "tragedy," in which "every sigh, every nuance, is prompted." But he also remarks that his own pleasure derives not simply from the poem itself but from the thought of Tsvetaeva witnessing his performance: "I sit and read it as though *you* were watching, and I love you, and I want you to love me" (*DNV* 149). The fantasy captures much about Pasternak's address to Tsvetaeva in these letters, in which he performs "Tsvetaeva" before her, composing, in the process, an image of himself. As he wrote in another letter, "I have begun to confuse two words to the point of meaninglessness: I and you" (*DNV* 195).

Pasternak goes on in this letter to theorize about how Tsvetaeva becomes present to him as he reads her poem. Reverting to the language of aesthetic philosophy, he defines "genius" as "the revelation of objectivity, the gift of identity with the world" (*DNV* 149). Knowing Tsvetaeva's aversion to this "lexicon," he apologizes for it and proceeds by way of example. Pushkin's *Eugene Onegin,* he says, illustrates the "paradox of objectivity" that distinguishes a work of genius: when Pushkin wrote the line, "but you know, my Tatiana is about to get married," he attributed an autonomous existence to a character of his own invention. In this sense, he created not a character but an objective entity. Pasternak discerns the same paradox at work in Tsvetaeva's "Poem of the End," but with a difference that has to do with her gender: "Everything recalled and introduced [into the poem], precious and memorable, stands as it was placed and governs itself in its aliveness, like his paradoxical Tatiana—but one musn't stop there and must add: you, too, are eternally with it all, there, in the middle of that all, in that Prague haunt, or standing on a bridge where mothers jump with their illegitimate newborns, and in exactly their hour. And precisely thus are you greater than yourself: that you are there, in the work, and not in its authoring" (*DNV* 150). Tsvetaeva, unlike Pushkin, does not author a poem but authors herself; her poem is not writing but unmediated self-expression. Moreover, Pasternak places her in the company of suicidal unmarried mothers, who, it must be noted, appear nowhere in "Poem of the End."[45] Her genius lies, that is, in her feminine expression of anguish. Pasternak's response to "Poem of the End" reveals what it was in Tsvetaeva's poetry that he recognized as also belonging to him: the lyricism of the woman in pain.

Not unexpectedly, Pasternak goes on to compare Tsvetaeva with Desbordes-Valmore: "How amazing that you are a woman. With your talent that is a rare occurrence! And now, instead of the chance to be a contemporary of Desbordes-Valmore (such a small chance in the lottery!)—the chance—to be your contemporary" (*DNV* 152–53). He made the same comparison when introducing her to Rilke: "She is Marina Tsvetaeva, a born poet of immense talent, similar in kind to Desbordes-Valmore" (*DL* 56). The hint of condescension is amplified in a letter Pasternak wrote to Josephine about the poem: "There, amid stormy shapelessness of middling quality, one constantly finds fragments of genuine, great, finished art that witness a talent that often reaches genius. Only Scriabin, Rilke, Mayakovsky, Cohen have moved me so much" (*DL* 46). Pasternak rehearses exactly Baudelaire's response to Desbordes-Valmore, representing the woman poet as derivative, as possessing "talent" that may occasionally rise to the level of male "genius." Like Baudelaire, he is driven thus to distinguish feminine and masculine writing by an ambivalent identification with the woman poet.[46]

"Poem of the End" offers rich material for such a reader. It is a blow-by-blow account of the last hours of an affair—Tsvetaeva's affair with Rodzevich—during which the lovers decide to part. Tsvetaeva herself described the poem to Pasternak as rendering her "feminine" response to the tragedy, in contrast to her other poem on the subject, "Poem of the Hill" ("Poema gory," 1924): "Poem of the End is one thing. Only Poem of the Hill is earlier and is the masculine aspect, written in the heat of the moment, immediately reaching the highest note, while Poem of the End is a woman's already erupting grief, springing tears, me when I lie down—not me when I get up! Poem of the Hill is the hill seen from another hill. Poem of the End is the hill on top of me, me under the hill" (*DNV* 218). The gender dynamics of "Poem of the End," however, are more interesting than Tsvetaeva allows here, if only by virtue of the fact that the poem features speaking roles for both the female and male protagonists.[47] "Poem of the End" does indeed portray "a woman's already erupting grief": the speaker battles her tears all through part 6, to succumb by part 7. The climax the poem builds toward, however, is the moment when her lover begins to weep. This moment marks the real "end of the end" (konets kontsu!), the event that finally reconciles her to their parting. The poem's dramatic climax, that is, centers on a weeping man. Tsvetaeva's poem actually features the hysterical male in the role of the lover, allowing Pasternak to enjoy his emotion—the emotion he performed in his earlier lyrics—without fear of being totally feminized.

"Poem of the End," after all, plays out the same love plot that structured *My Sister Life* and the relevant cycles of *Themes and Variations*. Like these cycles, Tsvetaeva's poem renders the prolonged process of the breakup. Unlike Pasternak, however, Tsvetaeva depicts the lovers in painful agreement that their needs are irreconcilable, and they part with dignity. She describes a tragedy, not a bitter disaster. Moreover, Tsvetaeva rewrites the familiar plot by making the woman the main actor: her lover wants to marry her, but she refuses on principle, detesting the bourgeois institution of marriage. (In the biographical context, this action has excruciating irony, since Tsvetaeva broke up with Rodzevich to save her marriage with Efron.) As Pasternak represented the love tragedy in his poems of 1917–18, it is precipitated not by high conviction but by a hysterical confusion whose source is the woman. In "The Sickness" and "The Breakup," he represents the male lover as wrecked and resentful, stricken with a disease from which he recovers alone. Pasternak, reading "Poem of the End," must have relished how Tsvetaeva freed up the male and female roles in the love plot and elevated it to the level of tragedy. He certainly remarked and approved Tsvetaeva's polemic against possessive love, quoting her lines about her lover: "Like a one-year-old child: 'give me' and 'mine'" (Ditia godovaloe: "dai" i "moi") (*DNV* 153).

That Pasternak read Tsvetaeva's poem in a personal light is apparent from his letters. As he had done once before, he christened her the muse of *My Sis-*

ter Life: "You are so beautiful, such a sister, such a my sister life, you came straight down to me out of the sky; you came in support at a time of spiritual extremity. You are mine and always were mine and all my life is because of you" (*DNV* 148). He goes on to contrast her to other women he has loved, namely, Elena Vinograd and his wife, Evgenia:

> My Sister Life was dedicated to a woman. The element of objectivity rushed to her in an unhealthy, insomniac, mind-clouding love. *She married someone else.* I could have hung around agonizing: as a result, *I also married someone else.* But I am talking to you. You know that life, whatever it's like, is always more noble and elevated than such libretto conventions. The high-speed, oncoming-train system of dramas isn't for me. My god, what am I telling you and why! My wife is a volatile, anxious, spoiled person. She can be attractive, but rarely so in recent days, since her anemia has gotten worse. At bottom, she is a good sort. Sometime in the nth generation this soul, too, like all the rest, will become a poet, armed with the whole sky. Would it not be shameful to ambush her and take advantage of the fact that she was caught prematurely and without means of defense? Therefore during our scenes—she gets the leading role, I retreat, make the sacrifice—*dissemble* (!!), while she speaks and feels libretto-style. But not another word about that. Not to you nor anyone else. It seems to me that the fate that handed you to me is *inoculated* against cares about this life. Here there will be no thrashing around, even libretto-style. (*DNV* 151)

Pasternak represents his relationships with other women as operatic love dramas. In particular, his marriage to Evgenia has been spoiled by her histrionics, by her inability to break out of the female role in the gender "libretto." Evgenia might have done better, he says, had she had the stature of a poet, the ideal condition toward which all of humanity is evolving ("this soul, too, like all the rest, will become a poet"). Tsvetaeva, of course, has already reached that level, assuring that their relations will remain free of such "thrashing around."

Pasternak, though, was still attempting to quell some "thrashing around" in Tsvetaeva's recent letters to him. Amid avowals of love, he reproaches her for some libretto-style behavior of her own: "Are you having a crisis? Why are you wallowing in humiliation?" (*DNV* 152). Apparently Tsvetaeva had accused him of being "like all the rest," a charge he counters by quoting the familiar stanza from "A Sublime Malady":

> All my life I wanted to be like everybody else,
> But the epoch in its beauty
> Is stronger than my whining,
> And wants to be like me.

In the context of Pasternak's poem, these lines represent the poet's creativity as a standard to which the revolution has yet to rise. He now quotes them to underscore a further claim that the poet is exceptionally advanced in his emotional life—that he is not like other men, and Tsvetaeva must not create him as such

("So you've created me like them?"). For his part, Pasternak affirms that he has not "created" Tsvetaeva, however much she "belongs" to him: "That you are terrifyingly mine and not created by me—that is the name of my feeling" (*DNV* 152).

Pasternak's anxiety that the two poets not "create" each other interestingly assorts with Tsvetaeva's desire for mutual rebirth. He appears to be resisting her desire, but in an earlier passage from the same letter, he renders their relationship through the image of a shared womb: "I love you so strongly, so *completely,* that in that feeling I become a thing, like someone swimming in a storm, and I need it to wash over me, turn me on my side, hang me by my heels—I'm swaddled by it, I become a child, the first and unique one in the world brought into being by you and me. I don't like the last three words. More later about the world. I can't say everything at once. Later you can edit and add to this" (*DNV* 148). The phrase "a child, the first and unique one" (pervym i edinstvennym) dates to their correspondence during 1924. Apparently Tsvetaeva first used this language when responding to the birth of Pasternak's son, stating that "a firstborn is always unique" (Pervenets vsegda edinstvennyi).[48] The poets used the same language when reflecting on how to rank poets, as "the first poet" or "the unique poet."[49] Despite this rhetoric, however, Pasternak resists suggesting that he is Tsvetaeva's child. His vision of being "swaddled" by fluids is a vision of being in the womb, but it is a metonymic womb: he is submerged in his "feeling" for her. Moreover, this womb is one he has helped create, a "world brought into being by you and me." Enacting this desire to co-generate, he offers her his text to edit, just as he had freely borrowed her language. But he also, as he says, dislikes the three words "you and me"—perhaps because the conjunction separates the two poets, but perhaps also because it conjoins them in the intimate task of creating themselves.

Pasternak reiterated his odd image of a womb shared with Tsvetaeva in a later, pivotal letter of April 20. At Pasternak's urging, Tsvetaeva had completed and mailed to him a questionnaire to be used for a proposed bibliographical dictionary of twentieth-century writers published by the State Academy of the Arts (Gosudarstvennaia akademiia khudozhestvennykh nauk). In her biographical sketch, Tsvetaeva identified her mother as being "of Polish aristocratic blood, a pupil of Rubinstein, exceptionally gifted in music. She died young. The poetry comes from her" (4:621; *DL* 65).[50] Pasternak's own mother, née Rozalia Kaufman, had Anton Rubinstein as her patron during her early career as a piano prodigy. As Pasternak told Tsvetaeva in his answering letter, Rubinstein once displayed his mother, then thirteen years old, to the orchestra of a Petersburg conservatory, announcing, "That's how you are supposed to play it" (*DNV* 185). Tsvetaeva's questionnaire revealed to Pasternak that the two poets had the same mother—that both, as he says, were "cooked down" in the amniotic fluid of music (v chem ty vyvarilas' i ia).

In the same letter, soon after making these remarks, Pasternak related a dream he had had about Tsvetaeva in which the two poets finally meet. The central image, which shifts and ramifies as Pasternak's description proceeds, is of a sheltering environment, another womb:

I dreamed about the beginning of summer in the city, a bright, immaculate hotel with no bedbugs or clutter, or maybe something like a building where I once worked. There were the same sorts of corridors downstairs. They told me someone was asking for me. Sensing it was you, I lightly ran along stairwells agitated by light and slid down the stairs. Truly, you stood there in a traveling outfit, in a haze of decisiveness, having appeared not suddenly but on wings, gliding, as I ran toward you. Who were you? A sketch of everything that in a decisive moment of feeling raises the woman you are holding to proportions physically incompatible with human size, as though she weren't a person but a sky with the beauty of all the clouds that ever floated above you.[51] But that was just a rudiment of your fascination. Your beauty, conveyed in the photograph—beauty in your special case—i.e., the manifestation of a great spirit in a woman, beat into the air around you before I fell into these waves of benevolent light and sound. This was the world's condition, called into being by you. It's hard to explain, but that's what gave the dream its quality of happiness and infinity. It was a harmony that for the first time in my life I experienced with the same power I have always experienced pain. I found myself in a world filled with passion for you, and didn't register my own harshness and vagueness. It was more first than first love and the simplest thing in the world. I loved you as I always *thought* I would love, long, long ago, to the nth degree. You were absolutely beautiful. You were in the dream and also in walls', floor's, ceiling's analogy of existence, that is, in the anthropomorphic unity of air and time—as Tsvetaeva, that is, as the language discovered in everything the poet listens to his entire life without hope of hearing an answer. You were an immense poet against a field of great, loving adoration, that is, the absolute *humanity of the elemental*, not among people or in the human use of the word ("the elemental"), but where you belong. (*DNV* 186–87)

The space first appears as an "immaculate hotel" where the poets have a sort of tryst, though not a sexual one, as the Russian original underscores. ("Immaculate" [bezgreshnaia] literally means "without sin.") They do not even meet privately; rather, Pasternak runs down a brightly illuminated staircase to find Tsvetaeva waiting below. She emanates "waves of benevolent light and sound" into which Pasternak falls, waves that recall the element in which Pasternak earlier imagined himself "swaddled."

This nurturing element then takes the shape of a room that is an analogy of, respectively, "existence," "Tsvetaeva," and "the language discovered in everything the poet listens to." Placed in this series, Tsvetaeva becomes a space that is isomorphic with being and language, a space within which Pasternak can live and write. She is the lyrical essence of poetry that has evaporated from his cultural surround ("The air is no longer charged with poetry"). She is the mother of his creativity. Pasternak's dream about Tsvetaeva as a poetic mother recalls Baudelaire's vision of Desbordes-Valmore, in whose poetry he finds "that warmth of the maternal nest, of which some among the sons of woman, less ungrateful than others, have kept the delicious memory."[52] When Baudelaire celebrates Desbordes-Valmore's femininity, that is, he de-eroticizes her, as Pasternak does in his dream of Tsvetaeva: their encounter is chaste, however suggestive the hotel setting.[53] His creation of Tsvetaeva as mother, though, has the added dimension of poetic rivalry. Pasternak was in the habit of imagining his own creativity in terms of female sexuality and fertility, while Tsvetaeva, in her earlier letters about her son's birth, had strongly asserted her procreative power. Pasternak's vision of sharing a womb with her was an attempt to diminish that power by also imagining her as a sibling, or even as his own child.[54]

Tsvetaeva's unique status as a mother/muse is highlighted when Pasternak turns to the subject of Elsa Triolet. In the culture of the period, Triolet and her sister Lily Brik were emblematic female muses. They inspired some of the canonic love tributes of Russian modernism: Viktor Shklovsky's *Zoo, or Letters Not about Love* (*Zoo, ili, pis'ma ne o liubvi*, 1923) concerns his spurned love for Triolet, while Brik was the longtime addressee of Mayakovsky's love poetry. Triolet emigrated after the revolution and married Louis Aragon; her leftist sympathies led her to visit Soviet Russia in 1926, when Pasternak encountered her in Moscow.[55] He apparently described the meeting to Tsvetaeva, provoking her to ask if he were attracted to Triolet, to which he responded,

> And you write about the woman with the dead fingers: "Perhaps you loved her?" And it's you seeing me and saying you know? But even if E[lsa] Iu[r'evna] were her complete opposite, *even then* there would have to be something exceptional, something that returns me from specific years and persons to the foundations of life, to the entrance, to the beginning—in other words, there would have to be you—to draw me from my path and lead me to something deserving of the term. After all, I'm not only married but I am still myself, and I am half child. I.e., it doesn't happen with me so frequently that it threatens to distort my life. And again, do you understand? There have been several times when Zhenya [Evgenia] suffered for no reason, i.e., when I started to fall in love and didn't make it even to the first step. There are *thousands* of females whom I would *have* to love if I gave myself free rein. I'm prepared to rush after any display of femininity, and my surroundings swarm with its appearance. Maybe I was born to realize that trait, and am shaped through powerful, almost absolute self-braking. (*DNV* 187)

In these paragraphs Pasternak configures the relations among his wife, Tsvetaeva, and the "thousands" of women who are potential love objects. These women, who include Elsa Triolet, he must and does resist out of loyalty to Evgenia. But he also does so out of loyalty to Tsvetaeva, whom he reassures by claiming that only she could draw him from his marriage toward a love "deserving of the term."

Just as he, Pasternak, does not take other women seriously, neither does Tsvetaeva have other men. After narrating his dream about their hotel encounter, Pasternak interprets it as confirming his sense that Tsvetaeva is loyal to her husband. He describes how, back in 1924, in his eagerness to learn more about her, he sought out one of Tsvetaeva's old lovers in Moscow, Evgeny Lann, only to dismiss him: "I didn't lend any significance to the Lanns, despite your attestation, despite your perhaps current protestation that the Lanns have weight in your heart. That's why only S[ergey] Ia[kovlevich] and my life exist for me" (*DNV* 187).[56] Pasternak names himself alongside Efron as though he were a second husband. The implication becomes explicit in his next letter, of May 5, when he names Tsvetaeva his wife: "I could and should have hidden from you until we met that now I will never be able to stop loving you, that you are my only legitimate sky, and my so very, very legitimate wife, that in that word, because of the strength that flows into it, I begin to hear a madness that never inhabited it before. Marina, my hair stands on end from pain and cold when I name you" (*DNV* 194). Tsvetaeva is not the other woman, as Elsa Triolet and "thousands of females" would be, but the other wife. Pasternak insists on the relationship's "legitimacy," which matches or even exceeds that of his own marriage. He thus creates a structure that had been in place for Tsvetaeva for some time. In an unfinished poem entered in her notebooks in May 1924, she wrote, "I won't hide . . . from you / That I live with your soul / With a passion sweeter than earthly passion! / (Even while I am with my husband and you are with your wife!)" (Ot tebia. . . ne skroiu, / Chto zhivu s tvoei dushoiu / V strasti, slashche chem zemnoi! / [S muzhem—pust' i pust'—s zhenoi!]).[57]

As we know, Pasternak's wife, Evgenia, was always troubled by his enduring and ambiguous tie with his "other wife." But when Pasternak's passionate interest in Tsvetaeva flared up again after he read "Poem of the End" in March 1926, it nearly precipitated a divorce. Pasternak remarked to Tsvetaeva that if he continued to write to her in this way, it would alienate him from his family—not because of Tsvetaeva or her letters but because of the new inspiration she had brought him (*DNV* 157). He declared to Tsvetaeva his intention of sending Evgenia and Evgeny abroad to his sister's in Munich for the summer so he could be alone to work. He also repeated his plan to "visit you and go with you to Rilke" the following summer. In this and other cryptic references to this plan, Pasternak did not explain how or why Rilke was involved; possibly he wanted Tsvetaeva to have the pleasure of hearing from Rilke herself before telling her the entire story. When she endorsed the idea of meeting in 1927, she spoke only about Pasternak's visit, asking how much money he would need and promising to set up readings for him in London and Paris (*DNV* 170).[58]

Pasternak, however, suddenly changed his plan after receiving the "first letter that made further existence without [her] unbearable" (*DNV* 188). This letter was the one containing Tsvetaeva's questionnaire, from which Pasternak learned about her musical mother. He now wanted to rush to Tsvetaeva immediately and put off the visit to Rilke. Of course, his chances of traveling abroad at all were small, as he discovered when he applied for a visa that spring and was refused.[59] But the very idea infuriated Evgenia, who, as Pasternak reported to Tsvetaeva, "has found out everything, mainly its scope and irrevocability" (*DNV* 194). When Evgenia and Evgeny received their visas a month later and left for Germany in late June, it was unclear whether they would rejoin Pasternak as a family.[60]

Pasternak wrote to Tsvetaeva about this new plan, putting it as a question: "*Should I come to you now or in a year?*" His reason for hesitating was that he needed to produce more work in order "to be something more *useful* in your life and fate" (*DNV* 188). Still, as he explained to Tsvetaeva, his resolve to wait would collapse unless she shored it up:

> If you don't stop me, then I will come with empty hands *only to you,* and can't even imagine *where else* I would go or *why.* Don't succumb to the romanticism that lives in you. It's bad, not good. *You yourself* are greater than that "*only,*" and I am like you. Meanwhile, if there is still fatedness in this world, and I saw it this spring, then there is still not that Russian air around us (and maybe not in the whole world) where one can rely on the humanity of chance, or better—on the unknown's being on the same footing with the poet. Here one must charge the air on one's own. And that will take a year. But I am almost certain that I'll come to you now, abandoning all work. In any case, until you bring me into line, I can't start anything. (*DNV* 189)

Pasternak disowns his agency while making his desire perfectly clear: he wants Tsvetaeva to put aside their romance and endorse his commitment to writing. He asks her, that is, to conform to his notion that the poet in her is stronger than the woman—the woman with whom he identifies when he represents himself as ruled by passion, as ready to "succumb to romanticism." "I am like you," he says, but not sufficiently to master his own femininity, as Tsvetaeva presumably is able to master hers. With startling directness, Pasternak reveals what is at stake for him in identifying with the female poet: she will lend him her creative agency. His sense of Tsvetaeva's power is so great that it allows him to rethink the possibilities of his situation as a Soviet poet, breathing an air that is devoid of lyricism. Against all of his theorizing about the poet as a passive entity, subject to the agency of inspiration, nature, and history, Pasternak now decides that "one must charge the air on own's own," empowered by Tsvetaeva's will.

Tsvetaeva's next letter opened with an unequivocal answer to Pasternak's question, telling him to come "In a year" (*DNV* 189). She later described the sequence of events: "In the summer of 1926, having read my Poem of the End somewhere, B. madly rushed to me, wanted to come here—I *turned him aside:* I didn't want a *general* catastrophe" (6:393). By speaking of a "general" catastrophe, she suggests a concern for their respective families. Her letter to Pasternak also reveals a desire to sustain the romance of distance. Although she speaks of his coming in a year, and even promises to help him do so, she also speaks of the pleasures of deferral ("You are a huge happiness that approaches slowly" [*DNV* 189]). This structure works differently for her now than it did in 1923. As Tsvetaeva herself remarks, she is no longer writing poems to him, poems that "call forth your soul" (*DNV* 191). The shift took place with the birth of her son, and in this letter she repeats the logic about love that she developed during her pregnancy: she is a mother, not a lover. Pasternak, she says, was correct to believe that she was devoted to Efron, though she would never marry now; her dream was always to have her lover's child and live alone. All she needs from Pasternak is for him to remain in place so that she has somewhere "to grow" and "to write." As she says, she would be happy even to receive "an empty envelope, as long as the address is written in your hand" (*DNV* 192).

Tsvetaeva urges the same equanimity on Pasternak. His recent letters to her were agitated, and he spoke openly about the state of his nerves. For years he had suffered from toothache, and the problem had recently resurfaced. In April he wrote to Tsvetaeva that the pain, triggered whenever he started writing well, had spread from the left to the right side of his jaw and was probably caused by an inflamed facial nerve (*DNV* 180). He marvelously described the experience as his father would have drawn it: "This is no toothache. This pain is so bad that under my father's pencil it would be rendered in two lines: the right side of my jaw bone and my left temple" (*DNV* 181). Tsvetaeva responded by trying to send him "a blue lamp for the neuralgia" along with her instruction not to come (*DNV* 192). At this point in 1926, she found herself in exactly the role she had rejected back in 1923, the role of the male poet's nanny. She now welcomed the role, reassuring him of her love and encouraging him to finish his 1905 poems as a "heroic deed" (podvig).

Pasternak was relieved by Tsvetaeva's refusal. He announced that she had "sat him down to work," and much of his letter concerns his writing plans for the summer, mainly finishing "Lieutenant Schmidt" and a projected novel based on "The Childhood of Luvers" (*DNV* 196).[61] There was nothing soothing, however, in the next letters Pasternak received from Tsvetaeva. She apparently wrote asking Pasternak to offer financial help to her old lover Sophia Parnok. Pasternak knew Parnok from working with her at "The Knot" (Uzel'), an artel formed in early 1926 to redress the lack of venues for publishing poetry, and he did not get along with her.[62] He now had even less reason to help her, since Tsvetaeva told him about their affair, quoting from one of her poems to Parnok:

> There are women.—Their hair like a helmet,
> Their fan with a subtle and fatal scent.
> They are thirty years old.—Oh why, why
> Did you need my Spartan child's soul?

> Есть женщины.—Их волосы, как шлем,
> Их веер пахнет гибельно и тонко.
> Им тридцать лет.—Зачем тебе, зачем
> Моя душа спартанского ребенка?

Tsvetaeva represented herself to Pasternak as a "Spartan child," referring both to her relative youth and innocence (Parnok was thirty at the time, Tsvetaeva twenty-three) and to the legend of a young boy who, rather than give up a fox cub he had concealed under his shirt, allowed it to eat his entrails.[63] In telling him this history, she was underscoring the trauma of sexual love, which she did not want to experience with Pasternak; she thus endorsed his vision of their meeting in an immaculate hotel (*DNV* 190). In any case, her story strongly activated Pasternak's habitual concern with violated womanhood. He was so disturbed by the revelation that he declared himself unable to talk about it.

Possibly more upsetting was an unexpected break in the chain he attempted to create between Rilke, Tsvetaeva, and himself. As Pasternak asked him to do, Rilke replied to him through Tsvetaeva. He mailed his letter to Pasternak to her in Paris, along with copies of his *Duino Elegies* and *Sonnets to Orpheus* inscribed to her. He also wrote her a warm note explaining how his connection with the Pasternaks had been renewed, and flirtatiously expressed dismay that during his recent eight-month stay in Paris, where he had enjoyed the company of Russian émigré friends, he failed to encounter her. Rilke certainly would have met or at least heard about Tsvetaeva had she been in Paris at the time; when she arrived in November 1925, she was welcomed as one of the emigration's great poets, and she gave a reading in February that was the event of the season. Rilke left Paris in August, however, repeating the pattern of missed meetings that defined Tsvetaeva and Pasternak's friendship. Rilke now proposed "making up for it" by arranging a meeting among the three of them: "Now, after Boris Pasternak's letter, I believe a meeting would bring both of you the deepest, innermost joy" (*DL* 83).

Tsvetaeva received Rilke's mailing on May 8. As Pasternak had asked her to do, she forwarded Rilke's letter to him, along with a sheet of paper on which she copied out the flattering things Rilke had said about him, though not Rilke's entire letter to her. These arrived in Moscow on May 18, and the next day Pasternak wrote her an anguished letter: "Yesterday your mailing of his words arrived: your absence, the palpable *silence* of your hand" (*DNV* 199). The letter exudes surprise and hurt, but he did not speak directly about his grievance until he wrote again on May 23. He would have liked, he says, to know all the details of Tsvetaeva's exchange with Rilke, including seeing the letters Rilke wrote to her. He now regretted submitting to her will and deciding not to make his trip to Europe, describing his superstitious logic: had Rilke's letter arrived in the same envelope as Tsvetaeva's refusal, Rilke's voice would have overpowered hers and induced him to come (*DNV* 202). Pasternak now felt entirely cut off from Rilke, and he declared several times that he was "not writing to Rilke." As for Tsvetaeva, though he tells her "nothing has changed," he speaks as though something between them had ended. He concluded his May 23 letter by sending greetings to Tsvetaeva's children and husband, and proposing that their families might become friends: "And this is no limitation but even more than we had before" (*DNV* 211).

Meanwhile, Tsvetaeva sent alarming reports of a quarrel with Rilke, with whom she had already exchanged three letters. On the very same day as Pasternak, Tsvetaeva wrote to say, "I'm not writing to Rilke" (*DNV* 213). When she first heard from Rilke, she wrote him an eloquent reply: "You are . . . the embodied fifth element: poetry itself, or (still not enough) you are that from which poetry arises and which is greater than you yourself" (*DL* 84). She also sent him copies of her *Poems to Blok* and *Psyche,* which she annotated to help him understand her Russian. She playfully dated her letter ahead by two days, so that it seemed to arrive the very day it was written, a device that delighted Rilke. He wrote an enthusiastic reply, which found her already embarked on another letter to him; his responsiveness emboldened her to continue in a more intimate tone, and to send a picture of herself and ask for one in return. Again Rilke replied promptly, on May 17, and in the same confiding manner. But he also talked about his worsening illness and warned that he might not be able to stay in touch. This caveat, accompanied by a confession that his Russian was not good enough to read her "difficult" poems, led Tsvetaeva to conclude that he was not genuinely interested in her, and she resolved not to write to him anymore. It now appeared to Pasternak that Tsvetaeva had possibly damaged his relations with Rilke, as Leonid Pasternak had feared when he learned that his son had introduced her to Rilke.[64]

The misunderstanding was soon cleared up, but only partially. In reply to Pasternak's reproaches, Tsvetaeva immediately sent him copies of Rilke's first two letters to her (though not the offending third letter). She explained that she was trying not to intrude on Pasternak's exchange with Rilke, an explanation Pasternak accepted but viewed critically: "I perfectly understood . . . the nobility and spiritual tactfulness of your reserve when forwarding [his letter]. But precisely the fact that you preferred this inborn gesture to an incidental slip (to *not* keep silent, to appear not as gold but as some unknown alloy) distressed me" (*DNV* 225). Pasternak found not that Tsvetaeva had acted wrongly but that she too categorically adhered to a gold standard of behavior. He nevertheless agreed to abide by her code: "We need to love each other according to your rules ('Gratitude')" (*DNV* 226). He was referring to her recently published aphorisms "On Gratitude" ("O blagodarnosti").[65] Tsvetaeva's rules are indeed categorical, demanding absolute delicacy in the relation between the donor and recipient of charity; in effect, she rejects the very sentiment of gratitude as demeaning.[66] Pasternak may have read Tsvetaeva's silent forwarding of Rilke's letter in that light, as a refusal to thank him for the gift of Rilke. In any case, the episode led Pasternak to reflect seriously on the differences in their views and behavior.

If Pasternak was prepared to accept Tsvetaeva's behavioral ethics, he was much less accepting of the "creative philosophy" (tvorcheskaia filosofiia) he discerned in her comments about Rilke. Initially Pasternak, eager to reaffirm their bond in his period of doubt, claimed that they still shared "the *same* solitude, the same journeys and searching, and the same favorite turns in the labyrinth of literature and history, and the same role" (*DNV* 208).[67] In speaking of their "same solitude," Pasternak was referring to their isolation in their respective milieus—Pasternak in Soviet Russia, Tsvetaeva in exile. But Tsvetaeva made different use of the notion of solitude in her May letters, weaving it into her mythology of the poet. Even before the events of 1926, Tsvetaeva was citing Rilke to assert the poets' isolation from the rest of humanity: "Und sind ihr ganzes Leben so allein" (4:18).[68] Rilke's "rejection" confirmed for her the notion of the poet's essential solitude. He was inaccessible not because he was ill, the reason he gave in the unshared third letter, but because he was a genuine poet, as she explained to Pasternak: "That meeting was a great wound, a blow to the heart, yes. All the more so because he is right (it's not his coldness! it's the coldness of the guardian divinity in him!), because in my best, highest, strongest, most renunciatory hours—I am the same" (*DNV* 207). Pasternak disagreed with what he called Tsvetaeva's "theses on solitude and creativity," once again not so much with their substance as with their rigid formulation: "You expressed them almost like a lie" (*DNV* 225). He understood them "in a lighter, more lifelike way," resisting what he perceived to be criticisms of Rilke. Having been reassured of Rilke's goodwill by his letters to Tsvetaeva, however, he felt "no need to go on about this anymore," and released her from any obligation to share Rilke's letters or even keep him informed about their exchange. As it happened, by the time he wrote this letter on June 10, Tsvetaeva had already revived her correspondence with Rilke, as she told him. She also, in what must have been a stunning piece of news for Pasternak, promised to send along "Rilke's elegy (to me)" (*DNV* 237).

Given Pasternak's concern with history, it is not surprising that he would resist the notion of the poet's essential isolation. Although, as he said in March, his historicism was "blown to pieces" by the impact of Rilke and Tsvetaeva, he persisted in his effort to bring together lyricism and history. But he now conceived of his new writing as contingent on his relations with the two poets who most powerfully exemplified lyricism; he urgently needed lyricism to sponsor his historical poems. For Pasternak, there was no question of visiting Rilke, or even communicating with him, until he had new work to show him.[69] This was how he described to Tsvetaeva the work he would complete before meeting her and Rilke in 1927: "This year is the measure, I will observe it. I'm talking *only* about work and preparation, about continuing my efforts directed at *returning* to history a generation that apparently has disappeared from it, and *to which you and I belong*" (*DNV* 188). That generation, he said in another letter, grew up with an art that was "socialist" (*DNV* 181). He also sent Tsvetaeva a poem he had written to her, along with his requiem for Larissa Reisner, a Bolshevik and Civil War hero whom Pasternak described as "the first and probably unique woman of the revolution" (*DNV* 176).[70] Tsvetaeva pointedly replied that in that case she, Tsvetaeva, "was—certainly—the first and unique exact opposite," and asked him not to write any more such poems to her (*DNV* 183). Nevertheless, he continued to involve Tsvetaeva in his ongoing work. After finishing part one of "Lieutenant Schmidt" he dedicated it to her in a fifteen-line poem containing the acrostic "To Marina Tsvetaeva" (Marine Tsvetaevoi).

After the episode with Rilke, Pasternak was more ready to remark their creative differences.[71] An occasion was supplied by Pasternak's receipt in early June of Tsvetaeva's long poem "The Pied Piper" ("Krysolov," 1925).[72] His first reply was that he needed time to respond "maturely and accurately" to the poem, possibly a month, since he was busy making preparations for Evgenia's and Evgeny's trip abroad. At the same time, he noted "frequent coincidences" between "The Pied Piper" and part one of "Lieutenant Schmidt," as well as the poems of his 1916 collection *Above the Barriers;* he considered sending these texts "on the condition that you won't say a word about them until I renew my human conversation with you" (*DNV* 222). Two days later he continued his letter in a burst of anxiety: "The coincidences of vocabulary and manner are such that I'm going to send what I proposed after all, so it won't seem like I wrote Schmidt and Barriers under the influence of The Pied Piper" (*DNV* 222). Earlier Pasternak had easily acknowledged the influence of "Poem of the End" on "Lieutenant Schmidt" (*DNV* 197). Clearly, though, he was uncomfortable about the resemblances between his poem and Tsvetaeva's "Pied Piper."

Pasternak's fear that Tsvetaeva's poem, published in 1925, could be perceived as influencing *Above the Barriers,* published in 1916, seems strange, though perhaps less so if one recalls that his first two books of poems were virtually unknown to readers of the 1920s.[73] In any case, what is noteworthy is Pasternak's impulse both to claim and to reject *Above the Barriers,* which he did in this letter to Tsvetaeva, and again later when he thoroughly revised it for a second edition.[74] *Above the Barriers* features his most experimental poetics, a poetics I have described as sharing many features with hysterical discourse. In his letter to Tsvetaeva, he lamented his "impermissible treatment of the word" and "terrible technical helplessness in the face of an internal pressure that is probably greater than in any of my other books" (*DNV* 223). *Above the Barriers,* he concluded, was wrongly considered by many to be his best book of poems, a mistake he compares to "the error of your creative *philosophy* as it surfaced in your last letters." Indeed, Pasternak's evaluation of his own early poems is polemically directed against Tsvetaeva; after all, he sent her the book because of "coincidences" with "The Pied Piper." He manages thereby to suggest that her mature poetics are those of Pasternak's immature youth, of which he takes a critical view.

What, then, of the similarities between his "Lieutenant Schmidt" and "The Pied Piper," which were the more immediate source of Pasternak's anxieties? The gap between his past and present writing was not so well defined, as he himself confessed: "As soon as one starts talking about it ['The Pied Piper'], you slip into talking about poetry in general; as soon as one starts talking about you, one's own regrets arise: the forces you set into play in this work are terribly familiar to me, and especially in the past. If I had not read 'The Pied Piper,' I would have been more sanguine in my compromised and already natural path" (*DNV* 232). The challenge of confronting Tsvetaeva's poem at this moment in his career is apparent from the labored, conscientious discussion of "The Pied Piper" he wrote over the next month, filling two long letters, which he self-mockingly compared to the work of Soviet literary scholars. What is at stake, again, is Pasternak's turn from lyricism ("the forces you set into play") to history ("my compromised and already natural path"). His commentary on "The Pied Piper," accordingly, focuses on the nature of its lyricism. Here for the first time Pasternak justifies his historical project by expressing a critical view of lyricism, or at least a particular brand of lyricism, rather than arguing that lyricism is culturally extinct.

Tsvetaeva's poem, which she labeled a "lyrical satire," is based on the familiar legend. It is a deeply felt diatribe against bourgeois society, fueled partly by her experience as an impoverished émigré. Hamelin, represented as a bourgeois paradise, is invaded by a starving army of Bolshevik rats. Once they achieve victory, the revolutionaries themselves decline into bourgeois complacency. The Pied Piper lures them out of Hamelin with visions of new revolutionary exploits and drowns them in a lake, thus saving them from further self-compromise. When the town refuses to compensate him, he leads his promised bride and Hamelin's children to their death, again cast as a fate far better than embourgeoisement. As Pasternak remarked, the two drowning scenes are the poem's focal points; they dramatize the frightening power of a lyricism that rejects this world. As Pasternak also remarked, the children's drowning scene, rendered in painfully realistic detail, "is a cruel and terrifying chapter" (*DNV* 248).

Pasternak began his first letter about "The Pied Piper" by declaring that he would refer to "A Sublime Malady," which he also appended (*DNV* 229).[75] He did not, in the end, talk about his poem, but it is clear why it came to mind. Both poems represent lyricism as an ideal toward which the revolution strives, and both shape this argument by appealing to Blok's representation of the revolution as an elemental phenomenon. Tsvetaeva's poem draws directly on Blok's poem "The Twelve" for chapter 4, in which the Piper leads the Bolshevik rats out of Hamelin. In this chapter, Tsvetaeva restages the march of the twelve while inverting its conclusion. Instead of Christ, it is the demonic Pied Piper who leads the revolutionaries, who go not to resurrection but to death. Tsvetaeva's rewriting affirms Blok's revolutionary romanticism, but in a paradoxical fashion: she insists on absolute commitment to his vision, the price of which is the loss of this world. The one figure who can sustain this commitment and survive is the Pied Piper, which is to say, the poet of the elemental.[76] By contrast, in "A Sublime Malady," Pasternak regrets Blok's acceptance of "elemental" revolutionary violence.

Pasternak's ambivalent response to "The Pied Piper" was essentially a response to Tsvetaeva's apotheosis of elemental lyricism. In his customary manner, he expressed that response indirectly. Pasternak focuses on the poem's formal properties; indeed, it is his argument that these are so powerfully employed that they destroy the poem's compositional unity. He understands, however, that this "imbalance" in the work is not like the "technical helplessness" of his early verse but a unique poetic achievement; Tsvetaeva has realized to perfection what he was attempting as a young poet. Her focus on "the physical side of speech" leads Pasternak to compare "The Pied Piper" to the futurists' "trans-sense" verse, but with an essential caveat: Tsvetaeva's is "the noblest form of *zaum*, that form which is contained in poetry through the ages" (*DNV* 233). Specifically, and idiosyncratically, Pasternak traces her form of *zaum* to Lermontov, to his "sound that is material to the point of nonsense." In this variety of *zaum*, form is generative; by analogy to the Pied Piper's song, it magically creates content. Such form operates as "movement," which is why Pasternak speaks of the phenomenon as Tsvetaeva's "poetic physics," and why he traces all of the poem's effects to its extraordinary rhythmic composition. Tsvetaeva is "a Wagnerian," whose rhythms build toward "frenzy" (osatanenie) and "possession" (oderzhimost'); their energy is so intense that they become "almost physical." Having been called into being, the rhythms then "begin to form *lyric judgments*," by which Pasternak means the poem's satiric thrust. In Pasternak's rendering, it is as though Tsvetaeva has called forth spirits who pronounce sentence on the contemporary world. More precisely, she has called forth lyricism itself, a lyricism that is musical, elemental, and demonic, a spirit of negation. With "The Pied Piper," Tsvetaeva has crafted verse (*stikhi*) that rhymes with the elemental (*stikhiia*), to quote Pasternak's line about Pushkin in "Themes and Variations" ("Stikhiia svobodnoi stikhii / S svobodnoi stikhiei stikha").

Although Pasternak begins his discussion of "The Pied Piper" by criticizing the absolute dominance of its formal energies, by the time he addresses the final chapter he is entirely swept away by them, and his critique becomes a declaration of love: "How I love you! How powerfully and for so long!" (*DNV* 248). Pasternak, that is, succumbs to the seduction of Tsvetaeva's lyricism, just as the children of Hamelin follow the Pied Piper. It is a seduction that is "fatal" for his own writing: "How precisely *because of that*, because of the nature of *that* passion, I am slow and unsuccessful and the way I am." As Pasternak labored over his reading of Tsvetaeva's poem, he continued to work on "Lieutenant Schmidt," and as he noted, there are "frequent coincidences" between the two works. Most obviously, though Pasternak did not comment on the fact, Tsvetaeva's poem also treats the subject of the revolution. It was indeed a coincidence and not a poetic dialogue: Tsvetaeva wrote "The Pied Piper" in early 1925 during the hiatus in their correspondence, at around the time Pasternak began his long poems about 1905. Pasternak must have been taken by surprise, since Tsvetaeva did not typically take contemporary history as a poetic subject.[77] In any case, he was confronted with Tsvetaeva's "lyrical judgment" about the revolution at the very time he was attempting to forge an appropriate poetic form for that event, one that placed it in historical perspective.

The two poets' very different statements about the revolution are highlighted by their use of strikingly similar poetic techniques—yet further coincidences between "Lieutenant Schmidt" and "The Pied Piper." Both poems are polymetrical, meaning that they employ a variety of shifting metrical patterns, and both are "polyphonic," that is, they weave other voices into the lyric narrative. (These features, not coincidentally, were showcased together in Blok's "The Twelve.") In her earlier fairy-tale poems Tsvetaeva had worked these two features into a dynamic narrative style that was fully realized in "The Pied Piper." Pasternak, however, was employing them in a long composition for the first time. A number of the poems from *Above the Barriers* were polymetrical, but he had written few since then, and his long poems were in classical meters.[78] ("A Sublime Malady" is written in iambic tetrameter, *Spektorsky* in iambic pentameter, and "1905" is anapestic.) Pasternak spoke to Tsvetaeva about his effort to break out of "ennui and arrhythmia" in a letter he wrote just before receiving "The Pied Piper": "Spektorsky is decisively bad. But I don't regret that with it and 1905, with the exception of two or three recent chapters of Schmidt, I crawled into such ennui and arrhythmia. I'll eat through that obstacle. And it's necessary: because it's in the nature of circumstances and inescapable and also because in the future it will free rhythm from being grafted onto inherited content. But such things you can't say in two words. You'll misunderstand me and decide that I'm dreaming about free verse, about the rhythmic casing? Oh, never, just the opposite. I'm talking about rhythm that carries the word for nine months" (*DNV* 210–11). Here Pasternak covets the power of the poet–mother, using the infant as a metaphor for an entirely new and organically evolved relation between form and content. But for Pasternak to give birth to such poetry, he must "free rhythm," which is what he was attempting with the polymetrism of "Lieutenant Schmidt." As Mikhail Gasparov has demonstrated, with "Lieutenant Schmidt," Pasternak deliberately returned to the avant-garde prosody of *Above the Barriers* in making the transition to his late, more simplified poetics.[79] What has not been sufficiently appreciated is how important a catalyst Tsvetaeva was in that process.

Pasternak's attempt to "free rhythm" produced shifting patterns that seem disordered in comparison to the practiced orchestration of Tsvetaeva's "Pied Piper." The poem's rhythm and rhyme schemes, as Iury Levin's thorough analysis has shown, often devolve into "open patterns" that are highly unpredictable.[80] Levin has linked the extreme polymetrism of "Lieutenant Schmidt" to the poem's second distinctive feature, its polyphony. Pasternak, unlike Tsvetaeva, does not typically ventriloquize other voices in his poetry or prose, and "Lieutenant Schmidt" represents his only major attempt to do so. The technique has a singular purpose in "Lieutenant Schmidt": to allow history to speak. By "history" I mean the historical record that Pasternak painstakingly consulted to write this poem. Levin has demonstrated Pasternak's extensive use of primary sources, primarily Schmidt's correspondence and memoirs by his paramour Zinaida Rizberg, by Schmidt's sisters, and by several participants in the Ochakov rebellion and subsequent trial. Pasternak did not rely on them simply to produce an accurate account of how events unfolded; in fact, he actually placed episodes out of sequence.[81] Rather, he imported language from his documentary sources directly into the poem. His emphasis on reproducing these texts in the poem accounts for some of its metrical diversity. For example, the first instance of nonclassical meter appears in part one, chapter 5, where phrases from the "October 17 Manifesto" constitute almost a "prose insertion."[82] Pasternak's unusual choice to write a polymetrical poem was linked to his equally unusual choice to quote other voices directly and indirectly. His willingness to let content dictate prosody is markedly different from what he observed about Tsvetaeva's *zaum,* in which form magically calls into being new content.

In some instances, Pasternak handles other voices in a manner similar to Tsvetaeva. Tsvetaeva's and Pasternak's poems are essentially poems about kinds of language, which are represented even when not being spoken. Like the novel as described by Mikhail Bakhtin, these poems represent the world as a world of languages, in which entities are defined as and through speech. At a deeper level, though, the image of a language is created through "double-voiced discourse," in which "the author does not speak in a given language (from which he distances himself to a greater or lesser degree), but he speaks, as it were, through language, a language that has somehow more or less materialized, become objectified, that he merely ventriloquizes."[83] A language both Tsvetaeva and Pasternak ventriloquize in these poems is revolutionary rhetoric—the speech of the revolutionary rats in chapters 3 and 4 of "The Pied Piper," and the language of the October 17 manifesto in part one, chapter 5, of "Lieutenant Schmidt." Like Tsvetaeva, Pasternak creates intonational distance on that language, highlighting its commonness and artificiality. It is a point Pasternak's narrator also steps forward to make directly, when he compares an agitator's words to "dumplings / Of unthinkable words ending in 'ism,' / That don't sound like Russian and you've never heard in your life" (kletski / Nemyslimykh slov s okonchaniem na izm, / Nerusskykh na slukh i neslykhannykh v zhizni).

This is, however, the only example of satiric discourse in Pasternak's poem, while such discourse pervades Tsvetaeva's. "The Pied Piper" stages an irreconcilable conflict between the poet's language and the other languages represented in the poem.[84] With her scorching satire, she makes what Pasternak called a "lyrical judgment," distancing the voice of the lyric poet from the voices of the social world. In fact, in the fantasy enacted by the poem's allegory, the lyric voice effectively silences all other voices. By contrast, Pasternak does not strongly objectify the languages of "Lieutenant Schmidt," with the noted exception of revolutionary propaganda. The voice of the lyric narrator is penetrated by other voices in a manner that appears truly dialogical. Levin, at least, reads it that way, arguing that Pasternak subordinated his own voice to historical and political voices in an act of self-refusal.[85] As Levin himself points out, however, many of these voices already sound like Pasternak's own. For example, the mannered, kitschy style of Schmidt's paramour Zinaida Rizberg, bits of whose memoir are included in part three, is "not entirely alien to Pasternak's own lyrical speech."[86] It seems more accurate, then, to say that Pasternak's "polyphony" is an exploration of aspects of his own discourse and, as I will argue, of precisely those aspects marked as feminine. This dynamic is evident in

Pasternak's treatment of Schmidt, who is the hero of the poem and whose letters and speeches are reproduced more accurately and extensively than any other documentary source.

Schmidt was one of the heroes of 1905, an officer of the Russian Imperial Navy who led a mutiny in the Crimea. (The more famous mutiny occurred on the *Potemkin*, which Pasternak treated in "1905"). He gained national renown when he was arrested for making an inflammatory speech at the funeral of demonstrators killed by the police. He was soon released from prison, only to be called upon by a group of sailors to lead their rebellion. Convinced that they would fail without broader national action, he attempted to dissuade them. He nevertheless agreed to take command when they were attacked by the main fleet, which quickly prevailed. Schmidt and several other officers were arrested, tried, and executed. In Bolshevik historiography Schmidt would not be the revolutionary hero of choice, both because he was from the intelligentsia rather than the working class and because he did not align himself with any particular party, although he called himself a socialist.[87] These very facts made him attractive to Pasternak, whose project in his historical poems was to establish the revolution's debt to the intelligentsia.

Schmidt was a typical nineteenth-century Russian *intelligent,* whose commitment to social justice often found expression in extraordinary acts of self-sacrifice. The intelligentsia's political idealism reached an apogee with the populist "going to the people" (*khozhdenie v narod*), when thousands of students moved to the countryside to work with the peasantry as doctors and teachers. Schmidt seems to have been cast in that mold; Pasternak includes mention, in his fictional "Letter to His Sister" ("Pis'mo k sestre"), of Schmidt's attempt to quit the navy to work in a factory making farm implements. Pasternak emphasized that Schmidt's politics were driven by compassion for the suffering of others, and especially for violated womanhood: "Forever forged within that boy's heart / Is the tormented visage of a woman / In the hands of Barkov's followers" (Navek rebenku v serdtse vkovan / Oblityi mukoi oblik zhenshchiny / V rukakh poklonnikov Barkova). (Ivan Semenovich Barkov was an eighteenth-century man of letters who was famous for his obscene poetry). The language is Pasternak's, but the sentiment is properly ascribed to Schmidt on the basis of his letters, and indeed was typically expressed by the conscience-stricken and somewhat prudish intelligentsia.

Perhaps less typically, Schmidt's compassion for women's suffering was part of a thoroughgoing identification with femininity. He was apparently sensitive and emotionally volatile, a fact he celebrated in one of his letters to Rizberg: "I don't want to be normal. . . . In my psychopathologism I sense more truth . . . than in all logical schemes."[88] Schmidt cried and fainted in public on several occasions, once when the rebellion was defeated and again during his trial. Pasternak, who included both episodes in "Lieutenant Schmidt," clearly was interested in this aspect of Schmidt's character. In fact, in the poem generally,

Pasternak casts Schmidt as a male hysteric, not only in his behavior but also in his discourse, which is not unlike his own lyric discourse. In his research for the long poems, Pasternak discovered in the historical record of the revolution a type for his own heightened emotionalism. This, then, is how Pasternak reconciled lyricism and history in "Lieutenant Schmidt"—by shaping a portrait of the revolutionary hero as a hysteric. It is a remarkable portrait, especially within the intensely masculinized culture of the Soviet 1920s.[89]

The poem as a whole presents what would be culturally tagged a "girl's" version of revolutionary history by framing the events with a love story. A similar mix of romance and history was present in *My Sister Life* and would be repeated in *Doctor Zhivago,* whose plot features the same coincidental meetings. "Lieutenant Schmidt" opens at a racetrack, where, as we learn in the second chapter, a letter from Schmidt to Rizberg, they met, lost sight of each other, and met again on the train back to the city. The love story, though, is immediately interrupted by history. As Schmidt writes his love letter in the early hours of the morning, Nature catches sight of Schmidt and recognizes him as a "kindred spirit" (rodimyi dukh). In another of Pasternak's renderings of the muse's visitation, she enters his window and "for lack of someone better / She enlists him as a hero" (Za neimeniem luchshego / On ei v geroi prochitsia). Schmidt is thus cast as nature's choice, though he is unremarkable and preoccupied with his budding romance. Pasternak further dramatizes the conflict between the personal and the historical in a later scene where Schmidt, on the verge of leaving for Petersburg to visit Rizberg, is deflected by an urgent message from the sailors that fatefully draws him into the rebellion. As Pasternak described the plot to Tsvetaeva, the poem relates "the transformation of a man into a hero for a cause in which he does not believe, his breakdown, and death" (*DNV* 223).

Schmidt's "transformation into a hero" is reflected in his language, which we first hear in his letter to Rizberg in chapter 2. His language is excited and self-conscious, studded with interruptions ("But about that later, later" [A vprochem, posle, posle]) and exclamations ("what room for faith!" [kakoe zdes' / Razdol'e vere!]). In the next chapter, the narrator describes Schmidt's work on the letter, as he cycles between "writing silliness" (pishet gluposti), trying to sleep, and splashing water on his face: "A wave of hysteria finds him / And again he's under the faucet" (Naidet volna klikushestva, / On syznova pod kran). The word Pasternak chooses for "hysteria" is not the Latin-derived *isterika* but the native Russian term *klikushestvo,* a term from peasant culture that describes extreme displays of affect in women. The narrator, that is, directly characterizes Schmidt's behavior as feminine. Pasternak's character Schmidt describes his own language as so excessive that he becomes frightening:

> My talkativeness
> Is noticeably growing.
> I'm afraid that my jabbering

> Might frighten you,
> And you'll stay silent, elusive woman,
> While I chatter myself out.

> Моя словоохотливость
> Заметно возрастет.
> Боюсь, не отпугнет ли вас
> Тогда моя болтливость,
> Вы отмолчитесь, скрытчица,
> Я ж выболтаюсь вдрызг.

Although Schmidt apologizes to Rizberg for his excessive verbiage, he goes on to say that it is no sign of "immaturity" (rebiachestvo) but conditioned by his situation: he urgently needs to see her before they are swallowed up by the unfolding political events. In *My Sister Life,* such language needed no justification but was the natural discourse of the poet in love as he addressed a similarly reticent beloved.

In the initial version of "Lieutenant Schmidt," the one Pasternak sent to Tsvetaeva, Schmidt's voice sounds again in two more letters to Rizberg that hew closely to the original documents. The title of the second of these, "A Masculine Letter" ("Muzhskoe pis'mo"), addresses the matter of how Schmidt's discourse is gendered. Written in the wake of his speech at the funeral of demonstrators killed by the police, the letter shows him in a mood of ecstatic self-congratulation, using his new fame to impress his girlfriend, as it were. He is uncharacteristically self-assertive, stepping confidently into the role of hero and lover: "And now I bravely confess / I love you, my very life!" (I teper', priznaius' smelo, / Ia liubliu vas, zhizn' moia!). Yet his masculine posture is undermined by his language, which has the same unstable urgency, repetitiveness, and exclamatory quality as before. Pasternak deliberately allows Schmidt's voice to sound like a hysterical voice.

Schmidt's "letters" stand in interesting contrast to Pasternak's representation of another verbal performance, the famous speech Schmidt gave at the funeral. Given Pasternak's reliance on the documents to write Schmidt's letters, it is noteworthy that he chose not to reproduce the speech. Although he does quote a few phrases, we do not hear the speech itself but hear it described in chapter 4, "The Elements" ("Stikhiia"). The title announces the character of Schmidt's performance, in which nature itself has a part:

> O whirlwind, tearing the phrases
> Like maples and elms! O wind,
> Sparing, of all connectors in the world,
> Only exclamations!
> You carry across the seething surface:
> "For memory's sake and the sake of future generations
> Not a step backward! Take this oath!"
> "We take it. Not a step!"

О вихрь, обрывающий фразы,
Как клены и вязы! О ветер,
Щадящий из связей на свете
Одни междометья!
Ты носишь бушующей гладью:
«Потомства и памяти ради
Ни пяди обратно! Клянитесь!»
«Клянемся. Ни пяди!»

This is recognizably Schmidt's exclamatory style, endorsed here as "natural." But though nature carries Schmidt's speech to his audience—the "seething surface"—it does so in fragments. Nature has shredded his language to the point where its content is virtually erased, "only exclamations" (odni mezhdometiia). Pasternak thus suggests that truly elemental, revolutionary speech is pure emotional sound. In a later scene, Pasternak describes another revolutionary oration, probably also given by Schmidt, that reaches the crowd beyond words (part two, chapter 1):

Their ecstasy wants to live and breathes
Not in words—but in their total loss.
It is a reckoning of giants.
He and the crowd get by without words.

Не словами,—полной их утратой
Хочет жить и дышит их восторг.
Зто объясненье исполинов.
Он и двор обходятся без слов.

Pasternak also "gets by without words" in these scenes, eschewing the documentary sources he so heavily relies on elsewhere in the poem. As he was aware, Schmidt's actual language could not plausibly achieve the kind of elemental power Pasternak wished to render here.[90] Rather than using Schmidt's words, Pasternak instead represents a kinship between Schmidt's hysteria and the high emotion of genuine revolutionary oratory.

Pasternak does, however, reproduce Schmidt's speech at his sentencing, and in more detail than any other source. This scene appears near the end of the poem, which Pasternak devotes to exposing the horror of the death penalty. The first lyrical argument against the death penalty appears in chapter 6, which describes nature grown unnatural at the prospect of an execution. (The weather grotesquely mixes different seasons into "a spiritual slop / of conceptions and agonies" [dushevnaia burda / Iz zachatii i agonii].) The next chapter describes the analogously disordered emotional state of the crowd that hears the lengthy sentence read out: "Faints, shouts, and fits of spasms. / It's read, and read, and read despite / The vertigo" (Obmoroki, kriki, skhvatki spasm / Chten'e, chten'e, chten'e, nesmotria na / Golovokruzhen'e). It is as though the crowd has taken over Schmidt's affect, as it did in the earlier speech scene.[91] Schmidt

himself, however, is uncharacteristically calm, as was the historical Schmidt.[92]
The eleven-stanza speech he pronounces after hearing his sentence ends with
this declaration:

> Placed at the edge of the abyss
> By the blind power of the law,
> I will feel no timidity,
> And my spirit will be unruffled.
>
> I know that the scaffold before which
> I will stand will be the boundary
> Between two different historical epochs,
> And I am glad of my election.
>
> Поставленный у пропасти
> Слепою властью буквы,
> Я не узнаю робости,
> И не смутится дух мой.
>
> Я знаю, что столб, у которого
> Я стану, будет гранью
> Двух разных эпох истории,
> И радуюсь избранью.

Schmidt's composure is reflected in the simple iambic trimeter, unusual in the
context of this poem. The meter is regularly observed throughout the speech,
except in the final stanza, which includes two lines of *dol'nik*. As Levin has
shown, in these lines Pasternak was following the rhythm of Schmidt's language, which he quotes verbatim here,[93] but the brief disruption may also serve
to convey a slight wavering of Schmidt's resolve. Largely, however, he appears
for the first time as a creature of will, as someone who now chooses what was
thrust upon him ("I was singled out from the ranks / By a wave of the elements
themselves" [Ia byl iz riada vydelen / Volnoi samoi stikhii]). Schmidt's transformation into a hero is now complete.

Schmidt's heroism is explicitly modeled on Christ's acceptance of the path or-
dained for him, in a kind of self-fashioning typical of the Russian populists.[94]
He speaks of his death sentence as a "Golgotha" and forgives his executioners
as "martyrs to dogma" (mucheniki dogmata). He also claims a part in usher-
ing in a new era for mankind; he stands at "the boundary of two different historical epochs." Schmidt's view of his historical role, however, is framed by the
theory of history Pasternak puts forward in a single authorial digression at the
end of part one, chapter 6:

> And eternally the step is taken
> From the Roman circuses to the Roman church,
> And we live by that same measure,
> We people of the catacombs and mines.

И вечно делается шаг
От римских цирков к римской церкви,
И мы живем по той же мерки,
Мы, люди катакомб и шахт.

Pasternak makes the birth of Christianity the model for all progressive histori-cal change, including the revolution. The revolution takes "the step" from em-pire to Christianity, from the rule of violence to faith, from slavery to freedom. But that step is "eternally taken," that is, never actually made, and Russia re-mains in the same historical limbo described at the beginning of "A Sublime Malady." As Pasternak interpreted the passage for Tsvetaeva, "one might think, looking at history, that idealism exists mostly so that it might be denied" (*DNV* 197).[95]

In fact, Pasternak leaves us with the impression not of Schmidt's courage but of the horror of his death. The final chapter describes the early morning arrival of a gunboat to take the two condemned officers from the prison boat to the place of execution. (Pointedly, Schmidt is no longer named, his identity oblit-erated by the death sentence.) After the clear iambs of Schmidt's speech, we are returned to the lyric narrator's irregular rhythms, here a trochaic meter in dif-ferent variations.[96] The contrast accompanies a marked change in affect, from Schmidt's calm to a general mood of anxiety. The action is nightmarish: the ships appear like monstrous creatures, as does the searchlight that crawls to-ward the hatch of the prisoners' cell and penetrates it "with a hiss"; the con-demned men throw themselves at the bars and are "impaled" on the light. When they are led away, their comrades' sobbing rises to such a volume that it "ex-tinguishes" the searchlight. The poem ends there, and we are left plunged in the prisoners' dark emotion.

The contrast at the poem's end between Schmidt's performance and the lyric narrator's returns us to the question of Pasternak's use of other voices in "Lieu-tenant Schmidt." Pasternak mostly worked to minimize stylistic differences between Schmidt's letters and speeches and his own lyric discourse.[97] Even without access to the source texts, the reader registers the kinship of these two voices, both of which speak with heightened pathos, however differently they achieve this effect. In Pasternak's lyric writing it is crafted through avant-garde prosody and figuration, while Schmidt, as scrupulously quoted by Pasternak, reaches for rhetorical clichés. But clearly Pasternak was alert to and fore-grounded their similar temperaments and discourses. He found in the histori-cal record a revolutionary hero who shared his passions and anxieties. Through him Pasternak described his own vision of heroism, rendering Schmidt's "trans-formation into a hero" as the shift from hysterical language to composed language.

Thus far, Pasternak's identification with Schmidt has been traced in the poem's discourse. But it is also attested to by a crucial topos. When Schmidt is chosen by Nature as her hero, she enters through the window as Schmidt is writ-ing at his desk. This is the classic scene of the poet's visitation by the muse, a scene Pasternak obsessively returns to in his writing. He even suggests that Nature seduces Schmidt: "Is it known how amorous / The homeless expanse is?" (Izvestno li, kak vliubchivo / Bezdomnoe prostranstvo?). This early scene, however, has a horrifying rhyme in the final chapter, when the searchlight penetrates the prisoners' cell, and the scene of inspiration becomes a scene of rape and murder. Although we understand that the perpetrator of violence is the state, it is not mentioned in the text. Rather, there is a complicity, or at least confusion, of nature and the state in the narrator's rhetorical figures (ships are beasts), as well as in the poem's general argument: nature selected Schmidt for the path that would end in his death at the hands of the state. Just as in "A Sublime Malady," Pasternak's insistence on regarding the revolution as a natural phenomenon comes up against its "elemental" violence. This conundrum informs Pasternak's ambivalent representation of nature as a threat as well as an inspiration. The muse, as she has been transformed in the course of postrevolutionary history, is to be feared as well as loved—hence Pasternak's regard for Schmidt as someone able to manage his terror.

Pasternak expressed a more optimistic view of the poet's relation to history in the dedication he wrote to Tsvetaeva in May after finishing part one of "Lieutenant Schmidt." The fifteen-line poem contained an acrostic of "To Marina Tsvetaeva" in the first letter of each line. When he sent the poem to her, Pasternak explained that it expressed his understanding "of the hero, of being fated to history, of passage through nature,—of my devotion to you" (*DNV* 201). The poem sets up a contrast between the disruptive hunt being prosecuted by the epoch (which I take to be the speaker quoted at the beginning) and the dreamlike forest in which it takes place:

> A flash of arms and legs, and after him:
> "Chase him through the dark of the ages! Bellow
> Louder horns! Halloo! Or else I'll quit
> The chase and plunge into the dream of boughs."
>
> But the horn ruins the dank beauty
> Of years as natural as forest leaves.
> Peace reigns, and every stump's a Saturn:
> Age revolving, circular trace.
>
> He should float off on verse into the dark of the ages:
> Such treasures lie in tree hollows, and in the mouth.
> This way, you drag him from lair to lair halloo,
> His moan's as natural as forest leaves.
>
> Epoch, why no desire for the hunt?
> Give reply with leaves, and stumps, and dream of boughs,
> And wind and grass to me and her.

Мельканье рук и ног и вслед ему:
«Ату его сквозь тьму времен! Резвей
Реви рога! Ату! А то возьму
И брошу гон и ринусь в сон ветвей».

Но рог крушит сырую красоту
Естественных, как листья леса, лет.
Царит покой, и что ни пень—Сатурн:
Вращающийся возраст, круглый след.

Ему б уплыть стихом во тьму времен.
Такие клады в дуплах и во рту.
А тут носи из лога в лог ату,
Естественный, как листья леса, стон.

Век, отчего травить охоты нет?
Ответь листвой, пнями, сном ветвей
И ветром и травою мне и ей.

In contrast to the action of the hunt, time in this environment is nonlinear, following the circular pattern inscribed in nature (the tree stump). It is the temporality of lyricism, which speaks as nature speaks ("Such treasures lie in tree hollows, and in the mouth"). But the poem's ending projects a rapprochement between lyricism and "the epoch," whose pursuit of the hero, after all, is diffident; it has no desire for the hunt. (Pasternak puns on the word *okhota*, which means both "desire" and "hunt"). It remains possible that the epoch may yet answer the poet in the poet's natural idiom, shared by "me and her."[98] In this hopeful scenario, both nature and postrevolutionary history are essentially benign, though not yet quite in synchrony.[99] There is no place in this dream for the violence of the elemental, in contrast to the story about Schmidt's destruction.

Pasternak wrote the dedication before reading "The Pied Piper," with its apotheosis of elemental lyricism. As he described it in his letters, the formal dynamism of Tsvetaeva's poem reminded him of his own poems in *Above the Barriers*. Tsvetaeva herself confirmed the resemblance by writing to praise one of these poems, "The Blizzard" ("Metel'," 1914),[100] whose incantatory power is like that of the Piper's song and similarly draws on Blok (*DNV* 193).[101] It may be that the display of lyrical force in "The Pied Piper" deepened Pasternak's doubts about his earlier work and confirmed him in his attempt to "give birth" to a new kind of lyricism. His ambivalence about elemental lyricism was perhaps also an ambivalence about the hysterical femininity he performed in his earlier lyrics. With his hero Schmidt, he imagined the possibility of speaking differently in the face of violence. Pasternak did not eschew femininity as such; Schmidt's heroism, modeled on Christ's, is a "feminine" heroism of submission to fate. But he wished to distance himself from hysteria both as a behavior and as a poetics, which involved distancing himself from Tsvetaeva's example.[102]

For her part, Tsvetaeva also felt a gap open up between them when she read part one of "Lieutenant Schmidt." (Likewise, she was baffled by his commentary on "The Pied Piper.") As Pasternak knew, Schmidt was one of her childhood heroes: on the questionnaire she filled out for him, she named Schmidt alongside Napoleon, of whom she made a lifelong cult.[103] Tsvetaeva's regard for the extraordinary individual, however, meant that Pasternak's all too human Schmidt was unrecognizable to her. In a strongly critical letter, she questioned Pasternak's attempt to recreate the historically actual Schmidt. The problem, in particular, was the use of Schmidt's letters, which she rightly suspected Pasternak had reproduced "almost verbatim" (*DNV* 239). It was Schmidt's discourse (slovesnost'), she said, that made it impossible to render him a hero. Tsvetaeva expressed herself more strongly in a series of later letters she probably did not send to Pasternak: "The Lieutenant Schmidt of your poem is deeply distasteful to me. He's a braggart, a chatterbox, a neurasthenic and a whiner" (*DNV* 269); "Schmidt moans. He slobbers. Schmidt is a whiner. Tears and mucus" (*DNV* 271). As these comments suggest, Tsvetaeva detected weakness in Schmidt's emotional style of expression, a weakness that made him ineligible for the hero's role. She advised Pasternak to include fewer letters in part two and to "let him grow more impressive before his death" (*DNV* 240).

Tsvetaeva, of course, was drawn to Pasternak precisely for the heightened emotionalism of his language. But her response to Pasternak's mingling of Schmidt's discourse and his own lyric discourse was to enforce the boundaries between them. Schmidt's language telegraphed to her weakness and vulnerability, while she perceived Pasternak's lyricism as suffused with energy, movement, and power, as she described them in "A Downpour of Light." In that essay she also registered Pasternak's "penetrability," which she no longer wished to see: "Why didn't you portray Schmidt of the 'hundred blinding photographs' that don't give you time to see what he is?" (*DNV* 239).[104] She did, however, still find traces of that powerful lyricism in "Lieutenant Schmidt" in the chapter titled "The Elemental" ("Stikhiia") ("Here large things are at work and not a small man" [*DNV* 239]). This is the chapter that renders Schmidt's speech at the funeral without his own words, precisely as Tsvetaeva wished: nature speaks for him, in a language that is "only exclamations!" (Odni mezhdomet'ia!). Pasternak's lyricism is marked here as elemental, as a force of nature, exactly as Tsvetaeva understood it to be. This true lyric discourse, she felt, must not be contaminated by the discourse of his hero. She therefore asked Pasternak to suppress his words: "I would like a *silent* Schmidt. A silent Schmidt and a speaking you" (*DNV* 240).

Tsvetaeva reiterated the difference between Pasternak and his hero with reference to Blok, recognizing that Pasternak was contending with Blok's legacy in his historical poems. She accused him of cultivating the wrong aspect of that legacy, that is, Blok's dutiful service to the revolution rather than his elemental lyricism: "Boris, I hate the intelligentsia, I don't consider myself part of it, so completely 'pince-nez.' I love the aristocracy and the people, the flower and the roots, Blok of the cloak and Blok of the expanses. Your Schmidt resembles Blok the *intelligent*. The same bad joke, the same lack of humor" (*DNV* 239). In distinguishing between the two Bloks, Tsvetaeva also neatly captured how differently the two poets responded to Blok in "Lieutenant Schmidt" and "The Pied Piper." Pasternak's hero, like Blok the *intelligent*, is the victim of an elemental force. Tsvetaeva's Pied Piper, like Blok the poet, wields an elemental lyricism. The two poems thus offer different imaginings of the poet's response to external threat, two different strategies for survival. Pasternak represents the poet's vulnerability, a condition he cannot change but may come to endure with calm. Tsvetaeva, by contrast, imagines the poet bearing the power of life and death. The contrast suggests that her dislike of Schmidt's "weakness" was a hysterical refusal of mortality, whether of Pasternak's or her own.

Pasternak answered Tsvetaeva's criticisms of "Lieutenant Schmidt" in a pained but resigned manner, saying that he agreed with her opinion "down to the smallest details" (*DNV* 257). It was "a great misfortune" to write badly, and even more painful to be "a parody of a human being and a parody of a lyric poet" (*DNV* 256–57). He asked Tsvetaeva's permission to remove the dedication so she would not be associated with such mediocrity.[105] Clearly, Tsvetaeva's criticism strongly activated his own self-criticism. Paradoxically, she thereby resolved his doubts about his historical poems: though he finished writing "Lieutenant Schmidt" and published it with "1905" as a book (titled *1905*), he no longer claimed that this work had any relation to genuine poetry. He followed Tsvetaeva's advice in his further work on "Lieutenant Schmidt," cutting Schmidt's letters from part one and allowing Schmidt to "grow more impressive before his death" in part three. As we have seen, however, Pasternak's version of heroism differed from Tsvetaeva's, and though she praised Schmidt's transformation, she continued to speak of him as "material for psychoanalysis" (*DNV* 349).

It was possibly Tsvetaeva's view of Schmidt's character that Pasternak registered most strongly. After all, she vehemently rejected a hero he had created as an alter ego. In fact, what is most striking about Pasternak's letter offering to withdraw the dedication is that its main subject was his own "weakness" and neuroses. It is as though he answered Tsvetaeva's attempt to separate Pasternak from his hero by saying, "but I am Schmidt." In an earlier letter, Pasternak had revealed his anxiety about spending the summer alone in Moscow after his wife and son left for Europe. In particular, he spoke about the torments of sexual temptation: "I'm afraid of freedom, I'm afraid of falling in love" (*DNV* 222). That remark set off a remarkably honest exchange about love and gender. Tsvetaeva, responding to Pasternak's confession and to her failure to share Rilke's letters with him, stated the paradoxical notion that one's love for each different person is absolute, a paradox she manages by claiming to be many people at once ("ich bin Viele") (*DNV* 238). Pasternak endorsed her idea, rephrasing it as the "momentary truth" of love. But whereas Tsvetaeva was talking about her love for Pasternak, Rilke, and her son, Pasternak expresses his longing to love all women, which he called "the loudest note in the universe"; he cannot understand, he says, how Adam's heart was constructed to make him love only one Eve (*DNV* 242). Pasternak had taken her thought in his own direction, and Tsvetaeva objected that his was not a universal leitmotif but a masculine one (muzhkoi leitmotiv), one she could not hear. If Pasternak could not understand Adam for loving only one woman, she could not understand Eve, for whom she expresses "Psyche's" contempt. Despite her objections, though, Tsvetaeva in the end conceded to Pasternak his masculine impulses, which she also linked to his Jewish blood. She advised him not to worry about his wife and son, and to "take everything you can—while you still want to take it!" (*DNV* 252–53).

At the same time Tsvetaeva was urging him to indulge his masculine nature, Pasternak wrote the dismayed letter about "Lieutenant Schmidt." Here he described himself not just as sexually obsessed but as in some way perverse: "I have some unhealthy inclinations that are paralyzed only by a lack of will. They are completely familiar to Freud, which I say for the sake of brevity, to indicate their type." These inclinations have to do with his professed femininity: "I have an abyss of feminine features. I know far too many aspects of what is called passivity" (*DNV* 257). Here for the first time Pasternak openly claimed his femininity before Tsvetaeva. She had discerned it in the poetry of *My Sister Life* and interpreted it in terms of her own hysterical femininity, her "phallic activity." But Pasternak's confession was more suggestive of Schmidt's "weakness," and there is no reason to believe that she would regard it any more sympathetically.

Pasternak's letter contained another statement that apparently troubled her more: "I need to tell you something about Zhenya [Evgenia]. I miss her terribly. Basically, I love her more than anything in the world" (*DNV* 258). For Tsvetaeva, the problem was not so much Pasternak's love for his wife as the changed nature of that love. Evgenia's absence from Moscow meant that she had replaced Tsvetaeva as Pasternak's romantic love: "Boris, there can be one woman here and another there, but both of them there, *two* 'there's,' is impossible and never happens" (*DNV* 259).[106] Pasternak had violated their arrangement, whereby he dallied with other women, lived with his wife, and had his "most legitimate" marriage with Tsvetaeva. She therefore asked him not to involve her anymore.

Pasternak obliged in his answering letter, declaring that they must stop writing to each other.[107] He did not envision a final break, saying that they were joined by "fate" and that he loves her "madly." He demanded her new address and said good-bye "until their full meeting" (*DNV* 260, 262). But at the moment he no longer wanted to engage with Tsvetaeva and begged her not to answer his letter but to let him have the last word. Without their correspondence, he said, he would experience his own version of Tsvetaeva's "soul meetings": "Once again, like this spring, with my spine, my temples and my whole right side I have felt the wafting of your presence beside me, the full hair-raising cold of your female Valkyrian nearness, the full pure slope of my tenderness toward your strength as it disappears into the distance" (*DNV* 263). Under pressure to articulate the differences that had brought the relationship into crisis, Pasternak distinguishes between two modes of femininity—his own "maidenly weakness," as he put it, and Tsvetaeva's terrifying Valkyrian force, which he can no longer safely confront. Pasternak's language reveals how much their attraction and tensions revolved around their different enactments of femininity.

Pasternak kept his word and stopped writing to Tsvetaeva, leaving her to ponder the meaning of his silence. In his last letter to her, he made a point of saying how much his friends in Lef admired her recent work, and that they wanted to reprint "Poem of the End" in their journal. Tsvetaeva protested that he and no one else was "My Russia, my Moscow" (*DNV* 268). Her letter documents her dawning realization that Pasternak's historical writing about the revolution truly was a complicated effort to endorse it. As she bluntly put it, "You are accepting a Communist Party card" and "you are leaving Russia and walking into letters [USSR] from which you will never return" (*DNV* 267). In response Tsvetaeva drew for him a clear line between poetry and socialism, a line she would not cross. In her effort to pull Pasternak back across that line, she wrote several more letters elaborating her critique of "Lieutenant Schmidt." She also sent him a copy of Rilke's elegy as a seal of her poetic authority and a reminder of what they shared. Pasternak answered none of these letters. Nevertheless, the blow of losing of Pasternak was cushioned, for a while at least, by her ongoing correspondence with Rilke.

5

The End of the End (1926–1935)

> With Boris this wouldn't be a double bed but the soul.
> I would simply sleep in the soul.
> —Tsvetaeva, letter to Pasternak
> (April 5, 1926)

> You are alone. . . . / And loneliness—is rococo.
> —Pasternak, *Spektorsky*

Tsvetaeva's correspondence with Pasternak in 1926 coincided with a new phase of her life in emigration. Not long after her triumphant arrival in Paris at the end of 1925, she was embroiled in a literary scandal that set the tone for the next fourteen years she spent in France. In April 1926 she published an essay, "The Poet on the Critic" ("Poet o kritike," 1926), in which she read a harsh lecture to émigré reviewers for their low cultural level and political prejudices, naming such eminences as Zinaida Gippius and Ivan Bunin and supplying a "bouquet" (tsvetnik) of exemplary quotations from the reviews of Georgy Adamovich. She also named one admirable exception, the literary scholar and critic Dmitry Sviatopolk-Mirsky. Mirsky, who had emigrated to England and become the main authority on Russian literature for the English audience, was as immoderate as Tsvetaeva in his attacks on émigré literary culture. He also strongly championed the writings of Pasternak and Tsvetaeva, whom he considered Russia's greatest living poets. Mirsky sought out Tsvetaeva when she came to Paris and arranged a reading for her in London in March.[1] He also joined forces with Tsvetaeva, Efron, and the music critic Piotr Suvchinsky to establish a journal to their own tastes and standards.

The journal was named *Milestones,* after Tsvetaeva's lyric collection. (Mirsky wanted to name it *The Pied Piper.*) The first number, which appeared in July 1926, featured Tsvetaeva's "Poem of the Hill" ("Poema gory," 1923) and the section "Rebellion at Sea" ("Morskoi miatezh") from Pasternak's "1905." The poets' photographs appeared together on the same page, as Tsvetaeva proudly wrote to Pasternak (*DNV* 255). Two more numbers of the journal would appear, but it was attacked on political grounds for its sympathetic treatment of "Soviet" writers such as Pasternak.[2] These attacks were unjustified and probably helped push Mirsky and Efron toward an increasingly pro-Soviet stance, not only culturally but politically as well. As a result, Tsvetaeva and her family were gradually ostracized by mainstream émigré society. In these circumstances, her link with Pasternak was all the more precious, but also more implicated in her evolving situation in émigré Russia. When they renewed their correspondence at the beginning of 1927, it centered on questions of poetry and politics.

While Pasternak stopped writing to her in July 1926, Tsvetaeva was still corresponding with Rilke. In the poems she wrote that summer, Tsvetaeva had already shifted her address from Pasternak to Rilke, from one male genius to another who was, in her eyes, even greater.[3] From mid-1926 to mid-1927, Tsvetaeva wrote a remarkable series of long lyric poems about encounters with the male genius. The theme of the "meeting," or more precisely the "missed meeting" (razminovenie), was the subject of many of her poems to Pasternak, most notably the poems of "Telegraph Wires." But if "Telegraph Wires" dramatizes the tragic thwarting of desire, these long poems, while premised on the same impossibility, resolutely ignore it, pressing language even harder to do what it cannot. These new long poems are structured as meetings accomplished within the space of the text, and this act of willing yielded the most powerful lyric writing of her career.

Tsvetaeva wrote the first of these poems to Pasternak in May, before the rift that took place at the end of July. The title, "From the Sea" ("S moria," 1926), refers to her location in St.-Gilles on the southern Atlantic coast of France, where she had gone with her family for the summer. (A full translation of "From the Sea" may be found in the Appendix.) In several long letters to Pasternak written at the same time, she describes her intense isolation and corresponding immersion in her "life with him": "So I live with you, mornings and nights, getting up into you, going to bed into you" (*DNV* 218). The bed, in fact, is where her encounter with Pasternak takes place in "From the Sea." The poem's conceit is that the two poets appear to each other in their dreams, a favorite notion of Tsvetaeva's, and one already featured in "Telegraph Wires" ("Though we're apart, no matter: all / Separations close in dreams. / Perhaps we'll see each other in a dream" [Khot' vroz', a vse zh sdaetsia: vse / Razroznennosti svodit son. / Avos' uvidimsia vo sne]).[4] The poem's opening stanzas have Tsvetaeva carried by the wind from St.-Gilles to Moscow, where she "jumps into" Pasternak's dream. She is dressed "in traveling clothes"—dressed, that is, as she was in Pasternak's dream about their meeting in an "immaculate" hotel.

Tsvetaeva carefully sustains the fiction of actual communication, down to noting the exact duration of her connection with Pasternak: she has only three minutes to speak, and she marks their passing ("Just a minute left for packing!" [Tol'ko minutu eshche na sbory]). The whole of this "mutual dream" (vzaimnyi son) will last six minutes, allowing, as she explicitly does, for Pasternak's response: "Each one gets three minutes— / So, six (a mutual dream)" (Kazh-domu po tri— / Shest' [son vzaimnyi]). Tsvetaeva, however, makes no attempt to represent Pasternak's side of the conversation, thus acknowledging that the dream's "mutuality"—its efficacy as a medium of communication—is a fiction.[5] In fact, she directly acknowledges the fantastic nature of the event in the opening stanza, when she arrives "by the North-South wind, / Impossible, I know!" (S Severo-Iuzhnym, / Znaiu: nemozhnym!). Yet she will proceed by sheer force of necessity: such a wind is "possible—if needed!" (Mozhnym— kol' nuzhnym!). Her wish to see Pasternak is simply that, a wish, and the poem fulfills it in the manner of a dream, through symbolic enactment.[6] Unlike a dream, however, the poem realizes a conscious wish. It is a willed, intentional act, as Tsvetaeva actually characterized her own dreams: "I don't have a dream, I dream it" (Mne son ne snitsia / Ia ego sniu).[7] Her notion might be character-ized as pre-Freudian, but it is probably better understood as counter-Freudian, as an effort not to unveil but to harness and control the unconscious. Hélène Cixous suggests something similar when she says about Tsvetaeva's writing: "The unconscious is at work, but so is the poet. A great multiplicity of signs, always very organized, prevails. She might be close to Genet's writings. In Tsve-taeva, there is so much work on language that it has the effect of a screen."[8] Tsvetaeva exercises her writerly agency with palpable force, simultaneously ex-posing and encoding psychological material in a kind of protective self-diag-nosis.[9] Her agency, however, remains confined to the text. As she formulated the problem in her essay on Pasternak, the poet's agency compensates for his passivity in life: "And because you perform no acts—all the mad action in your poems: nothing stays put" (*DNV* 40).

"From the Sea," more explicitly than any text considered thus far, deliber-ately rehearses a primary psychological dynamic: the creation of a self through language in relation to another. "Instead of a letter," as the poem's title origi-nally read (Vmesto pis'ma), she is sending herself: "Word of honor / It's me, not a letter!" (Chestnoe slovo / Ia, ne pis'mo!). In the early part of the poem, being is a matter of being seen: she is more visible in the dream than "under a postmark" (Za reshetkoi / Shtempel'noi). But when she instructs him on how to discern her face, her features have the aspect of a text. Her lips take the shape of the Russian character *iat'*, which Tsvetaeva, relying on a false etymological link to the first-person pronoun *ia*, uses as a sign for the authentic, individual self. (It is also an outlaw self; the letter *iat'* was eliminated by Soviet ortho-graphic reforms.) The self conveyed is, moreover, a perfect self: "Me—without a misspelling. / Me—without a blot" (Ia—bez opiski, / Ia—bez pomarki). The isomorphism among the poem, the dream, and the self is beautifully rendered in the way "From the Sea" concludes with a view of her face "fading out" at the end of her three-minute dream connection: "A nose, you thought? A promontory! / Eyebrows? No, rainbows, / Exoduses from— // Seen-ness" (Nos, dumal? Mys! / Brovi? Net, dugi, / Vykhody iz— // Zrimosti).

In a process that unfolds along with the poem, she composes herself from fragments—shells, stones, and other detritus washed ashore at St.-Gilles. She gathers them, just as she gathered debris for their "treasury of similes" in "Telegraph Wires," and offers them to Pasternak:

> Here, from the Ocean,
> Is a handful of play.
>
> Take it bit by bit, the way it was gathered.
> The sea played. To play is to be kind.
> The sea played and I took,
> The sea lost and I stowed
>
> In my collar, my cheek—tart, sea-tasting!
> The mouth is better than a case, if your hands
> Are full. Praise to the swell!
> The muse lost and the wave took.

> Вот с Океана,
> Горстка игры.
>
> Мало-помалу бери, как собран.
> Море играло. Играть—быть добрым.
> Море играло, а я брала,
> Море теряло, а я клала.
>
> Зá ворот, зá щеку,—терпко, мóрско!
> Рот лучше ящика, если горсти
> Заняты. Валу, звучи, хвала!
> Муза теряла, волна брала.

The process of composition, of self-composition, is a game she plays with Pasternak, which is to say that it is a collaboration. "From the Sea," that is, dramatizes her perennial fantasy of co-authoring herself with Pasternak.[10]

There is a third player in this game, however. The sea is, if not the source, then the enabling element of creativity, carrying material to Tsvetaeva, who in turn passes it on to Pasternak. What Tsvetaeva takes from the sea, she stores next to her skin ("in my collar") and in her mouth. This gesture has striking psychological content, associating poetic speech with an infant's urge to touch and ingest surrounding objects. Tsvetaeva underscores the association by imagining her "game" with Pasternak as a child's game, both in the poem itself and in her May 26 letter:

[I want to talk] about *us* today, from Moscow, or St.-Gilles,—I don't know which—watching the shabby vacationers' Vendée. (As one does in childhood, sitting with heads together, temple to temple, in the rain, watching people walk by.)

Boris, I don't live looking back, I don't impose my six-year-old or sixteen-year-old self on anyone—so why am I drawn into *your* childhood, why am I drawn to draw you into mine? (Childhood: a place where everything remains *the same* and *in the same place*.) Right now in the Vendée on May 26 I continually play a game with you, what do I mean game?—*games!*—I gather shells with you. (*DNV* 212)

Tsvetaeva imagines them as small children partly on the strength of their recent discovery about their musician mothers, a fact she inscribes in the poem: one of the shells they play with is shaped like "the G treble clef of childhood" (detstva skripichnyi kliuch). They are not just brother and sister but very young siblings. They play a game of spying on people with their heads pressed close together, "temple to temple." She envisioned a similar action earlier in the letter when describing her long-distance communion with him: "Boris, I talked to you continually, spoke into you—rejoiced—breathed. During moments when you were lost in thought for too long, I took your head in both hands and turned it: HERE!" (*DNV* 212). This fantasy about a childhood encounter would seem to be about the freedom to be physically intimate. With this removal of their relationship to the era of childhood, she does not so much renounce the eroticism of her address to Pasternak as return to its psychosexual origins in childhood.

While the sea sponsors their child's game, it also threatens it. Tsvetaeva and Pasternak's game of shells is played "at the tempo of 'le petit navire,'" which Ieva Vitins has identified as a French children's song in which a boatload of starving passengers draw straws to determine which of them will be eaten. The lot falls to a young boy, who is saved when the sea throws up thousands of fish in answer to his prayer.[11] This emergency scenario, in which famine threatens the sacrifice of a child, echoes the circumstances of Irina's death during the Civil War famine. The speaker of "From the Sea" lives in such a state of famine; the shells she stores in her cheek are "the bare bones of famished longing" (golodnoi toski obglodki). She threatens to devour the "young boy" Pasternak, but instead eats what the sea offers, meager as it is:

I'll gnaw a stone—I'll spare you,—
Better than a wave can

Камень—тебя щажу—
Лучше волны гложу

Stones are not enough to feed her, though, and she begins to consume herself. In the next stanzas, the debris she finds on the beach are fragments of her own experience and emotions—"the leftover bits of love," "the chewed ends of conscience" (liubvi okuski, ogryzki: sovesti). In Russian, as in English, one's conscience "gnaws," an idiom Tsvetaeva reverses by gnawing on her conscience. She takes the idiom to the point of semantic incoherence when she "gnaws" on her own tears, "which can't at all be gnawed" (Ne ugryzomuiu ni na stol'lko).

The speaker's redirection of her greed away from Pasternak and toward herself allows their game to proceed, as she turns from gathering fragments to sorting through them with him. This is the moment when she is co-authored by Pasternak, who completes whatever piece she supplies:

> Let's divide them up.
>
> Not whatever you like, but what I draw out.
> (May your son join us in bed
> And make a third in our game?)
> I'll pick first.
>
> Just sand, smooth, through my fingers.
> Wait a minute: the fragments of some stanza:
> "The underground temple of glory" . . .
> —Fine.—You'll finish the line yourself.
>
> Just sand, splashing, through my fingers.
> Wait a minute! the old skins of a rattlesnake,
> Of jealousy! Renewed,
> I call myself Pride.
>
> And I've crawled back to myself vindicated.
>
> Давай делить.
>
> Не что понравится, а что выну.
> (К нам на кровать твоего бы сына
> Третьим—нельзя ли в игру?)
> Первая—я беру.
>
> Только песок, между пальцев, ливкий.
> Стой-ка: какой-то строфы отрывки:
> «Славы подземный храм» . . .
> Ладно. Допишешь сам.
>
> Только песок, между пальцев, плеский.
> Стой-ка: гремучей змеи обноски,
> Ревности! Обновясь,
> Гордостью назвалась.
>
> И поползла себе с полным правом.

The site of the poets' collaboration is Pasternak's bed. Tsvetaeva had established this site in the poem's first stanzas when, as she enters Pasternak's dream, she "doesn't look" at who he's sleeping with (S kem—i ne glianu!— / Spish'). Now she invites his son to join them in bed for their game. The poem thus describes a familiar fantasy about displacing Evgenia as Pasternak's "most legitimate wife" and the mother of his child. This domestic scene makes the bed into an environment where the erotics of her relationship with Pasternak are the erotics of the family bed, which allow physical intimacy without sexual guilt. Like her vision of the two poets as children sitting "temple to temple," this fantasy is driven by a desire for rightful access to the other's body. (Tsvetaeva, after all, anchors their dream-communication to Pasternak's sleeping body, though presumably it could take place anywhere.) In this scenario she is beyond the love experience, beyond jealousy, has come into a self that is fully "vindicated" (s polnym pravom), a phrase that conveys Tsvetaeva's view of love as criminal as well as painful, so that recomposing herself also bestows absolution. This new self is the perfect, "unblotted" self that the poem creates.

By introducing Pasternak's son as a "third in our game," Tsvetaeva repeats the structure of their interaction with the sea. Yet another third party soon appears, the censor, who would scrutinize their exchange were it sent by mail. But the poets' dream-censor is the dawn, who indulgently looks the other way and lets her poem pass ("Some rhyming, dearie? / You've spilled a lot of ink!" [Virshi, golubchik? / Nu i cherno!]). This kindly figure stands in contrast to the sea, which reemerges with a threatening aspect. While the sea that earlier played with the poets was "kind," it now appears as an enormous mill that grinds everything in its path. Tsvetaeva borrowed this image of the sea from Pasternak's "1905," which she quotes in one of her May letters, stating that these lines were what brought her to the seashore: "'Everything palls. / Only you are not bound to grow tedious.' With that, for that, I came here" (*DNV* 213). The line comes from the section "Rebellion at Sea" ("Morskoi miatezh"), which Tsvetaeva had recently republished in the first number of *Milestones:*

> Everything palls.
> Only you are not bound to grow tedious.
> Days go by,
> And years go by,
> And thousands and thousands of years.
> In the white zeal of your waves,
> Hiding
> In the white pungence of the acacias,
> Perhaps it is you,
> Sea,
> Who will reduce and reduce them to naught.

> Приедается всё.
> Лишь тебе не дано примелькаться.
> Дни проходят,
> И годы проходят,
> И тысячи, тысячи лет.
> В белой рьяности волн,
> Прячась

В белую пряность акаций,
Может, ты-то их,
Море,
И сводишь, и сводишь на нет.

The Russian for "to pall" (*priedat'sia*) is based on the verb "to eat," and literally means "to be eaten up," that is, to lose one's substance. The suggestion of erosion is reinforced by the verb in the second line, "to grow tedious" (primel'kat'sia), with its echo of the word *mel'*, or "shallows." These meanings prepare for the final lines, where the irreducible sea "reduces to naught" human categories of time (days, years). Its unhurried, relentless action recalls the action of history in "A Sublime Malady," which is to say, the action of time itself.

When Tsvetaeva takes up Pasternak's image of a sea that erodes, she makes the same analogy with the passing of time:

Mill, you mill, you sea round-dance!
The mammoth, the butterfly—the sea has ground
Them all up. We can't speak badly—a pinch
Of dust—of the sea!

Мельня ты мельня, морское ко́ло!
Мамонта, бабочку,—все смололо
Море. О нем—щепоть
Праха—не нам молоть!

The dust's admiration for the grinding power of the sea/time marks its death-dealing agency. But Tsvetaeva, in the following stanzas, takes this conventional reflection on time and mortality in an entirely new direction. Time not only brings on death but also makes life itself a kind of death: "Immortality growing shallow— / That's life" (Obmelevaiushchee bessmert'e— / Zhizn'). Sustaining the rhetoric of diminishment, she locates life in the "shallows" of death: "Continents are only the sea's / Shallows. To be born (the point— / To multiply!)—is to run aground" (Materiki, eto prosto meli / Moria. Rodit'sia (tsel'— / Mnozhit'sia!)—sest' na mel').

This vision of a sea that "eats up" life is a final variation on the theme of starvation and ingestion. Like the plot of "le petit navire," it describes a reduced world of crisis and scarcity, in which the speaker survives on "the bare bones of famished longing." Thus starved, she becomes as rapacious as the sea-mill itself, a similarity Tsvetaeva underlines with another reference to Pasternak's "1905": she has "gone mad on the deserted slope" (osatanev na pustynnom spuske), echoing the sea's fury in Pasternak's poem ("The efficient surf / Goes mad / From the glut of work" [Rastoropnyi priboi / Sataneet / Ot prorvy rabot]). While earlier she redirected her aggression away from Pasternak and toward herself, here she unleashes it against the sea-mill. She is able to counter the sea's assault through that other aspect of her orality, her poetic gift. For the first time, her speaker directly addresses the sea, creating it as an interlocutor ("Mill, you mill"). Tsvetaeva also links the sea's grinding with speaking through clever use of idiomatic Russian. In the dust's utterance "we can't speak badly," the verb "molot′," which literally means "to grind," also describes a kind of gossipy chatter. (Speaking and chewing also merge in the articulatory aspect of these lines, whose "-ol" and "-om" sounds cause the reader to mouth them.) The sea, however, is silenced by the power of the speaker's utterance: "As soon as I speak out—it's quiet, / Sea!" (Kak tol′ko vygovorius′—i tikho, / More!). The sea then does recede, leaving behind its detritus, which the speaker consumes: "My tongue has ground so much—The sea's entire hem!" (Skol′ko iazyk smolol,— / Tselyi morskoi podol!).

The logic of this contest with the sea is familiar from the final poem of "Telegraph Wires," where the speaker escapes defeat through the power of poetic speech. While the threat appears existential in "From the Sea," the sea's function as both destroyer and nourisher recalls the ambivalent regard for the mother expressed in that earlier poem. The figure of the mother is at least phonically evoked in the stanzas about the sea-mill, in words such as "mamont," "babochka," and "materika." And just as she triumphs over "the other woman" in "Telegraph Wires," she tames the sea at the end of "From the Sea":

> The sea has grown tired, to be tired is to be kind.
> Eternity, ply the oar!
> Draw us. Let's sleep.
>
> Side by side, but not crowded.
> A fire, but no smoke.
> For this isn't dreaming together
> But mutual dreaming:
>
> In God, each in the other.
> A nose, you thought? A promontory!
> Eyebrows? No, rainbows,
> Exoduses from—
>
> Seen-ness.
>
> Море устало, устать—быть добрым.
> Вечность, махни веслом!
> Влечь нас. Давай уснем.
>
> Вплоть, а не тесно,
> Огнь, а не дымно.
> Ведь не совместный
> Сон, а взаимный:

В Боге, друг в друге.
Нос, думал? Мыс!
Брови? Нет, дуги,
Выходы из—

Зримости.

The poem-dream ends as children's play might end—with the poets falling asleep side by side. They are still in the boat of "le petit navire" but no longer under crisis conditions. This boat is also the family bed, in which Tsvetaeva and Pasternak may enjoy innocent physical intimacy without inciting the sea's rage. Similarly, the "fade-out" at the end of the poem is an escape from the censoring eye of the sea-mother.

Such a reading of the poem is urged by Tsvetaeva's May 25 letter to Pasternak, in which she declares her strong dislike of the sea, comparing it to her dislike of love. She refers to "the first time she disliked the sea," meaning her family's trip to the Italian shore as part of a failed cure for her mother's consumption. Tsvetaeva later recounted this story in her essay "My Pushkin" ("Moi Pushkin," 1937), where she once again invoked Pasternak's sea (5:90). In this letter to Pasternak, Tsvetaeva does not mention her mother's death but simply notes, "In childhood I loved [the sea], like I loved love" (*DNV* 216); she stopped loving love, that is, when her childhood ended along with her mother's life. Tsvetaeva's "dislike" of love is a form of loyalty to her mother, an agreement to live only on the detritus of her mother's abandonment. It is essentially an agreement not to live.

This is how Tsvetaeva herself, in the same letter, interpreted two of her earlier poems to Pasternak. Of "Eurydice to Orpheus," she says, as though just now making the discovery, that Eurydice caused Orpheus to turn back not out of weakness but by design, that she wanted to remain in Hades. Similarly, Marusya follows the vampire in order *"not to live"* (*DNV* 215). Eurydice and Marusya model the choice Tsvetaeva declares herself to make. She describes herself "resettling" from life into death, though "not as a shadow—not bloodless, but carrying with me so much blood that I would milk [nadoila] and overfeed [opoila] all of Hell. O, how my Hell would begin to speak!" (*DNV* 205). Tsvetaeva describes a primary, mutual dependency: *nadoit* means to acquire milk, as a child does from its mother; *opoit* means to injure with too much drink, or to poison. Her ambivalence is more openly expressed in the comments that follow: "For I myself am Marusya: honorable as one should be (confined as one can't be), keeping my word, shielding myself, avoiding happiness, half alive (more than that for others, but *in what way* I know only too well), myself not knowing why that's the way things are, complicit in my own subjugation, and even in going to that Kheruvimskaia—obeying a voice, someone else's will, and not my own" (*DNV* 206). The Kheruvimskaia is the hymn sung by the chorus at the conclusion of "The Swain" to the strains of which Marusya ascends with her lover. Tsvetaeva now describes her flight as a kind of abduction: she is "complicit in her own subjugation," obeying the will of "someone else." In making her renunciations, that is, Tsvetaeva was complying with the mother's demand.

The catalyst for these reflections was Rilke's "rejection" of her in mid-May, about which she complained bitterly to Pasternak. As recounted earlier, Rilke warned her that because of his poor health, he might not be able to keep up the correspondence. The wounded Tsvetaeva immediately wrote to Pasternak that their plan to visit Rilke was canceled because "he doesn't need me, and he doesn't need you" (*DNV* 207). Rilke, in short, is like the sea: "Boris, one thing: I DON'T LIKE THE SEA. I can't. So much space, and nowhere to walk. That's the first thing. It moves and I watch. Two. Boris, well it's actually the same scene, i.e., my forced, given immobility. My inertness. My—like it or not—patience. And at night! Cold, rushing, invisible, unloving, filled with itself—like Rilke! (Filled with himself or with divinity—same thing)" (*DNV* 213). Here Rilke's self-sufficiency is not just rejecting but paralyzing; in his presence, she has no agency. As her indictment unfolds further, she introduces a remarkable metaphor for the sea's plenitude: "It's a monstrous *bowl*! A *shallow* one, Boris! A huge flat-bottomed cradle that's continually pushing out babies (ships)." Rilke becomes a womb whose grotesque fertility blocks her own. As she goes on to say, he has "knocked her out of writing poems," in probably the only such instance of her writing life, and she announces that she is no longer writing to him (*DNV* 213). Like the sea-mother, Rilke has the power to sustain or to destroy her—to feed her or to eat her, to return to the rhetoric of "From the Sea."

In fact, Rilke makes an appearance near the end of the poem, in stanzas that formulate Tsvetaeva's relationship with the sea-mother:

> It just leaves things and doesn't ask us to take them . . .
> Strange that it's the receding tide that brings,
> Diminishment that puts things in your palm.
> Won't you recognize the notes

> Left for us, two or three each,
> At the hour when the god who brought them—floated away,
> Departed . . . Orpheus . . . Harpist . . .
> The sandbar is our musical score!

> Лишь оставляет, а брать не просит . . .
> Странно, что это—отлив приносит,
> Убыль, в ладонь, дает.
> Не узнаешь ли нот,

> Нам остающихся по две, по три
> В час, когда Бог их принесший—отлил,

Отбыл . . . Орфей . . . Арфист . . .
Отмель—наш нотный лист!

The departing god who leaves behind the musical score for Tsvetaeva's duet with Pasternak is both her pianist mother and Orpheus/Rilke. Like her departed mother, Rilke has abandoned her, and the trauma feeds her, though it is a starvation diet ("two or three [notes] each").

Tsvetaeva's rendering of Rilke as the all-powerful mother does not simply emerge from her own imaginary. It is also a perceptive reading of the poetic tradition she rewrites in "From the Sea." Her image of the sea derives from Pasternak's long poem "1905," as she said to him, and from Pushkin's "To the Sea" ("K moriu"), which her own title rewrites.[12] She also draws on Pasternak's own reading of Pushkin in his cycle "Themes and Variations." The "theme" of Pasternak's cycle is a famous painting by Ivan Aivazovsky and Ilya Repin that renders Pushkin in a romantic pose, standing on the rocky Crimean shore contemplating a wild surf.[13] Pasternak asserts the poet's affinity with the sea by punning on the opening line of Pushkin's poem, "Farewell, free element" (Proshchai, svobodnaia stikhiia):

> Two gods said farewell until tomorrow
> Two seas changed their expressions:
>
> The element of the free element
> And the free element of verse.
>
> Два бога прощались до завтра,
> Два моря менялись в лице:
>
> Стихия свободной стихии
> С свободной стихией стиха.

In the following poem, the first "Variation" ("Podrazhatel'naia"), Pushkin's encounter with the sea yields poetry, specifically, the opening chapters of *Eugene Onegin*. In Pasternak's bizarrely physiological imagining of that process, Pushkin appears to absorb the sea like a shell (rakovina), to expel it in a sob at the moment of inspiration.[14] Pasternak's image is a variation on the conclusion of Pushkin's "To the Sea," where the poet, reluctant to part with the sea, claims to carry it away inside him in a kind of pregancy.[15] In both of these texts, the poet absorbs the maternal element, a striking image for the appropriation of femininity.

Another Pasternak text, one Tsvetaeva did not know, supports her reading of the male poet's relation to a "maternal" sea. In a letter to his mother from 1911, the young Pasternak expressed the poet's frustration at confronting the sea: "Do you know what the Greeks called the sea? The Infertile One. Furthermore, they always put that word in a case that ends in *oio* and sounds like a wail: *atrugetoio*. That sea always seemed to me like bad taste, something primitive, like passions in a drama or a musical piece in octaves and chords, without counterpoint. . . . The sea works over itself. I don't know if it can inspire an artist. It seems to me you can only describe the sea realistically. Attempts to render the sea are always mediocre. Or you need to be a genius in order to make your way along the shore as if it were a field, bend to the sea, gather something, take it away, and grow it at home" (*DL* 121). Although Pasternak begins by calling the sea infertile, he goes on to complain like Tsvetaeva about its efficiency, which gets in the way of his own creative agency ("The sea works over itself"). But the genius, at least, may come away with something of his own to "grow." Pasternak was in his own contest with the sea-mother, the "elemental" nature he later imagined as violent as well as powerful. As I have remarked, Tsvetaeva was eager to read him as a poet of the elemental, and she later ranked his sea with Pushkin's.[16] But he was not himself the sea-mother, as she envisioned Rilke in 1926 and later envisioned Pushkin.[17]

Rilke was uniquely, even perfectly suited to play the poet-mother for Tsvetaeva. Most obviously, he was suited for the role because he was dying. In his second letter to her, Rilke informed her that he had been in a sanatorium since December, for half a year. Such a prolonged "cure" was reminiscent of her mother's, raising the specter of Rilke's death. He also suggested a vocation for her when he noted her address: "next to your beautiful name, next to this enchanting St.-Gilles = sur-vie (survie!)" (*DL* 89). Death and survival were the subject of Rilke's first substantive letter. It is generally thought that Tsvetaeva did not grasp how seriously ill Rilke was, though her answering letter, in which she took up the subject of "death and the poet," suggests otherwise. Tsvetaeva's knowledge that Rilke was dying helps account for the intensity of her attachment to him, which superseded her attachment to Pasternak.

She introduced the subject of the poet's death by telling Rilke about her polemic with Georgy Adamovich in "A Poet on the Critic." Among the many critical *mots* Tsvetaeva ridiculed in her essay was Adamovich's remark that the four years since Blok's death "have almost consoled us." Tsvetaeva countered that there is no consolation for the poet's death, in a statement whose logic is genuinely tortured (Tsvetaeva translated this passage from her essay into German for Rilke, not entirely precisely): "Every poet's death, even the most natural, is against Nature, i.e., *murder;* hence is unceasing, uninterrupted, eternally—within the moment—enduring. Pushkin, Blok, or to name all of them, *Orpheus,* can never have died, because he is right now (eternally!) dying. In every lover—anew, and in every lover—forever.[18] Therefore—no consolation until we have 'died' ourselves" (*DL* 93). The poet's death, being "against Nature," cannot take place. From that premise, Tsvetaeva concludes not that the poet lives forever but that he dies forever, thus achieving a paradoxical sort of immortality. Being immortal in this sense depends on a "lover," in whom the dead poet is resurrected. In this role, the lover is enjoined not simply to remember the dead poet but to remain inconsolable: "no consolation until we have 'died' ourselves." Just as the poet is always dying, the lover is always mourning. By thus refusing to complete the work of mourning, she avoids the finality of death. In speaking these thoughts to Rilke, Tsvetaeva tells him he will not die because she will always mourn him, which is also to say she will be his lover.

Tsvetaeva summed up her notion that the poet's vocation is to die by rewriting Rilke's famous line "It's Orpheus if it sings" (Ist's Orpheus, wenn es singt) to read "It's Orpheus if it dies" (wenn es stirbt) (*DL* 94). She thereby rendered Rilke's words still more Rilkean in an act of sympathetic co-authorship. As Tsvetaeva knew, Rilke was not merely a poet who was dying but the very "poet of death."[19] Rilke's perennial theme was the challenge of dying "the good death"; he sought to be open to death, to contemplate it without fear as a natural accompaniment of life. The poet is the one who is most open to death, as the one most engaged in transforming the visible into the invisible. As Maurice Blanchot has elegantly recapitulated Rilke's thought, "Orpheus is the process of transformation, not he who has overcome death but he who eternally dies, who is the urge to disappear, who disappears in the anguish of disappearing, an anguish which becomes song, speech which is the pure process of dying."[20] As Tsvetaeva said, "It's Orpheus if it dies," showing Rilke how well she understood him.

How well did she understand him, though? Even as she adopts Rilke's themes and language, Tsvetaeva does not accept his tuition about death.[21] The very notion of "eternal mourning" runs counter to Rilke's efforts to make the fact of death nothing to mourn. Moreover, Rilke's "openness" to all things, including and most especially death, is a solitary endeavor, while Tsvetaeva wishes to participate in his dying. The letter in which Rilke "rejected" her, in fact, was one in which he spoke about his solitude. These reflections arose in the context of his exchanging information with Tsvetaeva about their families. Rilke had asked about Tsvetaeva's children and was delighted by Alya's declaration, "Marina, thanks for the world," which Tsvetaeva included in one of the poems of *Psyche*. In that context, he confessed to not knowing whether his own daughter could make such an affirmation, since he had left his family after two years of marriage. He describes his solitude thereafter, which reached its "ultimate and uttermost state" when he retreated to Muzot in 1921. It was this solitude, he says, that allowed him to create *Duino Elegies* and *Sonnets to Orpheus*. This very solitude also, he suggests, caused his illness, an idea that would resonate with Tsvetaeva's view of the tragic cost of her poetic vocation. Even so, the thrust of Rilke's letter is to affirm the poet's solitude.

That Tsvetaeva felt excluded by Rilke's solitude is clear from the complaints she made to Pasternak. Rilke's total self-sufficiency meant that she could not be his Eckermann, as Tsvetaeva remarked to Pasternak: "Rilke is a hermit. Goethe in his old age needed only Eckermann (the latter's will for 'Faust II' and ears that recorded everything). Rilke has outgrown Eckermann, he doesn't need a mediator between God and 'Faust II'" (*DNV* 207). Rilke's autonomy, though, proves him to be an even greater poet than Goethe, whatever Tsvetaeva's personal disappointment. As she goes on to say, Rilke is right thus to exclude her, since that is the way of the genius.[22]

Even before the events of 1926, Tsvetaeva was citing Rilke to assert the poets' isolation from the rest of humanity: "Und sind ihr ganzes Leben so allein" (6:18). She speaks Rilke's line, however, with her own intonation. For her it is a painful sentence, one she manages to impose on herself only when she is like the genius. Her more typical choice is to be like Eckermann, to seek intimacy rather than solitude. But now that Rilke had personally declared his need for solitude, she was prepared to endorse his requirement even as it injured her. She was prepared, that is, to understand the solitude of abandonment as the solitude of lyric creativity.

After several weeks of self-disciplining, Tsvetaeva wrote to Rilke to assure him that she would not impose on him: "So, Rainer, it's over. I don't want to go to you. I don't want to want to" (*DL* 136). She was well rewarded for her compliance. Rilke replied immediately, though briefly, relying mainly on the impact of the gifts he enclosed ("Now that we have arrived at 'not wanting,' we deserve some mitigation" [*DL* 137]). He sent some photographs of himself, which Tsvetaeva had requested. He also sent a poem he wrote for her that same day, "Elegy for Marina Tsvetaeva-Efron" ("Elegie an Marina Zwetajewa-Efron," 1926). The elegy is a meditation on "non-wanting" love that reads like a lesson for Tsvetaeva, a lesson summed up by his phrase "Nothing belongs to us" (Nichts gehört uns). Rather than seeking to possess him, she should follow the poet's true path, laid out in the poem's final line: "Even in the time of waning, in the weeks of our change, / no one could ever again help us to fulfillment, except / our own solitary course over the sleepless landscape" (Auch in abnehmender Frist, auch in den Wochen der Wendung / niemand verhülfe uns je wieder zum Vollsein, als der / einsame eigene Gang über der schlaflosen Landschaft).[23]

Rilke's lecture to Tsvetaeva was one he had given many times before to women who formed attachments to him, often likewise on the basis of a correspondence.[24] His ideal of nonpossessive love was, along with death, his great theme.[25] In his representation, the ideal was easier to achieve for men than for women, who nevertheless might approach it through the experience of abandonment, as Rilke suggested in the first of his *Duino Elegies*: "[Sing] of those abandoned women, you envy them almost, / whom you found so much more loving than those who were gratified" ([Singe] Jene, du neidest sie fast, Verlassenen, die du / so viel liebender fandst als die Gestillten). The phrase "you envy them almost" captures Rilke's ambivalent identification with the feminine, a defining feature of his sensibility. Perhaps more than any other modern poet, Rilke performed the male feminine, both through his aesthetic and spiritual philosophies and through his conduct as an advocate for women artists.[26] In his elegy to Tsvetaeva, Rilke directly claims the feminine: "Oh how I understand you, female flower on the same / imperishable stalk. How powerfully I scatter myself into the night air / that in a moment will touch you" (O wie begreif ich dich, weibliche Blüte am gleichen / unvergänglichen Strauch. Wie streu ich mich stark in die Nachtluft, / die dich nächstens bestreift). Even as he locates himself "on the same stalk," however, he remains a masculine stamen, "scattering himself" like pollen over the female.

As a master of the feminine, Rilke often found himself in the position of exhorting women to achieve their ideal selves, as he found it necessary to exhort Tsvetaeva. His instruction puts the woman poet in a difficult double bind. In order to be a poet, she must not behave like a woman, which is to say she must not love the master if she is to be like him. Because the sentence of non-love is delivered by the beloved, it is difficult to obey. Tsvetaeva was deeply moved by Rilke's gift of the "Elegy," but she resisted its message and continued trying to love Rilke. Her letter of thanks opens with the confession that in withholding her correspondence with Rilke from Pasternak, she violated Rilke's injunction against possessive love: "Listen, Rainer, from the beginning, so you'll know. I am bad. Boris is good" (*DL* 151). She admits her wrongdoing and informs Rilke that she copied out and sent to Pasternak several of Rilke's letters to her. She was, though, "without remorse," continuing to insist on her right to a secret relationship with Rilke. His demand that she reveal their relationship to a third person "falsely situates" her; it "bends" her, she says, quoting one of Rilke's own lines, "for where I am bent, there I am a lie" (denn dort bin ich gelogen, wo ich gebogen bin).[27] To elaborate her experience of being "bent" or forced, Tsvetaeva turns to the rhetoric of the natural: "If I put my arms around a friend's neck, it is natural; if I tell of it, it's unnatural (to myself!). And when I make a poem about it, it's natural after all. . . . An inner right to secrecy. That isn't anybody's business, not even that of the neck that was encircled by my arms. *My* business. And consider, after all, that I'm a woman, married, children, etc." (*DL* 154). Tsvetaeva experiences Rilke's demand that she tell of their exchange as unnatural, as a violation of her privacy, which she attempts to preserve even in the midst of family life. She resists being "bent" by others' demands in those things that matter most, love and poetry. She thus reads back to Rilke his own lesson about the poet's solitude, though she achieves hers in the specific context of being "a woman, married, children, etc."

Rilke's reply similarly cast their sharpening disagreement in terms of gender: "You are right, Marina (isn't that a rare thing with a woman?), such a being-in-the-right in the most valid, the most carefree sense?" (*DL* 204). Even as he conceded her rightness, however, he continued to insist that she was wrong to exclude Pasternak. She was right to claim her autonomy, making her a "rare" woman. But she was also too feminine, wrongly succumbing to possessive love for Rilke. In her reply, Tsvetaeva accommodated the contradiction with agility, though also with a question mark. Summoning Goethe as an authority, she allowed that she might be both right and wrong, both natural and unnatural, both woman and not-woman: "About being in the right (having right on one's side). 'Even nature is unnatural' (Goethe); that's what you meant. I suppose! (Nature: right)" (*DL* 209).

The idea that nature can be unnatural derived not just from Goethe but from Tsvetaeva's mother. One of Tsvetaeva's May letters to Pasternak included a childhood reminiscence of her mother of the sort that would fill her later essay, "Mother and Music" ("Mat' i muzyka," 1934). The memory was triggered by Pasternak's anacrostic dedication of "Lieutenant Schmidt," which she praised for its "leitmotif of *the natural.*" She recalls her mother reading a fairy tale to her three young children, quizzing them about the identity of the "green princess." When Tsvetaeva correctly identified her as "nature," her mother rewarded her with a book of tales in which "the world was insistently divided into rich little girls and poor little boys, and the rich little girls, taking off their clothes (!), would dress the little boys in them (in what, skirts?). . . . In a word: NATURE (as so often) brought in its wake unnaturalness. Was that the bitter retribution for her own nature my mother had in mind when she gave [the book]? I don't know." (*DNV* 216).

Her mother's example of cross-dressing, which is specifically about boys wearing girls' clothes, aptly describes the male feminine. The male poet borrows the wealth of the feminine (the little girls are "rich"), thereby enriching himself. In her first letter to Rilke, Tsvetaeva wrote about Pasternak in precisely these terms: "He doesn't resemble his father by even the least little eyelash (the best a son can do: I only believe in mothers' boys [Muttersöhne]. You, too, are a mother's boy. A *man* taking after the *female* line and therefore so *rich* (duality)" (*DL* 86). Where, though, does that leave the mother's girl? The mother's unnatural law requires that she cede her femininity to the boy, leaving her naked in the wild. Rilke's law similarly demands that she relinquish her femininity (be a "rare" woman) to earn the title of poet. Both the mother and the male genius legislate a gender arrangement that leaves no place for Tsvetaeva except as the unnatural woman.

Tsvetaeva obeys and contests this law by representing herself to Rilke as the unnatural woman while defending her condition as "natural." This woman is none other than Psyche, whose identity Tsvetaeva now claims before Rilke: "Bodies are bored with me. They sense something and don't believe me (my body), although I do everything like everybody else. Too . . . altruistic, possibly, too . . . benevolent. Also trusting—*too much so*! Foreigners [Fremde] are trusting, savages, who know of no custom or law" (*DL* 207). As a foreigner, or savage, she is outside the law and is therefore unrecognizable as a love object. Tsvetaeva rehearses this argument in order to make an extraordinary request of Rilke:

> I want to sleep with you, fall asleep and sleep. That magnificent folk word, how deep, how true, how unequivocal, how exactly what it says. Just—sleep. And nothing more. No, one more thing: my head buried in your left shoulder, my arm around your right one—and that's all. No, another thing: and to know right into the deepest sleep that it is you. And more: how your heart sounds. And—to kiss your heart.
>
> Sometimes I think: I must exploit the chance that I am still (after all!) body. Soon I won't have any arms. (*DL* 206)

Tsvetaeva's specificity about how they will embrace underscores her claim that she intends "just sleep," without the sexual meaning of the phrase. Her reassurances, though, are designed to gain her access to Rilke's body. This letter to Rilke reveals like no other document what drives Tsvetaeva to identify herself as Psyche: she is bound to a cruel contract whereby she must deny her body's desire ("become soul") in order to enter the beloved's bed.[28]

That Tsvetaeva rehearsed this scene precisely with Rilke shows how attentively she read him. It was Rilke, after all, who introduced the subject of his body in his early letters to Tsvetaeva, describing the onset of his illness: "I have been, since a certain turning point in my being (which, around 1899 and 1900, coincided with my stay in Russia), without need of a doctor, accustomed to living in such perfect concord with it [his body] that I often could easily take it for a child of my soul: light and convenient it was, and easily brought into the spiritual realm, so often transcended that it had weight only out of politeness and not enough to frighten the invisible! So intimately mine: a friend and truly my bearer [Träger]; holder of my heart; capable of all my joys, diminishing none, making each more particularly mine; rendering them to me right at the intersection of my senses" (*DL* 103). Rilke represents his own body in the same fashion in which he renders bodies in his poetry, where, as Geoffrey Hartman has argued, "there is hardly a metaphor or simile that does not in some way derive from his sense of the physical."[29] As Hartman describes it, the Rilkean body is not a desiring body but one through which nature's "physical will" is realized. Its most perfect incarnation is the procreative female body, as Hartman suggests when he highlights Rilke's use of the verb *tragen* (to carry, bear), the same word Rilke used to describe his body to Tsvetaeva ("Träger"): "*Tragen* is the most pervasive of Rilke's gestures, even though it occurs less often as a word, for *tragen* is at the same time the most universal and least visible of signs. . . . *Tragen* represents the activity of Eurydice, of woman in general, but also perhaps of the man insofar as the body submits entirely to its fate. *Tragen*, as in 'Die Erwachsene,' is used with all its connotations as the act of simple physical support, of spiritual suffering, and of bringing to birth. It is implied in such symbols as the rider, staff, fruit, garland, doll, jug, fruit tree, and of course, mothers."[30] The mother's body is a body receptive to nature's "physical will," peaceful, detached, and wholly absorbed in the process unfolding inside her. That physical will, however, may be directed toward death as well as toward maturation—rather, toward death as a kind of maturation. As Hartmann uncomfortably notes, "Early death and maturity, rightly or wrongly, are identified by Rilke as two great types of physical fulfillment."[31] Hence, the exemplary significance of Eurydice, who, in Rilke's famous poem "Orpheus, Eurydice, Hermes," is pregnant with her own death: "She was within herself, like a woman with child" (Sie war in sich, wie Eine hoher Hoffnung).[32] Again, this is precisely how Rilke represents himself to Tsvetaeva. His body, which was "light and convenient" in health, has become heavy with his death: "My life is so curiously heavy in me" (*DL* 103; 205).

Rilke's identification with the pregnant woman was the most pronounced expression of his male feminine sensibility, to which Tsvetaeva was deeply responsive. As we have seen, the metaphorics of pregnancy were a crucial resource for Tsvetaeva in imagining her poetic strength and personal legitimacy. In "Telegraph Wires," she did so in contest with the "other woman," the powerful mother. In her exchange with Rilke, the powers of the mother are assimilated by the male genius to produce a figure of overwhelming psychological authority.[33] Moreover, Rilke inverts the metaphorics of pregnancy, making it the bearing of death rather than of life. When she climbs into bed with Rilke, she climbs into a scene Rilke dramatized in a poem titled "The Bed" ("Das Bett").[34] This obscure poem, as brilliantly analyzed by Andrzej Warminski, renders the painful hour of childbirth as recapitulating the hour of the sexual encounter and prefiguring the hour of death: "The poem answers the question: What is a bed? 'Liebesbett,' 'Wochenbett,' and 'Sterbebett' have become 'Das Bett.'"[35] The loving, birthing, dying woman is the authoritative image of femininity and of the poet which Rilke presents to Tsvetaeva, confirming her traumatic sense that her procreativity and creativity were implicated in death. Rilke's bed is comfortless, as his response to Tsvetaeva's request to sleep with him conveys: he invites her into "the sleep nest [das Schlaf-Nest], in which a great bird, a raptor of the spirit (no blinking!), settles" (*DL* 211).

Tsvetaeva accepted Rilke's "nest," supplying him with the Russian translation of the word in her answering letter. But she received no more letters from Rilke. She sent one more message into his silence when she changed addresses in November, a postcard asking, "I wonder if you still love me?" (*DL* 217). He died a few months later, on December 29, as Tsvetaeva learned with the rest of the reading public. Rilke's death prompted a lengthy period of mourning that took many forms. She wrote a "Posthumous Letter" ("Posmertnoe pis'mo") to Rilke (December 31, 1926); a new long poem, conceived as another such letter, "New Year's Greeting" ("Novogodnee," February 7, 1927);[36] an essay also addressed to Rilke, titled "Your Death" ("Tvoia smert'," February 27, 1927);[37] a second long poem, "Poem of the Air" ("Poema vozdukha," May 1927); and a translation into Russian of several of Rilke's letters (February 29, 1929). She also exchanged letters with Rilke's secretary, a Russian woman named Tatiana Chernosvitova, who forwarded to Tsvetaeva a Greek mythology Rilke had ordered for her before his death.[38] Tsvetaeva enjoined her to become the model secretary—Eckermann—by recording every detail of the last few months of Rilke's life: "Remember Eckermann's book, the only one of the many written about Goethe that gives us the living poet" (*DL* 227). Despite the connotations of her name ("black retinue"), Chernosvitova was not prepared to mourn Rilke in this way, as Tsvetaeva perceived after meeting her.[39]

Tsvetaeva mourned Rilke by seeking all possible means to continue their "correspondence," to join him in his nest. In her "Posthumous Letter," she asks about the nest: "I don't want to reread your letters or I will want to join you—there—and I dare not want such a thing. You know what this 'want' implies" (*DL* 222). The nest also figures in her poem "New Year's Greeting" ("Novogodnee," 1927), where it designates the high perch from which Rilke now looks down on earth. The poem describes an Orphic journey between the worlds of the living and the dead, whose boundary is erased in the poem's most famous line, "I have long taken life and death in quotation marks" (Zhizn′ i smert′ davno beru v kavychki). Tsvetaeva made a similar journey in a dream about Rilke which she had in the family nest, that is, in bed with her children Alya and Mur. In her dream, as she later described it to Pasternak, she encounters Rilke at an anthroposophical meeting presided over by Rudolph Steiner, and she appeals to Steiner's idea of the "transmigration of souls" to account for Rilke's presence: since he is only recently deceased, his body is intact and he remains close to earth, though he soon will be ascending beyond her reach.[40] When he thus visited her, she says he collaborated with her on finishing "New Year's Greeting," helping her fill twenty-four gaps in her poem.

Tsvetaeva's communion with the dead Rilke was most thoroughly imagined in her brilliant long poem, "Poem of the Air."[41] This was the last in the series of "meeting poems" Tsvetaeva wrote in connection with Pasternak and Rilke. After "From the Sea," she wrote "Attempt at a Room" ("Popytka komnaty," 1926), whose action is set in the hotel of Pasternak's dream. In that poem, the poet sits writing in her room when a male visitor arrives.[42] "Poem of the Air" begins with the same scenario:

> Well, here's the opening
> Couplet. The first nail.
> The door has gone noticeably quiet,
> Like a door a guest is standing behind.

> Ну, вот и двустишье
> Начальное. Первый гвоздь.
> Дверь явно затихла,
> Как дверь, за которой гость.

In this poem, however, the guest does not enter her room. Instead, Tsvetaeva leaves the space and joins Rilke on his ascent through seven distinct "heavens." There is another presence in the poem, however. Tsvetaeva's description of the gradually thinning air evokes her mother's death from consumption: "It was suffered out / In the stone bag / Of the lung. Inspect / The mucus" (Ot-stradano / V kamennom meshke / Legkogo! Issleduite / Sliz′!). As the poets ascend, they gradually shed their heavy mortal bodies and rise away from death. The poem's famous concluding image renders their flight as the flight of a spire from the stone body of a Gothic cathedral, which then also flies off in pursuit of its spire. As Alyssa Dinega has acutely observed, the image seems to describe "an allegory of a painful birth" when the church drops from its spire.[43] Read thus, the poem's conclusion renders the child's attempt to reverse her birth and join her lost mother.

"Poem of the Air" suggests that the mother's mortal body is the crucial context in which to understand Tsvetaeva's stagings of the loss of her own body, not only in this poem but at all such moments of "transcendence" in her work.

Her attempts to overcome the body express a horror of mortality; as she states in the poem, "The solid body is a dead body" (Tverdoe telo est' mertvoe telo). This dynamic appears with such clarity in "Poem of the Air," I believe, because Tsvetaeva found in Rilke her perfect lyric addressee. As I have argued, the loss of Rilke rehearsed the loss of her mother, the primary loss that structures her lyric address. Tsvetaeva always understood lyricism as generated by loss and experienced as trauma. It is a form of non-mourning of the sort Tsvetaeva described to Rilke, in which the lover is "always mourning" and the dead are "always dying." Within this perspective, Tsvetaeva's non-mourning of Rilke was the summit of lyrical achievement. Yet it also seems to have done some of the work of mourning, possibly because of the transference onto Rilke as a poet who so powerfully claimed the feminine. As Tsvetaeva put it to Pasternak, "After *such* a loss [she] remains invulnerable to anything except another SUCH loss," which she never will suffer, in fact, since she regards Rilke as not simply a lyric poet but lyricism itself (*DNV* 293). She wrote this as she was finishing "Poem of the Air," which she interpreted for Pasternak in a similar fashion: "Boris, I am writing a piece that will make your skin crawl. This piece is the beginning of my solitude, with it I'm getting out of something (withdrawing)" (*DNV* 351). This solitude is not a Rilkean solitude that sustains the poet's creativity but a new kind of solitude—the solitude of the end of mourning when the loss becomes real.

In other words, what Tsvetaeva was getting out of was lyricism. Her encounter with Rilke both confirmed her view of lyricism as a traumatic vocation and somehow moved her beyond it. Tsvetaeva largely had stopped writing lyric poems after 1925. As she later said to Pasternak, she knew "without sadness" that *After Russia* would be her last lyric collection (*DNV* 359). The long "meeting poems" she wrote in 1926–27 were the apotheosis of her lyricism, and they were followed by a writing crisis she repeatedly described in her letters to Pasternak.[44] She did work further on a trilogy of verse tragedies, writing "Phaedra" ("Fedra") in 1927, but did not complete the project.[45] She also worked on several historical poems in the late 1920s, a development Irina Shevelenko has persuasively ascribed to Pasternak's influence.[46] Tsvetaeva took up Pasternak's historicism with polemical intent, writing a hymn to the White Army's struggle in "Perekop" ("Perekop," 1928–29) and rendering the fate of the Romanovs in "Siberia" ("Sibir'," 1930). Her agenda was not simply to preserve the memory of those vanquished by the Bolsheviks but to contest what it means to write history. As Shevelenko has shown, Pasternak's political interest in history prompted Tsvetaeva to formulate her opposing view of history as "epos," or "epic": "Epos for her is that part of the past that survives the transformation into the eternal; it is a myth about history which incorporates the essential and drops the rest."[47] Thus Tsvetaeva, when she came to the end of lyricism, took up the question of history in her own way, first in her historical poems and then, more successfully, in the prose works to which she devoted most of her attention in the 1930s. In these essays, she writes a "family epic," returning to the autobiographism of her earliest writing.[48]

Tsvetaeva's encounter with Rilke also changed her relationship with Pasternak. In her new solitude, she immediately turned to Pasternak, ending a five-month silence. She wrote to him about Rilke's death as soon as she learned about it on December 31, and wrote again on January 1, 1927. She interpreted his death for Pasternak precisely as a blessing on their union: "I stubbornly insist on my relation to you, which Rilke's death definitively confirms. His death authorizes my right to be with you—more than a right, an order signed by his own hand" (*DNV* 289). Specifically, Rilke's death was a mandate for Tsvetaeva and Pasternak finally to accomplish their long-postponed meeting. Her proposal was concrete and specific: passports were cheap, she had read, and they could meet in London. She chose London because she knew Pasternak wanted to see the city; when she was there in March 1926, he wrote a long letter to her about his love of English literature, and she sent him an antiquarian map of the city. Pasternak replied to her letter in early February, and soon the poets were writing regularly again. As Pasternak said at the end of his letter, he was "chatting" with her "as though nothing had happened, as though we had parted yesterday" (*DNV* 284). Just as he had done a year earlier, Pasternak asked Tsvetaeva's advice on whether to come now or defer his trip for a year, expressing the same concern about doing "real work" (*DNV* 322). This time, however, he answered the question himself and declined Tsvetaeva's invitation.

Tsvetaeva accepted Pasternak's refusal with sadness, resignation, and a new perspective on the tragedy of separation. In an important letter of May 11, Tsvetaeva for the first time spoke of sexual love as a unique and desirable realm of experience.[49] The letter begins, "Boris, have you ever thought about that fact that there is an entire huge marvelous world that is forbidden to poetry and in which are revealed—were revealed, such immense laws" (*DNV* 336). This, at least, had been her experience as a poet, as she had earlier explained to Rilke. Representing herself to him as a bodiless Psyche, she described how writing about love gave her no access to it. More precisely, in attempting to know love through writing, she destroyed it: "I have always translated the body into the soul (*dis*-bodied it!), have so glorified 'physical love'—in order to be able to like it—that suddenly nothing was left of it" (*DL* 207). Here Tsvetaeva precisely analyzes her hysterical writing, writing that simultaneously is obsessed with the body and works to negate it. In this letter to Rilke she represents the dynamic as inevitable, and even as a dynamic she embraced. Not so in her letter to Pasternak, where she expresses a desire to know the body: "Boris, nothing is knowable together (everything—is forgotten together), neither honor, nor God, nor a tree. Only your *body, which is closed to you* (you have no entrance.) Think about it: the strangeness: an entire area of the soul, which I (you) cannot enter alone, I CANNOT ENTER ALONE. And it's not God who is needed, but a human being. Becoming through another person. *Sesam, ‹thue› dich auf*!!" (*DNV* 337). Tsvetaeva uses her familiar rhetoric about being channeled by the beloved. But this rhetoric now embraces the actual body, and the beloved is no longer a god but a human being. Moreover, the model is differently connoted, so that it describes not simply "moving through" each other but feeding each other. One of the "immense laws" of love she perceives is that the male lover, in slaking a woman's desire, slakes his own thirst: "The nourisher drinks" (Poiashchii p'et!) (*DNV* 336). With this imagining of mutual sustenance, Tsvetaeva moves beyond the "eat or be eaten" dynamic she represented in "From the Sea."

For Tsvetaeva, such love is possible only with another poet. In a later letter to Pasternak, she stated the full logic of her need to love a poet: only poets, used to contending with elemental force, are able to "poetically direct [napravliat']" love, fighting and succumbing to it like the progress of a poem, whose sound counters the meaning and whose meaning counters the sound" (*DNV* 372). Tsvetaeva's ideal love is a love whose anxieties and dangers are mastered the way a poet masters his elemental medium. The particular poet she needed was Pasternak, who in *My Sister Life* showed himself able to know the body through poetry. In her May letter, for the first time, Tsvetaeva spoke openly of Pasternak's poems as erotic: "Boris, you were already in this submerged [donnyi][50] world in *My Sister Life*—the fiery purity, the fiery purge of that book! At that time, when I wrote (badly, by the way), I hid it like a secret. But you didn't confine that world to nighttime but spread it through the whole day, drawing trees and clouds into it. You shared it out, stretched it out. Everyone has overlooked this in your book. I'm not talking about *Liebeslieder,* I'm talking about verse lines. There are lines that are identical, that act with equal force [ravnodeistvuiushchie]" (*DNV* 338). Back in 1922, Tsvetaeva had secretly written herself into Pasternak's erotic scenario, but now she declares her desire: "Someday take me into your bed, the most summery, leafy bed there is" (*DNV* 331). She wrote this, and her new reflections on love, in the wake of Pasternak's refusal to come to see her, which helps explain why she continued to imagine their love as a kind of writing (*DNV* 338–39). But what is new in these letters is Tsvetaeva's claim to Pasternak's sexual bed, in contrast to Rilke's cold nest.

Pasternak accepted Tsvetaeva's notion that Rilke's death authorized their relationship, but in a very different sense: it placed on him the responsibility of carrying forward Rilke's legacy, along with his sibling Tsvetaeva ("Do you grasp how crudely you and I have been orphaned?" [*DNV* 283]). What that meant for Pasternak was putting his historical poems behind him and taking up the defense of lyricism in Soviet culture. This was why, as he wrote to Tsvetaeva, he could not accept her invitation to visit her this year: "I am staying for another year. I'm endlessly happy and grateful that this has boiled over and I can write about it calmly, after two weeks of anxiety. Here's why I must stay: My visit to foreign territory must not simultaneously *coincide* with my return to myself: i.e., with a philosophy and tone which, of course, should go against everything here. I need to try to start this here, openly, in periodicals, locally, in conflict with the censors" (*DNV* 326). Pasternak's resolve in early 1927 to become a public apologist for lyricism was arguably not only a response to Rilke's death but also a capitulation to Tsvetaeva after their disagreements in 1926 over what and how Pasternak should be writing. He did go on to complete "Lieutenant Schmidt" but judged his effort to write historical poems no longer worth pursuing. His first act upon renewing his correspondence with Tsvetaeva was to send her everything he had written of part two of "Lieutenant Schmidt." As he wrote to her, he was able to finish it when he thought of it as being "in place of a letter" to Tsvetaeva on New Year's Eve (*DNV* 312). He wrote part three over the next few months, adjusting his portrayal of Schmidt in line with Tsvetaeva's demand for more heroism; he wrote it in a notebook she had sent him in 1926. Although Tsvetaeva warmly praised part three, he repeatedly agreed with her earlier low opinion of the poem, and when she declared her intention to write an essay about it, Pasternak begged her to desist.

While Pasternak was happy to put his historical poems behind him, he did not put aside his attempts to think through the poet's implication in exigent historical and political realities. Even as he embraced the cause of lyricism in his letter to Tsvetaeva, he also warned her, "You won't expect lyrics from me," rehearsing his familiar argument that lyricism was not yet historically possible in Soviet Russia, though it would become so in the future (*DNV* 327).[51] His defense of lyricism, that is, remained tied to his political hopes for a humane socialism. Tsvetaeva, disappointed as she was that Pasternak was not coming, accepted his reasoning in resigned tones: "But your argument (your reason) is justified . . . for I have long regarded as a truth the monstrous juxtaposition/ sound/harmony of 'you' and 'public spirit [obshchestvennost'].' In the end, it's simply, qu'en dire-t-on, goodness and concern. . . . I say that without malice or irony" (*DNV* 328). When she first registered the strength of his political commitments the previous fall, she wrote shocked and angry letters telling him that he was abandoning true poetry. She was now more reconciled to his choice and offered her best advice. She asked him not to listen to others' demands about his writing, including her own earlier demand that he write prose ("Dismiss the nannies, Boris"). He certainly should not heed the epoch, as she conveyed by rejecting his complaint about "lack of air" ("I believe only in the simple air you breathe with your lungs" [*DNV* 329]). She urged him to spend the summer alone somewhere far away from Moscow, somewhere in southern Russia, and "poems will come of their own accord—they can't not come" (*DNV* 331). Finally, she asked one thing for herself—that he someday make the trip to see her, "so it doesn't turn out like Orpheus and Eurydice" (*DNV* 328).

Over the next few years, Pasternak conscientiously pursued his defense of lyricism. Despite the general prohibition against praising Russian émigré writers and indeed any "bourgeois" writers in print, Pasternak managed to tell the story of his 1926 encounters with Tsvetaeva and Rilke in the pages of the Soviet journal *Reader and Writer* in early 1928.[52] He did so in the context of announcing that he was at work on an essay about Rilke, "about this amazing lyric poet and the unique world that, as with any true poet, his work creates." Pasternak had begun writing an article about Rilke in early 1927, not long after Rilke's death. But as he related in *Reader and Writer,* the article evolved into "an autobiographical fragment about how my views on art were formed" (*DL* 249). This fragment became part one of the book he would title *Safe Conduct*

(*Okhrannaia gramota*) when he finished it in 1931. The final version included an "afterword," cut by the censor, which took the form of a posthumous letter to Rilke. In a deliberate appeal to the genre in which Tsvetaeva mourned Rilke, Pasternak addressed the dead poet directly: "If you were alive today, I would write you this letter" (4:786). In Pasternak's case, the gesture had special poignancy, since Pasternak had never answered Rilke's note to him. As he explained in this posthumous letter, he had wanted to have new work to show Rilke before replying and was comforted by the thought that Tsvetaeva was acting in his place. The letter reads less like an apology than a confession of failure as a poet, and in fact he now offered the departed Rilke not new work but *My Sister Life*. Nevertheless, though Pasternak may have felt that he had fallen away from Rilke's poetic example, he took that example as his "safe conduct" through the politicized cultural environment of the late 1920s and early 1930s.

The main theme of Pasternak's correspondence with Tsvetaeva during 1927–29, and the defining context for this stage of their friendship, was the growing isolation of Soviet Russia. In the letter that revived their correspondence at the beginning of 1927, Pasternak spoke about the worsening political and cultural situation. He reported having read the first number of *Milestones* but warned Tsvetaeva not to send any other émigré periodicals by regular mail because they would be confiscated. He also told her about a scandal that unfolded in the fall concerning his acrostic dedication to her of "Lieutenant Schmidt." After hearing Tsvetaeva's criticisms of part one, Pasternak decided to remove the dedication. It nevertheless appeared at the head of the poem when it was published in the Soviet journal *New World* (*Novyi mir*). This journal, edited by the liberal Viacheslav Polonsky, had just endured official criticism for publishing Boris Pilniak's "Tale of the Unextinguished Moon" ("Povest' nepogashennoi luny," 1926). Polonsky, who had not noticed the acrostic, felt that Pasternak had placed him in jeopardy again by invoking the name of an émigré poet, a name that was "an aural ghost" in Russia, as Pasternak put it to Tsvetaeva. Pasternak quickly mended his friendship with Polonsky, who shared his moderate literary politics. In fact, at the time Pasternak was siding with Polonsky in a bitter conflict with Lef over the group's politicized literary agenda, in particular, Lef's demand that artists write in accordance with a "social command" (sotsial'nyi zakaz). Pasternak definitively broke his ties with Lef in May 1927, as he also related to Tsvetaeva. A year later he broke all personal ties with Mayakovsky for refusing to leave Lef. When Mayakovsky finally did leave the group, he formed the still more programmatic Ref, the Revolutionary Front of Art, which rejected all aesthetic criteria for political ones.[53] Whatever Mayakovsky's intentions, he thereby joined the general direction of Soviet cultural politics in the late 1920s toward the public persecution of artists on political grounds, a direction that convinced Pasternak that literature in Russia was dead.

At the same time, Pasternak was discovering new comrades abroad. Along with her first letters of 1927, Tsvetaeva forwarded to Pasternak a letter from Dmitry Sviatopolk-Mirsky, the literary scholar who was a family friend and a

fellow editor of *Milestones*. Because of a personal falling-out with Mirsky, Tsvetaeva tried to control his access to Pasternak.[54] Not just Mirsky, however, but
the entire *Milestones* group, including Tsvetaeva's husband, Efron, and her former lover Rodzevich, sought out Pasternak as a cultural link to Soviet Russia.
During the late 1920s they were becoming more deeply involved in Eurasianism, an émigré nationalist movement that identified the distinctive features of
Russian culture as "Asian" over and against the European culture within which
they were exiled. In 1928, Mirsky founded, and Efron edited, the newspaper
Eurasia (Evraziia), the organ of the movement. The politics of Eurasianism
were initially ill defined, but Efron's and Mirsky's sympathy for Russian socialism led in 1929 to a split in the movement between themselves and a group
of supporters of the Russian monarchy.[55] For Efron's circle, Pasternak was a
poet of the Russian revolution, and they warmly welcomed his poems about
1905. When the poems appeared as a book titled *1905* (1927), they received
inscribed copies through Tsvetaeva and wrote letters of praise to Pasternak in
Moscow.[56] Mirsky reviewed the book for the third issue of *Milestones* (1928),
stating that "Pasternak, the great revolutionary and transformer of Russian poetry, looks back on the entire previous tradition of the Russian revolutionary
martyrdom and gives it the aesthetic completeness it did not have the strength
to give itself."[57] Paradoxically, Pasternak's poems about the revolution found
their most receptive audience in Tsvetaeva's émigré milieu.

Still more paradoxically, this audience emerged just as Pasternak abandoned
his revolutionary poems, and with Tsvetaeva's encouragement. Once again, the
poets' correspondence became triangular, this time with the Eurasians, and in
particular Efron, who exchanged several letters with Pasternak over the course
of 1928–30. Pasternak, though he had never met Efron, always spoke about
him with warmth and admiration. When he sent Efron a copy of *1905* through
Tsvetaeva, he described the book as "the movement of kindred thoughts about
Russia" (*DNV* 434). His connection with Efron, that is, was based as much on
their shared vision of Russia as their shared love of Tsvetaeva. In his first letter
to Efron, Pasternak said that he considered Efron, Mirsky, and Suvchinsky "the
most upright and ingenuous of all the friends I might have or find there" (*DNV*
449); he wrote to Tsvetaeva, "I consider them and no one else the most in-
disputable and best friends I have in any circle or milieu" (*DNV* 457–58).
Pasternak was likely attracted by their nationalist pride in socialist Russia, un-
tarnished by the realities he was contending with on a daily basis. We know
enough about Pasternak's ambivalence toward contemporary history to doubt
that he fully shared the Eurasians' idealism. Rather than attempting to dispel
their illusions, however, he periodically sent messages and anecdotes about Soviet life to Efron, both directly and through Tsvetaeva, which suggested a hopeful future for Soviet Russia.

These stories were also intended for Tsvetaeva, who, as Pasternak knew, did
not share his and Efron's "kindred thoughts about Russia." When thanking
Pasternak for sending *1905* to Efron, Tsvetaeva remarked that Pasternak would

agree on more with Efron than with her (*DNV* 438). One of the most urgent questions about Tsvetaeva's years in Paris is whether and to what degree she shared her husband's politics, as he moved from being a Soviet sympathizer to a Soviet collaborator with links to the secret police (NKVD). Indisputably, Tsvetaeva respected Efron's principles and believed in his nobility of character. On this score she once compared him to Pasternak in a letter to a friend: "Now he [Efron] is . . . the *heart* of Eurasianism. The newspaper *Eurasia*, the only newspaper in the emigration (or in Russia)—is his idea, his child, his [illegible], his joy. In a way, in many ways, but mainly: with his conscience, his responsibility, his deeply serious nature, he is similar to Boris, but—more masculine. Boris, so to speak, is a feminine manifestation of the same essence" (7:314). Tsvetaeva's distinction between Pasternak and Efron recalls her criticism of "Lieutenant Schmidt," whose revolutionary hero she considered effeminate. Efron she regarded as a genuine, "masculine" hero. It is difficult to believe, however, that Tsvetaeva endorsed the same model as Efron when he opined that Pasternak should have chosen Ivan Kaliaev as his hero instead of Schmidt (*DNV* 239). Kaliaev was a member of the Socialist-Revolutionary Party who assassinated Grand Duke Sergey in 1905. Efron's own parents, Iakov Efron and Elizaveta Durnovo, were members of the same revolutionary movement; his father, a member of People's Will (Narodnaia volia), took part in an assassination, and his mother, a Socialist-Revolutionary, served time in prison for her activities.[58] That Efron imagined himself a hero in that same tradition was horrifyingly borne out by his later involvement in an assassination attempt against a former White Army general. Tsvetaeva's romantic maximalism, however, never extended to the realm of politics, and indeed was directed against that realm, as the allegory of "The Pied Piper" elaborates. Whatever her respect for Efron's, and Pasternak's, ideals, she refused to mythologize socialist Russia, much less any violence enacted in its name.[59]

Nonetheless, Tsvetaeva certainly shared the Eurasians' respect for the achievements of Soviet writers. She scandalized the émigré literary establishment by publishing in the pages of *Eurasia* a "welcome" to Vladimir Mayakovsky when he traveled to Paris in 1928 (7:350–51). She also believed that her true audience was back in Russia, despite the fact that she had been banished from the pages of Soviet publications. Most obviously, Tsvetaeva believed this because Pasternak himself was her true audience. But as we have seen, Pasternak also sent reports about showing or reading her work to Aseev and Mayakovsky. Now, in 1927, he gave her the same reassurances that she was a favorite in his circle, and that her long poems were circulating in handwritten copies (*DNV* 355).[60] Even as Pasternak's relations with Lef grew ever more conflicted, he continued to foster Tsvetaeva's connection with the group for a good reason: he wished to persuade this lyric genius to join his fight for lyricism in socialist Russia.

In late 1927, Pasternak became involved in a scheme to return Tsvetaeva and her family to Soviet Russia, a scheme apparently initiated by Tsvetaeva's sister

Anastasia. Tsvetaeva had not seen Anastasia since emigrating, though she wrote to her, often via Pasternak, who met Anastasia after his return from Berlin in 1923. In 1927, Anastasia received the highly unusual privilege of traveling abroad. She obtained a foreign visa on the strength of an invitation from Maxim Gorky to visit his estate in Sorrento, an invitation he also extended to Tsvetaeva. Gorky, a prominent writer of socialist convictions, had quarreled with the Bolsheviks after the revolution and emigrated to Italy, though as a familiar of Lenin he retained his prestige within the party. (He ended his exile in 1933 when he returned to Russia and helped shape the Stalinist literary doctrine of "socialist realism.") Gorky could not have been more alien to Tsvetaeva in his aesthetic and political sympathies, but his generosity may be explained by his old acquaintance with the Tsvetaev family. (The Tsvetaev girls had become friendly with Gorky's children in 1905 in the Crimea when their mother was taking the cure.)[61] In any case, Tsvetaeva responded with warmth and sent Gorky several of her books, which he predictably disliked, describing her poetry to Pasternak as "hysterical."[62] She did not travel to Sorrento, however. Instead, Anastasia made the trip from Sorrento to visit Tsvetaeva and her family in Meudon for two weeks in September.

Anastasia's visit yielded what Pasternak would refer to as "Asya's plan," a plan she concealed from Tsvetaeva. Asya was appalled by the conditions in which Tsvetaeva was living, worse than usual because most of the family came down with scarlet fever. For a long time it has been assumed that her plan was to arrange, with Gorky's help, for Soviet publication of Tsvetaeva's work, thus enhancing her income.[63] If it were simply a matter of publishing her work, however, there would have been no need for secrecy, since Tsvetaeva had already asked Gorky for help in this regard when she wrote to him.[64] Gorky himself believed that he was being asked to help Tsvetaeva return to Russia.[65] It seems likely that Asya, an ardent patriot, bonded with Efron during her visit and with him pursued a plan to bring the family back to Russia.[66]

Asya enlisted both Gorky's and Pasternak's aid, possibly even before she made the trip, to judge from Pasternak's letters at the time. He suggestively wrote to Tsvetaeva on September 8 that "if you were here, I would be completely happy with my homeland and either wouldn't think about 'abroad' at all, or only that part I need to for my parents and sisters" (*DNV* 381–82). When Asya wrote to him from Europe about Gorky's admiration for "The Childhood of Luvers," Pasternak sent Gorky a copy of *1905* inscribed to "the great expression and justification of the epoch," and they had a friendly exchange of letters.[67] When Asya returned to Moscow on October 12 and told Pasternak about Gorky's willingness to help Tsvetaeva, he wrote a thrilled letter to him, thanking him for his generosity and declaring his commitment to Tsvetaeva: "The role and lot of . . . M. Ts. are such that if you asked what I intend to *write* or do, I would answer: anything at all that could help her, and raise and return to Russia this great human being, who perhaps has not known how to put her gift on an equal footing with destiny, or, rather, the other way around."[68] Pas-

ternak wrote this to Gorky on October 13 and, possibly uncomfortable with
the idea of keeping a secret from Tsvetaeva, quoted it to her in a letter of October 15 (*DNV* 405). A few days later he wrote to her to say how much Gorky's
interest in Tsvetaeva had touched him, exclaiming, "Oh, if only you were here!"
(*DNV* 417). In the same letter he asked, "Do you know what Russia is now?"
and supplied an ecstatic answer. Russia is, he related, a peasant visiting Pasternak's cleaning woman with a copy of *My Sister Life* in his hands, a peasant who
was studying in a "Worker's Department" (rabfakul'tet). Could Tsvetaeva, he
asked, understand and take joy in this? (*DNV* 418).

Unfortunately, in his letter to Gorky, Pasternak also let drop that Asya had
conveyed Gorky's low opinion of *1905*, an indiscretion that angered Gorky.
Moreover, Gorky thought there was virtually no possibility of Tsvetaeva's receiving permission to return to Russia;[69] he offered instead to give her financial assistance. Alarmed by this turn of events, Pasternak asked Gorky to
withdraw from the plan and allow him to help Tsvetaeva by sending her money
through his family, which he did (5:222).[70] (Gorky not only withdrew but also
cut off his correspondence with Pasternak.)[71] This act of charity brought Tsvetaeva into a brief but heartfelt correspondence with Pasternak's parents and his
sister Josephine in Munich.[72] It also marked the beginning of what might be
termed the "philanthropic" years of their relationship, during which Pasternak
found ways to get material support to Tsvetaeva's family, mainly through the
generosity of his émigré friend Raisa Lomonosova.[73]

As the Gorky episode was unfolding without her knowledge, Tsvetaeva conceived her own remarkable plan—to make a trip to Russia (*DNV* 423). She ascribed the idea to Rodzevich, but most likely she was encouraged by Asya's
success in traveling abroad. When she broached the idea with Pasternak, he
warned her it would be difficult to get a visa, but he also reported that Aseev
was about to travel to see Gorky and intended to win him to Tsvetaeva's cause
with one of his dramatic readings of her long poems (*DNV* 433). She replied
by welcoming Aseev only as an emissary from Pasternak, repeating the rhetoric
of her earlier letter about finally "loving a human being" and discovering the
"America" of physical love. She said, as though she did, after all, know something about Asya's plan: "I wasn't talking about returning but about visiting.
These are very different things: 'may I visit you' and 'may I live with you'"
(*DNV* 438). Although she also spoke about her longing for Russia, Tsvetaeva
refused to contemplate returning there, as her family pressured her to do for the
next ten years.

The Gorky episode reveals that Tsvetaeva's conflict with her family was already opening in 1927, and that Pasternak was implicated in it. Although the
idea of Tsvetaeva's improbable visit to Russia in 1927 was dropped, the question of the family's return remained a pressing one. It was also a matter of rumor in both émigré and Soviet Russia. When Mayakovsky visited Paris in late
1928, he was accompanied by Tsvetaeva's old friend Pavel Antokolsky, who
visited her there. One or both of them spread news of her return to Soviet Russia, as Pasternak reported to her:

I don't know if Mayakovsky's stories fed the gossip going around the city, but since the spring, rumor of your supposed return has been growing more and more stubborn. Now, in a disordered way, I have some advice on the matter. Fragmentarily, from A. [Antokolsky], I learned about S's [Efron's] unique heroicizing of our affairs, and how little A. was able to satisfy him on that score. Well, S. Ia. [Efron] is of course closer to the truth than A., with the caveat that this truth is not given, not artificially contemplative, not romantic, but—to be achieved, growing thinly on the steep slopes of challenges, anti-romantic, Pushkinian and not Pushkinizing, i.e., a truth where the personally brilliant wholly and almost anonymously is smelted into the laboring massif of works and influences. (*DNV* 499–500)

Pasternak's letter is remarkable for the way it announces his "advice" on the question of Tsvetaeva's return to Russia. With absolute consistency, he hewed to his old argument: it is early to heroicize socialism; we are not there yet; in order to get there, we must bring genius ("the personally brilliant") to our cause. Not only did he wish for Tsvetaeva to return, he actually encouraged her to do so, in his own hesitant, oblique fashion. When Efron wrote to him in early 1930, apparently for help obtaining his Soviet citizenship, Pasternak declared to Tsvetaeva that he was "terribly glad to hear from him" (*DNV* 517).[74] Pasternak's reply to Efron himself was more anxious, reflecting the strain of holding to the "Pushkinian" course in a false environment, but he still concluded with a salute to the revolution (*DNV* 523). As he confessed to Tsvetaeva, he was ashamed to reveal his doubts to his more heroic companions abroad: "I write and sense that from afar you, and especially the men (S. Ia., D.P, P.P. [Efron, Mirsky, Suvchinsky]) must despise me for this funereal tone" (*DNV* 530).

Pasternak's main literary endeavors during the late 1920s and early 1930s were his "essay on Rilke" and his novel in verse, *Spektorsky*. Like the essay, the novel was "in its conception almost on the border of being a complete apologia for the poetic world," as he described it to Tsvetaeva (*DNV* 345). The two works were also more autobiographical than his earlier writings, a development that paralleled Tsvetaeva's own turn to the "family epic." He had begun the novel in March 1925, around the time he conceived and began writing his historical poems.[75] When the first three chapters appeared that year, his readers immediately recognized that Pasternak was writing a contemporary *Eugene Onegin*. Above and beyond Pasternak's choice of genre, his hero Spektorsky resembled the attractive but shiftless Onegin, and there was a carefully orchestrated interplay between the author's life and his hero's. Like the narrator of Pushkin's *Onegin*, Pasternak's narrator is his hero's contemporary and acquaintance; in this case, they are members of the Moscow intelligentsia during the period 1913–19. The novel begins with both characters having stayed up all night, which is also how Pushkin's hero arranges his time in the first chapter of *Onegin*. The reason for the narrator's night-owl existence is not directly given, but mention of a lamp and table suggests that he is a writer (though he is later described as a composer). In this first chapter, the narrator observes Spektorsky walking down the street after a night out; he does not actively fig-

Sergey Efron, 1937

Ariadna Efron, 1930s

ure in Spektorsky's story until the final chapter, where he crosses paths with him in a crucial plot twist.

The intersection between autobiography and fiction is likely what drew Pasternak to Pushkin's model: it allowed him to create a complicated relationship to his alter ego through the novel's composition, in contrast to "Lieutenant Schmidt," where his affinity with his hero was suggested discursively. Relatedly, in the novel the narrator's relation to Spektorsky has a temporal dimension, evolving in the course of Pasternak's incremental work on the novel. Like Pushkin, he wrote and published chapters as he finished them between 1925 and 1929. Unlike Pushkin, he gave the novel some closure by adding an introduction in 1930 and making revisions for the separate edition that appeared in 1931.

Pasternak's renewed relationship with Tsvetaeva in 1927 catalyzed a major shift in his work on the novel.[76] He wrote the first four chapters in 1925, publishing the first three together that same year. Chapter 1 shows Spektorsky returning home at dawn, late to meet his sister at the train station. Chapter 2 takes the action back to a year earlier, when Spektorsky had an affair with a woman named Olga Bukhteeva. Chapter 3 returns us to that morning in Moscow when Spektorsky's sister Natasha arrives on her own and cleans his apartment, while he remains in an Onegin-like state of ennui and depression. In Chapter 4 it emerges that Natasha is a revolutionary, and she quarrels with Spektorsky about his apoliticism before leaving for her home in the provinces. This is the chapter Pasternak sent to Tsvetaeva in May 1926 with a complaint about its "arrhythmia," which he was trying to combat with the polymetricism of "Lieutenant Schmidt." (*Spektorsky* is written in iambic pentameter, in four-line stanzas.)

Pasternak did not return to *Spektorsky* until he finished "Lieutenant Schmidt" in mid-1927. In the next chapter, chapter 5, he introduced two new characters. First, we meet another revolutionary, Sashka Balts, an acquaintance of Spektorsky's. When Spektorsky runs into Balts on the way to a tutoring job, Balts invites him to join an impromptu gathering at his apartment. The chapter closes with Spektorsky critically observing Balts's guests but drawn to an unidentified woman who appears similarly distanced from the others: "Possibly he wasn't the only one / Who didn't take it all so lightly" (Vozmozhno tut ne odnomu emu / Ne tak legko na eto vse smotrelos').[77] This new character is a poet named Maria Il'ina, whose name is a barely disguised version of "Marina." Pasternak, that is, drew Tsvetaeva into the world of *Spektorsky*, fundamentally altering its direction. From this point on, he conceived the novel as centrally about Spektorsky's relationship with Il'ina, and about his own relationship to Tsvetaeva. In 1927, *Spektorsky* became a vehicle for Pasternak to think through the events of 1926 and to give a definitive—and public—account of their relationship in its romantic and creative aspects. By introducing in this chapter the revolutionary thematic alongside Tsvetaeva, he also addressed the historical context of their exchange. With this telling of their story, Pasternak described the fate of poetry in postrevolutionary Russia.

The scene in which Il'ina first appears employs factual details from Pasternak's and Tsvetaeva's biographies. In January 1918, Pasternak and Tsvetaeva both attended a famous literary gathering where Mayakovsky read his poem "Man" ("Chelovek," 1918). (Pasternak later described the scene in *Safe Conduct* in a way that recalls Spektorsky's attraction to Il'ina: "I instinctively picked her out from among those present for her striking simplicity" [5:230].) Another fact underpins Spektorsky's meetings with Il'ina in the following chapters, where he visits her messy apartment. Pasternak visited Tsvetaeva once in her apartment on Borisoglebsky Lane in the fall of 1921 on a mission from Ehrenburg. Ehrenburg had recently discovered Sergey Efron in Prague and was helping Tsvetaeva emigrate to rejoin him; as Pasternak probably knew, he was delivering a letter from Efron.[78] He witnessed the poverty and disorder of Tsvetaeva's home, where she lived alone with Ariadna, having already lost Irina to the famine. When Tsvetaeva read the novel, she recognized her place on Borisoglebsky.[79]

Pasternak selectively transposed details from these episodes to 1913, the year in which the novel's action begins. The most important detail he retains is that Il'ina has a "foreign passport" and is on the brink of leaving Russia. The most striking omission he makes is that Il'ina has no husband or children, though this could also be a deliberate calculation; Pasternak might reasonably have believed that Tsvetaeva was still unmarried in 1913 and that he was staying close to the biographical record. (She actually married Efron in January 1912, the same year she gave birth to Ariadna.) Another detail bespeaks the precision with which Pasternak was handling biographical material. He accurately included mention of the death of Tsvetaeva's father in 1913, having learned it from the questionnaire she filled out for him in 1926. When Spektorsky meets Il'ina, she is in mourning for her father, who, like Ivan Tsvetaev, was a professor.

Pasternak's careful appeal to biographical fact suggests that he was inventing a retrospective scenario about what it would have been like to have an affair with Tsvetaeva in his youth. (Earlier, in a 1923 letter to Tsvetaeva, he had retrospectively imagined having a love affair with her instead of Elena Vinograd in 1917.) He transports their encounter to an earlier period when there was nothing to separate them—neither their respective marriages nor the historical event of the revolution, which was the reason Tsvetaeva finally used her "foreign passport." In thus elaborating a fantasy about their meeting, *Spektorsky* answers Tsvetaeva's "From the Sea," where she imagined the two poets "sleeping together."[80] Tsvetaeva's poem was a fantasy about an impossible tryst, whose impossibility is signified by its sexual innocence. Pasternak renders his fantasy in a novelistic mode, which is to say the affair has a locale, a history, and a full range of emotional, creative, and sexual connections. Remarkably, it involves a domestic arrangement: not long after Spektorsky's first visit, he moves into Il'ina's apartment. Contrary to Tsvetaeva's vision, Pasternak's fantasy involves both sleeping together and living together. Because his fantasy is articulated as a narrative, it also takes their relationship to a conclusion, that is, to their eventual parting. Pasternak's imagining of their affair is also an imagining of their "breakup." His account of how they parted ways evokes not only the personal and historical circumstances that dictated their many "missed meetings" but also the particulars of their falling-out in 1926.

The scenario Pasternak details in *Spektorsky*, in which the poets move in together, was a perennial subject of their correspondence. Tsvetaeva had always dismissed the idea that they could live together, while continuing to raise the question. It became particularly acute in late 1924–25, when, pregnant with Georgy, she was possessed by the thought of carrying Pasternak's child. As she explained to Pasternak then, she could not live with him because she is a Psyche, an entirely undomestic creature: "I've made my soul my home (maison roulante), but never made my home—a soul" (*DNV* 105).[81] She also cast Pasternak as a similarly unfettered spirit. In the 1926 letter in which she "freed" Pasternak to have affairs with other women, she explained, "I wouldn't be able to live with you not because of misunderstanding but because of understanding" (*DNV* 252). In her self-representation and her representation of Pasternak, Tsvetaeva hewed to the romantic notion that poets are beings incapable of domestic life. Such are the characters of Spektorsky and Il'ina in Pasternak's novel. Spektorsky, like the young Pasternak, is a composer; like him, and like the author, Il'ina begins her day at dusk. In creating this vision of a shared bohemianism, Pasternak was offering back to Tsvetaeva her vision of who he was—accepting, at least at this point in the novel, her co-authoring of himself as essentially like her.[82]

Pasternak's entire rendering of the affair in *Spektorsky* is a co-authored text that draws on the poems and letters they exchanged. Spektorsky's first meetings with Il'ina take place during "hours not entered in the lists" (v chasy, kotorykh v spiskakh net) and leave "no trace" (ne sled)—images drawn from the "treasury of similes" Tsvetaeva supplied in the lyrics of *After Russia*. These images mingle with those from his own lyrical treasury: their meeting times are set "in the sound of birds; / In the branches of rain; in the bird-cherry, and in thunder" (v shume ptits; / V kistiakh dozhdia; v cheremukhe i v grome). In a typically Pasternakian rendering of lovers' passion, nature "flies in the windows" during the nights Spektorsky spends in Il'ina's apartment:

> Here they kissed, in waking and accustomed reality.
> Here it was like smoke and rain shower, mist and din,
> Like smile to smile, mane to mane,
> Like pearls to pearls they clung.

> Тут целовались, наяву и вживе.
> Тут, точно дым и ливень, мга и гам,
> Улыбкою к улыбке, грива к гриве,
> Жемчужинами льнули к жемчугам.

The figures—"smoke and rain shower"—are familiar but, atypically for Pasternak, they are similes rather than metaphors. As such they do not veil, as Pasternak's figurative language usually does, the human actors and physical actions being described. This is a surprisingly forthright imagining of the poets' engagement as erotic, an imagining of the sort in which Tsvetaeva freely indulged in her lyrics. In fact, the imagery of the last two lines is Tsvetaevan and appears lifted from "The Tsar-Maiden," with its portrait of androgynous mythological lovers.[83]

The section describing the affair concludes with a favorite image of Tsvetaeva's, one that recalls the conclusion of "The Swain," where the lovers escape the world through flight: "And both flew off into the Empyrean, / Giving each other wings, that is, apart" (I oba unosilis' v empirei, / Vzaimookrylivshis', to est' vroz'). There is another subtext for these lines in a letter from Pasternak to Tsvetaeva. In October 1927, Pasternak, along with Evgenia, took his first flight on a plane, which he enthusiastically described to Tsvetaeva, asking her to join him someday on another ride: "The thunder and thrumming will deafen us, I won't be able to bother you, it will be solitude together, imposed by height" (*DNV* 407). The airplane metaphor made its way into his description of how earth flew into Il'ina's apartment "and thrust its tailfin / Parting a cloud like a sail" (Vletala v okna i vonzala kil', / Rasplastyvaia oblako, kak parus).[84]

Pasternak's imagery of flight and heights, glossed as "solitude together," is not characteristic of him and may be understood as a concession to Tsvetaeva as co-author of their relationship. He is most true to her in depicting the relationship as ultimately unrealizable; after Spektorsky and Il'ina's flight into the Empyrean, suddenly "now abysses yawned between them" (Teper' mezh nimi propasti ziiali). In fact, this line probably refers to a Tsvetaeva poem that appeared in *Milestones*, in which two lovers are two wings between whom "lay an abyss" (i bezdna prolegla).[85] Echoing a theme in Pasternak's and Tsvetaeva's correspondence, Spektorsky and Il'ina never give a definitive name to their relations: "and they would not let fall the word / Until they gave some shape to the whole wild affair" (i ne proroniat slova, / Poka ne splaviat ves' shurum-burum).[86] They contend with "the tyranny of the most confusing of confusions" (samodurstvom / Nerazberikhoi iz nerazberikh). In terms of the novel's plot, the relationship ends precisely because of a misunderstanding: Spektorsky leaves town for a few days without telling Il'ina, and she, feeling abandoned and hurt, finally decides to go abroad. That gap in communication also structured Pasternak's fantasy about flying in a plane with Tsvetaeva—the noise of the engines will prevent them from talking. He thereby suggests that in some essential way they cannot hear each other, however deep their kinship.

Pasternak's fictional version of his history with Tsvetaeva obliquely elaborates several causes for their separation. First, there is history, the event of the revolution. Despite his setting the action in 1913, Pasternak strongly evokes the circumstances of 1917–22, and not just through his picture of Il'ina/Tsvetaeva's messy apartment. Before we enter that space, Pasternak gives a five-stanza description of construction work going on around her building, which is being torn down and rebuilt. It is a scene of chaos and implied danger: "With horsepower, rebellious, ragtail, / The bicarbonate courtyard bubbled like a spring" (Mnogoloshadnyi, buinyi, goloshtannyi, / Dvuuglekislyi dvor kipel kliuchom); "Vocal chords were exposed. / The gravel's breathing opened its jaws wide" (Pokazyvalis' gorlovye sviazki. / Dykhanie shchebnia razevalo past'). It is, in other words, an allegorical picture of the revolution in progress, which threatens Il'ina/Tsvetaeva's home. Her apartment, in turn, connotes a last refuge for prerevolutionary "cultural relics," to use the rhetoric of the early Soviet culture wars. As Il'ina explains, her mess has meaning: "Any object you see here is a true story" (Ved' tut chto veshch', to byl'). The revolution's threat is realized in a later scene when Spektorsky returns to Moscow and finds the apartment not simply abandoned but torn up, strewn with building materials and tools. As we discover in the final chapter, Il'ina's detritus ended up on the scrap heap of history, in a warehouse for the belongings of those who died in or fled from the revolution. Pasternak thereby casts Tsvetaeva as a curator of Russian culture and history who became the revolution's victim.

Yet Il'ina/Tsvetaeva does not go quietly. She strongly objects to how things are unfolding around them, a stance that is somehow implicated in her estrangement from Spektorsky. We know her thoughts because the narrator quotes an entry from Il'ina's working notebook containing her reflections "about those days" (Ob etikh dniakh). Pasternak, that is, invented words for Tsvetaeva in his own iambic pentameter—a remarkable gambit even in the context of the poets' accustomed sharing of voices. He reveals intimate knowledge of her writing habits, including the fact that she used her notebooks for all kinds of jottings, and gives an evocative description of her handwriting:

> Among her poems there was an entry
> About those days, where the handwriting was prickly
> As thorns, and hatred, like silver nitrate,
> Furrowed the page with a fountain of blots.
>
> "The window is in scaffolding and—we, two caricatures,
> In order to avoid giving free shows,
> Will draw a curtain on the plasterers,
> But won't get out of the display window.
>
> It could be we'll prematurely ponder
> The unfathomable meaning of good and evil.
> But that's not the point. Life has its favorites.
> I think we aren't among them.
>
> This is a time of improvisations.
> But when will we start talking seriously?
> When will we, used up, take up our vocation
> In the field of buried dreams?

There's no way out. The older I grow, the more
Earth bursts into my daily environment
And drives away will and takes willessness
Under graveyards, ravines, and fields.

P.S All this needs to be confirmed.
I don't trust my thoughts—the weather changes every minute.
The day my things are at Shiperka's
I'll probably change my mind."

Среди ее стихов осталась запись
Об этих днях, где почерк был иглист,
Как тернии, и ненависть, как ляпис,
Фонтаном клякс избородила лист.

«Окно в лесах, и—две карикатуры,
Чтобы избегнуть даровых смотрин,
Мы занавесимся от штукатуров,
Но не уйдем из показных витрин.

Мы рано, может статься, углубимся
В неисследимый смысл добра и зла.
Но суть не в том. У жизни есть любимцы.
Мне кажется, мы не из их числа.

Теперь у нас пора импровизаций.
Когда же мы заговорим всерьез?
Когда, иссякнув, станем подвизаться
На поприще похороненных грез?

Исхода нет. Чем я зрелей, тем боле
В мой обиход врывается земля
И гонит волю и берет безволье
Под кладбища, овраги и поля.

P.S. Все это требует проверки.
Не верю мыслям,—семь погод на дню.
В тот день, как вещи будут у Шиперки,
Я, вероятно, их переменю.»

The vocabulary of this section is Pasternak's, and it expresses what he viewed as
Tsvetaeva's uncompromising nature—here, her attitude toward the revolution
whose "scaffolding" hangs outside her window and allows "the plasterers" to
look into her private world. This is not simply a violation of privacy, however;
her window is a "display window" because of the cultural authority of the poet.
Were the poet a less public figure, she would be less susceptible to compromise,

to becoming a "caricature." In the view Pasternak ascribes to Tsvetaeva, the historical situation places both of them in a false position, with the most serious ethical consequences ("It could be we'll prematurely ponder / The unfathomable meaning of good and evil"). Her solution is not to withdraw into privacy (to "draw a curtain") but to "get out of the display window" altogether, that is, to emigrate. The fact that Il'ina is speaking precisely about emigration is clear from the postscript, where she imagines leaving some of her things at the pawnshop (Shiperka's) to raise money for the trip. She hesitates to act on her convictions, on some level not wishing to leave. Like Tsvetaeva, however, she does not expect to be able to do as she wishes, regarding tragedy as the poet's inevitable fate: "Life has its favorites. / I think we aren't among them."

How is it, exactly, that the revolution places the poet in a false position? Il'ina remarks that it is "a time of improvisations," recalling Pasternak's repeated depictions of the revolution as a period of historical limbo, in which the shape of the future cannot be discerned. But the word "improvisation" is used here the way Tsvetaeva uses the word "rough draft" (chernovik), that is, to designate the incomplete, unsatisfactory strivings that characterize everyday life and, on a larger scale, human history. Il'ina the maximalist holds out for something better, more nearly perfect, more "serious." Her idealism is so extreme, and her disappointment so strong, that it yields a hatred that burns into the page like silver nitrate. Surely when Pasternak wrote these lines he was recalling, in particular, the vicious satire of "The Pied Piper," with its rejection of all compromised endeavors, including the revolution. In chapter 4 of Tsvetaeva's poem, the Piper accuses the revolutionaries of betraying their political ideal and calls them to rededicate themselves to it. Il'ina's own call to "take up our vocation / In the field of buried dreams" sounds rather like the Piper's call. And as he did in his response to "The Pied Piper," Pasternak resists Tsvetaeva's maximalism in these stanzas of *Spektorsky*.

Il'ina's exhortation to "take up our vocation" is expressed in the familiar, charged terms of agency and passivity. She describes her own maturing as a process of losing her will, or more precisely, having it taken away from her by "earth," as it "bursts into her daily environment" (V moi obikhod vryvaetsia zemlia). This is the third time in this scene Pasternak introduces the topos of inspiration as penetration through the window. First, during the poets' lovemaking, "[earth] flew into the windows" (vletala v okna), connoting both eroticism and lyric creativity. In a second instance, the revolution sets up its scaffolding outside her window, intruding on their privacy, just as it intruded on Lieutenant Schmidt's budding affair in the earlier poem. Nature, eroticism, lyricism, and revolution are figurally indistinguishable here, as they so often are for Pasternak. They are forces that cannot be resisted; as Il'ina says, nature "drives away will" (gonit vol'iu), in a process that both Tsvetaeva and Pasternak regarded as the process of poetic creativity.

But nature further "takes willessness / Under graveyards, ravines, and fields" (i beret bezvol'e / Pod kladbishcha, ovragi i polia). This action could be understood as recuperative, that is, as nature saving "willessness," or lyricism, from the site of history under construction and returning it to a natural Russian landscape that preserves the memory of generations. Such an interpretation accords with Pasternak's insistence on a history of the revolution that acknowledges its forebears. Nevertheless, what is most important for our reading of this scene is that Il'ina does not appear to be interested in this sort of recuperation but objects to being rendered "willess." Her impulse is to change her circumstances by an act of will rather than to succumb to the forces in play around her; she intends to emigrate rather than to "go underground," as it were. If Pasternak is suggesting that the poet can and should succumb, then he represents Il'ina/Tsvetaeva as making an unfortunate choice, as indeed he did in his letters of the period. As he wrote to Gorky in 1927, he would do anything to "return to Russia this great human being, who perhaps has not known how to put her gift on an equal footing with destiny, or, rather, the other way around" (*DL* 255).

At the very least, Il'ina makes a different choice than does Spektorsky, who as she writes this entry is occupied at the piano, "weaving the cord of his impromptus" (On plel svoikh ekspromptov kanitel'). The phrase suggests a tediously prolonged activity and echoes Il'ina's phrase "a time of improvisations." Spektorsky, that is, is in the same mode as contemporary history, trying out creative ideas without result. Il'ina's impatience is directed not just at their larger situation but at Spektorsky himself. Pasternak thus establishes a discord in the relationship before the episode that definitively ends it. One day Spektorsky stops by his own apartment, after spending all his time at Ili'na's, to discover that a telegram arrived ten days earlier announcing that his mother was deathly ill and he should come to Petersburg immediately. He rushes there and somehow, in the course of the two weeks it takes for his mother to improve, fails to let Il'ina know where he is. Il'ina abruptly decides to emigrate, and when Spektorsky returns to Moscow, she is gone. In this story about Spektorsky's disappearance, one hears an echo of Tsvetaeva's February 1923 letters, in which she begged Pasternak not to "disappear."[87]

In representing Spektorsky's failure to communicate with Il'ina, Pasternak oddly suggests that she was eclipsed by Spektorsky's mother: "When he blamed himself around Tver' / Concerned about Maria, he realized / What a mother is, and in childish superstition / Was startled by these simple feelings" (Kogda on ulichil sebia pod Tver'iu/ V zabotakh o Marii, to postig / Chto znachit mat', i v detskom suever'i / Sharakhnulsia ot etikh chuvstv prostykh). What draws him to his mother is the simplicity of a child's love, in contrast to the opaque quality of his feeling for Il'ina; she is not the maternal Tsvetaeva he dreamed about in 1926. This story about the end of their relationship also mitigates Spektorsky's guilt: he left Il'ina for his mother and not for another woman. As Pasternak establishes, "that this man / Was neither a Don Juan nor a deceiver, / Maria herself knew better than anyone" (Chto etot chelovek / Nikak ne Don Zhuan i ne obmanshchik, / Sama Maria znala lushche vsekh). Here Pasternak refers to Tsvetaeva's own characterization of him in 1925 as "too faithful" to be a Don Juan (*DNV* 106), which they both perhaps found confirmed by his fidelity to Evgenia, despite the temptations of the summer of 1926. Don Juan or no, Spektorsky's behavior traumatizes Il′ina, as Pasternak takes pains to describe:

> It maddened her that she did not know
> His home address. All she could do was live,
> Clothe herself in fury and lie to herself unconscionably
> In order to hide her suffering with a proud lie.
>
> And as soon as the lumps rose in her throat,
> She hurried to drown their weight
> In a frozen wail of pride
> And smashed her grief with rage.

> Бесило, что его домашний адрес
> Ей неизвестен. Оставалось жить,
> Рядиться в гнев и врать себе, не зазрясь,
> Чтоб скрыть страданье в горделивой лжи.
>
> И вот, лишь к горлу подступали клубья,
> Она спешила утопить их груз
> В оледенелом вопле самолюбья
> И яростью перешибала грусть.

Il′ina's helplessness leaves her hysterical, wailing, choking, and expressing violent emotion. Pasternak represents her hysteria as a strategy for managing trauma: she suppresses the "lumps in her throat" with a "frozen wail of pride." But he also judges it a strategy of deception, "a proud lie." Her lie seems to consist in hiding her suffering with "fury." Pasternak, that is, resists the hysteric's rage in this analysis of Il′ina's grief. Hers is a terrifying affect, like the corrosive hatred she symbolizes through her handwriting. More to the point, it is an affect that ends their relationship, since it is Il′ina's rage that impels her to leave Moscow, just as Tsvetaeva's upset over his confession of love for Evgenia led to the break in their correspondence in 1926.

Though Il′ina exits the novel at this point, the rage of the injured woman becomes the focus of the next and final chapters, chapters 8 and 9. They are set in 1919, six years after Il′ina's departure.[88] In chapter 8 the author reflects on the revolution and Civil War, but not in a narrative mode, which is to say that this chapter does not continue Spektorsky's story. This is precisely Pasternak's point—that during the revolution, the individual's fate is of no consequence ("Does [the reader], living in the grip of this picture, / Really believe in the story of the individual?" [Neuzhto, zhiv v okhvate toi kartiny, / On verit v byl′ otdel′nogo litsa?]). Instead, he presents an allegory about the period, an allegory that centers on sexual violence and woman's vengeance. Amidst the familiar rendering of the "bad weather" of revolution, the figure of a girl emerges: "Suddenly there's the cry of some girl in a basement" (Vdrug krik kakoi-to devushki v chulane). Then, the sunset, losing its "daughterly shame" (styd dochernii), becomes a Fury, breaking out the window with her heel and fleeing, followed by a "son's collar" (shivorot synovnii). The rhetoric of family was established in the preceding stanza, which describes revolution's epiphany about the kinship of all existence:

> Along the way it becomes clear: in this world
> There's no dust without a speck of kinship:
> Along with life these are bastard children—
> Courtyards and women, crows and firewood.

> Попутно выясняется: на свете
> Ни праха нет без пятнышка родства:
> Совместно с жизнью прижитые дети—
> Дворы и бабы, галки и дрова.

In the following stanzas it also becomes clear that this family excludes a generalized "you": the *intelligent* who is now isolated and spurned as a cultural relic ("You are alone . . . / And loneliness—is rococo" [Ty odinok . . . / A odinokost'—eto rokoko]). Worse, he becomes the victim of revolutionary violence: "Then you'll cry out. I'm not your fool! I'm being attacked!" (Togda ty v krik. Ia vam ne shut! Nasil'e!).[89] Here the rage of the raped girl leads to the violation of the *intelligent*. The girl's power is confirmed in a second allegorical scene, where she reappears as an Amazon—a woman on horseback in a "cherkess," fighting with the Red Army in the Civil War.

In this chapter of *Spektorsky*, Pasternak openly draws on the familiar plot about violence and gender to interpret the event of the revolution and to describe his own ambivalent stance toward it. In rendering the revolution's violence as the hysterical violence of the rape victim, Pasternak suggests that it is on some level justified and must be endured by the intelligentsia, however terrifying and possibly fatal. Here Pasternak makes clear that his view of the revolution as "elemental" is conditioned by a psychosexual logic: he responds to it as he responds to the spectacle of the hysterical woman, with sympathy and terror. That logic also underlay his representations of a feminized intelligentsia in "A Sublime Malady" and "Lieutenant Schmidt," where, however, it was not fully elaborated. In *Spektorsky*, Pasternak represents not only the *intelligent* but also the hysteric with whom he identifies as a victim of violence. But as the next and final chapter further establishes, the *intelligent* is also complicit in woman's suffering. In his novel, that is, Pasternak brings the drama of the heterosexual romance to his representation of revolutionary politics, in the end to define his own position as a traumatized lover of the revolution.[90]

Chapter 9 leaves behind the allegorical mode and returns us to the narrative. We learn that by 1919 Spektorsky has become a "literator," which roughly translates as "professional man of letters" and which in this context means that he belongs to an official Soviet organization. As such, he has been charged with sorting through the abandoned property of victims of the revolution, and in the course of that work he comes across some of Il'ina's belongings, including a photograph of himself. This is where the story ended when Pasternak wrote chapter 9 in 1929. The chapter thus repeats in novelistic detail the revolutionary allegory in which the injured woman returns. Just as Il'ina's hysterical anger against Spektorsky prefigured the appearance of the revolutionary Fury, she now also "pursues" him. The similarity between the two figures is reinforced by several subtexts in chapter 8. Fleishman has traced the line "And the sunset loses its daughterly shame" (I vot zaria teriaet styd dochernii) to a Tsvetaeva poem, a favorite of Pasternak's, in which she refers to herself as "the sky's daughter" (neba doch').[91] More obviously, the revolutionary Amazon is named "Marusya of the quiet backwaters"—"Marusya" being a version of "Maria" and the heroine of Tsvetaeva's "The Swain." The implication that Il'ina/Tsvetaeva is an injured sister of the revolution is surprising, but it does flow from the earlier narrative. After all, Il'ina left Russia because the historical revolution was not living up to its promises; her maximalism could be understood as the maximalism of revolutionary idealism. In Spektorsky's relationship with Il'ina, his "crime" would seem to be his role in catalyzing her decision to emigrate; he is guilty of helping divorce her from Russia when it most needs the poet's example. The results are tragic for all, as Spektorsky reflects when he comes upon the relics of their relationship: "Is her fate happier and more free than mine / Or more deathlike and slavish?" (Schastlivei moego li i svobodnei / Ili poraboshchennei i mertvei?).[92]

When Pasternak worked further on *Spektorsky* in 1930, he emphasized the suggested link between Il'ina and the revolution and thematized the tragedy of her emigration. He wrote a lengthy, twenty-six-stanza introduction that framed the entire novel as a response to Il'ina, introducing biographical material that still more securely identified her as Tsvetaeva. The introduction to *Spektorsky* well illustrates Pasternak's maxim, set forth in *Safe Conduct*, that the best art records its own birth.[93] The author describes his situation in 1924, the year Pasternak began writing *Spektorsky*. As the father of a new family, he says, he had stopped writing poetry in order to earn money with a day job—Pasternak's job at the Ministry of the Interior culling articles on Lenin from the foreign press. In the process, he says, he learned about Conrad, Proust, and the émigré poet Maria Il'ina. In describing the articles about Il'ina, Pasternak accurately represents émigré reviews of Tsvetaeva's work as brilliant but controversial, and Soviet criticisms of her as divorced from Russian concerns ("And the mainland argued with the islands, / Over whether she was an English or Russian author" [I s ostrovami sporil materik, / Angliiskii li ona il' russkii avtor]).

Pasternak alters the biographical record in this account of how he discovered Tsvetaeva: he says that he came across her name while looking for Lenin's. One might interpret Pasternak as suggesting that Tsvetaeva in some sense supplanted Lenin—that lyricism supplanted revolution—in his loyalties. More likely Pasternak was underscoring how, throughout the entire poem, he was linking Tsvetaeva and the revolution. As Lazar Fleishman has observed, the name "Il′ina" closely echoes "Lenin," as well as Lenin's patronymic, "Il′ich:" "This blasphemous 'identification' of Tsvetaeva with the leader of the revolution . . . corresponds to Pasternak's basic conviction that opposites coincide under the conditions of the revolutionary elemental."[94] I would say more specifically that Pasternak's rhyming of Tsvetaeva with Lenin is his most extraordinary formulation of the kinship between poetry and revolution. When Pasternak rewrote "A Sublime Malady" in 1928, he added a lengthy tribute to Lenin's speech at the Twentieth Congress, describing the power of his language in terms he usually reserves for the power of lyricism: "I remember that his way of speaking / Pierced the nape of my neck with a crest of sparks, / Like the rustle of balled lightening" (Ia pomniu, govorok ego / Pronzil mne iskrami zagrivok, / Kak shorokh moln′i sharovoi).[95] Tsvetaeva and Lenin are conjoined as masters of the elemental—Tsvetaeva in the realm of poetry, Lenin in that of oratory. They share the "sublime malady" of poetic and revolutionary inspiration, as expressed in the raw power of their language. As the introduction reminds us, both of these exemplary figures are now departed. With Lenin's death in 1924 and Tsvetaeva's emigration, Russia has suffered the double loss of true poetry and true revolution.

The author, however, remains inspired by their example. His discovery of Il′ina/Tsvetaeva returns him to writing after his stint as a librarian. And it turns him, in particular, to writing about his own past, as Pasternak does in *Spektorsky*. The stanzas that figuratively render that past are suffused with melancholy and end with the question, "Where is that house, that door, that childhood, where / Once the world cut through, dreaming?" (No gde zh tot dom, ta dver′, to detstvo, gde / Odnazhdy mir prorezyvalsia, grezias′?). With this introduction, Pasternak suggests that in returning to that past in *Spektorsky*, and in *Safe Conduct*, he is in some way answering Il′ina/Tsvetaeva's demand that they return to the ideals that shaped their art, ideals acquired in childhood. This choice is a lonely one, as the final stanza of the introduction conveys:

> An alien distance. An alien, alien rain shower
> Dropping from gutters over ruts and hats,
> And, by alienation turned into an oak,
> An alien artist, like Pushkin's miller.

> Чужая даль. Чужой, чужой из труб
> По рвам и шляпам шлепающий дождик,
> И, отчужденьем обращенный в дуб,
> Чужой, как мельник пушкинский, художник.

The word "alien" (chuzhoi) could also be translated as "foreign" or as "someone else's," and thus declares a despairing solidarity with Tsvetaeva, whose condition he shares: Soviet Russia is now as foreign to him as Tsvetaeva's place of exile in France.[96]

Pasternak's declaration of loyalty to Tsvetaeva is complicated in familiar ways by his reference to the miller in Pushkin's unfinished play "The Mermaid" ("Rusalka," 1829). In Pushkin's play, the miller is the father of a daughter who has been seduced by a prince. When the prince announces that he is marrying someone else, the miller's daughter is too shocked to protest, to the prince's relief ("I expected a storm, but the business went / Pretty smoothly" [Ia buri zhdal, no delo oboshlos' / Dovol'no tikho]). Once she recovers, though, she begins to rage hysterically and turns on her father: "My death / Will profit you" (Vprok tebe poidet / Moia gibel'). She then throws herself into the river, becomes a *rusalka,* and gives birth to a mermaid daughter. The prince, drawn to the river years later, finds the miller wandering there, gone mad with grief. The text breaks off with the suggestion that the prince will be seduced and drowned by the vengeful *rusalka.*

Pushkin's story parallels the story of Spektorsky and Il'ina and the political allegory of chapter 8, in which a wronged woman lashes back, sometimes at the wrong person. The new element introduced by Pushkin's drama is the figure of the father, who though not guilty of abuse is nevertheless accused of negligence and fully shares in his daughter's tragedy. This is the figure with whom the author chooses to identify, rather than with the abandoning seducer. Earlier in the introduction he represented himself as an inadequate father to his own family, which he struggles to support with his earnings at the library. He has also failed to save his "daughters"—Tsvetaeva and the revolution—from destroying themselves through violent, precipitous behavior. But Pasternak the father fully absorbs their pain, even presenting the hysterical symptom of paralysis. (He is "turned into an oak" [obrashchennyi v dub].) Like the miller, he is an anguished and obscurely guilty participant in a family tragedy.

The mood of the introduction, and of the last chapters, may be understood in the context of the worsening cultural situation, as Fleishman has amply shown.[97] Beginning in 1929, Soviet literary culture was dominated by RAPP (Russian Association of Proletarian Writers), the vehicle of party policy in literature. RAPP launched a broad campaign against the "fellow travelers," and singled out Evgeny Zamiatin and Boris Pilniak for publishing their work abroad. As it happened, the same issue of the émigré journal in which Zamiatin's offending story appeared also included portions of "Lieutenant Schmidt," supplied by Tsvetaeva, and Pasternak also started to come under attack. These events convinced Pasternak that literature in Soviet Russia was doomed, spurring him to complete *Spektorsky* and *Safe Conduct.*

Before publishing *Spektorsky* as a book in 1931, Pasternak wrote a new ending to chapter 9, in which the author reappears as a character. The author invites Spektorsky to visit him in his communal apartment. There Spektorsky encounters Olga Bukhteeva, the woman he had an affair with in 1912, as related in chapter 2. That earlier chapter emphasizes their sexual attraction, and even contains, as first published in 1925, an explicit six-stanza description of their time in bed. (It is also an illicit affair, since Olga is married, referred to once as "Karenina.") When, in chapter 9, Spektorsky is embarrassed to see her again, we surmise that things ended badly. The author diplomatically retreats, and from behind a door he hears and reports only fragments of their exchange. But he describes the general subject and tenor of their conversation:

> The conversation was about the swinishness of imaginary sphinxes,
> About principles and princes, but in balance
> There was just a vague echo of maternalism
> In the contempt, the tenderness, the pity, in it all.

> Был разговор о свинстве мнимых сфинксов,
> О принципах и принцах, но весом
> Был только темный призвук материнства
> В презреньи, в ласке, в жалости, во всем.

The phrase "principles and princes" once again invokes Pushkin's "The Mermaid." Like the *rusalka*'s, and like Il'ina's, Olga's shame and pain have resolved into something frightening. Olga, now a ranking party member and in official uniform, abuses Spektorsky, while subtly threatening violence: "She playfully adjusted her revolver / And expressed herself fully in that gesture" (Ona shutia obdernula revol'ver / I v etom zheste vyrazilas' vsia). She justifies her indignation by invoking her status as the daughter of nineteenth-century radicals, suggesting that his sexual offense is also a political offense, one she may now punish as a representative of the revolutionary state.[98] Yet Olga does not rage hysterically, nor does she seek vengeance, despite her feint with the revolver. Rather, the revolutionary Amazon feels some compassion for the weaker Spektorsky, and even maternal concern. Might she become the mother who frees Spektorsky from the compromised heterosexual romance, as his own mother did in drawing him away from Il'ina? Might she free him from his compromised politics and bring—force?—him into the revolutionary family? It appears possible that Spektorsky may be absolved and the victim's violence muted, that the Amazon will be transformed into the mother. We do not know where their conversation leads, however, because at this point the author falls asleep, and when he wakes up, Spektorsky and Olga have disappeared, bringing the novel to its conclusion.

The novel ends, like the introduction, with the author alone in a comfortless environment. The final stanzas emphasize, in particular, the absence of domestic comfort:

> I ran out, shivering, to open the door for a party official
> And rushed back as fast as I could.

> But I was frozen, there was no way to warm up,
> The warmth was gone from my bed.
> And only then did I remember what had happened.
> While I was sleeping both were long gone.

Zinaida Neigauz, 1930s (collection of E. B. Pasternak)

Я выбежал, дрожа, открыть партийцу
И бросился назад что было ног.

Но я прозяб, согреться было нечем,
Постельное тепло я упустил.
И тут лишь вспомнил я о происшедшем.
Пока я спал, обоих след простыл.

The absence of domesticity was a strongly established theme of Spektorsky's relationship with Il'ina. As Olga Raevsky-Hughes has remarked, in his depiction of their relationship, Pasternak embraced a bohemian vision of himself that contradicted his markedly domestic impulses.[99] These impulses surface even in Pasternak's portrayal of Spektorsky, who is dazzled by how his sister Natasha transformed his apartment: "When he opened his eyes in the evening, / He didn't immediately recognize his lair. / It was brighter than turquoise, / Finally reclaimed from the pawn shop" (Kogda on v sumerki otkryl glaza, / Ne srazu on uznal svoiu berlogu. / Ona byla svetlei chem biriuza / Po vykupe iz dolgogo zaloga). They also surface at the end of the novel, where our attention is focused on the author's cold bed.

The image evokes the hardships of 1919, but it also speaks to Pasternak's circumstances at the time of writing in 1931. In fact, the events of that year almost seem to extend *Spektorsky*'s narrative, leading the author to new and presumably better relationships in both the personal and political spheres. After the crises of 1926, Pasternak's marriage was stable, though plagued by the earlier tensions. In the summer of 1930, Pasternak befriended the pianist Genrikh Neigauz and his wife, Zinaida. He quickly fell in love with Zinaida and by the end of the year had moved out of the apartment he shared with Evgenia and his son. A year of chaos followed, during which Evgenia traveled to Germany and drew Pasternak's family into the situation, while Pasternak and Zinaida led a nomadic existence, staying in friends' apartments and making a trip to the Urals and then to Georgia. Back in Moscow at the end of 1931, Zinaida vacillated over leaving Neigauz and her two sons. When it appeared that she would end her affair with Pasternak, he attempted suicide in January 1932. This event decided Zinaida; she and Pasternak divorced their spouses and were married that year.

All of this transpired at a moment when the political situation appeared to be changing in a positive direction. By the spring of 1931, rumors of Stalin's dissatisfaction with RAPP were circulating and Pilniak actually received permission to travel abroad. (Such permission was denied to Pasternak in 1930, as he informed Tsvetaeva [*DNV* 526].) A year later, in spring 1932, the Central Committee issued a decree, "On Restructuring Literary Organizations," which abolished RAPP and welcomed the fellow travelers into the newly created Union of Soviet Writers. (Maxim Gorky returned from exile in 1933 to head the organization.) In sum, a new era of liberalization in the arts appeared to be under way. Pasternak's tendency to conflate the romantic and the political was strongly catalyzed by the confluence of his new hopes for Soviet culture and his new love. Pasternak openly addressed Zinaida Neigauz as a muse of socialist art: "I believe in you and I always know: you are the close partner of a great Russian creativity, lyrical in these years of socialist construction, inwardly terribly similar to it, its very sister."[100] His phrasing suggests a new conviction that lyricism was bound to socialism in the figure of the beloved woman. On the strength of that conviction, he returned to writing lyric poetry for the first time in more than a decade, and published a new lyric collection aptly titled *Second Birth* (*Vtoroe rozhdenie*, 1932). Like *My Sister Life,* these poems addressed a new romance. But they also expressed, in Fleishman's words, "Pasternak's readiness to accept Soviet reality as an inevitable and lawful model of socialism"[101]—or, as Zholkovsky put it in his important essay on *Second Birth,* a "dynamics of adaptation."[102]

As I have suggested, these dynamics were shaped in his earlier works of the 1920s, most explicitly in the work Pasternak had just completed, *Spektorsky.* In the novel, Pasternak laid out a logic of adaptation with the political allegory of chapter 8: if we imagine Russia as a victimized woman, then the revolution's violence is justified and must be endured by the intelligentsia, whether or not it was complicit in Russia's suffering. This logic of adaptation rests entirely on the premise of compassionate identification with the victimized woman. In the final poem of *Second Birth,* "In a springtime of ice" ("Vesenneiu poroiu l'da," 1931), Pasternak states this premise and the consequences of accepting it:

> And because from my earliest childhood
> I have been wounded by woman's fate,
> And the poet's trace is only the trace
> Of her paths, nothing more,
> And because I am moved only by her
> And she is now freed by us,
> I am entirely glad to be dissolved
> In revolutionary will.

> И так как с малых детских лет
> Я ранен женской долей,
> И след поэта—только след
> Ее путей, не боле,
> И так как я лишь ей задет
> И ей у нас раздолье,
> То весь я рад сойти на нет
> В революцьонной воле.

Pasternak now openly embraces the identification with the feminine that drives his lyric creativity. Crucially, Pasternak's "coming out" is linked to a historical change in the situation of woman: though woman's fate was always to suffer, she has now been liberated by socialism.[103] To identify with her, then, is no longer "wounding." Indeed, it makes him glad finally to succumb, like woman, to the masculine agency of the revolution ("revolutionary will"). There is a sign of lingering anxiety in the phrase "soiti na net," which I have translated as "be dissolved" but which more literally means "diminish to nothing." Nevertheless, the dominant impulse of the poem, and of the book as a whole, is to move beyond a traumatic past.

Pasternak's muse in *Second Birth* does indeed have a calm aspect. In "No one will be at home" ("Nikogo ne budet v dome," 1931), Pasternak once again rehearses the scene of inspiration as penetration into a domestic interior, but it has a new quality:

> But suddenly along the portiere
> There will run the trembling of an incursion.
> Measuring the silence with your steps
> You will enter like the future.
>
> You will appear at the door
> In something white, unfanciful,
> In something made straight from the materials
> From which snowflakes are sewn.
>
> Но нежданно по портьере
> Пробежит вторженья дрожь.
> Тишину шагами меря,
> Ты, как будущность, войдешь.
>
> Ты появишься у двери
> В чем-то белом, без причуд,
> В чем-то впрямь из тех материй,
> Из которых хлопья шьют.

This new muse has a human shape, rather than being rendered as a natural, elemental force. Relatedly, she is not violent; she does not break in but "measures the silence" with her steps. The muse, that is, is no longer a hysteric, no longer a disturbing but now a soothing presence. She augurs a new poetics, whose features are manifest in her dress—white and simple, made of the same "materials" as snow. She embodies the "unheard-of simplicity" (neslykhannaia prostota) Pasternak announced in the first cycle of the book, whose poems do, in fact, feature easier syntax, less complex figuration, and a more traditional poetic persona. Thus the erotic, the aesthetic, and the political are fused in these poems with unnatural perfection.

Pasternak rendered a similar image of the muse in part three of *Safe Conduct,* which he completed in 1931, alongside *Spektorsky* and the poems of *Second Birth.* It contains a short reflection on the topic of "the genius" and "the beauty," two words that are "identically banal" and "have so much in common" (4:234). He illustrates this point with an obscure allegorical tale. The beauty sets out on the road ("leaves through the gates") in a mood of expectation that derives from a sense of her own beauty and its kinship with the beauty of nature. It is, as Pasternak emphasizes, a healthy impulse: "She loves healthy nature in a healthy way and is not consciously aware that she will always count on the universe loving her back" (4:235). As she walks along, she encounters a man whom she takes for her beloved—mistakenly, the narrator suggests. Indeed, she then meets "her distant brother," with whom she experiences a total unity: "and whatever might happen, all the same, all the same the most perfect 'I am you' binds them with every conceivable tie in the world and proudly, youthfully, and exhaustedly stamps profile on profile, like a medal" (4:235). Pasternak supplies a vivid image for his identification with the feminine: the poet's profile is "stamped on" the profile of the female beauty. His rhetorical emphasis on health once again marks his desire to move beyond the mode of hysteria, which he now regards as lethal. It is important to note that this tale is interpolated into an account of Mayakovsky's suicide in 1930, the kind of unhealthy act Pasternak naturally wished to distance himself from. This account concludes *Safe Conduct*, in whose final pages Pasternak quotes Mayakovsky's famous lines, "Mama! Your son is beautifully ill!" By the end of the 1920s, Pasternak wished to replace the sublime malady with a more serene aesthetic ideal that would itself serve as "safe conduct" through the terrors of contemporary history.

Zinaida Neigauz was singularly well suited to inspire this evolution in Pasternak's imagining of his muse. Early on in their acquaintance, Zinaida, in a misguided attempt to deflect Pasternak's attentions, confided that she had been seduced at age fifteen by a middle-aged cousin, whose mistress she became for several years.[104] Despite her classic trauma, however, she appeared to be free of neuroses; Pasternak could indulge his fascination with the female victim without fear of hysterics. She also perhaps soothed Pasternak's anxiety about woman's artistic agency. Like Pasternak's mother, Rozalia, she possessed an unrealized musical gift; like her, she had been a piano student when she met her accomplished husband, Neigauz, and she put aside her music to marry him and raise a family. As Pasternak said to Tsvetaeva in 1926, he believed that his mother always regretted abandoning her music for domesticity. A similar tension surfaced in his marriage to Evgenia, whose pursuit of an artistic career took priority over creating domestic comfort, to Pasternak's enduring dissatisfaction. In Neigauz, however, Pasternak discovered a woman who, despite her gifts, was content to devote herself to family life. She was, moreover, Russian, and thereby free of the intrinsic tensions of Russian Jewish identity. The reality, of course, was that Pasternak was not cured by her presence; he suffered agonies over her sexual past and attempted suicide when she considered leaving him. But Zinaida Neigauz was indeed a new kind of "sister" to Pasternak—not Jewish but Russian, not hysterical but maternal, not my sister life but a sister of socialist Russia.[105]

Pasternak elaborated Zinaida's qualities in a most remarkable context—to the departed Rilke, in the unpublished "afterword" ("Posleslovie") to *Safe*

Conduct. As I have mentioned, the afterword takes the form of a "posthumous letter" in which he answered Rilke's 1926 letter. Without naming Evgenia and Zinaida, he contrasts their different kinds of beauty: Evgenia is beautiful only when happy, while Zinaida, "femininity itself," is beautiful under any circumstances "and doesn't fear grief as much as the first one" (4:787). In Zinaida, Pasternak celebrates a femininity that is invulnerable to traumatic emotion, a clear rejection of the pained but ecstatic lyricism of his earlier feminine identifications. What might seem a bizarre and inappropriate confession about his personal life actually emerged from Pasternak's reading of Rilke, which played a role in Pasternak's shift away from a hysterical poetics.

Most discussions of Pasternak's interest in Rilke attempt to discern how Rilke influenced him as a writer. These very discussions suggest, however, that Rilke's poetic example mattered less to Pasternak than his poetic philosophy.[106] This becomes apparent when we consider Pasternak's translations, which he did in 1929, of two requiems Rilke wrote and published together in 1908 as *Requiem*. Pasternak chose to translate the requiems as a way of composing his own requiem for Rilke. But, as Rimgaila Salys has shown in her essay on these translations, he also was drawn to the requiems as meditations on the causes of artistic failure.[107] They are, just as crucially, meditations on gender and artistic failure: the first was dedicated to a woman, the artist Paula Becker ("Requiem für eine Freundin"), the second to a young male poet, "Requiem für Wolf Graf von Kalckreuth." Kalckreuth was a gifted and unstable poet who killed himself at age nineteen. Pasternak published his translation of the poem as an addendum to part one of *Safe Conduct,* which details a series of crucial episodes in Pasternak's development as a young poet.[108] Clearly, Pasternak recognized in Kalckreuth his own ecstatic temperament, his own "earnest joy of your so strenuous longing" (die ernste Freude deiner strengen Sehnsucht). (Kalckreuth also happened to be the son of a highly regarded artist, as Pasternak learned from Rilke's wife, Clara Westhoff, through his father.) The Pasternak who translated the poem in 1929 was reflecting on his own excesses and failures as a young poet.

Rilke's requiem voices a gentle reproach to Kalckreuth for succumbing to his emotions and embracing a premature death. Kalckreuth perhaps would not have done so had he gained an understanding of genuine work: "had even something led you / to take your journey past some wakeful workshop / where men were hammering and day achieving / simply reality" (ja hätte nur dein Weg / vorbeigeführt an einer wachen Werkstatt, / wo Männer hämmern, wo der Tag sich schlicht / verwirklicht). Kalckreuth might then have brought that ethic to his poetic vocation, freeing himself from his painful emotions by crafting them into art, and avoiding the error of poets who,

> Like invalids,
> use a language full of woefulness
> to tell us where it hurts,

> instead of sternly transforming themselves into words,
> like the Stonemason imperturbably
> transposed himself into the imperturbable stone.

> Wie die Kranken
> gebrauchen sie die Sprache voller Wehleid,
> um zu beschreiben, wo es ihnen wehtut,
> statt hart sich in die Worte zu verwandeln,
> wie sich der Steinmetz einer Kathedrale
> verbissen umsetzt in des Steines Gleichmut.

Kalckreuth's "failure" is a failure to move beyond a hysterical poetics, beyond the "language of woefulness" employed by emotional invalids. He was too womanly, unable to acquire the masculine discipline of self-crafting. This is a message to which Pasternak was deeply responsive in the late 1920s, as he sought to make his feminine lyricism more consonant with the work of socialism.

If the Kalckreuth requiem is about tempering the male poet's femininity, the "Requiem für eine Freundin" elaborates the very principle of the male feminine. Rilke addresses the deceased Paula Becker to persuade her to stop haunting him and fully depart from this world. Her reluctance to die surprises him, since as an artist she had "done more transforming than any other woman" (die mehr / verwandelt hat als irgend eine Frau). She was able to achieve what Kalckreuth was incapable of achieving, that is, transposing herself into art; her self-portraits say "this is" rather than "this is me" (und sagte nicht: das bin ich; nein: dies ist). Why, then, her failure now to achieve full transformation through death? Rilke finds the answer in the fact that Becker died in childbirth. In the speaker's argument, the tragedy was not so much that Becker died but that she ever became pregnant. Her pregnancy, by drawing her away from art and into the realm of the body, enacts or predicts her failure to die properly. In a gruesomely drawn analogy, Rilke represents Becker's haunting as an attempt to give birth to herself, to call her blood back into her placenta. Her mistake could have been avoided had Becker remained with "the long work" which is art, and which in a final twist Rilke describes as a kind of pregnancy:

> Anyone who has lifted
> his blood into a work that takes years
> may find that he can't sustain it, the force of gravity
> is irresistible, and it falls back, worthless.
> For somewhere there is an ancient enmity
> between our daily life and the great work.
> Help me understand and say it.
>   Do not return. If you can bear to, stay
> dead with the dead. The dead have their own tasks.
> But help me, if you can without distraction,
> as what is farthest sometimes helps: in me.

> Jedem, der sein Blut
> hinauflob in ein Werk, das lange wird,
> kann es geschehen, daß ers nicht mehr hochhält
> und daß es geht nach seiner Schwere, wertlos.
> Denn irgenwo ist eine alte Feindschaft
> zwischen dem Leben und der großen Arbeit.
> Daß ich sie einseh und sie sage: hilf mir.
> > Komm nicht zurück. Wenn du's erträgst, so sei
> tot bei den Toten. Tote sind beschäftigt.
> Doch hilf mir so, daß es dich nicht zerstreut,
> wie mir das Fernste manchmal hilft: in mir.

Rilke, having begged the woman artist to stop trying to be born, enlists her aid in his own long work of giving birth to poems. His requiem ends with a convoluted, if not perverse, image of the male feminine, as he carries the dead woman artist inside him.

Rilke's "Requiem für eine Freundin" renders with exceptional power the figure of the poet-mother, the figure Tsvetaeva was contending with in her exchange with Rilke. In his reading of the poem, however, Pasternak appears to have identified with the poet as lover. Although the poem focuses on Becker's failure to die well, there is a moment when Rilke places the blame elsewhere with atypical directness:

> But now I must accuse:
> not the man who withdrew you from yourself
> (I cannot find him; he looks like everyone),
> but in this one man, I accuse: men.

> Doch jetzt klag ich an:
> den Einen nicht, der dich aus dir zurückzog,
> (ich find ihn nicht heraus, er ist wie alle)
> doch alle klag ich in ihm an: den Mann.

This is the moment in the poem that colored Pasternak's view of the requiem as "perhaps the strongest and most moral of everything said with a socialistic note in art of the last, prewar period. The petit bourgeois attitude is unmasked without naming it, par défaut" (*DL* 258). Pasternak understood the poem as a critique of men who confine women within the bourgeois institution of marriage. Such a critique was indeed leveled by many generations of European socialists, and in emphasizing its presence in Rilke's poem, Pasternak found yet another confluence of his poetic and political ideals.

Pasternak thus also found a perspective from which to view the failure of his own marriage.[109] The "one man" in whom Rilke accuses all men was the painter Otto Modersohn, who married Becker at the same time Rilke married her friend Clara Westhoff, also a painter. Rilke left Westhoff after only a year, while Modersohn sought to preserve his marriage even when Becker tried to leave him. While Pasternak knew nothing about Becker (and in fact she was not identified as Rilke's addressee in contemporary publications), he did know about Rilke's brief marriage. In a letter to his father concerning Leonid's correspondence with Rilke, Pasternak praised Rilke's concern for Clara even after their separation, saying that it was all "painfully similar to my entire situation, down to the smallest detail."[110] Pasternak directly identified his wife with Rilke's woman artist by borrowing an image from the requiem for a poem to Evgenia that appeared in *Second Birth*. In "Requiem für eine Freundin," Rilke describes Becker wearing amber beads (Bernsteinkugeln), a detail he himself borrowed from a nude self-portrait by Becker in which she wears only a heavy necklace. Pasternak interprets the amber stones as millstones, in the spirit of his understanding of the requiem:

> O marks left on women's necks
> From the fetishes hung upon them!
> How well I know them, how I understand,
> I who hang upon them.

> О ссадины вкруг женских шей
> От вешавшихся фетишей!
> Как я их знаю, как постиг,
> Я, вешающийся на них.

Pasternak's eager acknowledgment of his complicity in woman's suffering is not Rilkean and makes his identification with the feminine a more anxious matter. He also does not accept Rilke's solution, which is to remain solitary. Even as he endorses Rilke's critique of marriage, he refuses what he calls the requiem's "absurd" thesis, "an even bolder absurd than 'The Kreutzer Sonata'" (*DL* 258). For Pasternak, abstinence was not an option, as he proved by his affair with and quick marriage to Zinaida Neigauz. Even so, Pasternak continued to frame his choices in the terms of Rilke's instruction. Writing to his father about his love for Zinaida, he insists that although he does not live alone like Rilke, "the world of solitude . . . has not been injured or diminished when I have tried sharing it with her."[111] The strain of this claim shows the degree to which Pasternak wanted to understand his change of course in the late 1920s, his "second birth," as endorsed by Rilke.

During 1930, Pasternak exchanged a few letters with Tsvetaeva but said nothing about his unfolding domestic crisis. As Tsvetaeva related in a letter to their mutual friend Raisa Lomonosova, she learned about it from Pilniak in February 1931 when he visited Paris on his trip abroad. In the logic the poets elaborated together throughout the 1920s, her relationship with Pasternak was founded on their respective commitments to their families. In this letter and elsewhere she contrasts Pasternak's conduct to her own earlier conduct with Rodzevich. Tsvetaeva ended her affair with Rodzevich and remained in her marriage, in what she regarded as an act of fidelity to Pasternak. When Pasternak left his marriage, then, he betrayed Tsvetaeva, effectively ending their relationship:

> For eight years now (1923–1931), Boris and I have had a secret compact: to live in anticipation of being together. But the Catastrophe of a meeting was always deferred, like a storm that's somewhere behind the hills. Every now and then a clap of thunder, and then nothing—you go on.
> Understand me correctly: I, knowing myself, probably would not have left my family for Boris, but if I had gone—it would have been to him only. That's *my* view. Our actual encounter would have been above all a terrible anguish (I, my family—he, his family, my *pity*, his *conscience*). Now it won't happen at all. Boris isn't with Evgenia, whom he met before he knew me, Boris without Evgenia is also without me, Boris *with another woman who's not me* is not *my* Boris, just the best Russian poet. I relinquish him. (7:329)

She goes on to say that if she were living in Moscow, there wouldn't have been any Zinaida, "by the immense law of *kinship on all fronts:* MY SISTER LIFE" (7:329). In this instance, the power of her word was no match for the power of presence. But she perceived another factor at work as well. Having learned more from Pilniak about Zinaida and about Pasternak's jealous behavior with her, Tsvetaeva concluded that he had fallen in love with a different kind of sister: "Poor Boris, I'm afraid she's a regular Helen (My Sister Life)" (7:332). In yet another letter to Lomonosova, she observed that "he falls in love like a man. Like Pushkin. . . . [A] catastrophe is inevitable, since the girl has big eyes" (7:335). Tsvetaeva thus, like Pasternak but independently of him, interpreted his new love as a signal instance of "the poet and the beauty."[112]

Pasternak learned from Tsvetaeva's sister Asya that Tsvetaeva knew about Zinaida, and he wrote to her on March 5 with a straightforward account of what was happening. He also spoke of the poetry the affair had produced, namely two ballads, one to Genrikh Neigauz and one to Zinaida, which he copied out for Tsvetaeva ("They are sleeping in the dacha" ["Na dache spiat" 1931]). He expected that she would find this work "complete kitsch," but it was "my first strongly felt turn to lyricism after a years-long break" (*DNV* 531). In closing, he begged her not to reply with "an unreflective, unjust letter," at which moment he received a letter from her. (The letter is not extant.) Apparently Tsvetaeva did assert her claim on him—"Why are you reminding me about what we share? Did you really think it would be changed by anything?"—and complained about being the last to know. But her letter clearly was not what he had feared, nor was her next letter. She declared the ballad "good," though with the sharp observation that he had written it like one of the "sleeping sons" mentioned in the poem, a reference to Zinaida's two children (*DNV* 534). She also reviewed her own experience with Rodzevich in a way that reiterated her loyalty to Pasternak and the vision of love she had shaped with him. Instead of reproaching him, however, she relinquished him, as she put it to Lomonosova.

Pasternak wrote to her again in June of that year with more details of the unfolding drama, mainly concerning his family's turning against him, as they sheltered Evgenia and Evgeny in Munich. He oddly focuses on an emotional encounter with Genrikh Neigauz, with whom he spent all night at a party after one of Neigauz's performances. At the party he read, by popular demand, "The Pied Piper," which everyone greeted as brilliant, especially Neigauz, who was deeply moved and spent the next day devouring the poem. Pasternak celebrates this joining of two geniuses he loved, and yet the scene is overlaid with guilt at being a recent cause of pain to both owing to his relationship with Zinaida. He is complexly implicated in the hysterical romanticism of Neigauz's performance of Chopin and Schumann and of Tsvetaeva's "Pied Piper." In a postscript, he adds that "The Pied Piper" was also admired by two young men from the paper *Komsomol Truth,* whom he met on an official visit to a tractor factory in Chelyabinsk. His general strategy was to draw Tsvetaeva into all the currents of his changing life, as he made explicit when he said, "For the first time in all these years I have begun thinking about your return, have imagined it" (*DNV* 539).

Tsvetaeva's impulse, instead, was to distance herself. In her reply she tells him she has hung on her wall, above some driftwood she gathered from the shore at St.-Gilles, one of his father's drawings of the young Pasternak. Most would have put up the lover's image at the beginning of their affair, but Tsvetaeva's logic was different, as she explained:

> While I—that is, all the years until now—was sure we would meet, it never would have entered my head or my hand to thus make you visible—to me and to others. You were my secret—from all eyes, even my own. And only when I closed my eyes—did I see you—and I saw nothing else. I opened *my* eyes—into *yours.*
>
> It turns out that now I simply—have pulled you out of myself—and set you against the wall—like an artist sets up a canvas—maybe farther—and stepped back.[113]

She had always thought of herself as "carrying" Pasternak but now is ready to give birth to him, in an act she juxtaposes to his father's act of creating his image. As for returning to Russia, her reply was indirect but clear. She told Pasternak that Efron had just written him with a request, which Tsvetaeva did not describe, perhaps because of the subject's political sensitivity.[114] Efron was asking Pasternak to help him get his Soviet citizenship so he could return to Russia. Tsvetaeva gave Pasternak permission to fulfill Efron's request but did not include herself in the plan. She only remarked that people would criticize Efron for returning without his wife (*DNV* 541).[115]

Finally, Tsvetaeva mentioned that Mirsky was seriously ill and could no longer pay the rent for them, as he had done for several years, a comment that lends some credence to Pasternak's later claim that their correspondence stopped because of tensions over money. He wrote to Lomonosova in 1933: "I got desperate letters from M. I. Ts. asking for help with money, but we ourselves were

Portrait of Boris Pasternak by Leonid Pasternak, 1924 (collection of E. B. Pasternak)

in debt to all of our friends . . . and my correspondence with M. I. stopped. She mistook inability for lack of desire."[116] This last phrase is telling, and applies not just to this episode but to the relationship at its psychological and emotional core: she mistook inability for lack of desire. In any case, Pasternak felt his "inability" keenly. In 1933, in the absence of letters, Pasternak sent Tsvetaeva a new edition of his collected poems (*Stikhotvoreniia,* 1933) with the inscription: "To Marina. Forgive me. I kiss Serezha. Sergey Iakovlevich, you also forgive me. I would like what is most important to return. I haven't yet earned this. Forgive, forgive me. Forgive me" (*DNV* 543).

Pasternak's appeal provoked Tsvetaeva to renew their correspondence. She wrote on May 27: "Boris, I don't need to forgive you for not writing for 2 years (3 years?) but for the lines on p. 403, which are clearly *mine*—but not addressed to me? And I'm considering whether I can forgive, or even if I do—whether I will forgive (inside?)" (*DNV* 543). Tsvetaeva was referring to the poem "Beloved, the smoke of sugary speech, Like smoke from coal, is everywhere" ("Liubimaia, molvy slashchavoi, Kak uglia, vezdesushcha gar'," 1931). It is one of the poems addressed to Zinaida Neigauz in *Second Birth,* which was republished in the collection Pasternak sent. The offending lines appear in the penultimate stanza:

> And I would like us, after death,
> When we retreat into ourselves and depart,
> To be closer than the heart is to its auricle,
> And to be rhymed together.

> И я б хотел, чтоб после смерти,
> Как мы замкнемся и уйдем,
> Тесней, чем сердце и предсерьде,
> Зарифмовали нас вдвоем.

The conceit of the lovers "rhyming" after death comes from Tsvetaeva, from the first poem of her cycle "The Pair" ("Dvoe," 1924), in which the names of Helen and Achilles are rhymed in the next world. Tsvetaeva calls Pasternak's act "plagiarism," but worse, it was an absolute betrayal of their bond. Tsvetaeva had caught Pasternak rhyming with another woman, or as she carefully put it, "another being" (drugoe sushchestvo).[117]

Tsvetaeva's reading of *Second Birth* fundamentally changed her view of Pasternak. As she said, when she read these poems, "for the first time—I saw you differently" (*DNV* 545). What she meant by that is clear from her comments on a poem Pasternak addressed to Evgenia, "Don't be upset, don't cry, don't belabor" ("Ne volnuisia, ne plach', ne trudi," 1931). The poem, in which Pasternak urges the beloved to calm down and accept their separation, struck Tsvetaeva as "cruel" and "monstrously male" (izuverski-muzhskie stikhi). Tsvetaeva's fantasy about Pasternak as the male poet who transcends his gender came to grief, finally, with this poem about quelling a woman's hysterics.

Conclusion

Tsvetaeva and Pasternak finally met in the summer of 1935, when Pasternak was not so much permitted as forced to travel abroad. The period of apparent liberalization in the early 1930s ended in 1934 with the first wave of Stalin's purges, and Pasternak, as a public figure, was pressured from all sides, even by Stalin himself. After Osip Mandelstam was arrested that year, Pasternak got a phone call from Stalin, who asked whether Mandelstam was a genius; Pasternak deflected Stalin's question, saying that he had long wanted to have a conversation with him "about life and death," at which point Stalin hung up.[1] In 1935, Pasternak suffered a six-month bout of insomnia and an apparent nervous breakdown. He was recovering in a sanatorium when he was ordered onto a train to Paris as a delegate to the Congress of Writers in Defense of Culture, an international gathering to protest the rise of fascism. Pasternak arrived on June 24 and went directly to the congress, where he was greeted with an ovation. Tsvetaeva was there that day and met him in the corridor. She attended again the following day, when Pasternak gave his speech to the congress, which she helped transcribe. They met again at the hotel where he was staying, and at a clothing store, where Pasternak asked her to try on a dress he wished to buy for Zinaida.[2] Disappointed by their meeting, Tsvetaeva left town before the end of his stay. On June 28 she took her son to the Côte d'Azure, where she had rented a room for the summer, leaving Efron and her daughter Ariadna to attend to Pasternak until his departure on July 4.

The urgent topic of Pasternak's conversations with Tsvetaeva and her family was the question of their return to Russia. Placed in this difficult position and already in a terrible state, he could not give clear advice, as he later recalled:

> The members of Marina Tsvetaeva's family insisted that she should return to Russia. They were prompted partly by homesickness and sympathy with communism and the Soviet Union and partly by the consideration that Marina Tsvetaeva could never be happy in Paris and that she would perish living in a sort of vacuum without any readers to respond to her.

Marina Tsvetaeva asked me what I thought of it. I had no definite opinion to offer. I did not know what to say to her and I was very much afraid that she and her remarkable family would find things difficult and troubling in Russia. The general tragedy of the family infinitely exceeded my fears.[3]

To judge from Tsvetaeva's comments to a friend, however, Pasternak did convey something about what the family would find back in Russia: he told her that he "didn't dare refuse to come" and "was frightened," a confession she regarded with contempt (6:433).

Tsvetaeva's "non-meeting" with Pasternak, as she phrased it, caused her to grasp fully how fundamentally their paths had diverged, as she expressed in a letter to Pasternak's friend Nikolay Tikhonov, a Soviet poet whom she had met at the Congress:

> I get a strange feeling from Boris. I find him difficult because everything that is right to me, in his view—his, Boris's view—is sin, sickness.
>
> Just like when in answer to my tears (you, though, weren't there—if you had been there wouldn't have been any tears), he said "Why are you crying?" and I said, "*I'm* not crying, my eyes are crying." And he said, "If I'm not crying now, then it's because I have decided at all costs to resist hysteria and neurosis." (I was so surprised—that I immediately stopped crying.) "You—he said—will love the collective farms [Kolkhozy]."
>
> ... And I cried because Boris, the best lyric poet of our time, in my presence betrayed Lyricism when he called his entire self and everything in him a malady. (Even a "sublime" one. But he didn't even say that. Nor did he say that this malady is more precious to him than health and in general—more precious,—more rare and more precious than radium. This, you know, is my single *conviction:* my sureness.) (7:552)

Pasternak's loyalty to Soviet Russia had long been a contentious issue between them. What was new to Tsvetaeva, and what shocked her into tears, was Pasternak's repudiation of "hysteria" and "neurosis," which she tellingly interpreted as a rejection of lyricism. She did not perceive that Pasternak's struggle with traumatic feeling was a way of coping with the terrors of Stalinist Russia.

Tsvetaeva did not just speak to others about her disappointment but wrote directly to Pasternak in July, after his return to Moscow. As she equitably put it, "You were very good to me at our last meeting (non-meeting) and I was very foolish." Yet she still defended the right to "solitude" before the right of some "future of the people" (*DNV* 554–55). Pasternak wrote back in October to explain that he had been ill when he saw her in Paris and was only just recovering. In a touching fashion, he asks her to regard his breakdown as "only an interval" in his life and not as "the beginning of the end." He writes: "But let's say—suddenly I get better, and everything returns. And again I want to look ahead, and who would I see there, who by virtue of their strength and originality of the sort, for example, that Rilke had, who would I see except you? What do absolutes have to do with this? Is this romanticism permissible?"

(*DNV* 557). Even at this stage, deep into his project of creating a socialist lyricism, Pasternak still regarded Tsvetaeva as the exemplary lyric poet. In his effort to sustain his bond with her, Pasternak asked when she might come to Russia, and whether he might visit her again in Paris once his health was better (*DNV* 557).

Unfortunately for Pasternak, to demonstrate the seriousness of his illness, he also told Tsvetaeva that on his way back to Russia, he decided not to stop in Munich to see his parents, whom he had last seen twelve years before in Berlin.[4] For Tsvetaeva this truly was "the last devastating blow," as she put it in her answering letter (*DNV* 561). In this letter Tsvetaeva composed a finished critique of Pasternak's behavior that encompassed both his treatment of Evgenia and Evgeny and his treatment of his birth family. She provides a lengthy portrait of the poet as male narcissist. Responding to *Themes and Variations* back in 1923, she had distinguished Pasternak from his male peers, but she now casts him as the representative male poet:

About you. You can't be judged as a person, because in that case you're a criminal. For the life of me, I'll never understand how it's possible to ride past your mother on a train—past twelve years of waiting. And your mother won't understand—don't expect her to. It surpasses my understanding, our understanding, human understanding. In this I am your *opposite*: I would carry the train *on my back* to make that visit (though maybe I would be just as afraid and take just as little joy). Don't ask for understanding from your opposite. (There is no one more opposite. My supposed harshness.) And another related point: *all* of my loved ones— there were few—seemed incomparably gentler than me, even Rilke wrote to me: Du hast recht, doch Du bist hart—and that pained me, because I couldn't be otherwise. Now, taking stock, I see: my supposed cruelty was only a form, a contour of my essence, a necessary boundary for self-protection—from *your* softness, . . . for at the *last* minute—you took your hand away and left me, long ago cast out of the human family, one-on-one with my humanness. Among you, the inhuman, I was only human. . . .

I was myself (my soul) only in my notebooks and on isolated roads—which were rare, since my whole life I've been leading a child by the hand. Precisely because of that I've been worried all my life, have snapped and bitten all my life. I didn't have enough "gentleness" in my dealings with people, only enough for communication: (service, *useless* service) self-sacrifice. A *mother pelican* who, because of the feeding routine she herself established—was *mean*.—Well, there you have it.— . . .

But—and here is your vindication—only *such people* may do *such things*. Goethe was like you, Goethe who didn't go to Schiller's deathbed and who for ten years failed to visit his mother in Frankfurt—preserving himself for Faust II (or something else). But—parentheses!—at age 74 daring to fall in love and to get married— this time failing to preserve (physically!) his *heart*. For in that regard you are profligate, you are like "all the rest." And if I were not I, Rilke would have come from his deathbed—for a last chance to love! For you cure yourselves of it all (of yourself, of the awful horror of the inhuman, the divine, in you) like dogs cure themselves—through love, the simplest thing. And when Lomonosova wrote to me with anguish about your "lack of self-control," confusing you with Pushkin due to her

naïve benevolence and interpreting your new marriage as simple masculine passion—well yes, my dear—praise God! because this is his last lifeline.

Only *sex* makes you a human being, and *not* fatherhood.
So, Boris, hang on to your beautiful woman. (*DNV* 558–59)

Tsvetaeva had shaped her vision of the genius as "inhuman" during her encounter with Rilke. At the time, she aspired to become such a genius, though
she also registered her difference from Rilke, which she cast in terms of gender
("Consider, after all, that I'm a woman, married, children, etc."). After that encounter she essentially stopped writing lyric poetry, and years later, in this letter to Pasternak, she stated her conclusion that only the male poet can be a
genius because only the male poet is inhuman: it is his prerogative to disregard
the welfare of his family and find sustenance in a new love. Tsvetaeva, by contrast, saw herself as bound to family by her maternal vocation. For many years
after the birth of her son, she was able to imagine her poetic powers magnified
by her fertility. Now motherhood does not empower her but leaves her vulnerable; as she goes on to say, she fears being abandoned by her own son, just as
Pasternak rode past his mother. Tsvetaeva's ambivalent embrace of maternity
leaves her, finally, unable to imagine herself as a poet but only as a woman without a lifeline.[5]

In her last letter to Pasternak, Tsvetaeva declared that should he visit Paris,
he must not do so on her account, since "our story is over" (*DNV* 561). Their
story, of course, was not over, although their correspondence was. Tsvetaeva
continued her conversation with Pasternak in many of her writings. In one
example uncovered by Mikhail Gasparov and Omry Ronen, she polemicized
with Pasternak's hymn to domesticity in *Second Birth*.[6] Her poem "The Bus"
("Avtobus," 1936) makes a familiar critique of modernity and its faceless
masses—here, the passengers on the bus. The poem concludes with a conversation between Tsvetaeva and a companion, who compares a beautiful tree to
"a cauliflower in white sauce" (tsvetnaia kapusta pod sousom belym), to her
infinite contempt:

> You who could be so majestically
> Beloved, as eternally green (like moss!)—
> Will be known as a cauliflowery anonymity:
> I will avenge the flowering tree.

> Ты, который так царственно мог бы—любимым
> Быть, бессмертно-зеленым (подобным плющу!)—
> Неким цветно-капустным пойдешь анонимом
> По устам: за цветущее дерево—мщу.

Such "gastronomic" imagery appears only in the work of Boris Pasternak and
is especially prominent in *Second Birth*.[7] As Gasparov points out, Tsvetaeva en-

hanced the gastronomic theme when she worked on the poem in 1936, after her disappointing encounter with Pasternak in 1935. Omry Ronen, discussing the same subtext, has suggested that Tsvetaeva, in speaking of vengeance, had in mind not only Pasternak's habit of depicting nature as food but also his romantic habit of regarding it as feminine.[8] In other words, the tree in Tsvetaeva's poem is womankind, or Tsvetaeva herself. But there is another way of reading the final stanza. She distinguishes between a true Pasternak—the "eternally green" poet of nature—and a false one, the poet of the dinner table. She was perhaps avenging not so much womankind as the Pasternak she fell in love with when she read *My Sister Life*.

One can find similar attempts to recuperate her earlier vision of Pasternak in the essays on poetry she wrote in the 1930s.[9] The clearest example is her essay "Poets with a History and Poets without a History" (1934), a review of a volume of Pasternak's collected works from his earliest verse up through the poems of *Second Birth* (*Izbrannye stikhotvoreniia*, 1934). Tsvetaeva makes the distinction named in the title in order to cast Pasternak as a "poet without a history." Throughout his oeuvre, she argues, he expresses the same lyrical essence, which in his case is nature itself. In describing that lyrical essence, she recapitulates the insights of her earlier essay on *My Sister Life*, and indeed almost all of her examples are taken from that book or from *Themes and Variations*. When she briefly addresses *1905*, she argues that Pasternak's revolution is rendered through and as nature, and she casts *Second Birth* as a hymn to nature in the image of a beautiful woman. While she does not entirely suppress her criticisms—there is the old impatience with Lieutenant Schmidt, and the tartness about Pasternak's lectures to Evgenia in *Second Birth*—she concludes that Pasternak has not changed in any essential way. He remains the exemplar of a lyricism she describes with new directness as hysterical: "Pasternak cries about everything; every feeling that surges up brings forth his tears." These tears, though, are "above all an expression of strength." They are "neither feminine nor masculine tears—but lyrical tears" (5:418–19). This lyricism of pain as power is what Pasternak betrayed at their meeting in Paris when he renounced tears, hysteria, and neurosis.

Pasternak's renunciation of hysteria was bound up with his complexly evolving political commitments. He had observed the course of Soviet socialism with high hopes and strong disappointment but always with a desire for engagement. He had undergone a long process of assessing the viability of his brand of lyricism in the postrevolutionary environment. Already in "Lieutenant Schmidt" he imagined the authentic revolutionary hero as one who disciplines his hysteria, and his creative efforts in the late 1920s and early 1930s were directed toward bringing lyrical feeling into line with a more "classical" revolutionary ideal. After his "second birth," he actually seems to have cast himself as a kind of poet-adviser to Stalin, as Elena Korkina has argued.[10] Her interpretation helps explain his behavior during the phone call from Stalin, as well as several compromising acts he performed during the 1930s, including the publication of two poems in praise of Stalin in 1936. Even during this period, though, he remained aware of the standard of creativity he shared earlier with Tsvetaeva. Alongside the poems to Stalin as they appeared in *The Banner* (*Znamya*), Pasternak included a poem that contains clear references to Tsvetaeva, as Yury Levin has detected ("Vse naklonen'ia i zalogi," 1936).[11] Earlier, in *Spektorsky*, Pasternak had linked Tsvetaeva and Lenin as geniuses. Here Tsvetaeva is introduced as an antidote for his Stalin poems. The poem opens with the poet in need of "baking soda for his indigestion" (soda ot izzhogi), yet another of Pasternak's gastronomic images.

Tsvetaeva might not have read these poems, but she did read a speech he made in 1936 at a plenary session of the Writers' Board in which he intimated that Stalin might be a "genius" (4:638). Korkina has argued that an essay Tsvetaeva wrote about Pushkin in 1937, "Pushkin and Pugachev" ("Pushkin i Pugachev"), was actually an attempt to understand and justify Pasternak's fascination with Stalin.[12] Tsvetaeva interprets Pushkin's story "The Captain's Daughter" ("Kapitanskaia dochka," 1836) as one that reveals the poet's ambivalent love for the peasant rebel leader Emilian Pugachev, despite his full knowledge of Pugachev's criminal violence. She interprets this love as the poet's love for any powerful phenomenon, above and beyond ethical considerations.[13] She thus applies her notion of the poet's submission to an elemental force to explain Pasternak's relationship to Stalin. In a sense, she was forced to do so in order to sustain her understanding of poetic creativity, an understanding she developed largely in relation to Pasternak. But she could not see herself in the vision she worked so hard to articulate. As Irina Shevelenko has observed, Tsvetaeva drew for herself a line she would not cross when she wrote: "I don't want anything for which I wouldn't answer at 7 AM and for which (without which) I would not die at any time of day or night. For Pugachev—I would not die—therefore he is *not mine*."[14] It appears Tsvetaeva would rather conclude she is not a poet than relinquish her understanding of lyricism and of Pasternak as a true lyric poet.

Tsvetaeva was similarly loyal to her family against her own knowledge. In March 1937 her daughter Ariadna moved to Moscow, where she found employment as a journalist. Six months later she was suddenly joined by her father, who fled to Russia after his connection to an NKVD assassination plot was discovered. Tsvetaeva was interrogated by the French police, to whom she declared her husband's innocence.[15] After two more difficult years in Paris, she finally acceded to the wishes of her son Georgy, now a teenager, and followed her family to Russia on June 12, 1939. Within months of Tsvetaeva's return, both Ariadna and Sergey Efron were arrested. She never saw them again, though she did exchange some letters with Ariadna in prison. Efron was secretly executed in October 1941. Ariadna served time in the camps and then lived in forced exile until she was rehabilitated in 1955.

The story of Tsvetaeva's last years in Soviet Russia has been difficult to piece together, and much remains obscure, including the extent of her contact with

Tsvetaeva in Moscow, 1940

Pasternak.[16] According to Irma Kudrova, Pasternak occasionally saw Ariadna and Sergey in the years before their arrest, and in June 1939 he learned from them about Tsvetaeva's imminent arrival.[17] But the only evidence of their having met belongs to the period after her family's arrest. Pasternak helped her get a room in one of the Literary Fund's "houses" for writers during the winter and spring of 1939–40, and his son Evgeny recalls visiting Tsvetaeva there.[18] He then helped her find and pay for an apartment in Moscow. They probably did not see each other frequently, since Pasternak was living outside Moscow in

Peredelkino, where Tsvetaeva visited him once in the fall of 1940 (7:749). The recently published diaries of her son Georgy provide some new details, including Pasternak's efforts to enroll him in a good school.[19] The fifteen-year old Georgy was admiring and grateful, but also charmingly cynical about the "sincere but helpless Pasternak."[20] Possibly Pasternak's most valuable gifts to Tsvetaeva were the introductions he supplied: Tsvetaeva met many of the people they had spoken about in their letters, including Evgenia, the Neigauzes, and Nikolai Aseev, as well as a number of sympathetic Moscow literati.

That year of relative stability ended in August 1941. With the Germans marching on Moscow, members of the Writers' Union were evacuated to the south, and Tsvetaeva and Georgy traveled with them. Pasternak was there to see them onto the boat. His own family had already been evacuated to Chistopol, as had Aseev. Tsvetaeva and Georgy were directed to the smaller nearby town of Elabuga. Upon arriving, Tsvetaeva made a rushed effort to move to Chistopol, where the Writers' Union had more to offer in terms of housing and jobs. (Irma Kudrova has also speculated that she was being harrassed by the local representatives of the NKVD in Elabuga.) Tsvetaeva called on Aseev, and he made some efforts on her behalf, but by the time she returned to Elabuga, she was resolved to commit suicide. She hanged herself in their rented room on August 31, 1941. She left a note of apology to Georgy, and two other notes, one addressed to Aseev and one to the literary community, begging them to take Georgy into their care. Georgy spent another year in evacuation in Tashkent, and in 1943 he was mobilized and died at the front.

Years later, when Ariadna Efron read her brother's diaries, she concluded somewhat unfairly that Aseev was responsible for Tsvetaeva's suicide. But she had no such complaint against Pasternak, with whom she sustained a warm friendship through correspondence.[21] Pasternak himself was burdened by a confused sense of guilt, as he expressed in a letter to Nina Tabidze in March 1942: "Though I knew nothing and had nothing to do with it, I am, for all that, the only one to blame for this bitter sin of omission."[22] This feeling pervades a two-poem cycle he wrote two years after her death, in December 1943, titled "In Memory of Marina Tsvetaeva" ("Pamiati Mariny Tsvetavoi"). The cycle thematizes the inadequacy of his offering, and indeed in these poems "his tone was inadequate to the loss," as Joseph Brodsky has commented.[23] Brodsky offers this assessment to explain why Pasternak returned to finish the task of mourning in another two-poem cycle he wrote in 1949, titled "Magdalene" ("Magdalena"). These poems have none of the acrostics or telling allusions to Tsvetaeva of Pasternak's earlier poems, but Brodsky's speculation that they concern her is utterly persuasive. I rehearse only his essential points and recommend his essay, which follows the poets' meeting across the boundary between life and death.

The Magdalene poems belong to the "Gospel poems" that appear at the end of *Doctor Zhivago* as the creation of Pasternak's hero, Zhivago. As Konstantin Polivanov has shown, Tsvetaeva was a main prototype of the character of Lara, and her family's temperament and circumstances are reflected in the novel as well.[24] Brodsky detected an even deeper level of engagement in the Magdalene poems. He argues that Pasternak initially was responding to Rilke's "Pietà," in which the lyric speaker is Magdalene speaking to Christ.[25] Brodsky dismisses the first Magdalene poem as unsuccessful, and imagines Pasternak realizing he required "a timbre other than his own—a female timbre."[26] For that Pasternak turned to Tsvetaeva, who had already responded to Rilke's poem in the third poem of her own "Magdalene" cycle ("Magdalena"), written in 1923 during her obsession with Pasternak. Tsvetaeva's poem (like Rilke's) is a love poem, and a sensual one, in which Christ's feet, his body, and his entire being are "washed over" by Mary Magdalene. But she reverses the speaker and listener of Rilke's poem: in her poem, the lyric speaker is Christ addressing Mary. Brodsky argues that Tsvetaeva, by speaking in Christ's voice and thus "looking at herself from the outside," showed Pasternak a way to look at himself from the outside. Pasternak does just this in his second Magdalene poem, "People clean house for the feast day" ("U liudei pred prazdnikom uborka," 1949), in which the lyric speaker is Mary addressing Christ. As Brodsky says: "We are dealing here with an extremely radical relinquishment, with a shift into a different quality, into the other gender. This is no longer a literary conceit, nor is it a mask: this is not love poetry, but spiritual poetry."[27] For Pasternak, speaking the part of the suffering, sinful woman in Tsvetaeva's "female timbre" allows him to "experience Christ's loss as a personal loss." If Brodsky is right, in this instance Pasternak's performance of suffering femininity helped lead him to his spiritual ideal, an attainment in which Tsvetaeva had a part. Brodsky suggests, though he does not state it, that her credo of self-renunciation, in the Christian guise in which Pasternak perceived it, authorized Pasternak's later writings. In any case, Brodsky identifies a final instance in which the poets shared voices and genders in ways that profoundly shaped their writing.

During a crisis moment in August 1940, when Tsvetaeva wrote to a secretary of the Literary Fund for help in finding housing, she closed by saying, "I am not a hysteric, I am a completely healthy, simple person, ask Boris Leonidovich" (7:700). Pasternak probably regarded her at the time simply as fatally out of touch with reality.[28] Years later, when Pasternak wrote a reminiscence about Tsvetaeva in his 1956 autobiography, he gave an objective if not wholly accepting portrait of her and her writing as hysterical—as miming masculine force in works of exceptional power:

> Tsvetaeva was a woman with an active masculine soul, militant, resolute, and indomitable. Both in life and art she had an eager, avid, almost a rapacious need for definition and finality, and in pursuing this she outstripped everyone else.
>
> Apart from her few known works she wrote many others which are unknown in Russia, huge, stormy compositions, some in the style of Russian folklore, others on themes from well-known historical legends and myths.

Their publication will be a triumph and a revelation for our native poetry which, in a single moment, will be enriched by this overdue gift.

I believe that the reevaluation and the recognition which await Tsvetaeva will be very great.

We were friends.[29]

Appendix

Marina Tsvetaeva, "From the Sea" ("S moria," 1926)

By the North-South wind,
Impossible, I know!
But possible—if needed!
In clothes for traveling,

By a whirlwind,
That carries along a splinter!—
The dream lasts three
Minutes. Got to hurry.

I won't look who's in bed
With you! Three minutes.
Better than taking the long way
From the Ocean—to Moscow!

A lightening-fast
Track—a side track.
Out of my dream
I've jumped into yours.

I'm in your dream: am I distinct?
Visible? Clearer
Than under
A postmark? Am I worth—

Bond paper? Worth—
Postage?—Top dollar?

Word of honor
It's me, not a letter!

Behaving like a free
Caesura. A leap from a barge!
Without a censor—
Without even a stamp!

Hoodwinking everyone—
The shorthand of dream!
Here's something for you from the sea—
In place of a letter!

In place of a telegram.
The weight? You're not serious!
Altogether I don't weigh
Much—even with a whole

Lyre, with the heart of all the Cenci,
With the entire *other world*.
A dream weighs less
Than ten grams.

Each of us gets three minutes—
Six (a mutual dream).
See when you look:
A distinctive

Nose, a stubborn
Forehead, the letter of letters—
A Ѣ, a defiant Ѣ,
In the lips' signature.

Me—without a misspelling.
Me—without a blot.
I'd have liked to give you a handful
Of Alpine roses, and a shack

By the sea, but the waves
Are good-natured.
Here, from the Ocean,
Is a handful of play.

Take it bit by bit, the way it was gathered.
The sea played. To play is to be kind.

The sea played and I took,
The sea lost and I stowed

In my collar, my cheek—tart, sea-tasting!—
The mouth is better than a case, if your hands
Are full. Praise to the swell!
The muse lost and the wave took.

Crab-colored corals, read: shells.
The sea played, to play is to be foolish.
To think—gray braids!—
Is to be smart. Let's play!

Play shells. At the tempo of "le petit navire."
This one is like a heart, this one a lyre,
This one, now I've sorted through three piles,
Is the G treble clef of childhood.

I gathered them from a fisherman's boat.
They're the bare bones of famished longing.

I'll gnaw a stone—I'll spare you,—
Better than a wave can,

Gone mad here on the deserted slope.
This?—it's the leftover bits of love:

I won't bother to restore it:
Its bite was so shallow.

So it lies there, not entered in the lists.
These are the chewed ends, no longer of love:

Of conscience. Instead of shedding
Tears—I gnaw them,

Which can't at all be gnawed.
These are tomorrow's shards

Of our game. Don't see that.
It's sad, you know. Let's divide them up.

Not whatever you like but what I draw out.
(May your son join us in bed
And make a third in our game?)
I'll pick first.

Just sand, smooth, through my fingers.
Wait a minute: the fragments of some stanza:
"The underworld temple of glory . . ."
—Fine.—You'll finish the line yourself.

Just sand, splashing, through my fingers.
Wait a minute: the old skins of a rattlesnake:
Of jealousy! Renewed,
I call myself Pride

And I've crawled back to myself vindicated.
We're not Left Guardists—to be standing over
An eaten-out crabshell: it's not a crabshell:
It's the brick-red speckle of fame.

A modest whim:
A pebble. Pumice.
Slick as a critic.
Grey as a censor

At a revelation.
—The censors are asleep!—
Our poem's censor
Is the dawn.

(These dawns see better:
They're friends with the Castalian
Stream. They'll look the other way—
While we ruin pens . . .

"Some rhyming, dearie?
You've spilled a lot of ink!"
And without looking up:
They let it through!)

Mill, you mill, you sea round-dance!
The mammoth, the butterfly—the sea has ground
Them all up. We can't speak badly—a pinch
Of dust—of the sea!

As soon as I speak out—it's quiet,
Sea! Beautiful miller's wife,
Place where bits are washed up—
And we are swept out!

Schoolteachers! Windbags!
Continents are only the sea's
Shallows. To be born (the point—
To multiply!)—is to run aground.

On a welcoming shore, with peat, oil.
Immortality growing shallow—
That's life. No call for pride!
Life? A lack of water

Above sea level.
               I apologize in advance:

I've brought you so much rubbish,
So many marvels from beyond the sea:
Everything the tide washed up.

It just leaves things and doesn't ask us to take them . . .
Strange that it's the receding tide that brings,
Diminishment that puts things in your palm.
Won't you recognize the notes

Left for us, two or three each,
At the hour when the god who brought them—floated away,
Departed . . . Orpheus . . . Harpist . . .
The sandbar is our musical score!

—Just a minute left for gathering!
I've brought you so much nonsense:
My tongue has ground so much—
The sea's entire hem!

Just like the fisherman's wife, my neighbor.
But I've kept for you last of all
A gift on which there's a system.
It links the sea to Moscow,

Soviet Russia to the Ocean.
The Great Ocean itself
Sends greetings—from a royalist—
To a republican. Affix it to your cap.

And tell the peasants in the sheaves,
Who wear a cap with the reddest

Of red stars—don't believe: class
War!—wear the star of the seas!

Tell the workers and the people of all lands:
If you've fallen away from the star of Bethlehem,
And swiped—the sixth point,
You are destined—for the starfish:

The pagan, mythic star.
(I'm running on, but that's how long
The sea runs—along the sea bed.)
So inform the authorities

—I didn't ask their name and rank—
That on the stern of Russia's ship
Is an entire shipwreck:
A thing with five points.

Bare cliffs, elephants' ribs . . .
The sea has grown tired, to be tired is to be kind.
Eternity, ply the oar!
Draw us. Let's sleep.

Side by side, but not crowded.
A fire, but no smoke.
For this isn't dreaming together
But mutual dreaming:

In God, each in the other.
A nose, you thought? A promontory!
Eyebrows? No, rainbows,
Exoduses from—

Seen-ness.

Notes

Introduction

1. Ariadna Efron, *O Marine Tsvetaevoi* (Moscow: Sovetskii pisatel', 1989), 147.

2. Evgeny Pasternak, *Boris Pasternak, Materialy dlia biografii* (Moscow: Sovetskii pisatel', 1989), 171.

3. Christopher Barnes, *Boris Pasternak: A Literary Biography*, vol. 1, *1890–1928* (Cambridge: Cambridge University Press, 1989), 28.

4. Ibid., 22.

5. On the partly fictional nature of this reminiscence, see Boris Kats, *Muzykal'nye kliuchi k russkoi poezii* (St. Petersburg: Kompozitor, 1997), 137–144.

6. See Avril Pyman, *A History of Russian Symbolism* (Cambridge: Cambridge University Press, 1994), especially the final chapter.

7. Ivanov's *By the Stars* (*Po zvezdam*) appeared in 1909 and his *Furrows and Boundaries* (*Borozdy i mezhi*) in 1916; in 1910, Bely published *Symbolism* (*Simvolizm*) and *The Green Meadow* (*Lug Zelenyi*), and *Arabesques* (*Arabeski*) came out the following year.

8. Elaine Showalter, *Sexual Anarchy: Gender and Culture at the Fin de Siècle* (New York: Penguin, 1990). For a cultural history of the period in Russia, see Laura Engelstein, *The Keys to Happiness: Sex and the Search for Modernity in Fin-de-Siècle Russia* (Ithaca: Cornell University Press, 1992).

9. Vladislav Khodasevich, *Koleblemyi trenozhnik*, ed. V. G. Perel'muter (Moscow: Sovetskii pisatel', 1991), 272.

10. Roman Jakobson, "Marginal Notes on the Prose of Pasternak," in *Language in Literature*, ed. Krystyna Pomorska and Stephen Rudy (Cambridge: Harvard University Press, 1987), 306.

11. Svetlana Boym, "The Death of the Poetess," in *Death in Quotation Marks: Cultural Myths of the Modern Poet* (Cambridge: Harvard University Press, 1991), 200; Joseph Brodsky, "Footnote to a Poem," in *Less Than One* (New York: Farrar, Straus and Giroux, 1986), 195–267.

12. This line could also be translated "Be an absorbent Greek sponge." Pasternak also compared poetry to a sponge in two later works: his poem "I like the stubborn capriciousness" ("Mne po dushe stroptivyi norov," 1936) and his prose piece "Several Propositions" ("Neskol'ko polozhenii," 1922).

13. There is a vast critical literature on gender and European modernism. The most influential general discussion concerning English and American literature is probably Sandra M. Gilbert and Susan Gubar, *No Man's Land: The Place of the Woman Writer in the Twentieth*

Century (New Haven: Yale University Press, 1988). There is no comparable study of gender in Russian modernism, though Catriona Kelly discusses several modernist women writers in *A History of Russian Women's Writing, 1820–1992* (Oxford: Clarendon Press, 1993). Eric Naiman, in *Sex in Public: The Incarnation of Early Soviet Ideology* (Princeton: Princeton University Press, 1997), and Eliot Borenstein, in *Men without Women: Masculinity and Revolution in Russian Fiction, 1917–1929* (Durham: Duke University Press, 2000), focus on Soviet literature and culture of the 1920s. Alexander Etkind, in *Sodom i Psikheia: ocherki intellektual'noi istorii Serebrianogo veka,* (Moscow: ITs-Garant, 1996) treats sex and gender in Russian symbolism. On the same subject, Olga Matich has published a number of important essays and a book, *Erotic Utopia: The Decadent Imagination in the Russian Fin de Siècle* (Madison: University of Wisconsin Press, 2004), and Jenifer Presto's *Beyond the Flesh: Russian Symbolism and the Sublimation of Sex* (Madison: University of Wisconsin Press, 2006) addresses gender and the body in the work of Alexander Blok and Zinaida Gippius. (Neither of these sources was available during my work on this book.) Sibelan Forrester has written an invaluable essay, "Wooing the Other Woman: Gender in Women's Love Poetry in the Silver Age," in *Engendering Slavic Literatures,* ed. Pamela Chester and Sibelan Forrester (Bloomington: Indiana, 1996), 109–34. Svetlana Boym's *Death in Quotation Marks* remains the best general discussion of gender in the work of the post-symbolist Russian poets.

14. Anya Kroth was the first to put forward this thesis in "Androgyny as an Exemplary Feature of Marina Tsvetaeva's Dichotomous Poetic Vision," *Slavic Review* 38.4 (1979): 563–82.

15. Alyssa Dinega, *A Russian Psyche: The Poetic Mind of Marina Tsvetaeva* (Madison: University of Wisconsin Press, 2001); Diana Burgin, *Marina Tsvetaeva i transgressivnyi eros* (St. Petersburg: Inapress, 2000); Catriona Kelly, chapter on Tsvetaeva in *A History of Russian Women's Writing, 1820–1992* (Oxford: Clarendon Press, 1994); Barbara Heldt, chapter on Tsvetaeva in *Terrible Perfection: Women and Russian Literature* (Bloomington: Indiana University Press, 1987).

16. Hélène Cixous, "Poetry, Passion, and History: Marina Tsvetayeva," in *Readings: The Poetics of Blanchot, Joyce, Kafka, Kleist, Lispector, and Tsvetayeva,* ed. Verena Andermatt Conley (Minneapolis: University of Minnesota Press, 1991), 110–51, and "Difficult Joys," in *The Body and the Text,* ed. Helen Wilcox, Keith McWatters, Ann Thompson, and Linda R. Williams (New York: St. Martin's Press, 1990), 1–30; Boym, chapter on Tsvetaeva in *Death in Quotation Marks;* Sibelan Forrester, "Bells and Cupolas: The Formative Role of the Female Body in Marina Tsvetaeva's Poetry," *Slavic Review* 51.2 (summer 1992): 232–46; Stephanie Sandler, "Embodied Words: Gender in Tsvetaeva's Reading of Pushkin," *Slavic and East European Journal* 34.2 (summer 1990): 139–57.

17. See especially Alexander Zholkovsky, "Ekstaticheskie motivy Pasternaka v svete ego lichnoi mifologii," in *Boris Pasternak, 1890–1990,* ed. Lev Loseff (Northfield: The Russian School at Norwich University, 1991), 52–74, and "The 'Sinister' in the Poetic World of Pasternak," *International Journal of Slavic Linguistics and Poetics* 29 (1984): 109–31.

18. Christopher Barnes, "Boris Pasternak and Mary Queen of Scots: An Aspect of the Female Image," in *Scotland and the Slavs: Selected Papers from the Glasgow-90 East-West Forum,* ed. Peter Henry, Jim MacDonald, and Halina Moss (Nottingham: Astra Press, 1993), 25–38; Viacheslav V. Ivanov, "O teme zhenshchiny u Pasternaka," in *"Byt' znamenitym nekrasivo," Pasternakovskie chteniia,* vol. 1 (Moscow: Nasledie, 1992), 43–54.

19. Barbara Johnson, "Gender and Poetry: Charles Baudelaire and Marceline Desbordes-Valmore," in *The Feminist Difference: Literature, Psychoanalysis, Race, and Gender* (Cambridge: Harvard University Press, 1998), 101–28.

20. Luce Irigaray, *Speculum of the Other Woman,* trans. Gillian C. Gill (Ithaca: Cornell

University Press, 1985); Elisabeth Bronfen, *The Knotted Subject: Hysteria and Its Discontents* (Princeton: Princeton University Press, 1998); Juliet Mitchell, *Mad Men and Medusas: Reclaiming Hysteria* (New York: Basic Books, 2000).

21. Claire Kahane, *Passions of the Voice: Hysteria, Narrative, and the Figure of the Speaking Woman, 1850–1915* (Baltimore: Johns Hopkins University Press, 1995).

22. Ibid., xiv–v.

23. Ibid., 10.

24. Etkind has speculated that psychoanalysis in Russia was largley preempted by the Russian symbolist discourse on sex and love, though he also shows how that discourse absorbed psychoanalytic ideas, primarily from Otto Weininger. Alexander Etkind, *Eros nevozmozhnogo. Istoriia psikhoanaliza v Rossii* (St. Petersburg: Meduza, 1993).

25. Nina Gourianova, paper presented at the American Association for the Advancement of Slavic Studies, Toronto, 2003. On Freud in Russia, see James Rice, *Freud's Russia: National Identity in the Evolution of Psychoanalysis* (New Brunswick, N.J.: Transaction Publishers, 1993); and Martin Miller, *Freud and the Bolsheviks: Psychoanalysis in Imperial Russia and the Soviet Union* (New Haven: Yale University Press, 1998).

26. Irina Zherebkina, "Izobretenie isteriki," in *Strast': Zhenskoe telo i zhenskaia seksual'nost'* (St. Petersburg: Aleteiia, 2001), 12–81.

27. Quoted by Irina Shevelenko, *Literaturynyi put' Tsvetaevoi* (Moscow: Novoe literaturnoe obozrenie, 2002), 116.

28. Kahane, *Passions of the Voice*, 148.

29. G. S. Smith, "Marina Cvetaeva's 'Poèma gory': An Analysis," *Russian Literature* 6 (1978): 365–88.

30. For many years it was believed that most of their correspondence had been lost. Pasternak told the story in his autobiography "People and Propositions" ("Liudi i polozheniia," 1956–57), which I quote in a translation by Manya Harari (Boris Pasternak, *An Essay in Autobiography*, trans. Manya Harari [London: Collins and Harvill, 1959], 109–10):

> I had almost a hundred of her letters, written in reply to mine. . . . I lost them through excessive care to keep them safe.
>
> During the war, when I used to visit my family in the country to which they had been evacuated, a member of the staff of the Scriabin Museum, who was a great friend of mine and a great admirer of Tsvetaeva, offered to look after them together with some letters from my parents and a few from Gorky and Romain Rolland. She put them in the safe of the Museum—all except Tsvetaeva's; these she kept by her, never letting them out of her sight and not even trusting them to the fireproof safe.
>
> She lived all the year round in the country and took the letters with her every day, in a small attaché-case, to and from her work. One winter's evening she was going home utterly exhausted. When she was half-way home from the country station, walking through the wood, she realised that she had left the case in the coach of the suburban train. That was how Tsvetaeva's letters were borne away and vanished.

Fortunately, Tsvetaeva kept Pasternak's letters and copies of her own letters to Pasternak (sometimes in several versions), which were held in her archive at RGALI (Russian State Archive of Literature). These materials were not available to the public until 2000. All of these letters are now published as Marina Tsvetaeva and Boris Pasternak, *Dushi nachinaiut videt': Pism'a 1922–1936 goda*, ed. E. B. Korkina and I. D. Shevelenko (Moscow: Vagrius, 2004).

31. These letters were first published in German as Rainer Maria Rilke, Marina Zwetajewa, and Boris Pasternak, *Briefwechsel*, ed. Evgeny Pasternak, Elena Pasternak, and Konstantin M. Azadovsky (Frankfurt: Insel, 1983). They appeared in Russian as *Pis'ma 1926*

goda (Moscow: Kniga, 1990); this book was translated into English as *Letters, Summer 1926*, trans. Margaret Wettlin and Walter Arndt (San Diego: Harcourt Brace Jovanovich, 1985). An updated Russian version was published as Rainer Maria Rilke, *Dykhanie liriki* (Moscow: Art-Fleks, 2000), which has appeared in English with a preface by Susan Sontag, again as *Letters, Summer 1926* (New York: New York Review of Books, 2001).

1. The Girl Muse

1. Irina Shevelenko supplies the first general discussion of Tsvetaeva's reception of symbolism in her book *Literaturnyi put' Tsvetaevoi* (Moscow: Novoe literaturnoe obozrenie, 2002). R. D. B. Thomson and Omry Ronen have addressed symbolist influences on prosody and stylistics in Tsvetaeva's early work. See R. D. B. Thomson, "The Metrical and Strophic Inventiveness of Tsvetaeva's First Two Books," *Canadian Slavonic Studies* 30 (June 1988), 220–44; Omry Ronen, "Chasy uchenichestva Mariny Tsvetaevoi," *Novoe literaturnoe obozrenie* 1 (1992): 177–190.

2. Valery Briusov, "Zhenskaia poeziia," in *Marina Tsvetaeva v kritike sovremennikov*, ed. Lev Mnukhin, vol. 1, *1910–1941* (Moscow: Agraf, 2003), 23–27.

3. Shevelenko, *Literaturnyi put' Tsvetaevoi*, 65.

4. Alexander Etkind, *Eros nevozmozhnogo. Istoriia psikhoanaliza v Rossii* (St. Petersburg: Meduza, 1993).

5. For a lucid summary of Soloviev's theory of love, see the chapter on Soloviev in Irene Masing-Delic, *Abolishing Death* (Stanford: Stanford University Press, 1992).

6. On these sources, see M. H. Abrams, *Natural Supernaturalism: Tradition and Revolution in Romantic Literature* (New York: Norton, 1971).

7. M. H. Abrams, "The Apocalytic Marriage," ibid., 37–46, 294–96.

8. Samuel D. Cioran makes this point in *Vladimir Soloviev and the Knighthood of the Divine Sophia* (Waterloo: Wilfrid Laurier Press, 1977): "Obviously, homosexuality and lesbianism are denied any valid status in Soloviev's theory, not on purely moral grounds, but because they do not represent a union of opposite qualities, of two principles of male (active and producing) and female (passive and produced) conforming to his metaphysical scheme" (31).

9. Vladimir Soloviev, *Sochineniia v dvukh tomakh*, vol. 2 (Moscow: Mysl', 1988), 513. The translation is taken from *The Meaning of Love*, ed. and trans. Thomas Beyer (Stockbridge: Lindisfarne Press, 1985), 55.

10. See Olga Matich, "The Symbolist Meaning of Love: Theory and Practice," in *Creating Life: The Aesthetic Utopia of Russian Modernism*, ed. Irina Paperno and Joan Delaney Grossman (Stanford: Stanford University Press, 1994), 24–50.

11. See the essays in Paperno and Grossman, *Creating Life*.

12. Matich, "The Symbolist Meaning of Love," 31.

13. See Alexander Lavrov, "Andrei Bely and the Argonauts' Mythmaking," in Paperno and Grossman, *Creating Life*, 83–121.

14. For an account of Blok's marriage with Liubov Dmitrievna based on biographical materials, see Vladimir Orlov, "Istoriia odnoi liubvi," in *Puti i sud'by* (Moscow: Sovetskii pisatel', 1963), 579–667.

15. See Joan Delaney Grossman, "Briusov and Petrovskaia," in Paperno and Grossman, *Creating Life*, 122–50; S. S. Grechishkin and A. V. Lavrov, "Biograficheskie istochniki romana Briusova 'Ognennyi Angel,'" *Wiener Slawistischer Almanach* 1, 2 (1978): 79–108, 73–96. The Bely-Petrovskaya-Briusov triangle was also reflected in Bely's novel *The Silver Dove* (*Serebrianyi golub'*, 1910). See Maria Carlson, "The Silver Dove," in *Andrey Bely: Spirit of Symbolism* (Ithaca: Cornell University Press, 1987), 65–66.

16. Vladislav Khodasevich, "The End of Renata" ("Konets Renaty"), in *Koleblemyi tre-nozhnik,* ed. V. G. Perel'muter (Moscow: Sovetskii pisatel', 1991), 269–77. Khodasevich re-marks how Petrovskaya was viewed as Mendeleeva's demonic rival (273–74).

17. Eric Naiman, "Historectomies," in *Sexuality and the Body in Russian Culture,* ed. Jane T. Costlow, Stephanie Sandler, and Judith Vowles (Stanford: Stanford University Press, 1993), 264. See also Edith Clowes: "The whole project of balancing diverse human experience and total-unity is jeopardized, in my view, when Soloviev looks to biblical discourse to deal with the question of gender roles in the totalizing context of *vseedinstvo.* It is here that one, sin-gle, and what one might justifiably call 'masculine,' point of view becomes paramount" ("The Limits of Discourse: Soloviev's Language of Syzygy and the Project of Thinking Total-Unity," *Slavic Review* 55 [fall 1996]: 561).

18. Naiman, "Historectomies," 265.

19. Alan Richardson, "Romanticism and the Colonization of the Feminine," in *Romanti-cism and Feminism,* ed. Anne K. Mellor (Bloomington: Indiana University Press, 1988). See also Anne K. Mellor, *Romanticism and Gender* (London: Routledge, 1993). For a discussion of these issues in Russian romanticism, see Luc J. Beaudoin, *Resetting the Margins: Russian Romantic Verse Tales and the Idealized Woman* (New York: Peter Lang, 1997).

20. In his essay "The Poetry of Ia. P. Polonsky" ("Poeziia Ia. P. Polonskogo," 1896). Vladimir Soloviev, *Stikhotvoreniia. Estetika. Literaturnaia kritika* (Moscow: Kniga, 1990), 318–341.

21. "There is a Being, there is a feminine Shade, / Whom I desired in sorrowful visions" (Est' sushchestvo, est' zhenstvennaia Ten' / Zhelannaia v videniiakh pechal'nykh). The line actually reads, "There was a Being whom my spirit oft / Met on its visioned wanderings, far aloft" (*Complete Poems of Percy Bysshe Shelley* [New York: Modern Library, 1994], 468). On Balmont's translations of Shelley, see Martin Bidney, "Shelley in the Mind of the Russian Symbolist Bal'mont: Six Kinds of Influence/Appropriation," *Comparative Literature Studies* 25.1 (1988): 57–71.

22. Leslie Brisman, "Epipsychidion," in *Percy Bysshe Shelley: Modern Critical Views,* ed. Harold Bloom (New York: Chelsea House, 1985), 113. Brisman traces the convention to Dante, on whom Soloviev also drew for "Three Encounters."

23. Ia. P. Polonsky, *Stikhotvorniia i poemy v dvukh tomakh,* vol. 1 (Moscow: Khudozh-estvennaia literatura, 1986).

24. As reproduced by N. Iu. Griakalova in her essay "K genezisu obraznosti rannei liriki Bloka (Ia. Polonskii i Vl. Solov'ev)," in *Aleksandr Blok: Issledovaniia i materialy* (Leningrad: Nauka, 1991), 55.

25. Mellor, *Romanticism and Gender,* 26.

26. Karen Swann, "Harassing the Muse," in Mellor, *Romanticism and Feminism,* 81–92.

27. Blok's diaries and letters attest to his deep immersion in Soloviev's work, and studies of his early verse have traced numerous echoes of Soloviev's poetry. The most important of these studies is Zinaida Mints, "Poeticheskii ideal molodogo Bloka," *Blokovskii sbornik* 1 (Tartu, 1964): 196–98.

28. Alexander Blok, *Sobranie sochinenii v vos'mi tomakh,* vol. 7 (Moscow: Khudozh-estvennaia literatura, 1963), 52.

29. See Zinaida Mints, "Funktsiia reminisentsii v poetike A. Bloka," *Trudy po znakovym sistemam* 6 (Tartu, 1973): 408–10. See also Griakalova, "K genezisu obraznosti rannei liriki Bloka," 54, 59.

30. Lidia Ginzburg, *O lirike* (Moscow: Sovetskii pisatel', 1964), 278. See also Viktor Zhir-munsky, *Poeziia Aleksandra Bloka* (1922; reprint, Moscow: Serebrianyi vek, 1998); and Kor-ney Chukovsky, *Kniga ob Aleksandre Bloke* (1922; reprint, Paris: YMCA, 1976).

31. On the significance of Baudelaire for Russian symbolism, see Adrian Wanner, *Baude-*

laire in Russia (Jacksonville: University Press of Florida, 1996). See also the essays in *The Fruits of Evil: Baudelaire, Decadence, and Russia, Ulbandus* 8 (2004).

32. Joan Delaney Grossman, "Blok, Brjusov, and the 'Prekrasnaja dama,'" in *Aleksandr Blok Centennial Conference,* ed. Walter N. Vickery (Columbus, Ohio: Slavica, 1984), 159–77.

33. Ibid., 162.

34. Irene Masing-Delic, paper delivered at the Conference on Sex and Russian Civilization, University of Surrey, June 1996.

35. Barbara Johnson, "Gender and Poetry: Charles Baudelaire and Marceline Desbordes-Valmore," in *The Feminist Difference: Literature, Psychoanalysis, Race, and Gender* (Cambridge: Harvard University Press, 1998), 101–28.

36. Ibid., 121.

37. Ibid., 124.

38. See Sibelan Forrester, "Wooing the Other Woman: Gender in Women's Love Poetry in the Silver Age," in *Engendering Slavic Literatures,* ed. Pamela Chester and Sibelan Forrester (Bloomington: Indiana University Press, 1996), 109–34.

39. On Tsvetaeva's reading of Karolina Pavlova, see Tomas Venclova, "Almost a Hundred Years Later: Toward a Comparison of Karolina Pavlova and Marina Cvetaeva," in *Essays on Karolina Pavlova,* ed. Susanne Fusso and Alexander Lehrman (Evanston: Northwestern University Press, 2001), 187–214.

40. Barbara Heldt, *Terrible Perfection: Women and Russian Literature* (Bloomington: Indiana University Press, 1987).

41. Marie Bashkirtseff, *The Journal of a Young Artist, 1860–1884,* trans. Mary J. Serrano (New York: Cassell & Co., 1889), viii.

42. See her essay "Marina Tsvetaeva v 1911–1913 godakh: formirovanie avtorskogo samosoznaniia," *Blokovskii sbornik* 11 (Tartu, 1990): 50–66; and the first chapter of her *Literaturnyi put' Tsvetaevoi.*

43. Mnukhin, *Marina Tsvetaeva v kritike sovremennikov,* vol. 1 (Moscow: Agraf, 2003), 24.

44. Ibid., 24.

45. Ibid., 41.

46. Shevelenko, *Literaturnyi put' Tsvetaevoi,* 23.

47. Cf. Claire Kahane's reading of Olive Schreiner's novel *The Story of an African Farm* (1883), which "ambivalently embodies and attempts to recuperate the lost maternal object as language" (*Passions of the Voice: Hysteria, Narrative, and the Figure of the Speaking Woman, 1850–1915* [Baltimore: Johns Hopkins University Press, 1995], 90).

48. Ellis also presented her with his book of translations from Baudelaire, *Moe obnazhennoe serdtse* (Moscow: Diletant, 1907). She owned a copy of *Les fleurs du mal* in which she inscribed "Moscou, lisee 1908–09." *Marina Tsvetaeva. Fotoletopis' zhizni poeta* (Moscow: Ellis Lak, 2000), 32, 39.

49. "I published the book for reasons unrelated to literature but native to poetry—in lieu of a letter to a man with whom I had no other means to communicate" ("Geroi truda," 1925 [4:23]).

50. Ronen, "Chasy uchenichestva Mariny Tsvetaevoi," 93.

51. See Anna Saakiants's introduction to Marina Tsvetaeva, "Volshebstvo v stikhakh Briusova," *Den' poezii* (Moscow: Sovetskii pisatel', 1979), 32–34.

52. On this text, see Olga Hasty, "Valerii Briusov as Marina Tsvetaeva's Anti-Muse," *Vieldeutiges Nicht-zu-Ende-Sprechen,* ed. Arja Rosenholm and Frank Göpfert (Gopfert-Fichtenwalde, 2002), 191–204.

53. Mnukhin, *Marina Tsvetaeva v kritike sovremennikov,* 27–28.

54. Ibid., 28.

55. Anastasia Tsvetaeva, *Vospominania*, 3rd ed (Moscow: Sovetskii pisatel', 1984), 231.

56. Ellis, *Argo* (Moscow: Musaget, 1914), 29.

57. Tsvetaeva had earlier rendered her refusal of Ellis in one of the poems of *Evening Album*, "The Mistake" ("Oshibka," 1910).

58. Mnukhin, *Marina Tsvetaeva v kritike sovremennikov,* 35–36.

59. Omry Ronen has detected the influence of both Zinaida Gippius and Mirra Lokhvitskaia in Tsvetaeva's early verse. Jane Taubman cites documentary evidence that Tsvetaeva read Lokhvitskaia in her "Tsvetaeva and the Feminine Tradition," in *Marina Tsvetaeva: One Hundred Years,* ed. Viktoria Schweitzer, Jane A. Taubman, Peter Scotto, and Tatyana Babyonyshev (Berkeley: Berkeley Slavic Specialties, 1994), 80. Tomas Venclova has speculated that Tsvetaeva might have known Karolina Pavlova's work, pointing out that Tsvetaeva's title repeats the Latin title of Pavlova's 1854 poem "Laterna Magica" ("Almost a Hundred Years Later," 189). If this is so, it would appear that Pavlova's voicing of unhappiness in love was less useful to Tsvetaeva at this stage of her career than Desbordes-Valmore's, perhaps because it was so bitter.

60. Johnson, "Gender and Poetry."

61. Ibid., 104, 108.

62. Ibid., 126–27.

63. Ibid.

64. See the collection of essays on this period, *Borisogleb'e Mariny Tsvetaevoi: sbornik dokladov* (Moscow: Dom-muzei Mariny Tsvetavoi, 1999).

65. Olga G. Revzina, "Samosoznanie Mariny Tsvetaevoi v Borisoglebskii period," ibid., 103.

66. See S. Poliakova, *Zakatnye ony dni: Tsvetaeva i Parnok* (Ann Arbor: Ardis, 1983); Diana Lewis Burgin, "After the Ball Is Over: Sophia Parnok's Creative Relationship with Marina Tsvetaeva," *Russian Review* 47.4 (1988): 425–44; and Forrester, "Wooing the Other Woman."

67. Diana Lewis Burgin, *Sophia Parnok: The Life and Work of Russia's Sappho* (New York: New York University Press, 1994).

68. Diana Lewis Burgin, "Laid Out in Lavender: Perceptions of Lesbian Love in Russian Literature and Criticism of the Silver Age, 1893–1917," in Costlow, Sandler, and Vowles, *Sexuality and the Body in Russian Culture,* 198.

69. This is another borrowing from Blok, who used Andersen's tale in his famous cycle "Snow Mask" ("Snezhnaia maska," 1907).

70. Sibelan Forrester, "Bells and Cupolas: The Formative Role of the Female Body in Marina Tsvetaeva's Poetry," *Slavic Review* 51.2 (summer 1992): 232–46. Forrester remarks how Tsvetaeva's relationships with Parnok and Akhmatova are structured as mother-daughter relationships.

71. Ibid., 235.

72. Ibid., 246.

73. Matich, "Symbolist Meaning of Love," 28–29.

74. Tsvetaeva later gathered the observations about love she noted in her diary during 1917–19 and published them as "About Love" ("O liubvi") in the émigré newspaper *Days* in Berlin (*Dni*, December 5, 1925).

75. On these plays, see Simon Karlinsky, "Kuzmin, Gumilev, and Cvetaeva as Neo–romantic Playwrights," in *Studies in the Life and Works of Mixail Kuzmin,* ed. John Malmstad, Wiener Slawistischer Almanach, vol. 24 (Vienna: Gesellschaft zur Forderung slawistischer Studien, 1989), 17–30; and Peter Scotto, "Toward a Reading of Tsvetaeva's 'Feniks,'" in Schweitzer et al., *Tsvetaeva: One Hundred Years,* 194–201.

76. Jane Taubman, *A Life through Poetry: Tsvetaeva's Lyric Diary* (Ann Arbor: Ardis, 1989), 127.

77. Shevelenko, *Literaturnyi put' Tsvetaevoi,* 137.

78. The phrase "lastochka tvoia—Psikheia" is taken from Mandelstam's poem "When Psyche-life descends to the shadows" ("Kogda Psikheia-zhizn' spuskaets'ia k teniam," 1920).

79. Shevelenko, *Literaturnyi put' Tsvetaevoi,* 43.

80. Ibid., 168.

81. See Tsvetaeva's (and Alya's) notes from that period in "Zapisnaia knizhka 7, 1919–1920," in *Neizdannoe. Zapisnye knizhki v dvukh tomakh,* vol. 2 (Moscow: Ellis Lak, 2001), 7–94.

82. Her first long poem was the poem to Ellis mentioned earlier, "The Enchanter" ("Charodei").

83. See chapter 3 of Michael Makin, *Marina Tsvetaeva: Poetics of Appropriation* (Oxford: Clarendon Press, 1993). See also G. S. Smith, "Characters and Narrative Modes in Marina Tsvetaeva's 'Tsar'-devitsa,'" *Oxford Slavonic Papers,* n.s. 12 (1979): 117–34.

84. See Elena Korkina, "Liricheskii siuzhet v fol'klornykh poemakh Mariny Cvetaevoi," *Russkaia literatura* 4 (1987): 161–68.

85. She once listed his poem "Song of the Gypsy Girl" ("Pesnia tsyganki," ca. 1850) as one of her favorites. Marina Tsvetaeva, *Neizdannoe. Svodnye tetradi* (Moscow: Ellis Lak, 1997), 290. Michael Makin believes that Tsvetaeva knew Polonsky's "Tsar-Maiden," citing the lines in which her tsar-maiden's kiss leaves a mark (pechat') on the tsarevich's forehead. One should note, however, that this detail is a typical folktale motif (Griakalova, "K genezisu," 55).

86. Anya M. Kroth first explored this aspect of the poem in "Androgyny as an Exemplary Feature of Marina Tsvetaeva's Dichotomous Poetic Vision," *Slavic Review* 38.4 (1979): 566.

87. Shevelenko, *Literaturnyi put' Tsvetaevoi,* 169.

88. Smith, "Characters and Narrative Modes in Marina Tsvetaeva's 'Tsar'-devitsa,'" 133.

89. "In the poem 'On a Red Steed' (1921), encoded in the dedication to Akhmatova which was later removed, there appears the image, complex and dynamic in its iconicity, of Tsvetaeva's 'deified' Blok—creator of 'The Twelve,' of George the Victor of the Revolution, purest and most dispassionate Genius of poetry, inhabitant of those heights which Tsvetaeva thought herself incapable of reaching." Ariadna Efron, *O Marine Tsvetaevoi* (Moscow: Sovetskii pisatel', 1989), 92.

90. Ibid. There are several echoes of "The Twelve" in "On a Red Steed," as David Bethea has remarked ("'This Sex Which Is Not One' versus This Poet Which Is 'Less Than One': Tsvetaeva, Brodsky, and Exilic Desire," in *Joseph Brodsky and the Creation of Exile* [Princeton: Princeton University Press, 1994], 186).

91. Blok's death in 1921 inspired a second cycle of poems, which Tsvetaeva published together with the 1916 cycle as a separate volume, *Poems to Blok (Stikhi k Bloku,* 1922). On Tsvetaeva's poems to Blok, see V. N. Golitsyna, "Tsvetaeva o Bloke," *Tvorchestvo A. A. Bloka i russkaia kul'tura XX veka* (Tartu: Tartuskii gosudarstvennyi universitet, 1975), 135–40; and "M. Tsvetaeva ob Al. Bloke (tsikl 'Stikhi k Bloku')," *Blokovskii sbornik* 9 (Tartu, 1989): 99–113; David Sloane, "'Stikhi k Bloku': Cvetaeva's Poetic Dialogue with Blok," in *New Studies in Russian Language and Literature,* ed. Anna Lisa Crone and Catherine V. Chvany (Columbus: Slavica Publishers, 1987), 258–70.

92. This opening section appeared only in the poem's first publication in her collection *Parting (Razluka,* 1922).

93. Simon Karlinsky has suggested that the closest model for the poem may be Vladimir Soloviev's "Three Encounters" ("Tri svidaniia," 1898). Simon Karlinsky, *Marina Cvetaeva: Her Life and Art* (Berkeley: University of California Press, 1966), 210.

94. Shevelenko, *Literaturnyi put' Tsvetaevoi,* 174.

95. Bethea, "This Sex," 186.

96. Shevelenko, *Literaturnyi put' Tsvetaevoi,* 173. The passage appears in Tsvetaeva, *Neizdannoe. Zapisnye knizhki,* 25.

97. I have argued in another context that this is a pervasive and defining pattern in Tsvetaeva's lyric poetry. Catherine Ciepiela, "The Demanding Woman Poet: On Resisting Marina Tsvetaeva," *PMLA* III (May 1996): 421–34.

98. Kahane, *Passions of the Voice,* 36.

99. Ibid., 37.

100. This dynamic closely resembles that of Olive Shreiner's *Story of an African Farm* as described by Kahane: "Here, Lyndall's maternal rejection of the child not only ties her to Schreiner's own 'cold and unloving mother,' but also indicates the daughter's more general rejection of a maternal identity and of the infant as emblem of her desire. There is, however, a psychic cost to this rejection that the novel continually demonstrates" (ibid., 88).

101. Karlinsky, *Marina Cvetaeva,* 190.

102. Kahane, *Passions of the Voice,* 16.

103. Ibid., 41.

104. Blok used this very phrase with a negative cast, as Sergei Hackel discusses in his book *The Poet and the Revolution: Aleksandr Blok's 'The Twelve'* (Oxford: Clarendon, 1975), 122–24. My thanks to Michael Wachtel for this information.

105. Andrey Bely, "The Poetess-Singer" ("Poetessa-pevitsa"), *Golos rossii,* no. 971 (May 21, 1922); reprinted in *Voprosy literatury* 4 (1982): 276–77.

106. Thomas Beyer has made a detailed study of Bely's response to Tsvetaeva in "Marina Cvetaeva and Andrei Belyi: 'Razluka' and 'Posle Razluki,'" *Wiener Slawistischer Almanach* 35 (1995): 97–132. See also Viacheslav V. Ivanov's comments on Tsvetaeva and Bely in "O vozdeistvii 'esteticheskogo eksperimenta' Andreia Belogo," in *Andrei Belyi. Problemy tvorchestva* (Moscow: Sovetskii pisatel', 1988), 361–63; for a general discussion of their friendship, see, in the same volume, Anna Saakiants, "Vstrecha poetov. Andrei Belyi i Marina Cvetaeva," 367–85.

107. Tsvetaeva, in her memoir of Bely, recalls his saying, "It will be a whole book: 'After Parting'—after the parting—with her, and your 'Parting'" (4:254).

108. As L. V. Zubova has shown, Tsvetaeva often uses the plural to signal absence of distinction or individuality (*Poeziia Mariny Tsvetaevoi* [Leningrad: Leningrad University, 1989], 28).

109. Efron, *O Marine Tsvetaevoi,* 142.

110. Elena Aizenstein has worked out that she received her copy of *My Sister Life* on July 1 (*Borisu Pasternaku—navstrechu! O knige Mariny Tsvetaevoi "Posle Rossii"* [St. Petersburg: Neva, 2000], 24).

111. As translated by Angela Livingstone in Marina Tsvetaeva, *Art in the Light of Conscience: Eight Essays on Poetry by Marina Tsvetaeva* (Cambridge: Harvard University Press, 1992), 24–25, with my amendations.

112. From David Burliuk et al., "Poshchechina obshchestvennomu vkusu," in *Manifesty i programmy russkikh futuristov* (Munich: Wilhelm Fink, 1967), 50.

113. Luce Irigaray, *Speculum of the Other Woman,* trans. Gillian C. Gill (Ithaca: Cornell University Press, 1985), 72.

2. The Boy Poet

1. This translation is from Boris Pasternak, *Collected Short Prose,* trans. Christopher Barnes (New York: Praeger, 1977), 22, with my amendations.

2. See Lazar Fleishman's discussion "Avtobiograficheskoe i 'Avgust' Pasternaka," in *Stat'i o Pasternake* (Bremen: K-Presse, 1977), 103–17.

3. See Lazar Fleishman, *Boris Pasternak: The Poet and His Politics* (Cambridge: Harvard University Press, 1990), 32–33.

4. Ibid., 56.

5. As quoted by A. V. Lavrov, "Andrei Bely i Boris Pasternak: Vzgliad cherez 'Marburg,'" in *Themes and Variations: In Honor of Lazar Fleishman,* ed. Konstantin Polivanov, Irina Shevelenko, and Andrey Ustinov (Stanford: Department of Slavic Languages and Literatures, Stanford University, 1994), 46.

6. Fleishman, *Boris Pasternak,* 48.

7. Pasternak, however, did attend a lecture Bely gave at the Moscow Religious-Philosophical Society in November. Ibid., 47.

8. Viacheslav V. Ivanov, "O vozdeistvii 'esteticheskogo eksperimenta' Andreia Belogo (V. Khlebnikov, V. Maiakovskii, M. Tsvetaeva, B. Pasternak)," in *Andrei Belyi: Problemy tvorchestva* (Moscow: Sovetskii pisatel', 1988), 359.

9. He requested in a letter of July 26, 1912, that his friend Alexander Shtikh send him complete collections of Briusov, Blok, Sologub, and Ivanov (5:71–72).

10. Mikhail Gasparov and Konstantin Polivanov identify numerous symbolist subtexts in their commentary to Pasternak's first book of poems, *"Bliznets v tuchakh" Borisa Pasternaka: opyt kommentariia* (Moscow: RGGU, Institut Vysshikh gumanitarnykh issledovanii, 2005). See also V. S. Baevsky, "Temy i variatsii. Ob istoriko-kul'turnom kontekste poezii B. Pasternaka," *Voprosy literatury* 10 (1987): 30–59; and Igor Smirnov, *Porozhdenie interteksta (Elementy intertekstual'nogo analiza s primerami iz tvorchestva B. L. Pasternaka)* (St. Petersburg: Iazykovoi tsentr, 1995).

11. Bobrov's essay "On the Lyric Theme" ("O liricheskoi teme," 1913) also explicitly developed ideas first articulated by Ivanov. See Fleishman, *Boris Pasternak,* 57.

12. See Christopher Barnes's account of this development in *Boris Pasternak: A Literary Biography,* vol. 1 (Cambridge: Cambridge University Press, 1989), 158–60.

13. Pasternak expressed mixed feelings about Aseev's introduction in a letter of July 1, 1914, to Alexander Shtikh (5:80–81).

14. On the gender politics of the European avant-garde, see Susan Rubin Suleiman, *Subversive Intent: Gender, Politics, and the Avant-Garde* (Cambridge: Harvard University Press, 1990). On gender and cross-dressing in Mayakovsky's work, see Svetlana Boym, *Death in Quotation Marks* (Cambridge: Harvard University Press, 1991).

15. Lazar Fleishman, "K kharakteristike rannego Pasternaka," in *Stat'i o Pasternake,* 8.

16. Fleishman, *Boris Pasternak,* 42.

17. Pasternak was well versed in German romantic literature and philosophy, main sources of symbolist imagery and thought. Boris Paramonov has persuasively described Pasternak's romanticism as deriving from Schelling's *Naturphilosophie,* in which man is envisioned as part of a spiritualized universe ("Pasternak protiv romantizma," in *Boris Pasternak, 1890– 1990,* ed. Lev Loseff [Northfield: Russian School of Norwich University, 1991], 11–25). Karen Evans-Romaine has traced many of Pasternak's concepts and images to Novalis, Hoffmann, and Heine, among them the notion of the poet's madness or spiritual illness (*Boris Pasternak and the Tradition of German Romanticism* [Munich: Otto Sagner, 1997]).

18. Barnes, *Boris Pasternak,* 151–52. See also Viacheslav V. Ivanov, "Pasternak i bessmertie. 1913 god," *Krug chteniia* 5 (1995): 46–47. On Ivanov's reception of Nietzsche, see Edith Clowes, *The Revolution of Moral Consciousness: Nietzsche in Russian Literature, 1890–1914* (DeKalb: Northern Illinois University Press, 1988), 134–41. On Ivanov's reception of German literature, see Michael Wachtel, *Russian Symbolism and Literary Tradition* (Madison: University of Wisconsin Press, 1994).

19. Viacheslav Ivanov, *Po zvezdam* (1909; reprint, Letchworth: Bradda Books, 1971), 250.

20. Ivanov's essay and other symbolist writings also supply the context in which to under-

stand Pasternak's use of the term "realist" for artists squarely situated in the romantic tradition—artists such as Blok, Verlaine, and Chopin. As Ivanov states in his essay, "Romanticism is a variety of realism, which has many forms" (ibid., 264). Contemporary scholarship on the period has emphasized the realist bent of symbolism: "Russian Symbolists saw their attempts to merge art and life as a revival of romanticism. However, they operated in the culture that had passed through and responded to the experience of realism. Realism was worked into their aesthetics." Irina Paperno, "The Meaning of Art: Symbolist Theories," in *Creating Life: The Aesthetic Utopia of Russian Modernism* (Stanford: Stanford University Press, 1994), 22.

21. Ivanov, *Po zvezdam*, 252.

22. Angela Livingstone, "'Fausta chto-li, Gamleta-li': The Meaning of Faust in Pasternak's Poetry," in *The European Foundations of Russian Modernism*, ed. Peter Barta (Lewiston: Edwin Mellen Press, 1991), 183.

23. I quote this passage, with some changes, as translated by Angela Livingstone in Boris Pasternak, *Pasternak on Art and Creativity*, ed. Angela Livingstone (Cambridge: Cambridge University Press, 1985), 33. I have restored the sentence in brackets, which appears in the original version I cite.

24. Here Pasternak violates grammar ("byl'" is grammatically feminine) and engenders "fact" as masculine heaviness.

25. Michel Aucouturier, *Pasternak par lui-même* (Paris: Éditions Duseuil, 1963), 32.

26. E. B. Pasternak, "Pervye opyty Borisa Pasternaka," in *Trudy po znakovym sistemam*, 4 (1969): 239–81. See also Elena Pasternak, "Dopolnenie k publikatsii pervykh opytov B. Pasternaka. Perevody iz Rilke," *Trudy po znakovym sistemam* 6 (Tartu, 1973): 546–48.

27. Anna Ljunggren made this observation in her discussion of Rilke's influence on Pasternak in *Juvenilia B. Pasternaka: 6 fragmentov o Relikvimini* (Stockholm: University of Stockholm, 1984), 95–117. Lunggren traces Pasternak's representation of lyricism as movement to Rilke's *Notebooks of Malte Laurids Brigge* (*Die Aufzeichnungen des Malte Laurids Brigge*, 1910). See also Larissa Rudova's analysis of Rilke's influence on Pasternak's prose in chapter 2 of *Pasternak's Short Fiction and the Cultural Vanguard* (New York: Peter Lang, 1994), 43–78.

28. See Christopher Barnes, "Boris Pasternak and Rainer Maria Rilke," *Forum for Modern Language Studies* 8.1 (1972): 61–78; and Walter Arndt, "Pasternak's Version of Early Rilke Poems," in Loseff, *Boris Pasternak, 1890–1990*, 168–77.

29. Donald Rayfield, "Unicorns and Gazelles: Pasternak, Rilke, and the Georgian Poets," *Forum for Modern Language Studies* 26.4 (1990): 377.

30. See Helen Sword's discussion of Rilke in "Leda and the Modernists," *PMLA* 107 (March 1992): 305–18.

31. Baevsky has found specific echoes in *A Twin in Clouds* of Blok's cycle "A Terrifying World" ("Strashnyi mir," 1907). V. S. Baevsky, "Lirika Pasternaka v istoriko-kul'turnom kontekste," *Izvestiia Akademii nauk. Seriia literatury i iazyka* 47 (1988): 138–39. Ivanov also has identified several Blok subtexts for these early poems. Viacheslav V., "O teme zhenshchiny u Pasternaka," "*Byt' znamenitym nekrasivo*," *Pasternakovskie chteniia*, vol. 1 (Moscow: Nasledie, 1992), 43–54.

32. Elena Pasternak, "Iz pervykh prozaicheskikh opytov Borisa Pasternaka. Publikatsiia II," in *Boris Pasternak: Essays*, ed. Nils Åke Nilsson (Stockholm: Almqvist & Wiksell International, 1976), 29.

33. Z. G. Mints and A. P. Iulova, "Iz kommentarii k tsiklu Bloka 'Snezhnaia maska,'" in *Tipologiia literaturnykh vzaimodeistvii* (Tartu: Tartuskii gosudarstvennyi universitet, 1983), 99–108.

34. E. B. Pasternak, "Pasternak o Bloke," *Blokovskii sbornik* 2 (Tartu, 1972): 448.

35. Christopher Barnes has suggested that the representation of women in their work ac-

tually evolves in a similar fashion ("Boris Pasternak and Mary Queen of Scots: An Aspect of the Female Image," in *Scotland and the Slavs: Selected Papers from the Glasgow-90 East-West Forum,* ed. Peter Henry, Jim MacDonald, and Halina Moss [Nottingham: Astra Press, 1993], 35).

36. Ivanov, "O teme zhenshchiny u Pasternaka."

37. Most commentators have downplayed this aspect of the story. Two exceptions are Susan Layton, "Poetic Vision in Pasternak's 'The Childhood of Luvers,'" *Slavic and East European Journal* 22.2 (1978): 163–74; and Judit Barothy, "The Androgynous Mind: A Contrastive Analysis of Virgina Woolf's 'To the Lighthouse' and Boris Pasternak's 'Zhenya Luvers' Childhood,'" *The Anachronist* (1996): 79–97.

38. Omry Ronen, "'What Makes a Woman an Amazon': Pasternak, Cvetaeva, and the Heritage of Heinrich von Kleist," paper presented at the American Association for Teachers of Slavic and East European Languages, Seattle, 1992.

39. To my knowledge, this is Pasternak's only published reference to Freud. There is no question, however, that Pasternak was acquainted with Freudian thought. Pasternak's friend and fellow futurist Aleksei Kruchenykh was an important advocate of Freud's work in the teens. Nina Gourianova, paper presented at the American Association for the Advancement of Slavic Studies, Toronto, 2003.

40. Boris Pasternak, Marina Tsvetaeva, and Rainer Maria Rilke, *Letters: Summer 1926,* trans. Margaret Wettlin, Walter Arndt, and Jamie Gambrell (New York: New York Review Books, 2001), 235.

41. Ivanov, for example, addressed a wintry landscape as a "dead czarevna" in his poem of that title ("Mertvaia tsarevna," 1907). V. S. Baevsky has identified this poem as a subtext for a later Pasternak poem, "After the Blizzard" ("Posle v'iugi," 1957) ("Temy i variatsii," 52).

42. This detail is autobiographical, as we learn from Pasternak's "People and Propositions" ("Liudi i polozheniia," 1956), where a strong childhood memory is the "stuffed bears in the coachmakers' windows in Carriage Lane" (4:296–97). As Ivanov has shown, the same detail appears in *Doctor Zhivago* and is linked to Lara's sexual trauma. Lara, as an underaged girl, remembers the "stuffed bears" ("medvezh'ie chuchela") sold on Karetnyi Lane before visiting the man who will seduce and torment her ("O teme zhenshchiny u Pasternaka").

43. Pasternak directly addressed the loss of virginity as traumatic in an earlier poem, "Yesterday a naked child was smashed / Like the statuette of a god" ("Vchera, kak boga statuetka, / Nagoi rebenok byl razbit," 1913). The poem bears an epigraph from Sappho: "Virginity, virginity, / Where are you leaving me for?" (1:440).

44. "Randbemerkungen zur Prosa des Dichters Pasternak" (1935). This essay appears in translation as "Marginal Notes on Pasternak's Prose" in Roman Jakobson, *Language in Literature,* ed. Krystyna Pomorska and Stephen Rudy (Cambridge: Harvard University Press, 1987), 301–17. It appeared earlier in *Pasternak,* ed. Donald Davie and Angela Livingstone (London: Macmillan, 1969), 135–51.

45. Jakobson, "Marginal Notes," 313–14. On Pasternak's lyric subject, see also Andrey Sinyavsky, "Predislovie," *Stikhotvoreniia i poemy* (Moscow: Sovetskii pisatel', 1965).

46. Jakobson himself understood how his insights might serve a similar kind of argument: "Mechanists of the psycho-analytical school would find the sources of Pasternak's thematic material in his confession that he had languished shamefully long 'in the sphere of mistakes made by the childish imagination, boyish perversions and the hungers of youth.' From these assumptions they would infer not only the repeated theme of passive exaltation and the inevitable falls, not only the poet's agitated recourse to motifs of adolescent development, but also his metonymical deviations around every fixed object" ("Marginal Notes," 315).

47. Alexander Zholkovsky, "'Window' in the Poetic World of Boris Pasternak," in *Themes*

and Texts: Toward a Poetics of Expressiveness (Ithaca: Cornell University Press, 1984), 135–58. This essay previously appeared in Russian as "Mesto okna v poeticheskom mire Pasternaka," *Russian Literature* 7 (1978): 1–38.

48. Zholkovsky, "'Window,'" 143–44.

49. M. L. Gasparov, "Rifma i zhanr v stikhakh Pasternaka," in *Pasternakovskie chteniia*, vol. 2 (Moscow: Nasledie, 1998), 63–70.

50. On Pasternak's syntax, see Fiona Björling, "Aspects of Poetic Syntax: Analysis of the Poem 'Sestra moja—žizn' i segodnja v razlive' by Boris Pasternak," in Nilsson, *Boris Pasternak: Essays*, 162–79.

51. Fleishman, *Boris Pasternak*, 106.

52. For a detailed analysis of Pasternak's evolving poetics, see M. L. Gasparov, "Evoliutsiia stikha B. Pasternaka," in *Literature, Culture, and Society in the Modern Age: In Honor of Joseph Frank*, pt. 2, ed. Edward J. Brown, Stanford Slavic Studies 4:2 (Stanford: Department of Slavic Languages and Literatures, Stanford University, 1992), 136–56. There he writes about Pasternak's effort in *My Sister Life* to write an "improved version" of *Above the Barriers* (150).

53. For readings of "The Mirror," see Fleishman, "K kharakteristike rannego Pasternaka"; and Anna Ljunggren, "'Sad' i 'Ia sam': Smysl i kompozitsiia stikhotvoreniia 'Zerkalo,'" in *Boris Pasternak and His Times*, ed. Lazar Fleishman, Modern Literature and Culture, vol. 25 (Berkeley: Berkeley Slavic Specialties, 1989), 224–37.

54. Ljunggren, "'Sad' i 'Ia sam,'" 230.

55. Boris Gasparov, "Byt kak kategoriia poetiki Pasternaka," in Polivanov, Shevelenko, and Ustinov, *Themes and Variations*, 56–69.

56. This translation is from Boris Pasternak, *An Essay in Autobiography*, trans. Manya Harari (London: Collins and Harvill, 1959), 45.

57. Fleishman, *Boris Pasternak*, 12–13.

58. As quoted by Irigaray, *Speculum of the Other Woman*, trans. Gillian C. Gill (Ithaca: Cornell University Press, 1985), 61.

59. Boris Gasparov, "Ob odnom ritmiko-muzykal'nom motive v proze Pasternaka (Istoriia odnoi trioli)," in *Studies in Poetics*, ed. Elena Semeka-Pankratov (Columbus: Slavica, 1995), 233–59.

60. Katherine Tiernan O'Connor, *Boris Pasternak's "My Sister Life"* (Ann Arbor: Ardis, 1988), 38.

61. Michel Aucouturier, "Pol i 'poshlost'': tema pola u Pasternaka," in *Pasternakovskie chteniia*, vol. 2, 74.

62. O'Connor, *Boris Pasternak's "My Sister Life,"* 43.

63. Sigmund Freud, "An Autobiographical Study," in *The Freud Reader*, ed. Peter Gay (New York: Norton, 1989), 24.

64. O'Connor, *Boris Pasternak's "My Sister Life."*

65. Ibid., 13.

66. On "the prosaic" in Pasternak's poetry, see Gasparov, "Byt kak kategoriia poetiki Pasternaka."

67. Iury Tynianov, "The Interregnum" ("Promezhutok") in *Arkhaisty i novatory* (1929; reprint, Ann Arbor: Ardis, 1985), 565.

68. Nils Åke Nilsson, "'With Oars at Rest' and the Poetic Tradition," in Nilsson, *Boris Pasternak: Essays*, 195.

69. See also O'Connor, *Boris Pasternak's "My Sister Life,"* 182; and Elena V. Pasternak, "Leto 1917 goda. 'Sestra moia—zhizn' i 'Doktor Zhivago,'" *Zvezda* 2 (1990): 158–65.

70. Quoted by Evgeny Pasternak, *Boris Pasternak. Materialy dlia biografii* (Moscow: Sovetskii pisatel', 1989), 294.

71. Iury Tynianov discusses Fet's importance for Pasternak in his essay "The Interregnum."

72. Smirnov, *Porozhdenie interteksta,* 102–6.

73. Alexander Blok, *Sobranie sochinenii,* vol. 7 (Moscow: Khudozhestvennaia literatura, 1963), 35.

74. Smirnov, *Porozhdenie interteksta,* 102–6.

75. On Pasternak's interest in this fact, see Timothy Sergay, "'Blizhe k suti, k miru Bloka': The *Mise-en-Scène* of Boris Pasternak's 'Hamlet' and Pasternak's Blokian—Christological Ideal," *Russian Review* 64 (July 2005): 401–21.

76. Boris Eichenbaum, for example, in his tribute to Blok just after the latter's death in 1921, called him "the Knight of the Beautiful Lady—Hamlet" ("Sud'ba Bloka," *Skvoz' literaturu* [1924, 'S-Gravenhage: Mouton & Co., 1962]: 218.)

77. In the same context, he noted and cross-referenced five of the "Ophelia" poems and spoke in his notes of Blok's "Hamletism." E. B. Pasternak, "Pasternak o Bloke," 447–53.

78. Katherine Tiernan O'Connor, "Elena, Helen of Troy, and the Eternal Feminine: Epigraphs and Intertextuality in 'Sestra moia—zhizn,'" in Fleishman, *Boris Pasternak and His Times,* 212–23. The prosody of Pasternak's "To Helen" also originates with Goethe, via Lermontov: the model for the Russian three-foot trochaic meter is Lermontov's imitation of Goethe's "Über allen Gipfeln," "Gornye vershiny." Pasternak, however, changes Lermontov's rhyme scheme (alternating masculine and feminine rhymes) to include daring hyperdactylic rhymes ("plavala kak" = "navoloka"). On this meter, see Mikhail Gasparov, *Russkie stikhi 1890-kh–1925-ogo godov v kommentariiakh* (Moscow: Vysshaia shkola, 1993), 222.

79. Elena Pasternak has characterized Elena Vinograd as hysterical, linking her state to a sexual affair she earlier had with her cousin, Pasternak's friend Alexander Shtikh ("Leto 1917 goda"). It was to Shtikh that Pasternak dedicated his poem about the loss of virginity (see note 43).

80. Iu. I. Levin, "O nekotorykh chertakh plana soderzhaniia v poeticheskikh tekstakh," in *Strukturnaia tipologiia iazykov* (Moscow: Nauka, 1966), 205–6.

81. For a reading of how this poem modernizes a romantic topos, see Iury M. Lotman, "Analiz dvukh stikhotvorenii," in *Teksty sovetskogo literaturovedcheskogo strukturalizma* (Munich: Wilhem Fink Verlag, 1971), 101–224. The section on Pasternak was reprinted as "Analiz stikhotvoreniia B. Pasternaka 'Zamestitel'nitsa,'" in Lotman, *O poetakh i poezii* (St. Petersburg: Iskusstvo, 1996), 718–30.

82. Elaine Showalter, "Representing Ophelia: Women, Madness, and the Responsibilities of Feminist Criticism," in *Shakespeare and the Question of Theory,* ed. Patricia Parker and Geoffrey Hartman (Methuen: New York, 1985), 86.

83. See Elaine Showalter, *The Female Malady: Women, Madness, and English Culture, 1830–1980* (New York: Penguin, 1985).

84. Donald Plank, "Readings of *My Sister Life,*" *Russian Literature Triquarterly* 2 (1972): 323–37. As many commentators have remarked, sound is densely orchestrated in these poems. See Kahane, Chapter 1, *Passions of the Voice* on speech disturbances as hysterical symptoms.

85. Katherine Tiernan O'Connor, "Boris Pasternak's 'My Sister Life': The Book Behind the Verse," *Slavic Review* 37.3 (1978): 409.

86. Nikolai Vilmont, *O Borise Pasternake* (Moscow: Sovetskii pisatel', 1989), 78–79.

87. Vladimir Alfonsov, *Poeziia Borisa Pasternaka* (St. Petersburg: Saga, 2001), 122–132.

88. Although the events described in the cycle are chronologically prior to the unhappy year described in "The Sickness," Pasternak reversed the order in which the cycles appear so that the cure follows the illness.

89. Alexander Zholkovsky, "Ekstaticheskie motivy Pasternaka v svete ego lichnoi mifologii," in Loseff, *Boris Pasternak, 1890–1990,* 52–74.

90. The poem originally belonged to a four-poem Faust cycle. On the history of the Faust cycle, see Evgeny Pasternak, *Boris Pasternak,* 343.

91. Jane K. Brown, *Goethe's "Faust": The German Tragedy* (Ithaca: Cornell University Press, 1986), 106.

92. Evgeny Pasternak, in his biography of his father, has said the poem "portrays the horrifying triumph of masculine force over feminine unguardedness and innocence" (*Boris Pasternak,* 343).

93. This "cure" is already suggested in "To Helen," where the poet imagines striking her.

94. Alexander Zholkovsky has similarly argued that Pasternak's identification with women is neither simple nor exclusive, that an "active," "Mayakovskian" element in his work is just as strong as the "passive," "feminine" element" ("The 'Sinister' in the Poetic World of Pasternak," *International Journal of Slavic Linguistics and Poetics* 29 [1884]: 109–31). More recently, he has described Pasternak's rhetoric as sadomasochistic ("Ekstaticheskie motivy Pasternaka v svete ego lichnosti," 62). Zholkovsky, however, discusses this dynamic as though it were unique to Pasternak's writing, while I believe it is properly understood within a literary tradition of male lyric masochism.

95. Omry Ronen, "Chasy unchenichestva Mariny Tsvetaevoi," *Novoe literaturnoe obozrenie* 1 (1992): 185–86. Ronen indicates that Pasternak and Tsvetaeva knew these lines from the symbolist poet Konstantin Balmont, who used them as the epigraph to his poem "The Marsh" ("Boloto").

96. About Pasternak's interest in Mary Stuart, see Barnes, "Boris Pasternak and Mary Queen of Scots."

97. Mario Praz, *The Romantic Agony,* trans. Angus Davidson (Oxford: Oxford University Press, 1970), 230.

98. See Sibelan Forrester's discussion of the essay in "Marina Tsvetaeva as Literary Critic and Critic of Literary Critics," in *Russian Writers on Russian Writers,* ed. Faith Wizgell (Oxford: Berg, 1994), 81–98.

99. Alexander Bakhrakh, review of *Epopeia* 3, *Novaia Russkaia Kniga* 1 (January 1923): 20–21.

100. Georgy Ivanov, "Pochtovyi iashchik," *Tsekh poetov* 4 (1923): 70.

101. Osip Mandelstam, "Zametki o poezii," in *Sobranie sochinenii,* 3 vols. (New York: Interlanguage Literary Associates, 1971), 2:264. On the breathing motif in Mandelstam's work, see chapter 4 of Nancy Pollak, *Mandelstam the Reader* (Baltimore: Johns Hopkins University Press, 1995).

102. O'Connor, "Boris Pasternak's 'My Sister Life,'" 402.

103. A. K. Zholkovsky, "O zaglavnom trope knigi 'Sestra moia—zhizn,'" in *Poetry and Revolution. Boris Pasternak's "My Sister Life",* ed. Lazar Fleishman, Stanford Slavic Studies 21 (Stanford: Department of Slavic Languages and Literatures, Stanford University, 1999), 30–31.

104. In a later letter to Pasternak, Tsvetaeva said, "I still love you, pressing my brow into your shoulder and your palm, do you remember like I did in my first poem to you, in which I consciously spoke in your (secret!) language?" (*DNV* 113).

105. I am indebted to Dale Peterson for suggesting the relevance of the Pygmalion myth.

3. The Romance of Distance

1. 1. Christopher Barnes, *Boris Pasternak,* vol. 1 (Cambridge: Cambridge University Press, 1989), 313.

2. Evgeny Pasternak, *Boris Pasternak: Materialy dlia biografii* (Moscow: Sovetskii pisatel', 1989), 386.

3. Leonid and Rozalia Pasternak remained in Germany until 1938, when they joined their daughter Lydia in England. They planned to return to Russia, but Rozalia died in 1939. Leonid Pasternak died in Oxford in 1945. See Leonid Pasternak, *The Memoirs of Leonid Pasternak,* trans. Jennifer Bradshaw (London: Quartet Books, 1982), 70–78, and E. B. Paster-

nak and E. V. Pasternak, "Rodstvenniki za granitsei," *V krugu Zhivago. Pasternakovskii sbornik,* ed. Lazar Fleishman (Stanford: Department of Slavic Languages and Literatures, Stanford University, 2000), 24–37.

4. Letter to V. P. Polonsky, January 10, 1923 (5:139).

5. Ibid., 138. See Viktor Shklovsky's portrait of Pasternak:

Pasternak is uneasy in Berlin. He's a man of Western culture—at least, he understands it: he lived at one time in Germany. Now he has a fine young wife with him, yet he's still very uneasy. It seems to me that he feels among us an absence of propulsion—and I say this not merely to make the letter circular. We are refugees. No, not refugees but fugitives—and now squatters.

> For the time being anyway.
> Russian Berlin is going nowhere. It has no destiny.
> No propulsion.

Viktor Shklovsky, *Zoo, or Letters Not about Love,* trans. Richard Sheldon (Ithaca: Cornell University Press, 1971), 63.

6. Tsvetaeva had a friendly acquaintance with Mayakovsky. She wrote a poem to him ("Mayakovskomu") on September 18, 1921, which she read to him and which he liked (2:497). By her own later account, she ran into Mayakovsky not long before she emigrated and asked him what message she could deliver to Europe, to which he replied, "[Tell them] that truth is here" (7:351).

7. About his time in Moscow, Ehrenburg stated, "I would spend time with Tsvetaeva and Pasternak—I love them dearly" (*Novaia russkaia kniga* 4 [April 1922]: 45).

8. Ehrenburg's accompanying note read: "Dear Marina, I'm sending you a letter from Pasternak. At his request I read the letter and I'm delighted for him. I'm also delighted for you" (6:280, 1:1).

9. Ehrenburg was to become Soviet culture's ambassador to the West for several decades. On Ehrenburg's lengthy, politically agile career, see biographies by Anatol Goldberg, *Ilya Ehrenburg* (New York: Viking, 1984), and Joshua Rubenstein, *Tangled Loyalties* (New York: HarperCollins, 1996).

10. See Tsvetaeva's letters to Ehrenburg (6:211–16).

11. "Au-dessus de la mêlée," *Russkaia kniga,* nos. 7–8 (July–August 1921): 2.

12. See Ilya Ehrenburg's anthologies *Poets of Revolutionary Moscow* (*Poety revoliutsionnoi Moskvy*) and *Portraits of Russian Poets* (*Portrety russkikh poetov*), both of which appeared in Berlin in 1922. See also his essays "O nekotorykh priznakakh rastsveta rossiiskoi poezii," *Novaia russkaia kniga* 9 (September 1921): 1–5; and "Novaia proza," *Novaia russkaia kniga* 9 (September 1922): 1–3.

13. Ilya Ehenburg, *Portrety russkikh poetov,* reprint ed. (Munich: Wilhelm Fink, 1972), 151.

14. See her letter to Roman Gul of February 9, 1923 (6:518–19).

15. Vishniak published the cycle in his journal *Epos* (*Epopeia*). Tsvetaeva had "involved" Pasternak in the affair even earlier, when she replied to his first letter in Vishniak's presence (*Neizdannoe. Svodnye tetradi* [Moscow: Ellis Lak, 1997], 98). It appears Pasternak did learn about the affair, since he later mentioned her "bitter and delicate" (gor'kii i stesnitel'nyi) reason for leaving Berlin (*DNV* 27).

16. She actually completed the poem somewhat earlier, on December 24, 1922.

17. N. K. Teletova, "Tragediia 'Faust' Gete i poema 'Molodets' Tsvetaevoi," *Russkaia literatura* 1 (2000): 78–102.

18. Michael Wachtel, *Russian Symbolism and Literary Tradition* (Madison: University of Wisconsin Press, 1994), 94–95.

19. Michael Makin, "Text and Violence in Tsvetaeva's 'Molodets,'" in *Discontinuous Discourses in Modern Russian Literature,* ed. Catriona Kelly, Michael Makin, and David Shepherd (New York: St. Martin's, 1989), 115–35.

20. Ibid., 132.

21. Tsvetaeva, *Neizdannoe. Svodnye tetradi,* 161.

22. Quoted in Tsvetaeva's *Sobranie sochinenii* (6:282, 3:7).

23. Under the heading "Poems to You," Tsvetaeva listed in her notebook "Ne nado ee oklikat'," "Net, pravdy ne osparivai," "Emigrant," "Dusha," the three-poem cycle "Skifskie," "Liutnia," "Ot ruki moei ne vzygrival," and "Opereniem zim" (*Neizdannoe. Svodnye tetradi,* 121).

24. Neither Pasternak's inventory nor his accompanying postcard is extant. Tsvetaeva acknowledged receiving his postcard in a postcard she sent on February 15 (*DNV* 43).

25. For most of the passage the poet's gender is not grammatically clear, since Tsvetaeva uses the plural. When she switches to the singular, however, she uses the masculine pronoun ("kogda emu khotelos' est'"), and her target is clearly the male poet. (She names Osip Mendelstam and Tikhon Churilin as examples.)

26. See the page reproduced in Pasternak, *Boris Pasternak,* 383.

27. Viacheslav V. Ivanov mistakenly claims she did so in his "O vzaimootnoshenii dinamicheskogo issledovaniia evoliutsii iazyka, teksta, i kul'tury," in *Issledovanie po strukture teksta,* ed. T. V. Tsivian (Moscow: Nauka, 1987), 13.

28. See note 26.

29. Tsvetaeva, *Neizdannoe. Svodnye tetradi,* 119. The notebook versions of extant letters tend to be longer. Tsvetaeva wrote in a later letter to Pasternak: "I always write my letters to you (this one too) in my notebook quickly, like the draft of a poem. Only the final version never comes out, just two drafts, one for you and one for me" (*DNV* 168). As Irina Shevelenko states in her preface to Tsvetaeva's correspondence with Pasternak, it is not always clear what she actually sent him (*DNV* 8).

30. See R. D. B. Thomson's analysis of how the prosody of "Ne nado ee oklikat'" echoes Pasternak's ("Cvetaeva and Pasternak, 1922–24," in *Boris Pasternak and His Times,* ed. Lazar Fleishman [Berkeley: Berkeley Slavic Specialties, 1989], 63–64).

31. Viacheslav V. Ivanov, "O teme zhenshchiny u Pasternaka," in *Byt' znamenitym nekrasivo, Pasternakovskie chteniia,* vol. 1 (Moscow: Nasledie, 1992), 48. For another reading of this poem, see Antonina F. Gove, "The Poet's Self: Images of Soul in Four Poems of Pasternak," *Slavic and East European Journal* 27.2 (summer 1983): 185–99.

32. Jane Taubman first discussed the February poems in relation to Pasternak in "Dvukh solov'ev poedinok," in *Actes du 1er colloque international (Lausanne, 30.VI.–3.VII. 1982),* ed. Robin Kemball, Efim Etkind, and Leonid Heller (Bern: Peter Lang, 1991), 160–69.

33. Pasternak used the word in this sense in one of his early poems, "Lyric Expanse" ("Liricheskii prostor").

34. "Polnoglasie" is actually a linguistic term for the way Russian and other North Slavic languages added vowels to certain consonant clusters, and Tsvetaeva possibly employs it to assert her Russianness.

35. The stanza about the dead muse does not appear in the version published in *After Russia (Posle Rossii,* 1928).

36. As Michael Wachtel has pointed out to me, this phrase evokes Blok's poem "A girl sang in the church choir" ("Devushka pela v tserkovnom khore," 1906), in which the girl sings while illuminated by a ray of light. Tsvetaeva's poem shares some central features with Blok's, which is also set in a church (though an Orthodox one) and features a weeping boy positioned above the singing girl.

37. Here Tsvetaeva either displays uncanny intuition or reveals that she had read Paster-

nak's *Above the Barriers,* which contained a cycle titled "Paganini's Violin" ("Skripka Paganini"). Pasternak later quoted a poem from this cycle in a letter to Tsvetaeva *(DNV* 95).

38. These poems appear in the cycle "N. N. V" (1920). A native source for such imagery in Tsvetaeva's work is Russian sectarianism (as opposed to Russian Orthodoxy): "The soul that knows no bounds, / The soul of a flagellant and fanatic" ("Dusha, ne znaiushchaia mery, / Dusha khlysta i izuvera," 1921). Tsvetaeva once remarked that Russian culture had no language for love, in the context of arguing that no Russian poets are truly Russian in the sources of their inspiration: "Even the early Akhmatova, the Akhmatova of her first book, if she mentions Russia, mentions it as a guest—from the land of Love, which is also exotica in Russia" ("A Living Word about a Living Man" ["Zhivoe o zhivom," 1932]) (4:211).

39. Marina Tsvetaeva, *After Russia,* trans. Michael Naydan (Ann Arbor: Ardis, 1992), 237. Dido appears nowhere in Tsvetaeva's work, but she combines elements of Tsvetaeva's favorite mythological heroines, Ariadne and Phaedra, to whom she would devote entire verse tragedies.

40. Tsvetaeva later repeated this image of cascading notes in her cycle "Streams" ("Ruch'i," May 1923) to invoke a performance by Paganini: "Rumbling with prophesies, with the *pizzicatos* of the unrepentant violinist . . . like a burst necklace!" (Proritsaniiami rokocha, / Neraskaiannogo skripacha / Piccikata'mi . . . Razryvom bus!).

41. Pasternak refers to the train trips featured in *My Sister Life.* See especially the title poem, "My sister is life and today in a flood" ("Sestra moia—zhizn' i segodnia v razlive").

42. She had used the story to model her romantic relationship with Vishniak ("Otrok," 1922) and would use it again in poems to Konstantin Rodzevich ("Ovrag," 1923). She was probably inspired to do so by Rainer Maria Rilke, whose cycle "David Sings before Saul" ("David singt vor Saul") represents them both as hypermasculine and heterosexual but also in love with each other.

43. On the importance of shifts of address in Tsvetaeva's work, see Catherine Ciepiela, "Inclined toward the Other: Tsvetaeva's Lyric Address," in *Critical Essays on the Prose and Poetry of Modern Slavic Women,* ed. Nina Efimov, Christine Tomei, and Richard Chapple (Lewiston, Maine: Mellen Press, 1998), 135–53.

44. The basic meaning of the Greek *aggelos* is "messenger" and may designate both good and evil spirits. Tsvetaeva's poetic etymology is accurate, since the word is related to the Latin *angelus.*

45. Tsvetaeva may have had in mind an unfinished long poem about Azrail by the nineteenth-century romantic poet Mikhail Lermontov, to whom Pasternak dedicated *My Sister Life.*

46. Alyssa W. Dinega, chapter 2, *A Russian Psyche: The Poetic Mind of Marina Tsvetaeva* (Madison: University of Wisconsin Press, 2001).

47. The poem is "You pass by on the way to West of the Sun" ("Ty prokhodish' na Zapad Solntsa").

48. The day before, in a letter to Gul, she explained that she would visit Berlin in early May if a publisher were found for her memoir of revolutionary Moscow, "Earthly Signs" ("Zemnye primety") (6:520).

49. *Boris Pasternak i Sergei Bobrov: pis'ma chetyrekh desiatiletii,* ed. M. A. Rashkovskaia, Stanford Slavic Studies 10 (Stanford: Department of Slavic Languages and Literatures, Stanford University, 1996), 126.

50. Ibid., 135.

51. Ibid., 138.

52. Quoted in Pasternak, *Boris Pasternak,* 384–85.

53. Boris Pasternak, *Sushchestvovan'ia tkan' skvoznaia: Perepiska s Evgeniei Pasternak,* ed. E. B. Pasternak (Moscow: Novoe literaturnoe obozrenie, 1998), 193.

54. She also wrote a short letter at the end of February, but it is not clear whether she sent it to him (*DNV* 44).

55. Tsvetaeva here brings together Goethe and Mikhail Lermontov, the two poetic spirits who presided over the creation of *My Sister Life*.

56. Avital Ronell, *Dictations: On Haunted Writing* (Bloomington: Indiana University Press, 1986).

57. Ibid., 78.

58. Ibid., 66–67.

59. Sigmund Freud, "Mourning and Melancholia," in *The Standard Edition of the Complete Psychological Works of Sigmund Freud,* vol. 14, ed. James Strachey (London: Hogarth Press, 1957), 243–58.

60. Letter to O. E. Kolbasina-Chernova of January 8, 1925 (6:708).

61. "Prorva" also names a glutton, an image that becomes central in her later poem to Pasternak, "From the Sea" ("S moria," 1926).

62. She wrote the first poem on March 17, the day before Pasternak's announced departure; Pasternak actually left on March 21 (Pasternak, *Boris Pasternak,* 386). She added nine more poems before finishing the cycle in mid-April.

63. Ieva Vitins has demonstrated the relevance of the Psyche myth to the structure of the cycle ("The Structure of Marina Cvetaeva's 'Provoda': From Eros to Psyche," *Russian Literature Journal* 41 [1987]: 143–56).

64. The poems are "Ophelia to Hamlet" ("Ofelia—Gamletu," February 28, 1923) and her cycle "Phaedra" ("Fedra," March 7–11, 1923).

65. In an earlier letter to Pasternak, Tsvetaeva stated, "By the way, for me the word is a conveyor of voice, not at all of meaning, intent!" (*DNV* 24).

66. "Mother and Music" ("Mat' i muzyka," 1934) (5:21–22).

67. The truncated word could also be a noun or a conjugated verb, but this would break the pattern of quoted utterances being either cries or commands.

68. Bruce T. Holl, "'The Wildest of Disharmonies': A Lacanian Reading of Marina Tsvetaeva's 'Provoda' Cycle in the Context of its Other Meanings," *Slavic and East European Journal* 40.1 (1996): 27–44.

69. Tsvetaeva plays on the Russian idiom "to speak rashly" ("brosat' na veter slova; govorit' na veter").

70. Even before receiving Pasternak's letter, Tsvetaeva was very interested in Evgenia. In the same letter in which she asked Gul to procure a copy of Eckermann, she said, "I would like to know what his wife is like" (6:525).

71. He also turned down her "tender and insistent request" (*DNV* 53) to read her February poems in the train on the way back to Moscow, again invoking his wife's sensitivity. Tsvetaeva had enclosed the February poems with her March 9–10 letter. She also sent her recently published collection *Craft* with the inscription "To my celestial [zaoblachnomu] friend—my celestial brother—Boris Pasternak" (6:281, 1:17).

72. As Olga Hasty has shown, Tsvetaeva drew on Rilke's "Orpheus. Eurydike. Hermes" (1904) for her image of Eurydice (*Tsvetaeva's Orphic Journeys in the Worlds of the Word* [Evanston: Northwestern University Press, 1996], 52). Tsvetaeva's Eurydice, however, remains agitated by passion, while Rilke's is wholly absorbed with the gestation of her death and therefore indifferent to Orpheus' presence. Her treatment of the myth more resembles Briusov's in his poem "Orpheus and Eurydice" ("Orfei i Evridika," 1904).

73. Tsvetaeva did, however, include the poem in the cycle when she sent it to Pasternak in 1924.

74. See her later remark in her notebooks: "Thoughts and lines (To Boris). We will meet once we are dead" (*Neizdannoe. Svodnye tetradi,* 347).

75. See, for example, Ieva Vitins: "By contrast, a controlled evenness of emotional tone and diction informs the second half of the cycle. Stoic resignation represses physical contentiousness as an otherwordly orientation takes precedence, and a reflective mode dominates over the dialogical" ("The Structure of Marina Cvetaeva's 'Provoda,'" 150).

76. In her later essay "Story about Sonechka" ("Povest' o Sonechke," 1937), Tsvetaeva attributed this phrase to her friend Sonya Gallidei (4:310–11). Svetlana Boym has argued that Gallidei represents for Tsvetaeva "the voice of the poetess," which she describes as the voice of an exaggerated femininity, or what I am terming hysterical femininity (*Death in Quotation Marks* [Cambridge: Harvard University Press, 1991], 217).

77. Jane Taubman rightly speculated that Tsvetaeva knew of Evgenia's pregnancy in her discussion of "Telegraph Wires" in *A Life through Poetry: Marina Tsvetaeva's Lyric Diary* (Columbus: Slavica, 1988), 194.

78. Tsvetaeva also quoted the phrase in the version of "Brozhu—ne dom zhe plotnichat'" that she sent to Pasternak: "Thus non-living children avenge themselves: / Destroy yourself, they tempt, unfurl yourself, they tempt" (Tak nezhivye deti mstiat: / Razbeisia, l'stiat, razveisia, l'stiat) (*DNV* 92). She rewrote these two lines for the poem's publication in *After Russia*.

79. Several of the poems Tsvetaeva wrote in the months following Pasternak's departure feature erotic brother-sister pairings, namely, "The Brother" ("Brat," July 13, 1923) and "The Dagger" ("Klinok," August 18, 1923) ("But there are—passionate sisters! / But there is—brotherly passion!" [No byvaiut—strastnye sestry! / No byvaet—bratskaia strast'!]).

80. In her memoir of her mother, Ariadna Efron states that Pasternak broke the silence sometime in 1924 to announce the birth of his son. Apparently Tsvetaeva replied, saying, "A firstborn is always *unique,* no matter how many brothers he has!" and praising him for naming the child Evgeny because it marked his maternal legacy (*O Marine Tsvetaevoi* [Moscow: Sovetskii pisatel', 1989], 153). These letters do not appear in the published correspondence.

81. Elena Aizenstein has written a helpful book that sequentially interprets each poem of *After Russia* in terms of Tsvetaeva's relationship to Pasternak (*Borisu Pasternaku—navstrechu!* [St. Petersburg: "Neva," 2000]).

82. See Barbara Heldt's discussion of this poem in *Terrible Perfection* (Bloomington: Indiana University Press, 1987), 135–37.

83. Tsvetaeva also possibly refers to Andersen's tale "The Ice Maiden," in which the Maiden lures victims into glacial crevasses, where their bodies are perfectly preserved. Irene Masing-Delic has identified this tale as an important subtext for Blok's cycle "The Snow-Mask" ("Snezhnaia maska," 1907) (*A. Blok's "The Snow Mask": An Interpretation* [Stockholm: Almqvist & Wiksell, 1970], 92–93).

84. Tsvetaeva documented her distress in a diary-like "Bulletin of an Illness" and in a famous poem, "The Letter" ("Pis'mo," August 11, 1923).

85. See Tsvetaeva's letter to Roman Gul of March 30, 1924 (6:533).

86. These included her cycle "Ariadna" ("Ostavlennoi byt'" and "O vsemi golosami rakovin"), her cycle "Neskol'ko slov" ("Ty obo mne ne dumai nikogda," "La-don' v ladon'," and "Provodami prodlennaia dal'"), "Sestra," "Sivilla-mladentsu," "Dialog Gamleta s sovest'iu," "Rasshchelina," "Zanaves," "Pis'mo," "Sakhara," "Brat," and "Klinok." She also included three unfinished poems, "Magdalina," "Pobeg," and "Brozhu—ne dom zhe plotnichat'" (*DNV* 72–92).

87. Roman Gul apparently served as courier until she received Pasternak's new mailing address: "Tsvetaeva sent to me in Berlin her letters to B. Pasternak with the request to forward them to him in Moscow, sending them to the address of a writer acquaintance of mine. I sent three or four letters that way until M. I. received an 'exact Moscow address' from Pasternak" (6:545).

88. Pasternak, *Sushchestvovan'ia tkan' skvoznaia*, 40. Pasternak continued to inform Evgenia about his correspondence with Tsvetaeva, which remained a sore point, as his correspondence with Evgenia reveals. That May, Evgenia and their infant son joined her parents first in Petersburg, then at a dacha for the summer; Pasternak remained in Moscow to pursue his writing.

89. *Russkii Sovremennik* 3 (1924). Pasternak especially admired "The Curtain" (*DNV* 96). For a reading of this poem, see Tomas Venclova, "M. I. Tsvetaeva, 'Zanaves,'" in *Neustoichivoe ravnovesie: vosem' russkikh poeticheskikh tekstov* (New Haven: Yale University Press, 1986), 135–47.

90. Pasternak, *Sushchestvovan'ia tkan' skvoznaia*, 97.

91. She sent "The Pair" (July 1924) to Pasternak sometime in the summer of 1924, or so she recalled in a later letter to him (*DNV* 218).

92. Thomson remarks this shift in his "Cvetaeva and Pasternak, 1922–1924."

93. Omry Ronen, "Chasy uchenichestva Mariny Tsvetaevoi," *Novoe literaturnoe obozrenie* 1 (1992): 188.

94. Tsvetaeva forwarded the letter on June 29 to Roman Gul to deliver for her (6:538–39). We know that Tsvetaeva told Pasternak about her pregnancy from the contents of her next letter, written in October, and a letter she wrote to her friend Olga Kolbasina around the same time: "I haven't written since June, and to my last letter—about my future Boris—I didn't get an answer, I want to *make sure*" (6:693).

95. These lines appear in the notebook version of the letter (*Neizdannoe. Svodnye tetradi*, 309) and were cut from the version Tsvetaeva sent to Pasternak.

96. Tsvetaeva also associated her son, Georgy, with Rodzevich, who was not his father. In 1933, Tsvetaeva remarked that "the afterword to the Hill (There are gaps in my memory—blanks) was written Feb. 1, 1924. Exactly a year later—maybe to the hour—Mur was born" (*Neizdannoe. Svodnye tetradi*, 282). By "afterword to the Hill," Tsvetaeva means "Poem of the End."

97. "Sealed like the mouth of an oracle— / Is your mouth, which has divined for many. / Woman, what have you hidden from surveillance / Between your tongue and palate?" (Zapechatlennyi, kak rot orakula— / Rot tvoi, gadavshii mnogim. / Zhenshchina, chto ot dozoru spriatala / Mezh iazykom i nebom?).

98. "Adalis" was a pen name purportedly invented by Briusov. Her real name was Adelina Efimova Efron, the name of her adoptive parents (who were not related to Tsvetaeva's husband).

99. Tsvetaeva mistakenly identifies it as "To the Girls" ("Devushkam"). "The Woman" appeared as the third poem of the cycle "Sonnets and Tercets" ("Sonety i tertsiny," 1901–3) in *Puti i pereput'ia* but is not found in the standard edition of his collected works. Valery Briusov, *Sobranie sochinenii v semi tomakh* [Moscow: Khudozhestvennaia literatura, 1973].

100. See also her two-poem cycle "Bethlehem" ("Vifleem," December 6, 1921), which was accidentally excluded from *Poems to Blok* (*Stikhi k Bloku*, 1922).

101. She was still repeating the story of Blok's son to Gul in 1924 (6:536).

102. Tsvetaeva once claimed, in a letter to Bakhrakh, to be Blok's great unrealized love: "After Blok's death I frequently met him on all of Moscow's nighttime bridges; *I knew* that he was wandering there and—perhaps—waiting, I was his greatest love, though he didn't know me, a great love destined for him—and never realized" (6:606).

103. Tsvetaeva told the story of Blok's son to Pasternak in 1923, in the context of asking him to deliver a gift to Nolle-Kogan (6:240). She later grouped Pasternak's son with Blok's in a letter to Gul, saying that whoever delivered her letter to Pasternak would see "both little boys" (6:533).

104. Tsvetaeva possibly borrowed the image from Rilke's "Eine Sybille," in which she is "tall and hollow and burnt out" (hoch und hohl und ausgebrannt). Rilke's Sybil, however, is

nightmarishly pregnant "with words, which left unchecked / would multiply in her against her will" (von den Worten, die sich unbewacht / wider ihren Willen in ihr mehrten. (Rainer Maria Rilke, *New Poems [1908]: The Other Part,* trans. Edward Snow [New York: Farrar, Straus and Giroux, 1993]). Tsvetaeva invoked the Annunciation in yet another poem to Pasternak, "With the plumage of winters" ("Opereniem zim," February 17, 1923), which she originally included with "Azrael" in a cycle of that title.

105. Olga Peters Hasty has interpreted the cycle as describing a feminine prototype of the poet who can perform Orpheus' mediating action between the divine and the mortal (see chapter 4, "The Sybil," in *Tsvetaeva's Orphic Journeys in the Worlds of the Word* [Evanston: Northwestern University Press: 1996]).

106. Tsvetaeva also had visions of bringing their sons together ("They will be friends" [*DNV* 111]) and imagined Pasternak living with her son in the event of her death (*DNV* 107).

107. Tsvetaeva derived a similar notion from her reading of Pasternak's story "Aerial Ways" ("Vozdushnye puti," 1923) in 1924: "I remember your words about fatherhood in your amazing 'Aerial Ways.' I would suggest this formula: Around the world (the sailor) and around the universe (the father). Because the cradle is the only authentic universe: the not-yet-realized, i.e., *limitless* person. And my only conception of the infinite is you, Boris. Not because I love you, my love is because of that" (DNV 111).

108. This is attested by Pasternak's letter, written a year later, on July 2, 1925: "A month ago I received your letter, Marina. God knows how it reached me. I've been told you answered my letter last year. But that one never arrived" (*DNV* 113).

109. Tsvetaeva received it on June 10 (*Neizdannoe. Svodnye tetradi,* 379). The editors of her collected works incorrectly indicate July (6:285).

110. See her letter to Franz Kubka of August 26, 1925 (7:24). Tsvetaeva also republished "Aerial Ways" in the Prague émigré journal edited by her husband, Efron, *Our Own Paths* (*Svoimi putiami* 6–7 [1925]).

111. Tsvetaeva, *Neizdannoe. Svodnye tetradi,* 361.

112. Ibid., 352–53.

4. Lyricism and History

1. Pasternak also wrote about the revolution in two works from 1917 that remained unfinished: "Dramatic Fragments" ("Dramaticheskie fragmenty") and the story "Lovelessness" ("Bezliubie"). A poem, "The Russian Revolution" ("Russkaia revoliutsiia"), remained unpublished. On this poem, see Lazar Fleishman, "Pasternak i Lenin," in *Literature, Culture, and Society in the Modern Age,* pt. 2, Stanford Slavic Studies 4:2 (Stanford: Department of Slavic Languages and Literatures, Stanford University, 1992), 97–135. See also Christopher Barnes, "Pasternak's Revolutionary Year," *Forum for Modern Language Studies,* 11 (October, 1975), 46–60.

2. Enthusiastic reviewers of *My Sister Life* consistently described it as "contemporary," among them Valery Briusov ("Vchera, segodnia i zavtra russkoi poezii," *Pechat' i revoliutsiia* 7 [1922]: 57).

3. See Tsvetaeva's letter to Gul of March 30, 1924 (6:533). On that occasion she also gave Kerensky a copy of her *Psyche* (*Psikheia,* 1923), inscribed "To the Romantic of the Revolution—Alexander Fedorovich Kerensky—with all my heart. Marina Tsvetaeva. Prague, Feb. 1924" (6:545).

4. It is possible, though very unlikely, that Tsvetaeva knew the third of these fragments, "Dialogue" ("Dialoga"), which was published in *The Banner of Labor* (*Znamia truda,* May 17, 1918).

5. Pasternak thus revised his earlier assertion, in "The Black Goblet" ("Chernyi bokal,"

1915), that historical concerns are alien to lyric poetry: "We must not be deceived: reality is disintegrating. As it disintegrates, it gathers at two opposite poles: Lyricism and History. They are equally a priori and absolute" (4:358).

6. Quoted by Clare Cavanagh in *Osip Mandelstam and the Modernist Creation of Tradition* (Princeton: Princeton University Press, 1995), 189.

7. Pasternak published a poem from *Themes and Variations* in the first issue, and wrote an occasional poem, "May the First" ("1 maia," 1923), for the second.

8. Halina Stephan, *"Lef" and the Left Front of Arts* (Munich: Otto Sagner, 1981), 97. Of course, their rejection of lyricism was not entirely consistent. Mayakovsky continued to write lyrical long poems dramatizing his sufferings in love, though he did so with ambivalence: "About This" ("Pro eto," 1923) appeared in *Lef* with an introduction apologizing for its personal theme.

9. Among the genre terms used by Lef were the ballad, ode, epistle, hymn, and song. See Stephan's discussion (ibid., 110).

10. Like his fellow Lefists, Mayakovsky and Aseev, Pasternak had attempted the long poem earlier in his career.

11. In a reported conversation with Tikhonov, another Lef poet, Pasternak discussed his effort "to push lyric material over longer distances" without resorting to plot. Evgeny Pasternak, *Boris Pasternak: Materialy dlia biografii* (Moscow: Sovetskii pisatel', 1989), 391. Iury Tynianov compared Pasternak's approach to Pushkin's in his 1924 survey of recent achievements in Russian poetry, "Interregnum" ("Promezhutok," 1924): "His 'Sublime Malady' presents an epic poem outside plot, as the slow rocking, the slow nurturing of a theme—and its thorough realization. And it is clear that Pasternak is confronting Pushkin's poetic word and trying to renew the principles of Pushkin's image (the basis for Pushkin's epic poetry)" (*Arkhaisty i novatory*, reprint ed. [Ann Arbor: Ardis, 1985], 579). As for contemporary examples, Christopher Barnes has compared "A Sublime Malady" to Mandelstam's "Finder of a Horseshoe," "Slate Ode," and "Jan. 1, 1924," all from 1923–24 (*Boris Pasternak*, vol. 1 [Cambridge: Cambridge University Press, 1989], 326).

12. Ilya Serman, "'Vysokaia bolezn'' i problema eposa v 1920-e gody," in *Boris Pasternak, 1890–1990*, ed. Lev Loseff (Northfield: Russian School at Norwich University, 1991), 81–82. In *Safe Conduct*, Pasternak states in two different contexts that "150,000,000" marked the point when he no longer accepted Mayakovsky's poetry (4:220, 231).

13. Pasternak later changed the line to "The moving rebus flickers" ("Mel'kaet dvizhushchiisia rebus"). In my discussion, I refer to the poem as it was first published in *Lef*, since presumably this was the version Pasternak shared with Tsvetaeva in 1926 (1:554–63).

14. Osip Mandel'shtam, *Sobranie sochinenii v trekh tomakh*, vol. 2, ed. G. P. Struve and V. A. Filippov (New York: Inter-Language Literary Associates, 1971), 210.

15. Fleishman has argued that Pasternak suspends the polarity between "poetry" and "revolution." Lazar Fleishman, *Boris Pasternak v dvadtsatye gody* (Munich: Wilhelm Fink, 1981), 30–34.

16. See L. K. Dogopolov, *Poemy Bloka i russkaia poema kontsa XIX–nachala XX vekov* (Moscow: Pushkinskii dom, 1964), esp. chap. 5, "'Dvenadtsat'' i vozrozhdenie epicheskoi poemy," 145–88.

17. Barnes, *Boris Pasternak*, 59–60.

18. For a reading of how the poem stabilizes prosodically, see Efim Etkind, "Demokratiia, opoiasannaia burei: Kompozitsiia poemy A. Bloka 'Dvenadtsat','" in *Materiia stikha* (Paris: Institut d'études slaves, 1978), 114–33.

19. See Kevin Platt's argument that in *My Sister Life*, "Pasternak rejected both the boundless orgiastic Scythian release and the Bolshevik thunder of a new era, and instead created his own, novelized vision of revolution" ("Revolution and the Shape of Time in 'My Sister Life,'"

in *Poetry and Revolution: Boris Pasternak's "My Sister Life,"* Stanford Slavic Studies, vol. 21 [Stanford: Department of Slavic Literatures and Languages, Stanford University, 1999], 143).

20. Throughout his career, Blok conflated love and revolution as "elemental" forces. See Z. G. Mints and A. P. Iulova, "Iz kommentarii k tsiklu Bloka 'Snezhnaia maska,'" in *Tipologiia literaturnykh vzaimodeistvii* (Tartu: Tartuskii gosudarstvennyi universitet, 1983) 99–108.

21. For other discussions of Blok's importance for "A Sublime Malady," see I. V. Fomenko, "Zametki k interpretatsii 'Vysokoi bolezni' (O romanticheskikh tendentsiiakh v tvorchestve B. L. Pasternaka)," in *Romantizm v russkoi i zarubezhnoi literature* (Kalinin: Kalininskii gosudarstvennyi universitet, 1979), 94–105; Serman, "'Vysokaia bolezn'' i problema eposa v 1920-e gody"; and Olga R. Hughes, *The Poetic World of Boris Pasternak* (Princeton: Princeton University Press, 1974), 82–84.

22. Alexander Blok, "Intelligentsia i revoliutsiia," in *Sobranie sochinenii v vos'mi tomakh,* vol. 6 (Moscow: Khudozhestvennaia literatura, 1962), 20.

23. Pasternak's notion resembles the psychopoetics of "the rape of the intelligentsia" in the work of the Nietzschean Marxists. In their writings, and in Soviet culture generally, the intelligentsia was coded as feminine, a proper object for the masculine aggression of the proletariat. Igal Halfin, "The Rape of the Intelligentsia: A Proletarian Foundational Myth," *Russian Review* 56.1 (January 1997): 90–109.

24. Pasternak was particularly horrified by the Bolsheviks' use of the death penalty, which figures in his story "Aerial Ways" ("Vozdushnye puti," 1924).

25. He did so using the same contrast between silence and sound that structures the lyrical argument of "A Sublime Malady": "And it was silent as the heart of a catacomb, / You could hear the beating of hearts. And in that silence / One imagined: in the distance a courier raced, the sealed orders / Shook, and the country imagined it heard a trigger being pulled" (A zdes' stoiala tish', kak v serdtse katakomby, / Byl slyshen boi serdets. I v etoi tishine / Pochudilos': vdali, kur'erskii nessia, plomby / Triaslis', i vzvod kurkov mereshchilsia strane). See Fleishman's discussion of the poem in "Pasternak i Lenin."

26. When Pasternak rewrote the poem in 1928, he celebrated the power of Lenin's speech. For an analysis of the changes Pasternak made to the poem, see Serman, "'Vysokaia bolezn'' i problema eposa v 1920-e gody." See also Pasternak's later characterization of Lenin in the unpublished portions of "People and Propositions" ("Liudi i polozheniia," 1956–57) (4:789).

27. On Pasternak's evolving relations with Lef, see Fleishman, *Boris Pasternak v dvadtsatye gody.*

28. Konstantin Polivanov, "K 'intimizatsii istorii': Zametki o 'Deviat'sot piatom gode' Borisa Pasternaka," in *Themes and Variations: In Honor of Lazar Fleishman* (Stanford: Department of Slavic Languages and Literatures, Stanford University, 1994), 71–80; Iury Levin, "Zametki o 'Leitenante Schmidte' B. L. Pasternaka," in *Boris Pasternak: Essays,* ed. Nils Åke Nilsson (Stockholm: Almqvist & Wiksell, 1976), 85–161.

29. For a discussion of Blok's work on the poem, see L. K. Dolgopolov, *Aleksandr Blok* (Leningrad: Akademiia Nauk, 1978), 107–30.

30. Letter of June 17, 1926, in Boris Pasternak, *Pis'ma k roditeliam i sestram* (Moscow: Novoe literaturnae obozrenie, 2004), 301.

31. Tsvetaeva was reading Rilke as early as 1915, and in her essay "On Germany" ("O Germanii," 1919) mentioned Rilke alongside Blok. But it appears that she first read him seriously after emigrating. She told Rilke himself that she read *Die frühen Gedichte* in Prague, and quotations from *Das Stundenbuch* appear in her writings from the 1920s (*DL* 85). Her copy of *Das Buch der Bilder* was inscribed by her on August 1, 1922, upon her arrival in

Prague. Konstantin Azadovsky, *Nebesnaia arka: Marina Tsvetaeva i Rainer Maria Rilke* (St. Petersburg: Akropol', 1992), 19.

32. As he goes on to say, "And again in this longing for form which our time mercilessly lacks, there is for me, just as in my thoughts about you and Scriabin, a constant and troubling point" (*DNV* 140). Earlier in his letter, Pasternak links Tsvetaeva and Scriabin as artists representing "one of the poles of talent, and the one that once again seems to me all-embracing and extreme" (*DNV* 139).

33. Pasternak later cut this description from the poem (1:698–99).

34. A comment of Pasternak's suggests she openly rejected his historical project. When asking her opinion of "1905," he wrote that his interest in the genre "is broader and more serious than you suggested (and you presented in a caricatured way it did not deserve)" (*DNV* 141).

35. For a discussion of Tsvetaeva's interest in Esenin's suicide, see Olga Peters Hasty, "Reading Suicide: Tsvetaeva on Esenin and Maiakovskii," *Slavic Review* 50.4 (winter 1991): 836–46.

36. Quoted by Anna Saakiants, *Marina Tsvetaeva: Zhizn' i tvorchestvo* (Moscow: Ellis Lak, 1997), 431.

37. Pasternak later recalled this sequence of events in a letter to Tsvetaeva of January 5, 1928: "I suddenly remembered that my 'ty' with you was preceded by your proposal to cut off a relationship you considered an insulting and unworthy error on your part" (*DNV* 450).

38. Until the recent publication of letters from Tsvetaeva's archive, the year 1926 was the best-documented period of her correspondence with Pasternak. Both poets took special care to preserve these letters because they involved Rilke. They were first published in German as Rainer Maria Rilke, Marina Zwetajewa, and Boris Pasternak, *Briefwechsel*, ed. Evgeny Pasternak, Elena Pasternak, and Konstantin M. Azadovsky (Frankfurt: Insel, 1983). They appeared in Russian as *Pis'ma 1926 goda* (Moscow: Kniga, 1990); this book was translated into English as *Letters, Summer 1926*, trans. Margaret Wettlin and Walter Arndt (San Diego: Harcourt Brace Jovanovich, 1985). An updated Russian version was published as Rainer Maria Rilke, *Dykhanie liriki* (Moscow: Art-Fleks, 2000), which appeared in English with a preface by Susan Sontag, again as *Letters, Summer 1926* (New York: New York Review of Books, 2001). This volume includes not only the poets' letters but commentary and materials that contextualize their correspondence, making it the most convenient source to cite when discussing the events of the summer of 1926. (I do, however, continue to cite Tsvetaeva's correspondence with Pasternak in the more complete *Dushi nachinaut videt'* [*DNV*].) I cite the Russian edition, *Dykhanie liriki* (*DL*), because it contains the fewest translated materials. I have consulted the German edition in making my translations of Rilke's correspondence with the Pasternaks and Tsvetaeva, which was conducted in German. Tsvetaeva's correspondence with Rilke also may be found in *Nebesnaia arka*, ed. Konstantin Azadovsky (St. Petersburg: Arkopol', 1992). Full versions of the letters between Pasternak and his family may be found in Pasternak, *Pis'ma roditeliam i sestram*.

39. To judge from Pasternak's March 25 letter to Tsvetaeva, the date was March 21 ("for four evenings in a row").

40. Published under the title *Portrety russkikh poetov* (Berlin, 1922). In his letter Rilke also noted Hélène Iswolsky's French translations of some of Pasternak's poems in the winter issue of Paul Valéry's *Commerce* (*DL* 33).

41. In drawing Tsvetaeva into the circle, Pasternak had pragmatic considerations as well as poetic ones. Rilke could not write directly to Pasternak, since Switzerland did not have diplomatic relations with the USSR. Nor did Pasternak wish to rely further on his family, though he did send this particular letter through them, which they once again circulated among themselves, thus delaying its arrival in Switzerland until the beginning of May.

42. Tsvetaeva sent him "The Swain" with her letter of May 26, 1925, inscribed "To Boris Pasternak. Marina Tsvetaeva. Prague, May 1925" (6:285). In that same letter she promised to send "Poem of the Hill," "Poem of the End," and "Theseus," but either she did not or the mail went astray.

43. Compare Pasternak's "I wanted to go outside to see what happened to the air and sky as soon as a poet named another poet" (*DNV* 185) to Tsvetaeva's "When we meet it truly will be a mountain coming to the mountain: Moses'—and Zeus'" (*DNV* 112). (Tsvetaeva is also playing on a Russian idiom, "Mountains don't meet, but friends will" [Gora s goroi ne skhoditsia, a chelovek s chelovekom soidetsia].)

44. Pasternak addressed a poem to Tsvetaeva on the subject that he sent with his letter of April 11. The poem, titled "Not villagers in an opera" ("Ne opernye poseliane"), concludes with the following message:

> Just don't go getting tragic,
> Or climbing up on a steam pipe.
> Is that a way out of this trivial muck?
> You won't write poems in the grave.
>
> You're still a virgin land.
> And death is your pseudonym.
> You musn't give in. Don't print,
> Don't publish under that name.
>
> Но только не лезь на котурны,
> Ни на паровую трубу.
> Исход ли из гущи мишурной?
> Ты их не напишешь в гробу.
>
> Ты все еще край непочатый.
> А смерть—это твой псевдоним.
> Сдаваться нельзя. Не печатай
> И не издавайся под ним.

Pasternak again expressed his concern on May 5, asking why she wrote in a questionnaire, "Life is a train station, soon I will leave, for where—I will not say." In this case, it was Tsvetaeva's sister Asya who interpreted the remark literally, leading Pasternak to question Tsvetaeva about it (*DNV* 194). Tsvetaeva apparently calmed his fears: "You answered my question about the last phrase of your questionnaire. Thank God" (*DNV* 199). Asya, however, continued to attribute suicidal yearnings to her sister, pointing to the conclusion of "The Swain." In her letter to Pasternak of May 22, Tsvetaeva says: "Yes, about 'The Swain,' if you remember—you are correct and not Asya. 'Borya, because of his extraordinary goodness, saw in the ending only freedom and was glad for you'" (*DNV* 205).

45. In fact, Tsvetaeva's speaker rejects suicide: "I won't—jump off! / To dive in would mean // Letting go of your hand" (Ne—broshus' vniz'! / Nyriat'—otpuskat' by ruku // Pri—shlos').

46. Barbara Johnson, "Gender and Poetry: Charles Baudelaire and Marceline Desbordes-Valmore," in *Feminist Difference: Literature, Psychoanalysis, Race, and Gender* (Cambridge: Harvard University Press, 1998), 101–28. Pasternak makes this gendering explicit in a letter to Voloshin, where he describes "Poem of the End" as "written by a great poet, un-femininely well, with great feeling and, what is more important, with great knowledge of the nature of that feeling" (*Ezhegodnik Rukopisnogo otdela Pushkinskogo Doma na 1979 god* [Leningrad: Nauka,1981], 194).

47. Tsvetaeva also remarked to Pasternak, "'Poem of the End' is sheer (forgive the crudeness) masculine power, the power of passion, the power of love, blind power that suddenly *also* turns out to be soul" (*DNV* 190). As always, Tsvetaeva understands active desire as masculine.

48. Ariadna Efron quotes this phrase in her memoir (*O Marine Tsvetaevoi*, 153). This letter does not appear in the edition of Tsvetaeva's correspondence with Pasternak.

49. Pasternak remarked that Briusov and not Annensky was "the first poet" of his generation (*DNV* 115). Tsvetaeva quoted and glossed this statement in her essay on Briusov, "A Hero of Labor": "Yes, incomparable poet, you are right: 'A *unique* poet is never the first poet'" (*Edinstvennyi ne byvaet pervym*) (4:19). Tsvetaeva means to say that being first is less important than being unique. As it happens, "uniqueness" was a vexed issue in Pasternak's relations with Briusov, whose late poetry strongly imitated Pasternak's style. See E. B. Pasternak, "Pasternak i Briusov. K istorii otnoshenii," *Russia. Rossiya* 3 (1977): 239–65; and Fleishman, *Boris Pasternak v dvadtsatye gody,* 34–39.

50. In fact, Maria Mein studied not with Rubinstein himself but with one of his students.

51. This image was perhaps inspired by a line from "Poem of the End," which Pasternak had quoted in his March 25 letter: "And suddenly there's you, not created by me, who are by nature penetrated by every shudder—'exaggeratedly, that is / to your full height'" (*DNV* 152). It also recalls Helen of Troy's transformation into a large cloud at the end of *Faust,* part two.

52. Johnson, "Gender and Poetry," 127.

53. Ibid., 108.

54. Katherine Tiernan O'Connor makes this suggestion in "Reflections on the Genesis of the Pasternak-Tsvetaeva-Rilke Correspondence," in *Readings in Russian Literature,* UCLA Slavic Studies, n.s., vol. 1, ed. Ronald Vroon and John E. Malmstad (Moscow: Nauka, 1993), 264.

55. Triolet was herself a novelist who became a successful French author. She also translated Tsvetaeva's poetry into French (*Poèmes* [Paris: Gallimard, 1968]).

56. Pasternak remarked in a letter to Evgenia from June 23, 1924, "There's something repulsive in Lann" (*Sushchestvovania tkan' skvoznaia: perepiska s Evgeniei Pasternak* [Moscow: Novoe literaturnoe obozrenie, 1998], 97). Tsvetaeva was romantically involved with Evgeny Lann while living in Moscow, separated from Efron by the Civil War. Remarkably, she made the same analysis of the relationship to Lann himself. In a letter to him, she quoted a conversation with Alya when she said that from Lann she wanted only a letter but wanted Efron in person (6:171).

57. Marina Tsvetaeva, *Neizdannoe. Svodnye tetradi* (Moscow: Ellis Lak, 1997), 294.

58. It is also possible, of course, that Pasternak told Tsvetaeva about Rilke in a non-extant letter and Tsvetaeva was avoiding the subject.

59. Pasternak, *Sushchestvovania tkan' skvoznaia,* 133.

60. See chapter 2 of Pasternak, *Sushchestvovania tkan' skvoznaia.*

61. Pasternak did not finish this novel and later destroyed the manuscript.

62. Parnok probably was not inclined to like Pasternak, since she was always wary of Tsvetaeva's involvements with male poets. In a poem she wrote during their affair, she imagines Tsvetaeva as a Bettina von Arnim who will leave her for some future "Goethe," and it appears that one of the reasons for their breakup was Osip Mandelstam's infatuation with Tsvetaeva in early 1916. Although the two women did not communicate thereafter, Parnok knew about Tsvetaeva's friendship with Pasternak. In her 1924 review essay on *Themes and Variations,* Parnok warned Tsvetaeva (and Mandelstam) against becoming epigones of Pasternak, clearly having read Tsvetaeva's "Downpour of Light" ("Pasternak i drugie," *Russkii sovremennik* 2 [1924]; reprinted with restored cuts in *Literaturnoe obozrenie* 11 [1990]: 86–92). Parnok also knew about Pasternak's answering passion, since she attended one of his private

readings of "Poem of the End" that very spring. Diana Lewis Burgin, *Sophia Parnok: The Life and Work of Russia's Sappho* (New York: New York University Press, 1994), 213. Parnok once described Tsvetaeva's poem as "very talented, but quite unbridled." Sophia Parnok, *Sobranie sochinenii* (Ann Arbor: Ardis, 1979), 355.

63. Poliakova points out in her commentary that Karolina Pavlova drew on this legend in her poem "We met strangely. Amid the salon circle" ("My stranno soshlis'. Sred' salonnogo kruga," 1854) (*Zakatnye ony dni: Cvetaeva i Parnok* [Ann Arbor: Ardis, 1983], 120–21). See Tomas Venclova's discussion of this poem in "Almost a Hundred Years Later: Toward a Comparison of Karolina Pavlova and Marina Cvetaeva," in *Essays on Karolina Pavlova*, ed. Susanne Fusso and Alexander Lehrman (Evanston: Northwestern University Press, 2001), 199–203.

64. Leonid Pasternak wrote to his son that, while his behavior seemed unconventional to him, "perhaps among you poets it's accepted to exchange books without being personally acquainted" (*DL* 61). Pasternak later wrote to reassure his parents that Tsvetaeva had behaved properly, enclosing Rilke's letter to him and excerpts from Rilke's first letter to Tsvetaeva (*DL* 157).

65. This piece appeared in the first issue of the émigré journal *The Well-Intentioned* (*Blagonamerennyi*) in 1926.

66. See Olga Raevsky-Hughes, "Marina Tsvetaeva on Wealth and Gratitude," in *For SK: in Celebration of the Life and Career of Simon Karlinsky*, ed. Michael S. Flier and Robert P. Hughes, Modern Russian Literature and Culture, vol. 33 (Berkeley: Berkeley Slavic Specialties, 1994), 247–52.

67. He also sent her a copy of his poetic credo "Several Propositions" ("Neskol'ko polozhenii," 1922), with the comment "Is this not you?" (*DNV* 211).

68. The lines are from the poem "Und du erbst das Grün" in Rilke's *Book of Hours* (*Das Stundenbuch*, 1905).

69. Pasternak continued to worry that he was offending Rilke with his silence, but as he put it to his father, "I need to be completely myself and gather my thoughts in order to answer him." Pasternak, *Pis'ma k roditeliam i sestram*, 306.

70. The poem to Tsvetaeva was "Not villagers in an opera" ("Ne opernye poseliane," 1926) (see note 44). The final version of the poem to Reisner was titled "In Memory of Reisner" ("Pamiati Reisner," 1926).

71. Pasternak did have earlier reservations about some of Tsvetaeva's work but had downplayed them. This is especially apparent in his response to "The Swain" (*DNV* 131–32).

72. Ilya Ehrenburg delivered "The Pied Piper," "Poem of the Hill," and several other gifts from Tsvetaeva: a photograph of herself, a notebook, a sweater, and some money, probably the fee for *Milestone*'s publication of a chapter of "1905" (*DNV* 221).

73. Fleishman, *Boris Pasternak v dvadtsatye gody*, 94.

74. For an analysis of these revisions, see Fleishman, chapter 5, *Boris Pasternak v dvadtsatye gody*.

75. Tsvetaeva already knew the poem and had recently quoted it back to him in her letter of May 22. Pasternak also mentions a piece he wrote in 1916 titled "Someone Else's Fate" ("Chuzhaia sud'ba"), which has not been identified. Evgeny Pasternak believes that it was incorporated into "A Story" ("Povest'") (*Boris Pasternak*, 444).

76. For a more detailed exposition of this argument, see my article "Leading the Revolution: Tsvetaeva's 'Pied Piper' and Blok's 'The Twelve,'" in *Marina Tsvetaeva: One Hundred Years*, ed. Viktoria Schweitzer, Jane A. Taubman, Peter Scotto, and Tatyana Babyonyshev, Modern Russian Literature and Culture, vol. 32 (Berkeley: Berkeley Slavic Specialties, 1994), 111–30.

77. Tsvetaeva had written a book of poems about the Civil War, *The Swans' Encampment*

(*Lebedinyi stan,* 1917–21), which appeared only posthumously, in 1957. Pasternak seems to have heard of the poems by early 1926, when he asked Tsvetaeva about them. See Tsvetaeva's letters nos. 44–45.

78. M. L. Gasparov, "Évoliutsia stikha B. Pasternaka," in *Literature, Culture, and Society in the Modern Age: In Honor of Joseph Frank,* ed. Edward J. Brown, Stanford Slavic Studies, 4:2, (Stanford: Department of Slavic Languages and Literatures, Stanford University 1992), 136–56.

79. Ibid. See also M. L. Gasparov, "Rifma i zhanr v stikhakh Pasternaka," in *Pasternakovskie chteniia,* vol. 2 (Moscow: Nasledie, 1998), 63–70.

80. Iury I. Levin, "Zametki o 'Leitenante Schmidte,'" in Nilsson, *Boris Pasternak: Essays,* 85–161.

81. Ibid., 126.

82. Ibid., 112.

83. Mikhail Bakhtin, "Slovo v romane," in *Voprosy literatury i estetiki* (Moscow: Khudozhestvennaia literatura, 1975), 112.

84. See my article "Taking Monologism Seriously: Bakhtin and Tsvetaeva's 'The Pied Piper,'" *Slavic Review* 53.4 (winter 1994): 1010–24.

85. Levin, "Zametki o 'Leitenante Schmidte,'" 97–98.

86. Ibid., 152.

87. Ibid., 158 n. 46.

88. Levin, "Zametki o 'Leitenante Schmidte,'" 129.

89. See Eric Naiman, *Sex in Public: The Incarnation of Early Soviet Ideology* (Princeton: Princeton University Press, 1997); and Eliot Borenstein, *Men without Women: Masculinity and Revolution in Russian Fiction, 1917–1929* (Durham: Duke University Press, 2000).

90. Pasternak later described Schmidt's style as "phrase-mongering" (frazerstvo) and "self-exposing oratory" (samooblachaiushchaia krasnorechivost') (*DL* 197).

91. Even the guards share this condition: "The guards put aside / Their half-dead rifles / And wiped their shaking cheek bones / With their fists" (Konvoinye otstavili / Poluzhivye ruzh'ia / I terli kulakami / Triasushchies'ia skuly).

92. Levin, "Zametki o 'Leitanante Schmidte,'" 146.

93. Ibid., 87.

94. For a helpful discussion, see chap. 4 of Joseph Frank, *Dostoevsky: The Mantle of the Prophet (1871–1881)* (Princeton: Princeton University Press, 2002), 65–86.

95. The entire passage reads: "In the theme there's your influence (the Jew, the cross and so on from 'Poem of the End'). But you took this as a symbol and in its eternal aspect, tragically, but I take it precisely as the constant transition, the almost ornamental canon of *history*: the arena becoming the first rows of the amphitheater, the labor camp becoming the government, or even better: one might think, looking at history, that idealism exists mostly so it might be refuted" (*DNV* 197). Remarking on the influence of "Poem of the End," Pasternak refers to the famous line "In this most Christian of worlds / Poets are Jews!" (V sem khristianneishem iz mirov / Poety—zhidy!). On the motif of crucifixion in the poem, see Tomas Venclova, "'Poéma gory' i 'Poéma kontsa' Mariny Tsvetaevoi kak Vetkhii i Novyi Zavet," in Schweitzer, Taubman, Scotto, and Babyonyshev, *Marina Tsvetaeva: One Hundred Years,* 147–61.

96. Levin, "Zametki o 'Leitenante Schmidte,'" 87.

97. Ibid., 152–53.

98. Appropriately, the dedication ends on the feminine pronoun "her" (ei), "the same ring-like, narrow, and compelling word" that concluded another poem he wrote and sent "in the same strange mood." This poem, a political poem about workers' strikes in London, inscribed yet again his desired union with history ("You will build the pillar, history, and as the days

move on, / I will meet the day when I'll be meeting her" [Ty zizhdesh' stolb, istoriia, i v pered-vizhke dnei / Ia svizhus' s dnem, v kotoryi svizhus' s nei]).

99. By contrast, two later poems that use the same imagery of the hunt render a nightmarish vision of the epoch: "When the fatal snap of a creaking pine" ("Kogda smertel'nyi tresk sosny skripuchei"), originally titled "Istoriia" (1927), and "Strapping archer, careful hunter" ("Ros-lyi strelok, ostorozhnyi okhotnik," 1928). Pasternak sent both poems to Tsvetaeva (*DNV* 387–88, 493). For a reading of the latter poem, see Iury Levin, "Razbor odnogo malopopu-liarnogo stikhotvoreniia B. Pasternaka," *Russian Literature* 6 (1978): 39–43.

100. Irina Shevelenko has speculated that Tsvetaeva read this poem in Pasternak's *Selected Poems* (*Izbrannye stikhi,* 1926) (*DNV* 608). She received *Above the Barriers* later, on June 21 (*DNV* 235).

101. As Igor Smirnov has established, Pasternak's "Blizzard" draws on Blok's "Snow Mask," as well as Pushkin's "Demons" ("Besy," 1830) (*Porozhdenie interteksta,* 2nd ed. [St. Petersburg: Sankt-Peterburgskii gosudarstvennyi universitet, 1995], 106).

102. When Pasternak thoroughly revised *Above the Barriers* for a second edition in 1928, he wrote to Tsvetaeva that the "new poetics" displayed there might render him alien to her. He described that new poetics as developing themes "like prose does," and mentioned Rilke as an influence (*DNV* 492–93).

103. Pasternak somehow knew earlier about Tsvetaeva's admiration for Schmidt. In a let-ter of January 5, 1926, he says, "I know you were infatuated with him" (*DNV* 132). In her letter of May 23, Tsvetaeva told him that she had met Schmidt's son in Prague and claimed to have seen Schmidt "in Yalta on the wharf" in the summer of 1905, when her family was visiting the Crimea (*DNV* 207).

104. Tsvetaeva refers to a line from Pasternak's poem "Storm, Instantaneous Forever" ("Groza, momental'naia navek") in *My Sister Life.*

105. Tsvetaeva apparently asked Pasternak not to remove the dedication (*DNV* 621).

106. See also her letter to Rilke of August 14, 1926 (*DL* 210).

107. The editors of the 1926 correspondence state that Tsvetaeva called a halt to their cor-respondence, to which the extant fragment of the letter does not attest. In fact, she may have offered to come to Pasternak. In his next letter, Pasternak says that he would never return her "promises to come to me" (*DNV* 260–61).

5. The End of the End

1. For an account of Mirsky's acquaintance with Tsvetaeva, see G. S. Smith, *D. S. Mirsky: A Russian-English Life (1890–1939)* (Oxford: Oxford University Press, 2000), and his "Ma-rina Tsvetaeva i D. Sviatopolk Mirskii," in *Actes du 1er colloque international (Lausanne, 30.VI.3–3.VII.1982),* ed. Robin Kemball, Efim Etkind, and Leonid Heller (Bern: Peter Lang, 1991), 192–206.

2. On the impact of *Milestones* within émigré culture, see Irina Shevelenko, *Literaturnyi put' Tsvetaevoi* (Moscow: Novoe literaturnoe obozrenie, 2002), 305–34.

3. Tsvetaeva made that claim back in 1925 during her exchange with Pasternak about ru-mors of Rilke's death. She told Pasternak about reading Rilke alongside *My Sister Life* in Berlin and deciding, "There's someone even greater than Pasternak" (*DNV* 127).

4. She spoke of dream communication to Pasternak at the beginning of their correspon-dence: "My favorite form of communication is unearthly: the dream: seeing in a dream. My second favorite is correspondence. The letter as a kind of unearthly communication, less per-fect than a dream, but with the same laws" (*DNV* 23). She also periodically described to Pas-ternak dreams she had about him. (See, for example, her letter of September 1925 [*DNV* 126].) On the significance of dreams in Tsvetaeva's work, see E. O. Aizenstein, *Sny Mariny Tsvetaevoi* (St. Petersburg: Akademicheskii proekt, 2003).

5. Tsvetaeva said as much in a preface to her translation of some of Rilke's letters: "A dream is rarely a dialogue, almost always a monologue: of our longing for a thing, or the longing of a thing for us. There are no mutual dreams. Either I draw someone into my dream, or someone enters my dream. A matter of one person, not two" (5:317).

6. "Every dream is an interpretation of a wish." Sigmund Freud, *Interpretation of Dreams* (New York: Avon, 1965), 155.

7. Marina Tsvetaeva, *Neizdannoe. Svodnye tetradi* (Moscow: Ellis Lak, 1997), 154.

8. Hélène Cixous, *Readings: The Poetics of Blanchot, Joyce, Kafka, Kleist, Lispector, and Tsvetayeva* (Minneapolis: University of Minnesota Press, 1991), 191.

9. Cf. Tsvetaeva's own statement about the different functions of dreams and poems: "There are things that can appear only in a dream. The same things can appear in poetry. There's a kind of encoding in the dream and the poetic line, rather: the transparency of a dream = the encoding of the poetic line." Quoted by Elena Korkina, "Poeticheskii mir Mariny Tsvetaevoi," in Marina Tsvetaeva, *Stikhotvoreniia i poemy* (Leningrad: Biblioteka Poeta, 1990), 27.

10. Ieva Vitins has argued that the poem enacts a Nietzschean view of creativity, in which the artist experiences a Dionysian shattering of self and is recomposed through an Apollonian imposition of form. This model, however, cannot account for the poem's representation of that process as a game involving other players ("Marina Cvetaeva's Poèma 'S morja,'" in Kemball, Etkind, and Heller, *Marina Tsvetaeva: Actes du 1er colloque international*).

11. Ibid., 253.

12. See Simon Karlinsky, "Pasternak, Pushkin i okean v poème Mariny Tsvetaevoi 'S morja,'" in *Boris Pasternak and His Times,* ed. Lazar Fleishman, Modern Russian Literature and Culture, vol. 25 (Berkeley: Berkeley Slavic Specialties, 1989), 46–57. As Ieva Vitins has established, the poem also contains references to other poets, among them Akhmatova and Mandelstam ("Marina Cvetaeva's Poèma 'S morja'").

13. Karlinsky notes that Tsvetaeva set her own earlier poem about Pushkin (1913) in the same locale ("Pasternak, Pushkin," 50).

14. The poem concludes with this action:

> Even with a knife
> You can't pry from the shell
> That which keeps love's pain fresh.
> That most happy sob
> That gushed out and created a reef,
> Reddening the corals' lips,
> And died on the polyp's mouths. . . .

> Из створок
> Не вызвать и клинком ножа
> Того, чем боль любви свежа.
> Того счастливейшего всхлипа,
> Что хлынул вон и создал риф,
> Кораллам губы обагрив,
> И замер на устах полипа.

15. The poem's final lines are, "Into the forests, into silent wildernesses, / I, filled with you, will bear / Your crags, your coves, / And glitter and shadow and murmuring waves" (V lesa, v pustyni molchalivy / Perenesu, toboiu poln, / Tvoi skaly, tvoi zalivy, / I blesk, i ten', i govor voln). As translated by Stephanie Sandler, who discusses the poem in *Distant Pleasures: Pushkin and the Writing of Exile* (Stanford: Stanford University Press, 1989), 57–76.

16. "To Pasternak is given living hills, the living sea (and what a sea! the first sea in Rus-

sian literature after the sea of the free elements and equal to Pushkin's)" ("Epic and Lyric in Contemporary Russia" ["Epos i lirika v sovremennoi Rossii," 1932]) (5:381). Tsvetaeva, however, near the end of "From the Sea," rejects the political connotation of Pasternak's rendering of the sea in "1905"; she predicts that the Soviet "ship of state" will be destroyed by the elemental sea.

17. See Hélène Cixous's reading of Tsvetaeva's image of Pushkin in "My Pushkin": "Actually Tsvetaeva was born out of the womb of Pushkin—the woman womb of Pushkin" ("Difficult Joys," in *The Body and the Text: Hélène Cixous, Reading and Teaching,* ed. Helen Wilcox, Keith McWatters, Ann Thompson, and Linda R. Williams [New York: St. Martin's Press, 1990], 16). See also Stephanie Sandler, "Marina Tsvetaeva's Pushkin and the Poet's Identities," in *Commemorating Pushkin: Russia's Myth of a National Poet* (Stanford: Stanford University Press, 2004), 214–65.

18. This sentence is in Russian in the original (Rainer Maria Rilke, *Briefwechsel,* 116).

19. Les Calvedt, "Mitten im Schreiben sind wir mitten im Tod," in *Unreading Rilke,* ed. Hartmut Heep (New York: Peter Lang, 2001), 127.

20. Maurice Blanchot, "Rilke and Death," in *The Siren's Song: Selected Essays by Maurice Blanchot,* trans. Sacha Rabinovitch, ed. Gabriel Josipovici (Bloomington: Indiana University Press, 1982), 161.

21. See Olga Hasty's discussion of Tsvetaeva's misunderstanding of Rilke in chapter 6 of *Tsvetaeva's Orphic Journeys in the Worlds of the Word* (Evanston: Northwestern University Press, 1996). Hasty argues that they had different visions of the poet-as-Orpheus: "Tsvetaeva encounters a joyous, life- and death-affirming poet who differs significantly from the tragic figure she herself envisioned" (144). I view Rilke's philosophy and his influence on Tsvetaeva more critically, as reinforcing an association between death and femininity.

22. In fact, she claimed to Pasternak that she stated Rilke's credo back to him: "I wrote to him: I won't lessen myself, that won't make you greater (and doesn't make me less!), that will make you only *more solitary,* for on the island *where we were born—all—are like us*" (*DNV* 214). She did not, in fact, write this to Rilke, but fell silent for two weeks.

23. I quote Rilke's poems in Stephen Mitchell's translation, to which I have made adjustments (*The Selected Poetry of Rainer Maria Rilke* [New York: Vintage, 1989]).

24. See Patricia Brodsky, *Rainer Maria Rilke* (Boston: Twayne, 1988).

25. Rilke's writings on love have been gathered and translated by John L. Mood, *Rilke on Love and Other Difficulties* (New York: Norton, 1975). See also William Gass, "Throw the Emptiness Out of Your Arms: Rilke's Doctrine of Nonpossessive Love," in *The Philosophy of Erotic Love,* ed. Robert C. Solomon and Kathleen M. Higgens (Lawrence: University of Kansas Press, 1991), 451–66.

26. See Anna Tavis, "Russia in Rilke: Rainer Maria Rilke's Correspondence with Marina Tsvetaeva," *Slavic Review* 52.3 (fall 1993): 494–511.

27. "Ich bin auf der Welt zu allein," from the *Book of Hours, First Book* (*Das Buch vom mönchischen Leben. Erstes Buch,* 1899).

28. Diana Burgin has noted a similar dynamic in Tsvetaeva's imagining of Pushkin (*Marina Tsvetaeva i transgressivnyi eros* [St. Petersburg: Inapress, 2000], 206).

29. Geoffrey Hartman, *The Unmediated Vision: An Interpretation of Wordsworth, Hopkins, Rilke, and Valéry* (New York: Harcourt Brace, 1966), 91.

30. Ibid., 91. This list of symbols largely derives from the tenth Duino Elegy, which names a string of constellations that ends with "the clear sparkling *M* / that stands for Mothers" (das klar erglänzende M / das die Mütter bedeutet).

31. Ibid., 85.

32. Tsvetaeva read this poem carefully, as Olga Hasty has shown (*Tsvetaeva's Orphic Journeys,* 52).

33. She attempts to counter his authority by speaking to Rilke as his mother: "You are my darling grown-up boy" (*DL* 222).

34. The poem is from *New Poems: The Other Part* (*Neue Gedichte, Anderer Teil,* 1908).

35. Andrzej Warminski, "Rilke's 'Das Bett,'" in *Rilke: the Alchemy of Alienation,* ed. Frank Baron, Ernst S. Dick, and Warren R. Maurer (Lawrence: Regents Press of Kansas, 1980), 165.

36. See Joseph Brodsky's reading of this poem in his "Footnote to a Poem," in *Less Than One* (New York: Farrar, Straus and Giroux, 1986), 195–267, and Olga Hasty's in chapter 7 of *Tsvetaeva's Orphic Journeys,* 163–222.

37. See Olga Hasty, "'Your Death'—The Living Water of Cvetaeva's Art," *Russian Literature* 13 (1983): 41–64.

38. She also later had an exchange of letters with Rilke's literary executor, Nanny Wunderly-Volkart, and Rilke's daughter Ruth Sieber-Rilke.

39. See her letter to Wunderly-Volkart (7:359).

40. Tsvetaeva actually met Steiner in Prague. Tsvetaeva criticism in Russia has begun to emphasize the influence on Tsvetaeva of Russian religious and mystical philosophy. See, for example, Zinaida Mirkina, *Nevidimyi sobor* (Moscow: Universitetskaia kniga, 1999). Several critics have argued that anthroposophical notions shape the action of "Poema vozdukha." See essays by T. V. Kuznetsova, S. B. Dzhimbinov, and O. A. Kling in the published proceedings of a conference on the poem, *Poèma Vozdukha Mariny Tsvetaevoi* (Moscow: Dom-muzei Mariny Tsvetaevoi, 1994). See also Alexandra Smith, "Surpassing Acmeism?—The Lost Key to Cvetaeva's 'Poem of the Air,'" *Russian Literature* 45 (1999): 209–22.

41. On "Poem of the Air," see the collection of articles cited in note 40. See also Mikhail Gasparov, "'Poema vozdukha' Mariny Tsvetaevoi: opyty interpretatsii," in *Trudy po znakovym sistemam 15* (Tartu, 1982): 122–140; and Alyssa Dinega's chapter on Rilke in *A Russian Psyche: The Poetic Mind of Marina Tsvetaeva* (Madison: University of Wisconsin Press, 2001).

42. See Catriona Kelly's reading of this poem in *A History of Russian Women's Writing, 1820–1992* (Oxford: Clarendon Press, 1994), 305–7.

43. Dinega, *A Russian Psyche,* 175. Alexandra Smith has discussed Tsvetaeva's image of the Gothic cathedral as polemically directed toward the Acmeists in "Surpassing Acmeism?—The Lost Key to Cvetaeva's 'Poem of the Air.'"

44. See especially her letter of March 4, 1928 (*DNV* 473–76).

45. Tsvetaeva conceived the trilogy in 1923 and finished the first play, "Ariadne," in 1924.

46. Irina Shevelenko, "The Artist in History, the Artist on History: The Pasternak-Tsvetaeva Dialogue in the 1920s," paper presented at the American Association of Teachers of Slavic and East European Languages, New York, December 2002.

47. Ibid.

48. See Shevelenko's excellent discussion in *Literaturnyi put' Tsvetaevoi,* 350–81.

49. This letter was published for the first time in Rainer Maria Rilke, *Dykhanie liriki* (Moscow: Art-Fleks, 2000), 251–54.

50. Tsvetaeva refers to her earlier statement that this "whole world . . . will sink to the bottom" (*DNV* 337).

51. That year he did, however, write five poems, in connection with which he said, "I sense that for me history has returned to nature, where it belongs" (*DNV* 384). The poems, which he sent to Tsvetaeva in September 1927, were "Lilies of the Valley" ("Landyshi"), "Space" ("Prostranstvo"), "Istoriia" ("History"), "Storm's Approach" ("Priblizhen'e grozy"), and "Lilac" ("Siren'").

52. "Sovetskie pisateli o pisateliakh i chitateliakh," *Chitatel' i pisatel'* 4–5 (February 11, 1928) (4:623).

53. These developments are related in illuminating detail by Lazar Fleishman in chapters 4, 5, and 6 of *Boris Pasternak v dvadtsatye gody* (Munich: Wilhelm Fink, 1981).

54. Tsvetaeva first forwarded a letter from Mirsky to Pasternak on June 12, 1926.

55. For an account of the Eurasian "schism," including Tsvetaeva's involvement in it, see Irina Shevelenko, "K istorii evraziiskogo raskola 1929 goda," in *Themes and Variations: In Honor of Lazar Fleishman,* Stanford Slavic Studies, vol. 8 (Stanford: Department of Slavic Languages and Literatures, Stanford University, 1994), 376–416. The schism was partly precipitated by Tsvetaeva's "welcome" to Mayakovsky, which appeared in the newspaper *Eurasia* on November 24, 1928 (7:350–51).

56. Pasternak refers to their letters in his correspondence (5:234). Several of these letters have been published. See Lazar Fleishman, "Iz Pasternakovskoi perepiski," in *Slavica Hierosolymitana,* vols. 5–6 (Jerusalem: Magnum Press, 1981), 535–41; and V. M. Kozovoi, "Pervyi vzroslyi poet: iz perepiski B. Pasternaka i P. Suvchinskogo," *Literaturnoe obozrenie* 12 (1990): 99–103.

57. D. S. Mirsky, *Uncollected Writings on Russian Literature,* ed. G. S. Smith (Berkeley: Berkeley Slavic Specialties, 1989), 287.

58. Anna Saakiants, *Marina Tsvetaeva. Zhizn' i tvorchestvo* (Moscow: Ellis Lak, 1997), 25.

59. Alexandra Smith has argued otherwise in her interesting essay "Between Art and Politics: Tsvetaeva's Story 'The Chinaman' and Its Link with the Eurasian Movement in the 1920s–30s," *Soviet and Post-Soviet Review* 28.3 (2001): 269–85.

60. In an example of the mind-bending politics of the period, Pasternak tells her he read in a hack Soviet journal an excerpt from an émigré journal declaring Tsvetaeva's popularity in Soviet Russia—a claim the Soviet journal, of course, disputed.

61. See Simon Karlinsky, *Marina Tsvetaeva: The Woman, Her World, and Her Poetry* (Cambridge: Cambridge University Press, 1985), 21.

62. "Gor'kii–B. L. Pasternak," in *Literaturnoe nasledstvo. Gor'kii i sovetskie pisateli* (Moscow: Akademia Nauk, 1963), 301.

63. See the accounts in *Dykhanie liriki, DL* 254–55; and Saakiants, *Marina Tsvetaeva,* 487–88.

64. The editors of *Dykhanie liriki* quote Tsvetaeva saying to Gorky, referring to *After Russia:* "The thing should return to its birthplace. Here no one needs it, but in Russia I am still remembered" (*DL* 254). These sentences do not appear in Tsvetaeva's letters to Gorky as published in *Sobranie sochinenii.*

65. See his letter to Pasternak of October 19, 1927 ("Gor'kii–B. L. Pasternak," 302).

66. In her memoir, Anastasia Tsvetaeva recalls suggesting to her sister that she return to Russia, an idea Tsvetaeva dismissed (*Vospominaniia* [Moscow: Sovetskii pisatel', 1984], 693).

67. Pasternak, "Gor'kii–B. L. Pasternak," 297 n. 1.

68. Ibid., 300.

69. Ibid., 302.

70. This and several other letters to Gorky do not appear in the correspondence published in *Gor'kii i sovetskie pisateli.*

71. Pasternak later gave Tsvetaeva a full account of the "Gorky epic" in a letter of January 5, 1928, though still without clarifying the nature of the plan.

72. Tsvetaeva's correspondence with Pasternak's parents may be found in her collected works (6:294–301).

73. Tsvetaeva's correspondence with Lomonosova may be found in her collected works (7:313–49). Pasternak's letters to the Lomonosovs, and those of his family, have been published as "Neotsenimyi podarok: Perepiska Pasternakov i Lomonosovykh (1925–1970)," in *Minuvshee: Istoricheskii al'manakh,* nos. 15–17 (Moscow: Atheneum Feniks, 1994), 193–247; 150–208; 358–408, respectively.

74. In the same letter Pasternak reported to Tsvetaeva that "he learned for the first time about Sviatopolk's serious desire to return here (Prokofiev spoke only about Suvchinsky)" (*DNV* 517). Mirsky and Suvchinsky had recently visited Gorky in Sorrento. In the end, Mirsky received Soviet citizenship, while Suvchinsky did not. See G. S. Smith's account in *D. S. Mirsky*, 164–167.

75. Earlier, in 1922, he wrote two fragments related to the novel, "Three Chapters from a Tale" ("Tri glavy iz povesti") and "Spektorsky's Notes" ("Iz zapisok Spektorskogo").

76. Olga Raevsky-Hughes was the first to discuss Tsvetaeva's presence in *Spektorsky* in her essay "Boris Pasternak i Marina Tsvetaeva (k istorii druzhby)," *Vestnik russkogo studencheskogo khristianskogo dvizheniia* 100 (1971): 281–305. Fleishman supplies a more in-depth analysis in his chapter on the novel in *Boris Pasternak v dvadtsatye gody*, which I refer to extensively in my discussion.

77. I quote from the first version of chapter 5, written in December 1927 (1:572–75). Pasternak reworked this chapter for the 1931 edition. See Fleishman, *Boris Pasternak v dvadtsatye gody*, 156–69.

78. Pasternak spoke of having delivered Efron's letters in a letter to Tsvetaeva of March 31, 1928 (*DNV* 481).

79. In her marginalia to *Spektorsky*, Tsvetaeva remarked, "Like my Borisoglebsky of 1917–1922" (*Mir Pasternaka*, ed. E. S. Levitin, N. A. Borisovskaia, and V. V. Leonovich [Moscow: Sovetskii pisatel', 1989], 172.)

80. Pasternak read "From the Sea" not long before he finished chapter 5. See his letter of October 15, 1927 (*DNV* 406.) When he rewrote chapter 5 in 1931, he added a specific reference to Tsvetaeva's poem, describing Il'ina as "a girl with hair à la Cenci" (devushka s pricheskoi à la Chenchi). In "From the Sea," Tsvetaeva's lyric speaker has "the heart of all the Cencis" (s serdtsem Chenchi, / Vsekh).

81. Tsvetaeva spoke to Pasternak about her hatred of housework: "It's like a rote lesson, like the Our Father, which you can't get wrong because you don't understand a word. Not a syllable" (*DNV* 204).

82. Interestingly, Tsvetaeva identified Spektorsky not as Pasternak but as Evgeny Lann in the marginalia on her copy of *Spektorsky* (Levitin, Borisovskaia, and Leonovich, *Mir Pasternaka*, 172).

83. Pasternak, though, keeps gender difference in play with the anagrammatic "mga" and "gam," which share the same sounds and semantics but have different grammatical gender. One commentator has described the scene as incestuous. L. L. Gorelik, *"Spektorsky" Borisa Pasternaka* (Smolensk: Smolenskii gosudarstvennyi pedagogicheskii institut, 1997), 12.

84. At this point Pasternak knew about Tsvetaeva's "Poem of the Air" but had not read it. See his letter of July 27, 1927 (*DNV* 366).

85. "Like right and left hands" ("Kak pravaia i levaia ruka," 1918). Tsvetaeva underlined Pasternak's lines in her copy of the novel (Levitin, Borisovskaia, and Leonovich, *Mir Pasternaka*, 172).

86. In a letter of 1928, apparently under some pressure from Tsvetaeva, Pasternak warned her away from using "that word": "For if you touch that word, like a cork in a bottle of kvass, that will be the end" (*DNV* 479).

87. There is also an afterecho in the plot of *Doctor Zhivago*, where Zhivago leaves Lara knowing they will not be reunited. See Raevsky-Hughes, "Boris Pasternak i Marina Tsvetaeva," 301.

88. The intervening years of the war and revolution, which Spektorsky spends in the provinces with his sister, are treated in a related prose work titled "A Story" ("Povest'," 1929). Il'ina is mentioned once in the story, when Spektorsky describes her to his new love

interest, Anna Arild: "Maria doesn't need anything. Maria is immortal. Maria is not a woman" (4:133).

89. Fleishman has identified a subtext for this line in Pushkin's remark about the Decembrists, "And I too could have been like a jester" (*Boris Pasternak v dvadtsatye gody,* 151).

90. Boris Paramonov has similarly described Pasternak's ambivalent representation of the revolution as a woman's "rebellion against violence and as violence itself" in his essay "Pasternak protiv romantizma," in *Boris Pasternak, 1890–1990,* ed. Lev Loseff (Northfield: Russian School of Norwich University, 1991), 22.

91. Fleishman, *Boris Pasternak v dvadtsatye gody,* 165. Pasternak mentioned this very poem ("Znaiu, umru na zare") in a letter of June 29, 1928, as the inspiration for his poem "Roslyi strelok, ostorozhnyi okhotnik" (*DNV* 493).

92. Pasternak compared their "slavery" in a letter of January 10, 1928: "But your *woman's* slavery isn't as grotesque as my masculine (citizen's, etc.) slavery. Building water mains" (*DNV* 461).

93. "The best works of world literature, while narrating the most various things, actually tell about their own birth" (4:186).

94. Fleishman, *Boris Pasternak v dvadtsatye gody,* 169.

95. See also his comment about Lenin in his 1956 autobiography: "the incomparable daring of [his] address to the seething element of the people" (4:789).

96. Pasternak also expressed this despairing solidarity with Tsvetaeva in two poems he wrote to her during 1929. They were published in a group of four poems addressed to cherished contemporaries—Tsvetaeva, Akhmatova, and Meierhold. In a gesture that perhaps followed from Pasternak's linking of Tsvetaeva with the poetics of *Above the Barriers,* he asked her permission to include the poems to her in the new, revised edition of the book (*DNV* 526). (The second poem presumably did not get past the censor because it contained another acrostic of her name.) When the book appeared in 1931, he inscribed the first poem, "You are justified, turning out your pockets" ("Ty vprave, vyvernuv karman," 1929), in the copy he gave to her. The poem, whose leitmotif is the phrase "It's all the same to me" (Mne vse ravno), declares the poet's indifference to his worldly surroundings and imagines a Tsvetaevan escape through upward flight. Tsvetaeva later borrowed Pasternak's leitmotif to write a powerful poem about the alienation of life in emigration, "Nostalgia for the homeland!" ("Toska po rodine!" 1934).

97. See Fleishman's chapter on *Spektorsky,* 134–70.

98. Almost all of Olga's reported speech concerns her revolutionary bloodline: "I am the daughter of People's Will members. / *You didn't understand that then?*" (Ia doch' narodovol'tsev. / *Vy etogo ne poniali togda?*); "I am by birth a patriot" (Ia rodom—patriotka).

99. Raevsky-Hughes, "Boris Pasternak i Marina Tsvetaeva," 294–95.

100. As quoted in Christopher Barnes, *Boris Pasternak: A Literary Biography,* vol. 2 (Cambridge: Cambridge University Press, 1998), 50.

101. Lazar Fleishman, *Boris Pasternak: The Poet and His Politics* (Cambridge: Harvard University Press, 1990), 164.

102. Alexander Zholkovsky, "The Dynamics of Adaptation: Pasternak's Second Birth," in *Text Counter Text: Rereadings in Russian Literary History* (Stanford: Stanford University Press, 1994).

103. There is also a hint of Eurasianism in the poem, perhaps in solidarity with Efron and Mirsky: "The soul is leaving the West, / She has nothing to do there" (Ukhodit s Zapada dusha, / Ei nechego tam delat'). Tsvetaeva wrote to Pasternak that she was offended by these lines, thinking they referred to her (*DNV* 544).

104. Barnes, *Boris Pasternak,* 40–41.

105. See Pasternak's letter to Tsvetaeva in 1928, where Pasternak casts himself as Russia's difficult boyfriend: "Now I'm going to say some stupid things. But permit them their thought, their ideal. The more complete I become, the closer I come to truth, the more I talk about the motherland, the more I become a piece of it. All the more so when I cause her suffering, when she has a difficult time with me, when shy (and thus more comprehensible to me and beautiful), she will hide what she knows and turn away from me each time there come between us her natural suitors, before whose lightness and simplicity she will be ashamed of the difficulties I rewarded her with" (*DNV* 491–92). In Pasternak's statement that his rivals are more "natural" and therefore provide less cause for shame, one senses a consciousness of both his Jewishness and his "compromised" masculinity. His difference makes for a difficult relationship with Russia, but it is a relationship that is already far evolved and that he pursues without apology. The most striking thing about this allegory is the demeanor of the beloved, who responds to the suffering Pasternak inflicts on her not with hysterical rage but with becoming shyness.

106. On Pasternak's idiosyncratic appeal to Rilke's example in "Safe Conduct," see R. Miller-Budnitskaia, "O filosofii iskusstva Borisa Pasternaka i R. M. Rilke," *Zvezda* 5 (1932): 160–68; Angela Livingstone, "Some Affinities in the Prose of the Poets Rilke and Pasternak," *Forum for Modern Language Studies* 19 (July 1983): 274–88; Serafima Roll, "Rilke, Death, and Writing in Boris Pasternak's *Safe Conduct*," *Germano-Slavica* 7.1 (1991): 13–24; and the chapters on "Safe Conduct" in Fleishman, *Boris Pasternak v dvadtsatye gody.*

107. Rimgaila Salys, "Love, Death, and Creation: Boris Pasternak and the Two Rilke Requiems," *Russian Review* 55 (April 1996): 267.

108. See Fleishman's discussion of how the Kalckreuth requiem relates to *Safe Conduct* (*Boris Pasternak v dvadtsatye gody,* 192–96).

109. Salys, "Love, Death, and Creation," 273.

110. Ibid.

111. Ibid., 278.

112. Tsvetaeva already treated this theme with respect to Pushkin in her essay "Natalia Goncharova" (1929). The name belongs both to Pushkin's wife, whose beauty provoked the jealousy that led him into a fatal duel, and to one of her later relatives, the modernist painter Natalia Goncharova, with whom Tsvetaeva became friends in Paris. (Goncharova made a series of lithographs for Tsvetaeva's French translation of "The Swain," "Le Gars.") In her essay, Tsvetaeva polemically reintroduces the woman artist into the equation of the genius and the beauty, a three-way dynamic that was shaped by the history of her relations with Pasternak. On this essay, see Liza Knapp, "Tsvetaeva and the Two Natal'ia Goncharovas: Dual Life," in *Cultural Mythologies of Russian Modernism,* ed. Boris Gasparov, Robert P. Hughes, and Irina Paperno (Berkeley: University of California Press, 1992), 88–108; and Stephanie Sandler, "Marina Tsvetaeva's Pushkin and the Poet's Identities" in *Commemorating Pushkin: Russia's Myth of a National Poet* (Stanford: Stanford University Press, 2004), 245–51.

113. Tsvetaeva, *Neizdannoe. Svodnye tetradi,* 442. This version differs from the letter published in *DNV* 540.

114. Efron asked both Pasternak and Gorky for help. See his letter of June 29 to his sister, ibid., 606 n. 771.

115. Nevertheless, just a year later Tsvetaeva also applied for citizenship. Shevelenko, *Literaturnyi put' Tsvetaevoi,* 391.

116. Pasternak et al., "Neotsenimyi podarok: Perepiska Pasternakov i Lomonosovykh (1925–1970)," *Minuvshee* 16 (1994): 206.

117. Pasternak had earlier "rhymed" with Larisa Reisner in the draft of "In Memory of Reisner" he shared with Tsvetaeva in April 1926:

> I must blend everything there is in me of Boris,
> For years departing from a dream,
> With your remote position, Larissa,
> Just as sound rhymes our names.

> Смешаться всем, что есть во мне Бориса,
> Годами отходящего от сна,
> С твоей глухой позицией, Ларисса,
> Как звук рифмует наши имена.

Tsvetaeva did not take offense in this case. As she explained, "Boris" and Larisa" were only rhymed by "sound," while her name and Pasternak's were rhymed by "meaning" (*DNV* 183).

Conclusion

1. See Nadezhda Mandelstam's account of this episode in *Hope against Hope: A Memoir,* trans. Max Hayward (New York: Atheneum, 1970), 145–49. See also Evgeny Pasternak, *Biografiia* (Moscow: Tsitadel; 1997), 494–95.

2. Anna Saakiants, *Marina Tsvetaeva. Zhizn' i tvorchestvo* (Moscow: Ellis Lak, 1997), 619.

3. I quote from this essay in Manya Harari's translation, with small adjustments. Boris Pasternak, *An Essay in Autobiography,* trans. Manya Harari (London: Collins and Harvill Press, 1959), 107–8.

4. As Pasternak explained in a letter he wrote to his parents from Paris, the Soviet delegation decided not to travel back through Germany for political reasons, and he had "neither the courage nor the strength" to make the trip on his own. Boris Pasternak, *Pis'ma k roditeliam i sestram, 1907–1960* (Moscow: Novoe literaturnoe obozrenie, 2004), 636–37.

5. Tsvetaeva continued to speak of lyric creativity as maternity in her last letter to Pasternak (March 1936): "Why are you announcing that you will write differently? That's your business—with your womb. Whose business is it? ('I've given birth to all dark-haired kids but now I've *decided* to have a *redhead*.' Or is that something already being practiced there?)" (*DNV* 563).

6. Mikhail Gasparov, "'Gastronomicheskii' peizazh v poème Mariny Tsvetaevoi 'Avtobus,'" *Russkaia rech'* 4 (1990): 20–26; Omry Ronen, "Chasy uchenichestva Mariny Tsvetaevoi," *Novoe literaturnoe obozrenie* 1 (1992): 188–89. Svetlana El'nitskaia has developed and broadened their insights in "O nekotorykh osobennostiakh Tsvetaevskogo anti-gastronomizma i nepriiatiia 'stroitel'stva zhizni' v ee lirike 1930-kh godov," *Wiener Slawistischer Almanach* 46 (2000): 45–118.

7. Karen Evans-Romaine has documented the persistent presence of gastronomic or culinary imagery in Pasternak's work (*Boris Pasternak and the Tradition of German Romanticism* [Munich: Otto Sagner, 1997], 72).

8. Ronen, "Chasy uchenichestva Mariny Tsvetaevoi," 189.

9. See El'nitskaia, "O nekotorykh osobennostiakh Tsvetaevskogo anti-gastronomizma"; and Irina Shevelenko's discussion of Tsvetaeva's late prose in chapter 5 of *Literaturnyi put' Tsvetaevoi* (Moscow: Novoe literaturnoe obozrenie, 2002).

10. Elena Korkina, "Pushkinskaia tema v sud'be Pasternaka i Tsvetaevoi v 1930-e gody," in *Marina Tsvetaeva: Pesn' zhizni* (Paris: YMCA Press, 1996), 102–26. A shorter version of this essay appeared earlier as "Pushkin i Pugachev: liricheskoe rassledovanie Mariny Tsvetaevoi," in *Marina Tsvetaeva: One Hundred Years,* ed. Viktoria Schweitzer, Jane Taubman, Peter Scotto, and Tatyana Babyonyshev, Modern Russian Literature and Cultures 32 (Berkeley: Berkeley Slavic Specialties, 1994), 221–29. For another account of Pasternak's actions in

the 1930s, see Lazar Fleishman, *Boris Pasternak v tridtsatye gody* (Jerusalem: Magnes Press, 1984).

11. Iu. I. Levin, "Zametki k stikhotvoreniiu B. Pasternaka 'Vse naklonen'ia i zalogi,'" in *Byt' znamenitym nekrasivo, Pasternakovskie chteniia,* vol. 1 (Moscow: Nasledie, 1992), 67–75.

12. Korkina, "Pushkinskaia tema."

13. Tsvetaeva fully unfolded this idea in her essay "Art in the Light of Conscience" ("Iskusstvo pri svete sovesti," 1932). It would be useful, I believe, to compare Tsvetaeva's reflections on art and "power" to those Pasternak expressed in *Safe Conduct.*

14. Shevelenko, *Literaturnyi put' Tsvetaevoi,* 411.

15. The protocols of her interrogation have been published in translation in Irma Kudrova, *The Death of a Poet: The Last Days of Marina Tsvetaeva,* trans. Mary Ann Szporluk (Woodstock: Overlook Duckworth, 2004).

16. For accounts of Tsvetaeva's final years in Soviet Russia, see Maria Belkina, *Skreshchenie sudeb,* 2nd ed. (Moscow: "Rudomino," 1992); and Irma Kudrova, *Gibel' Mariny Tsvetaevoi* (Moscow: Nezavisimaia gazeta, 1995), which has been translated into English as *The Death of a Poet.*

17. Kudrova, *Gibel' Mariny Tsvetaevoi,* 73.

18. Saakiants, *Marina Tsvetaeva,* 712.

19. Georgy Efron, *Dnevniki v dvukh tomakh* (Moscow: Vagrius, 2004).

20. Ibid., 1:64.

21. Ariadna Efron, *Pis'ma iz ssylki (1948–1957)* (Paris: YMCA Press, 1985).

22. As quoted by Jane Taubman in "Marina Tsvetaeva and Boris Pasternak: Toward the History of a Friendship," *Russian Literature Triquarterly* 2 (1972): 304–21.

23. Joseph Brodsky, "A Footnote to a Commentary," in *Rereading Russian Poetry,* ed. Stephanie Sandler (New Haven: Yale University Press, 1999), 192. This essay first appeared in Russian as "Primechanie k kommentariiu," in Schweitzer, et al., *One Hundred Years,* 262–84.

24. Konstantin M. Polivanov, "Marina Tsvetaeva v romane Borisa Pasternaka *Doktor Zhivago,*" *De Visu* (1992): 52–57, and "Eshche raz o *Doktor Zhivago* i Marine Tsvetaevoi," in *V krugu Zhivago: Pasternakovskii sbornik,* ed. Lazar Fleishman (Stanford: Department of Slavic Languages and Literatures, Stanford University, 2000), 171–83.

25. As Brodsky points out, Rilke conflates the Virgin Mother and Magdalene ("Footnote," 188).

26. Ibid., 186.

27. Ibid., 189.

28. Saakiants reports that Pasternak, who delivered Tsvetaeva's letter to the official, added an alarmed letter of explanation (*Marina Tsvetaeva,* 712).

29. Pasternak, *An Essay in Autobiography,* 109.

Index

Italic page numbers refer to illustrations.

Solntsa"), 270n47; "Your Death" ("Tvoia
smert'," 1927), 196; "The Youth" ("Otrok,"
1922), 85. *See also* "Downpour of Light, A"
("Svetovoi liven'") (Tsvetaeva); *Evening Album (Vechernyi al'bom,* 1910) (Tsvetaeva);
"From the Sea" ("S moria," 1926) (Tsvetaeva); *Milestones (Versty,* 1921) (Tsvetaeva);
"On a Red Steed" ("Na krasnom kone,"
1921) (Tsvetaeva); "Poem of the End" ("Poema kontsa," 1924) (Tsvetaeva); "Swain,
The" ("Molodets," 1922) (Tsvetaeva); "Telegraph Wires" ("Provoda," 1923) (Tsvetaeva)
Turgeneva, Asya, 20, 39
"Twelve, The" ("Dvenadtsat'," 1918) (Blok):
and Pasternak's "January 1919," 137; and
Pasternak's "Lieutenant Schmidt," 164;
and Pasternak's "A Sublime Malady," 139;
and Tsvetaeva's "On a Red Steed," 33,
260n90; and Tsvetaeva's "The Pied Piper,"
162, 164

Union of Soviet Writers, 225, 244

Victorian culture, 7, 38, 61
Vinograd, Elena: as hysterical, 266n79; as
muse, 50, 68, 131; Pasternak's affair with,

64, 71; photograph of, 67; and poetry of
Pasternak, 66; Tsvetaeva compared to, 151,
211
Vishniak, Abram, 39–41, 85, 90, 268n15,
270n42
Vishniak, Vera, 85
Vitins, Ieva, 182, 271n63, 272n75, 283nn10,
12
voice: and poetry of Pasternak, 164, 165–66,
168, 171, 174, 175, 214–15, 245; and poetry of Tsvetaeva, 39, 92–93, 94–97, 98,
100–101, 109, 110–11, 126–27, 165
Voloshin, Maximilian, 10–11, 16, 17, 26, 27,
29, 278n46

Weininger, Otto, 11, 24, 51, 255n24; *Sex and
Character (Geschlecht und Charakter,*
1903), 11
Westhoff, Clara, 229, 231, 232
women poets: as influence on Tsvetaeva, 25–
26, 28–29, 259n59; of Russian fin de siècle
culture, 16
Woolf, Virginia, *Orlando,* 6

Zholkovsky, Alexander, 7, 72, 80–81, 226,
267n94